Street by Street

KU-043-458

WEST KENT

PLUS BIGGIN HILL, ORPINGTON, OXTED, TILBURY

Enlarged Areas Chatham, Gillingham, Maidstone, Rochester, Royal Tunbridge Wells, Sevenoaks

lst edition May 2001

© Automobile Association Developments Limited 2001

This product includes map data licensed from Ordnance Survey® with the permission of the Controller of Her Majesty's Stationery Office. © Crown copyright 2000. All rights reserved. Licence No: 399221.

Published by AA Publishing (a trading name of Automobile Association Developments Limited, whose registered office is Norfolk House, Priestley Road, Basingstoke, Hampshire, RG24 9NY. Registered number 1878835).

Mapping produced by the Cartographic Department of The Automobile Association.

A CIP Catalogue record for this book is available from the British Library.

Printed by in Italy by Printer Trento srl

The contents of this atlas are believed to be correct at the time of the latest revision. However, the publishers cannot be held responsible for loss occasioned to any person acting or refraining from action as a result of any material in this atlas, nor for any errors, omissions or changes in such material. The publishers would welcome information to correct any errors or omissions and to keep this atlas up to date. Please write to Publishing, The Automobile Association, Fanum House, Basing View, Basingstoke, Hampshire, RG21 4EA.

Ref: MD101

Key to map pages ii-iii

Key to map symbols iv-1

Enlarged scale pages 2-11

Street by Street 12-247

Index – towns & villages 248-251

Index – streets 252-290

Index – featured places 290-298

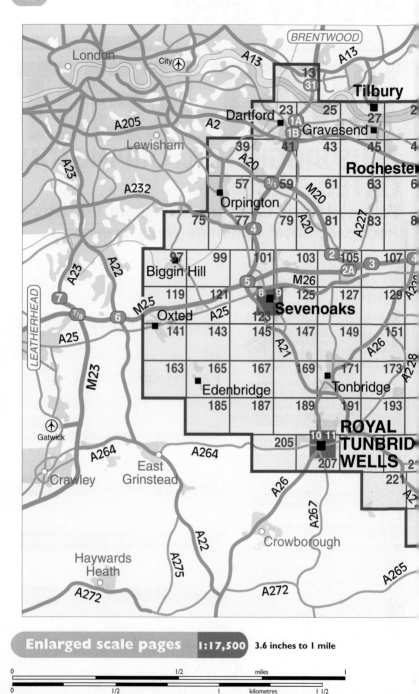

Enlarged scale pages | **1:17,500** | 3.6 inches to 1 mile

| 0 | 1/2 | miles | 1 |
| 0 | 1/2 | 1 | kilometres | 1 1/2 |

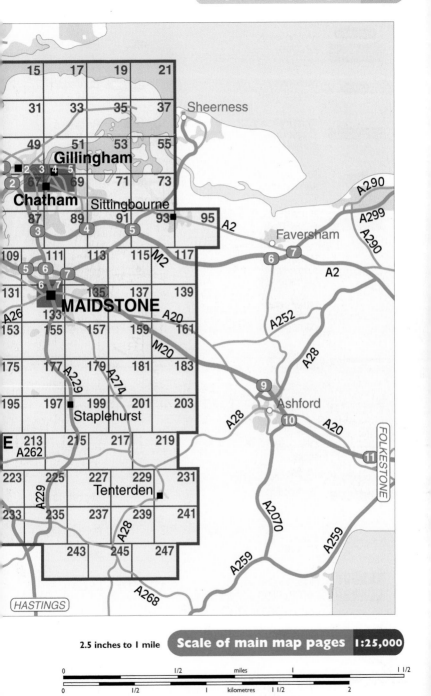

| 15 | 17 | 19 | 21 |

Sheerness

| 31 | 33 | 35 | 37 |

| 49 | 51 | 53 | 55 |

Gillingham

2 3 4 5

2

67 69 | 71 | 73 |

Chatham

Sittingbourne

| 87 | 89 | 91 | 93 | 95 | A2

3 4 5

Faversham

| 109 | 111 | 113 | 115 | 117 |

5 6 7

M2

6 7

A290

A299

A290

6 7

A2

| 131 | 135 | 137 | 139 |

MAIDSTONE

133 A20

A26

A252

| 153 | 155 | 157 | 159 | 161 |

M20

A28

| 175 | 177 | 179 | 181 | 183 |

A229 A274

| 195 | 197 | 199 | 201 | 203 |

9

Staplehurst

A28

Ashford

10

A20

E 213 | 215 | 217 | 219 |
A262

11

FOLKESTONE

| 223 | 225 | 227 | 229 | 231 |

A229

Tenterden

| 233 | 235 | 237 | 239 | 241 |

A28

A2070

A259

| 243 | 245 | 247 |

A259

A268

(HASTINGS)

2.5 inches to 1 mile **Scale of main map pages** 1:25,000

| 0 | 1/2 | miles | 1 | 1 1/2 |

| 0 | 1/2 | 1 | kilometres | 1 1/2 | 2 |

iv

Junction 9	Motorway & junction	P+🚌	Park & Ride
Services	Motorway service area	🚌	Bus/coach station
	Primary road single/dual carriageway		Railway & main railway station
Services	Primary road service area		Railway & minor railway station
	A road single/dual carriageway	⊖	Underground station
	B road single/dual carriageway	⊖	Light railway & station
	Other road single/dual carriageway	++++++++	Preserved private railway
	Restricted road	*LC*	Level crossing
	Private road	•—•—•—	Tramway
← ←	One way street	---------	Ferry route
	Pedestrian street	....	Airport runway
==========	Track/ footpath	—·—·—·—	Boundaries- borough/ district
	Road under construction	\\\\\\\\\	Mounds
]- - - -[	Road tunnel	**93**	Page continuation 1:25,000
P	Parking	**7**	Page continuation to enlarged scale 1:17,500

River/canal lake, pier		Toilet with disabled facilities	
Aqueduct lock, weir		Petrol station	
465 ▲ Winter Hill Peak (with height in metres)		Public house	PH
Beach		Post Office	PO
Coniferous woodland		Public library	
Broadleaved woodland		Tourist Information Centre	
Mixed woodland		Castle	
Park		Historic house/ building	
Cemetery		National Trust property	Wakehurst Place NT
Built-up area		Museum/ art gallery	M
Featured building		Church/chapel	†
City wall		Country park	
Accident & Emergency hospital	A&E	Theatre/ performing arts	
Toilet		Cinema	

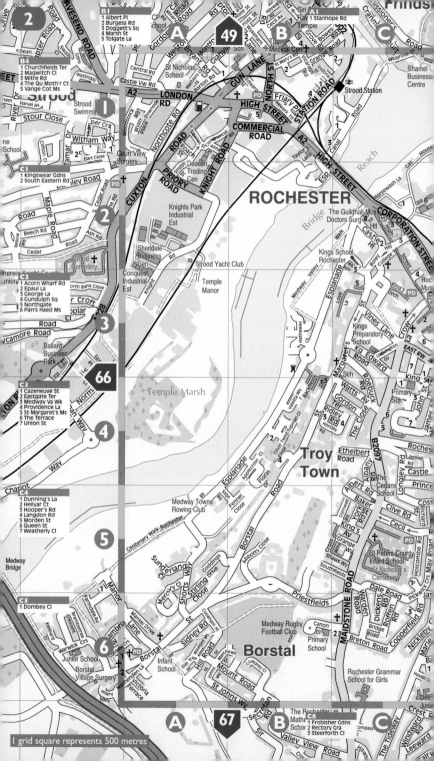

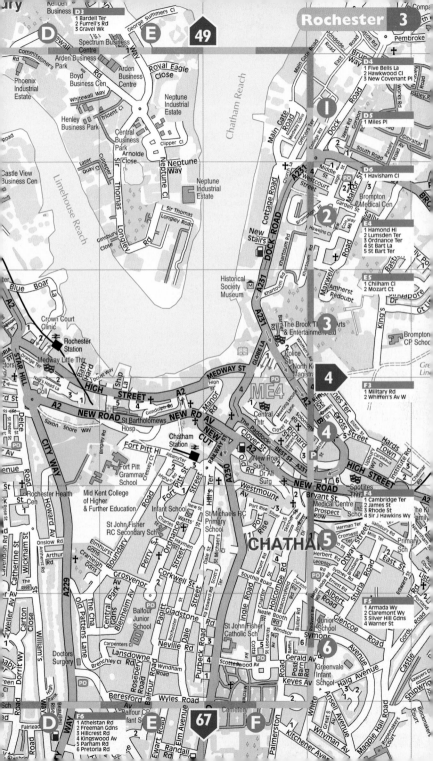

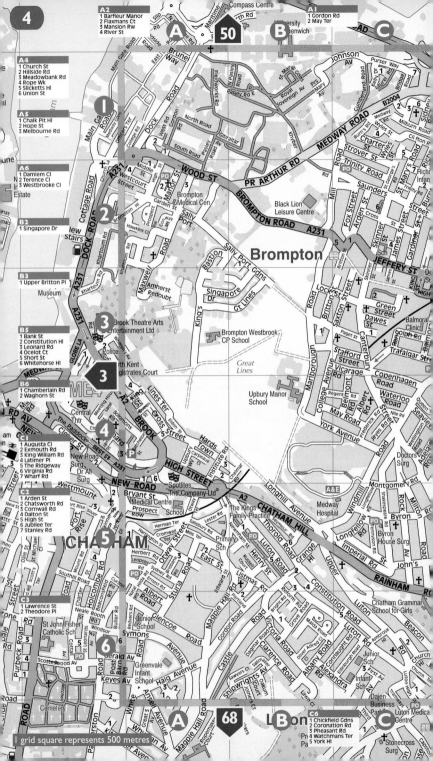

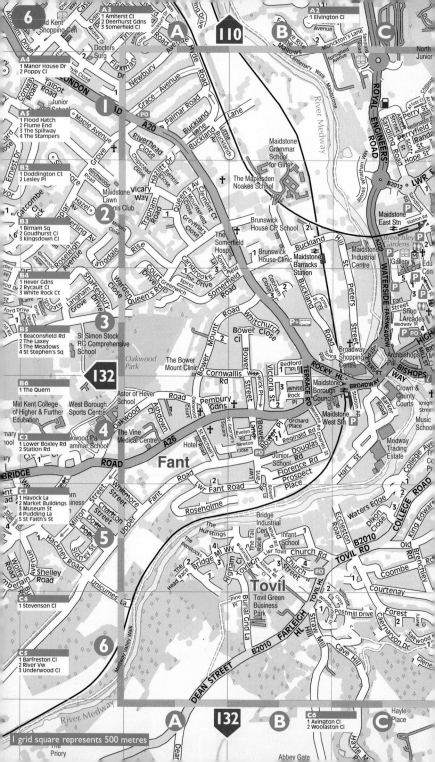

I grid square represents 500 metres

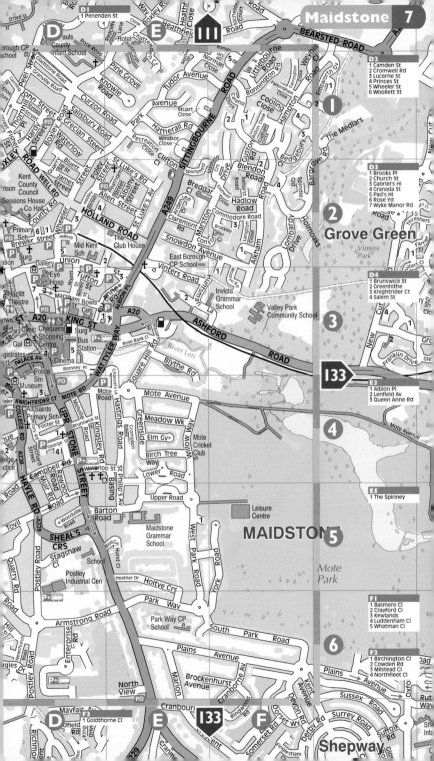

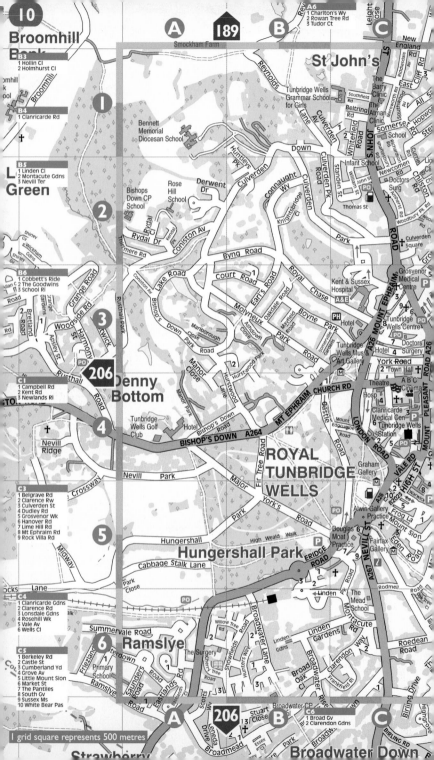

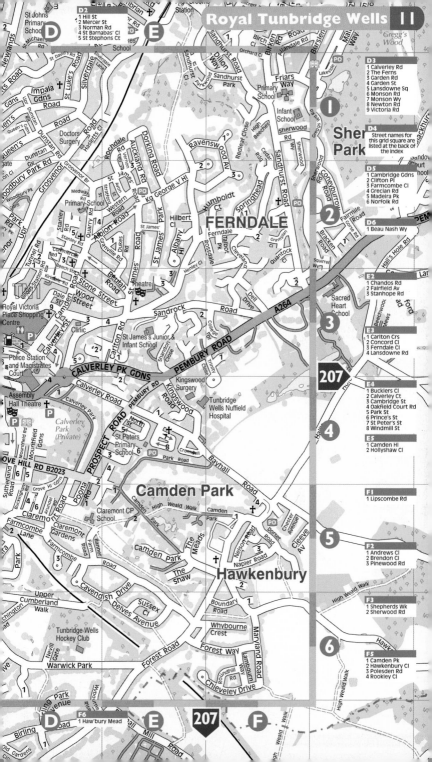

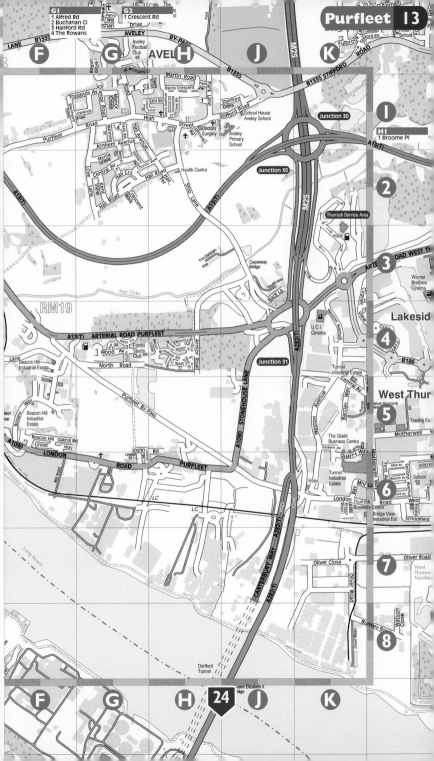

G1
1 Alfred Rd
2 Buchanan Cl
3 Hanford Rd
4 The Rowans

G2
1 Crescent Rd

H1
1 Broome Pl

F **G** AVEL**H** **J** M25 **K**

I

2

3 ROAD WEST T

4

5 West Thur

6

7 Oliver Road

8

Lakesid

West Thur

Motherwell

West
Thurrock
Marshes

Aveley
St Michaels Cl
Martin Road
Stifford Road
Stanford
School House
Aveley School
Junction 30
Aveley
Primary
School
Thurrock Service Area
Hotel
Doctors
Surgery
Health Centre
Junction 30

Toplands Av
Manor
Close
Grange Road
Lowlands
High
Street
Arnhem Avenue
Purfleet
Central Av
Hall Crs
Hall Road
Love
Lane
Kent
Ship Lane
Crescent
Hall Road

Aveley Football Club
AVELEY
BY-PASS
B1335
B1335
B1335 STIFFORD ROAD
A13(T)
A13(T)

The Caravan
site
Causeway
Bridge
South Way
Back La

Mar Dyke
RM19

M25
Junction 31
A282(T)

ARTERIAL ROAD PURFLEET
A13(T)
Fondu
Sports
Club
Wood Av
North
Road
Armor Road
Purfleet By-Pass

U C 1
Cinema
Weston Avenue
Cramer
View

Warner
Brothers
Cinema

B186

Trading Es

Beacon Hill
Industrial Estate
Lane
Beacon Hill
Industrial
Estate
Botany
Way
Oakhill Way
Oakhill
Way
Linnet
Way
LONDON
Joslin Rd
Lindsell
ROAD
PURFLEET
A1090
A1090

STONEHOUSE LANE

Tunnel
Industrial Estate
Central Av
Barclay
The Glade
Business Centre
Eastern
Quarry
Hotel
Tunnel
Industrial
Estate
London
Thurrock
Business Centre
Bridge View
Industrial Est
Road

Weston
Avenue
Motherwell Way
West Thurrock Way
Fifth Av
Fourth Av
Third Av
Second Avenue
First Av
Schoolfield
West
Essex

LC
LC
Long Reach

CANTERBURY WAY
A282(T)

Oliver Close
Oliver Road
Oliver Road

Burnley Road
Watson
Close

Dartford
Tunnel
Queen Elizabeth II
Bridge
24

F **G** **H** **J** **K**

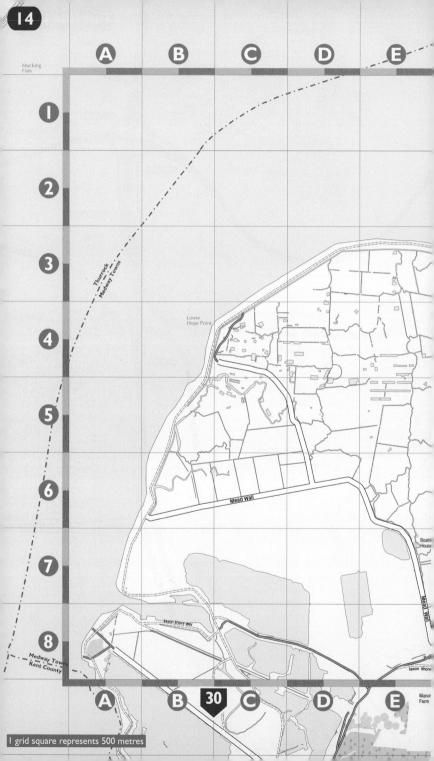

F G H J K

Blythe
Sands

1

2

River   Thames

3

4

16

5

Cliffe
Marshes

Cliffe Fleet

6

7

Ryestreet Common

8

Pickle's
Way
Church   Road
Morse   Close
Reed   Street
Rookery Crescent
Cliffe
Common   Lane
Buttway Lane
Swingate
Avenue
Wadlands
Road
Chancery Rd
Rye Street
Farm
Swan Shore Way

West
Freet

G

St Helens C of E
Primary School

H

31

J

K

St Helens Road
Marsh Crescent
Wharf
Thatcher's Lane
Church Street
Turner Street
Millcroft

Swan Shore Way

Cooling

Cooling

West Point

St Mary's
Hoo

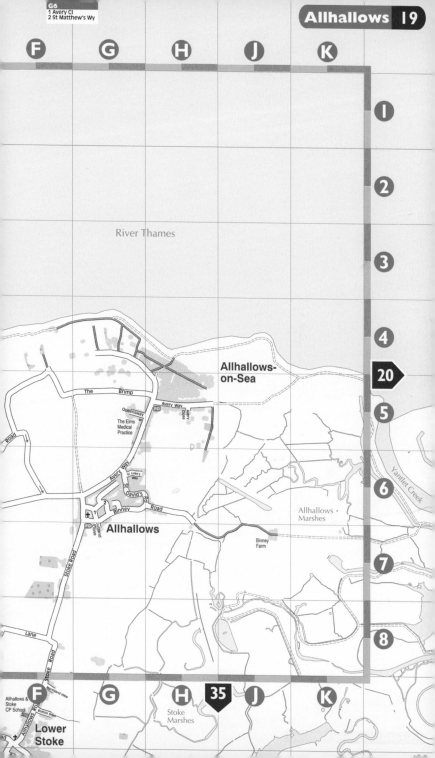

G6
1 Avery Cl
2 St Matthew's Wy

River Thames

Allhallows-
on-Sea

The Brimp

Queensway

Avery Way

Avery Close

The Elms
Medical
Practice

St Luke's Way

David's

Binney Road

Allhallows

Jutland Close

Allhallows Marshes

Binney Farm

Stoke Road

Road

Lane

Allhallows &
Stoke
CP School

Maryland View

Buxton Drive

Almond Rd

**Lower
Stoke**

**Stoke
Marshes**

Yantlet Creek

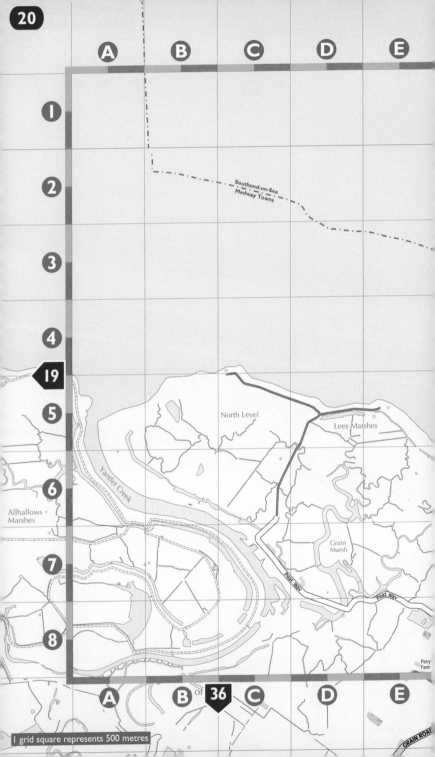

1

2

Southend-on-Sea
Medway Towns

3

4

19

North Level

5

Lees Marshes

Yantlet Creek

6

Allhallows
Marshes

Grain
Marsh

7

Peat Way

Peat Way

8

Perry
Farm

GRAIN ROAD

1 grid square represents 500 metres

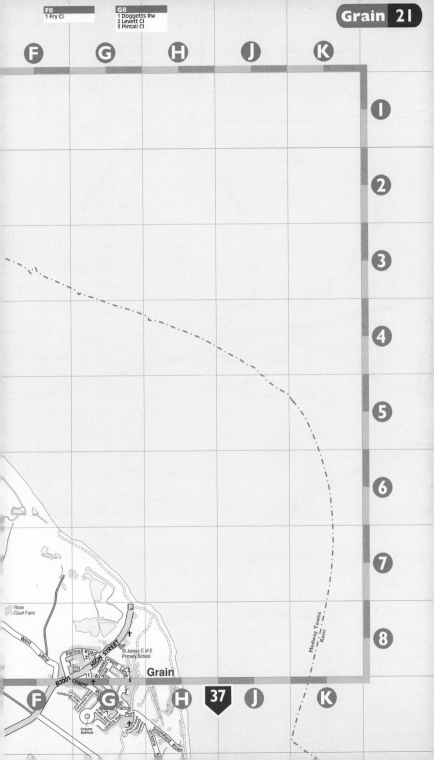

F G H J K

1
2
3
4
5
6
7
8

Rose
Court Farm

West
Lane

Pannell Road

HIGH STREET

St James C of E
Primary School

St James Green Lane

Chapel

B2001

Edinburgh Rd

Colemans Road

Victoria Rd

Grayne
Avenue

Port

Grain

Medway Towns
Kent

F G H **37** J K

F3
1 Crest Vw

F4
1 Borland Cl
2 Cutty Sark Ct
3 Riverview Rd
4 Wheatley Cl

F **G** **H** **J** **K**

I

G4
1 Admirals Wk
2 Skippers Cl

2

G5
1 Starboard Av

3

Kraft
Industrial
Estate

H5
1 Austen Cl
2 Bevans Cl
3 Johnsons Wy

Kraft Industrial Estate

GALLEY HILL ROAD

4
Swanscombe
Station

26

HOPE RD

Doctors Surger

5

1 Craylands Sq

New Swan Valley
Community
Schl

6

K5
1 Madden Cl
2 Mayfield
3 Wallace Gdns

7

8

Stone Ness

Thurrock
Kent County

King
Edward Rd
Kestner
Industrial Est

HIGH STREET

Sara Crs

B255

STATION ROAD

Eagles
Road

Greenhithe for
Bluewater Stn

Ivy Bower Surgery

Greenhithe
Health Clinic

Greenhithe

Knockhall

Park Terrace

B255

A226

Breakness

Mounts Rd

Knockhall
Road

Valley Vw

Spring
Vale

Cross Ct

whites

Ansley Wy

Alkerden Lane

Stone
Castle

Parkway

B255

Lime Tree
Av

Bean
Lane

Bean

HIGH STREET

Brenchley
Way

The Surgery

Fallowfield

Beacon Drive

Beacon
Lane

Stone
Lane

43

The Moors

Stonewood

Jolly
Lane

Oakwood Rd

F **G** **H** **J** **K**

LONDON ROAD A226

A226

Manor Way

Pilgrims Road

Craylands
Lane

Swanscombe
Business Centre

Galley Hill
Industrial Estate

All Saints

DA10

Swanscombe

Craylands
Lane

Lewis Rd

Milton
Rd

Ames

Gasson
Rd

Moore
Rd

Broad Rd

Gyny
Road

Broadfield Rd

Manor
Rd

Durham
Way

Leonard Avenue

St Paul's

Cemetery

Keary Rd

Albert Rd

Castle Rd Vernon

ROMAN ROAD

A296

A2(T) A2(T)

Rosherville

Perry Street

New House

F · G · H · J · K

East
Tilbury
Marshes

ay Towns
t County

Coalhouse
Point

Saxon Shore Way

Shorne Marshes

Canal Road

Road

Queen's
Farm

Lower Higham Road

Queens Farm

Lower Road

King's Farm

East Court
Manor

Lane

Lower Road

CHESTER ROAD

Church Lane

Green Lane

47 Green
Farm

Hill Farm

F · G · H · **47** · J · K

I 1
2
3
4
30
5
6
7
8

G1
1 Chesterton Rd

G6
1 Mallingdene Cl
2 Masefield Dr
3 Newbury Cl

G7
1 Dorchester Cl

F **G** **H** **15** **J** **K**

Pickle's Way

Buttway Lane

West Street

Cliffe

Swingate Avenue

Wadlands Road

Chancery Rd

St Helens C of E Primary School

CHURCH STREET

Turner Street

Millcroft Road

Norwood Close

Higham Road

Cooling Road

Rectory Road

Buckland Farm

South Bank

STATION ROAD

B2000

Simonds Road

Buckland Road

Cooling

I

Saxon shore way

Rye Street Farm

Cooling Road

Berry Court Farm

Gattons Farm

Cooling Court Farm

2

3

4

32

New Barn Farm

Cooling Street

Cooling Street

Perry Hill Farm

Perry Hill

Spendiff Farm

5

Merry Boys Road

Cooling Common

6

Cliffe Woods Surgery

Wentworth Drive

Milton Avenue

Mortimers Avenue

Shaw Cl

Cliffe Woods C P School

Cliffe Woods

Great Chattenden Wood

LODGE

Ladyclose Avenue

Parkside

Tennyson Avenue

Brewer Road

Broomead Rd

View Road

Goodwin Close

Ashwood Close

Road

7

North Terrace

Central Ter

8

TOWN ROAD

Ham River Hill

Common Road

Lee Green

B2000

View Road

LOCHAT ROAD

Swinton Av

F **G** **H** **49** **J** **K** Chattenden

Mockbeggar

Hill

Bunters Hill Rd

Common Road

Street

Kirby Road

Chattenden Lane

F G H **17** J **K**

Hoo

I

Newlands Farm

Ratcliffe Highway

ME3

Clinchstreet Farm

Clinch Street

Walnut Tree Farm

Saxon Shore Way

2

Turkey Hall Farm

Bellwood Court

MALMAYNES

Saxon Shore Way

Northwood Avenue

Thames AV

Medway Avenue

Harrison Drive

Eden Rd

Goodword

Leaman Close

Willowbank Drive

The Street

A228

High Halstow

The

Christmas Lane

3

Fenn Street

4

Ratcliffe Highway

A228

Solomons Farm

Sharnal Street

34

Cold Arbour

5

Tunbridge Hill

Roper's Green Lane

6

LC

PATCLIFFE HIGHWAY

Stoke Road

Belunce Farm

7

Roper's Lane

Tile Barn Farm

Kingshill Drive

Waters Road

Wylie

Bell's Lane

St Werburgh Medical Centre

Trellin Road

Saxon Shore Way

Jacob's Lane

Stoke Road

Estcol Road

Kingsnorth

8

F G H **51** J **K**

Peel Cl

Flack Gdns

Coombe

Witt Road

Road

Elms lical tre

Brookside

Church Road

Court Road

Abbots

Abbot's Court

Saxon Shore Way

F2
1 Denison Ms
2 Grebe Cl
3 High St
4 Little Oakham Ct

F3
1 Anchorage Cl

F G H **19** J K

Lane

Stoke Road

Allhallows &
Stoke
CP School

Marshland View

Buxton Drive

**Lower
Stoke**

Allhallows Road

Stoke Marshes

I

A228

GRAIN ROAD

A228

2

LC

3

**Middle
Stoke**

Burrows Lane

Colemans Tree

4

36

5

Stoke Saltings

Elphinstone
Point

6

Stoke Ooze

7

Sharp
Ness

8

**Burntwick
Island**

Oakham
Marsh

F G H **53** J K

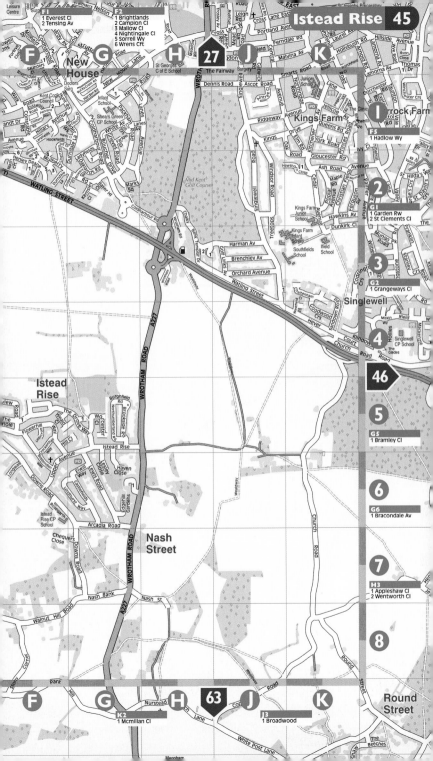

F1
1 Everest Cl
2 Tensing Av

F2
1 Brightlands
2 Campion Cl
3 Mallow Cl
4 Nightingale Cl
5 Sorrell Wy
6 Wrens Cft

F **G** New House **H** **27** The Fairway **J** **K**

St Georges C of E School

I Brock Farm
F5
1 Hadlow Wy

2
G1
1 Garden Rw
2 St Clements Cl

3
G2
1 Grangeways Cl

Singlewell

4
Singlewell CP School
The Glades

46

5
G5
1 Bramley Cl

6
G6
1 Bracondale Av

7
H3
1 Appleshaw Cl
2 Wentworth Cl

8

Kings Farm

Mid Kent Golf Course

Istead Rise

Nash Street

F **G** **H** **63** **J** **K** Round Street
K2
1 Mcmillan Cl

J3
1 Broadwood

F5
1 Goldsworth Dr
2 Rosemount Ct
3 Sherbourne Dr

F6
1 Morgan Rd

F7
1 Stanhope Rd

Chattenden

G5
1 Smetham Gdns

G6
1 Florence St
2 Martin Rd
3 Millpond Cl
4 St Michaels Ct

G7
1 Albert Pl
2 Burgess Rd
3 Doggett's Sq
4 Marsh St
5 Tolgate La

Lower

Mockbeggar

Noke Street

Wainscott

H5
1 Mayfair
2 Thirlmere Cl

Upper Up

H6
1 Murray Rd
2 Peckham Cl
3 Watermill Cl

Frindsbury

H7
1 Kingswear Gdns
2 South Eastern Rd

Strood Station

ROCHESTER

H8
1 Acorn Wharf Rd
2 Epaul La
3 George La
4 Gundulph Sq
5 Northgate
6 Parrs Haed Ms

K6
1 Chaucer Cl

J4
1 Jarrett Av

J3
1 Greenfields Cl

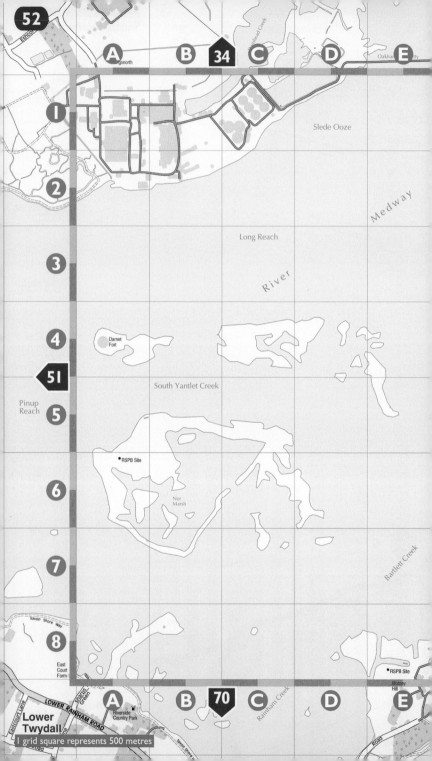

I grid square represents 500 metres

F G H **47** J K

I
2
3
4
66
5
6
7
8

Lodge Farm

Kent County
Medway Towns
Great Wood

Warren Road

Lower Bush

Bush Road

North Downs Way

Popilicans Road
Nine Acres
Charles
Whitesmakers
Ladywood RD
Bush Road

Upper Lodge Road

North Downs Way

Upper Bush

Court Lodge

Cuxton County Infant School
Woodhurst Cl
St Mary's

Red Wood

Kent County
Medway Towns

North Wood

Dean Farm

ROCHESTER ROAD

North Downs Way

Wingate Wood

North Halling
A228

Pilgrims Road

FORMBY RD

Horseholders Wood

New Town

Kent Road

F G H **85** J K

Upper Halling

Primrose Road
Grove Road
The Street

Road

Vicarage Cl

A228
Cem

Halling Station

Marsh Road Marsh Road

High Street
Low Meadow

Halling

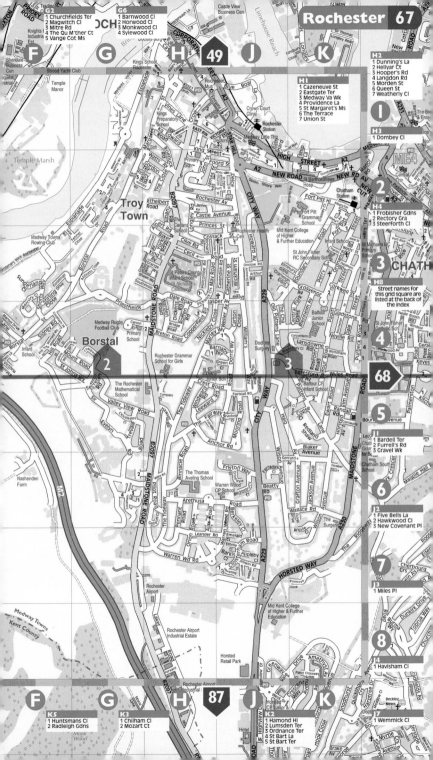

F7
1 The Coach Dr

G7
1 Bramble Bank

F G H **63** J K

Priestwood

Horn's Oak Road

Chandler's Hill

Chandler's Road

David Street

Priestwood Road

Priestwood Green

I
H6
1 Croftside
2 Stonecroft

Heron Hill Lane

2
I6
1 Admers Wy

St Francis Rd

Harvel

Harvel Street

3

South Street

Chapman's Hill

Wilsons Way

Leith Lane

Ridge Lane

Harvel Lane

Culverstone GM Primary School

Willow Walk

Willow Wood Road

Prospect Lane

School Lane

Ridge Wood

Ridge Lane

Valley Lane

4

Culverstone Green

Mountfield Close

Carter's Hill Lane

Whitehorn Lane

Conifer Drive

Beechwood Drive

St Francis Rd

Harvel Lane

84

White Horse Road

Roundgate

5

WROTHAM ROAD

Silver Birch Av

The Shieling

Antnam Close

Meadow Lane

Avenue

Beech Gardens

Brookdene

Whitefoot Lane

Beechwood Drive

Echofield Style

Harvel Lane

Vigo Rugby Club

Open Green

Whitehorse Wood

6

Oak Farm Lane

GRAVESEND ROAD

Newlands Lane

Vigo Village

Harvel Road

Bank

Churchside

Timber Woodside

Downs Wood

The Gallop

Vigo CP School

Ash Keys

Fern Down

The Copse

Highview

Highview

Common Road

Erskine

Hornbeams

Chestnut La

Waterlow Road

Kent County Council

7

Harvel Road

The Covert

North Downs Way

Trosley Country Park

Pilgrims Way

Pinesfield Lane

Westerly

8

Coldrum Lane

Taylors Lane

Downsway

Green Lane

F G H **106** J K

Ryarsh Wood

Trottiscliffe

The Street

School Lane

Church

Trottiscliffe C of E Primary School

Pilgrims Way

88

I grid square represents 500 metres

Hempstead

Wigmore

Park Wood

Lidsing

Bredhurst

Dunn Street

Kemsley Street

Scragged Oak

Lower Cox Street

Junction 4

Medway Towns
Kent County

Little Halstead Farm

Bredhurst Hurst

Monkdown Wood

Newlands Wood

Pollyfield

Grange Farm

G2
1 Honeysuckle Cl

H1
1 Green Bank Cl

H2
1 Thistledown Cl

H3
1 Martin Ct

I2
1 Black Rock Gdns
2 Coppice Ct
3 Stalham Ct

F G H 69 J K

I

2

3

4

90

5

6

7

8

F G H 112 J K

A   B   75   C   D   E

I   Luxted

Bird House Lane

Luxted Road

Hang Grove Hill

Downe Road

Cudham Lane North

Mace Farm

Hostye F

Mace

Lane

2   Church Hill   Cemetery   Angas Home   Cacket's Farm

Charles Darwin School

Luxted Road

Aldous Street

Berry's Hill

Cudham Lane South

Cudham

Cacket's Lane

3   Cudham School   Berry's Green Road

Berry's Green

Aperfield

Juniper Rose

4   New Barn Farm

97

5   Belvedere   St Winifred Road   Isabelle Road

Woodbury Close

Horns Green

6   South Street   A233 MAIN ROAD

Cudham Frith

Scot Lodg

7   Southwood   Bombers Farm   Bombers Lane   Silversted Lane

Cudham Grange

Grays Road

8   Tatsfield Lane   Buckhurst Road

Hawley's Corner

Grays Road   Grays Farm   Silversted Lane

Black's Road   The A

A233

A   B   120   C   D   E

Chestnut   BERHAM   HILL   TN16

Betsom's Hill

Pig's House

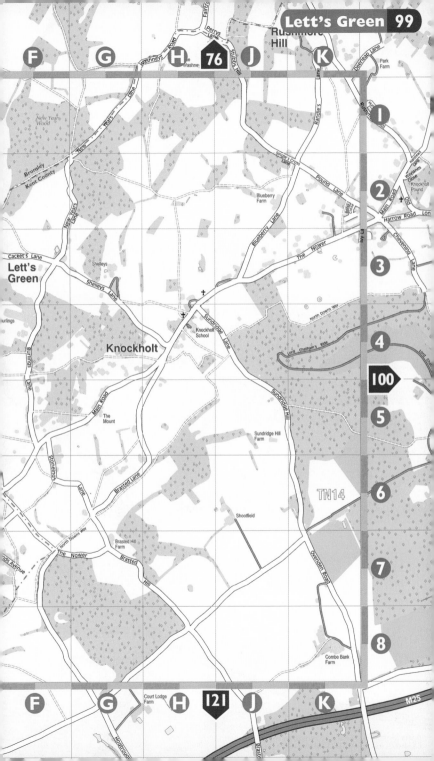

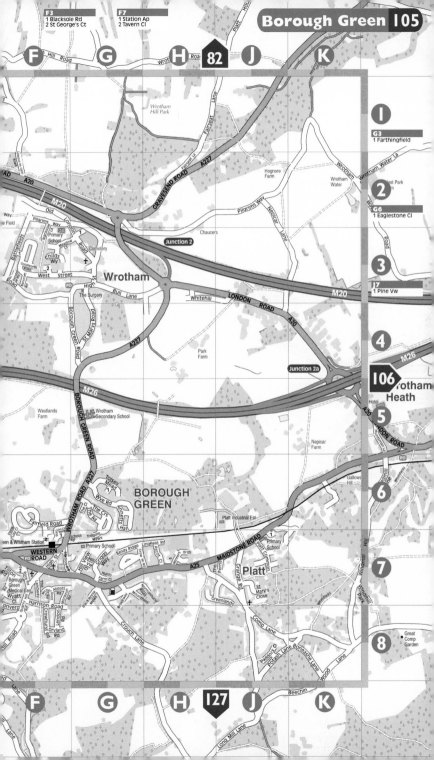

A B 83 C D E

I

Horsholm La

Wrotham Water La

West Park Farm

Wrotham Water

2

Wrotham Water Road

Ford Lane

Green Lane

The Street

School Lane

Church Lane

Trottiscliffe

Trottiscliffe C of E Primary School

Addington Lane

Westway

Trottiscliffe Road

†

Coldrum Lane

Pinesfield Lane

3

M20

M20

Junction 3

The Chost

Park Road

A20

M26

Westfield Farm

Westway

St Vincents Lane

St Vincents

West Malling Golf Club

†

LONDON

4

Junction 2a

105

A20 LONDON ROAD

Hotel

Wrotham Heath

Nepicar Farm

Sandy Lane

Westbury

Clearway

Aldon

Moorlands Wood

Aldon Lane

5

Gallows Hill

PO

Windmill Lane

Westbury

Windmill Hill

Windmill Park Hill

B2016

Teston Road

6

Highlands

7

Comp Farm

Comp Lane

Orchard Place Business Centre

Boneyote Lane

WOOD Lane

Waterford

8

Great Comp Garden

Comp

Beechin

A B 128 C D E

1 grid square represents 500 metres

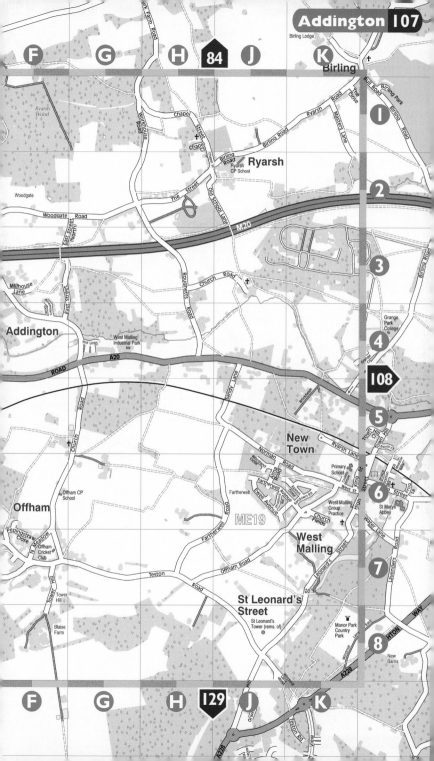

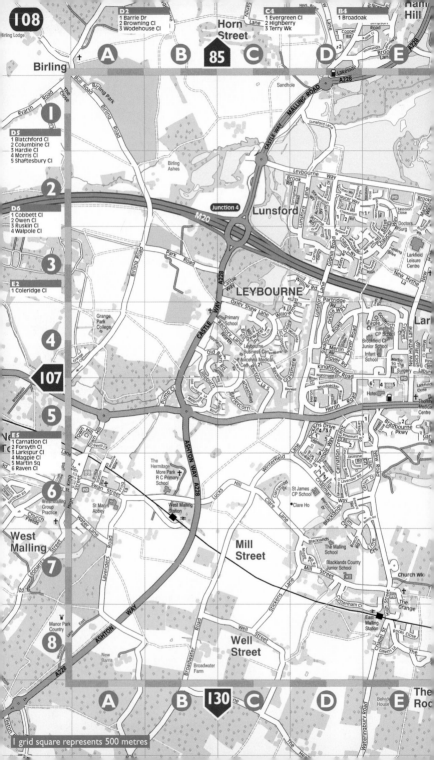

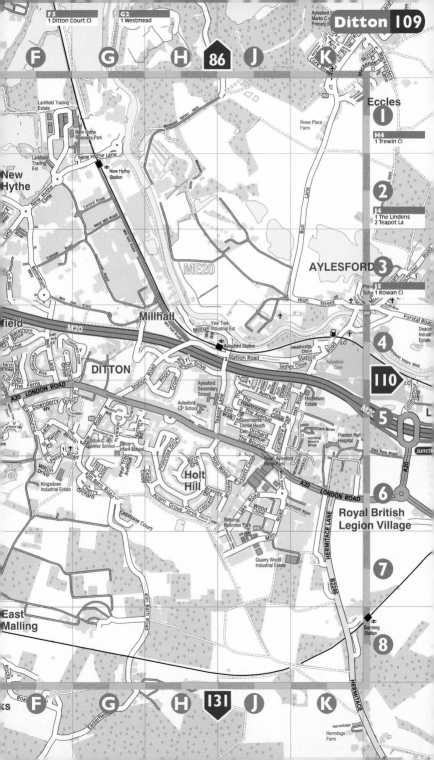

F5
1 Ditton Court Cl

G2
1 Westmead

F **G** **H** 86 **J** **K**

Aylesford S
Marks C o
Primary S

Skinners
Cork Street
Mackenders

Eccles
I

H4
1 Trewin Cl

2

J4
1 The Lindens
2 Teapot La

AYLESFORD **3**

J5
1 Rowan Cl

4

Rowe Place
Farm

Larkfield Trading
Estate

New Hythe
Business Park

New Hythe Lane
New Hythe Lane

New Hythe
Station

New
Hythe

Larkfield
Trading
Est

Central Road

West Mill Road

College Road

ME20

Deacor
Industr
Estate

High Street

Forstal Road

110

M20 Millhall
Industrial Est

Yew Tree
Millhall
Millhall Industrial Est

Aylesford Station

Station Road

Heathcote
Close
Sedley Close

Station

Aylesford
Cem

M20 **5**

L

DITTON

A20 LONDON ROAD

Aylesford
Secondary
School

Aylesford
CP School

Ditton C of E
Junior School

Ditton
Infant School

The Avenue
The Hawthorns
The Avenue
The Bounds

Horsefarm
Estate

Clark Mews

Admiral Moore
Drive

Preston Hall
Hospital

East Park Road

6

Holt
Hill

Kingsdown
Industrial Estate

Cherry
Orchard

Eadstone Court

Kiln Barn Road

South Aylesford
Retail Park

A20 LONDON ROAD

Royal British
Legion Village

East
Malling

Britannia
Business Park

Quarry Wood
Industrial Estate

HERMITAGE LANE

A229

7

Barming
Station

8

F **G** **H** 131 **J** **K**

HERMITAGE

Hermitage Court
Hermitage
Farm

I

G7
1 The Hedges

2

G8
1 Penenden St

3

H6
1 Ashburnham Rd
2 Clewson Ri
3 Harbourland Cl
4 Staplers Ct

4

I 12

5

H7
1 Woodlands Cl

6

J8
1 Basmere Cl
2 Crayford Cl
3 Kewlands
4 Luddenham Cl
5 Whatman Cl

7 Junction 7

K8
1 Netley Cl
2 Newenden Cl

8

Abbey
Gate

Boxley

Sandling

Harbourland

Penenden Heath

Grove Green

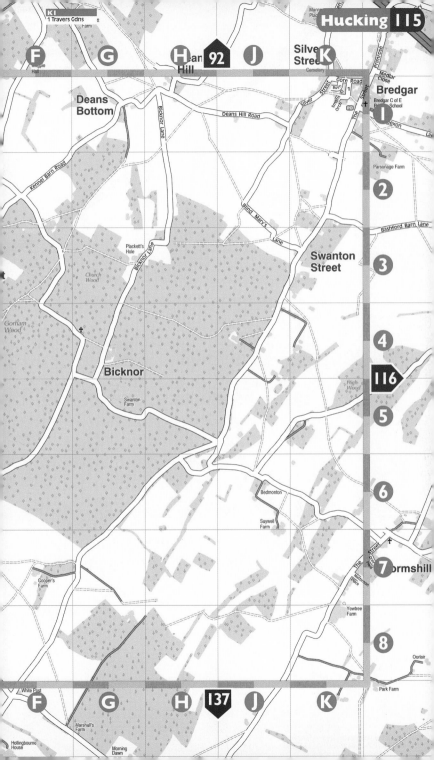

A B **96** C D E

I

2

3

4

5

6

7

8

A B **140** C D E

CROYDON ROAD

B269

B2024

North Downs Way

TITSEY HILL

North Downs Way

The Ridge

Vanguard Way

Chalkpit La

Flint House

North Downs Way

Greensand Way

Greensand Way

M25

Water Lane

Pilchfort Lane

Vanguard Way

Titsey Park

Crells Farm

Tatsfield Lane

Southfields

Wickers Way

Stoneview

Road

Dorans Way

Dorans Way

Chalkpit Lane

Westlands Way

Oakshaw La

Central Wy

Creastands Wy

Gordons Wy

Barnett's

Stilgrove Road

Westlands Cl

WG Shaw

Chichele Road

Oxted & Limpsfield Hospital

St Marys Middle School

Downs Way School

Limpsfield

Limpsfield Grange

Limpsfield Grange School

Park Road

Bluehouse Lane

Bluehouse Gardens

Oxted County School

New Ldg

Cresham Cl

Granville Road

Limpsfield Lawn Tennis Club

Detillens Lane

WESTERHAM

Bluehouse Road

Beatrice Road

Amy Rd

Oxted Gallery

Oxted Health Centre

Snatts

Brassey Hill

Barrow Green Court

Barrow Green Farm

Barrow Green Road

Sandy Lane

Hookwood La

St Mary's Cl

Station Rd

Church Lane

Alan Carter Gallery

OXTED

Oxted Station

East Hill

Old La

Uvedale Road

Brassey Road

The Priory

Peter Av

The

Hoskins

Harwood La

Farm Pk

Willow Br

M25

140

Harrowbrook

High St

PH

West Hill Bank

Ridlands Rise

Clair

GODSTONE ROAD

Quarry Close

Quarry

Woodland Rise

Woodland

Road

Greensand Way

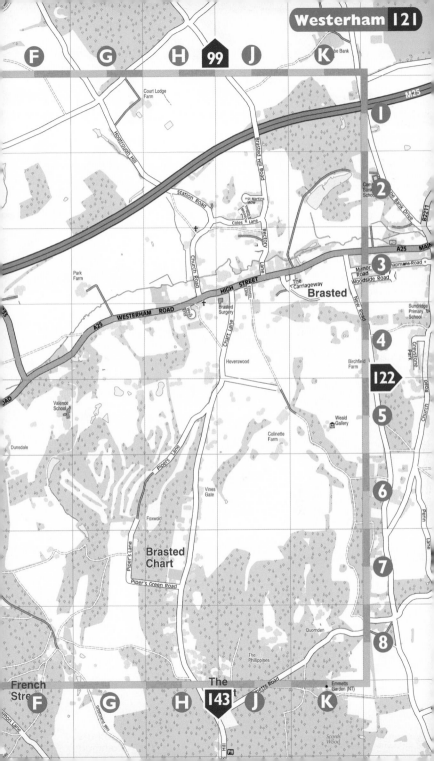

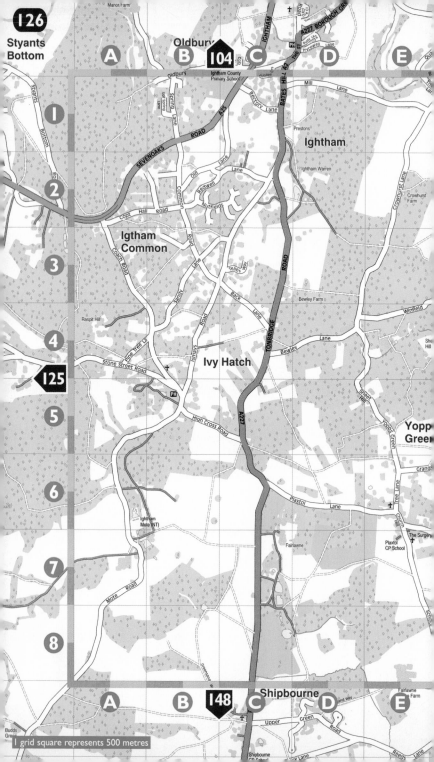

126
Styants Bottom

A   B   C   D   E

104

Oldbury

Manor Farm

Ightham County Primary School

Oldbury

1

Upper Spring Lane

Spring Lane

SEVENOAKS ROAD

Rectory Lane

Mill Lane

Ightham

Prestons

2

Copt Hall Road

Old Redwell Lane

Lane

Nutfields

Ightham Warren

Crowhurst Farm

Igtham Common

Coach Road

Sandy Lane

Common Road

Redwell Lane

Tebbs Way

Bewley Farm

3

Raspit Hill

Back Lane

TONBRIDGE ROAD

Winfield

Bewley Lane

She
Hill

4

125

Pine Tree Ln

Stone Street Road

St Leus Road

Ivy Hatch

PH

Street Hill

Tops Green

**Yopp
Gree**

5

High Cross Road

A227

Grange

6

Ightham Mote (NT)

Plaxtol Lane

Tree Lane

Church Hill

The Surgery

Plaxtol CP School

7

Mote Road

Fairlawne

8

Greensand W

Fairlawne Farm

Budds
Green

A   B   **148**   C   D   E

Shipbourne

Green Road

Upper Green

Fairlawne Way

Shipbourne CP School

Reed's

1 grid square represents 500 metres

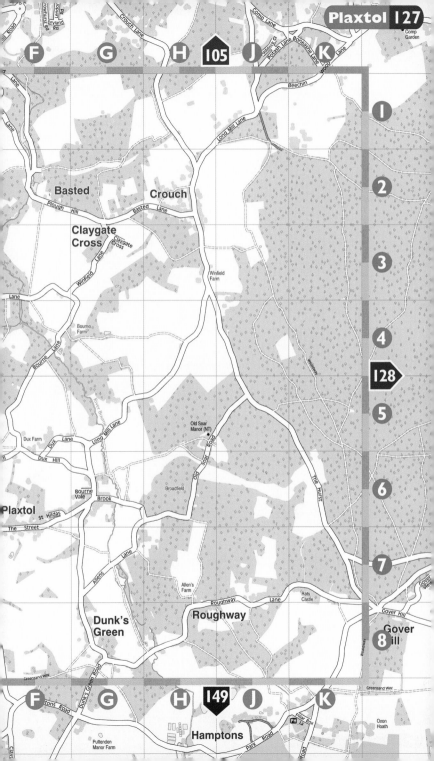

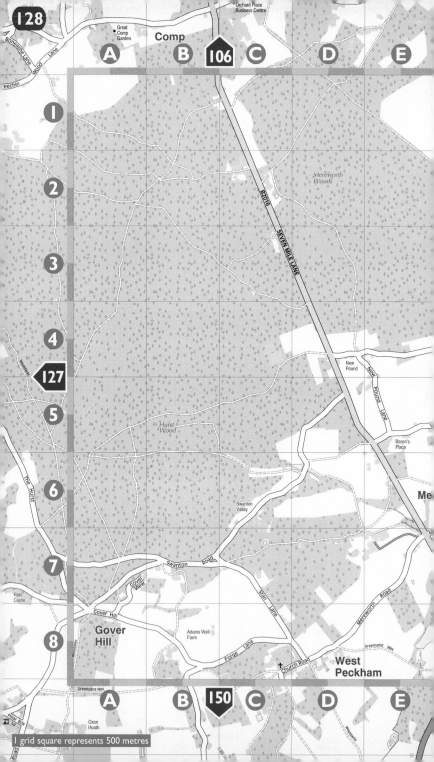

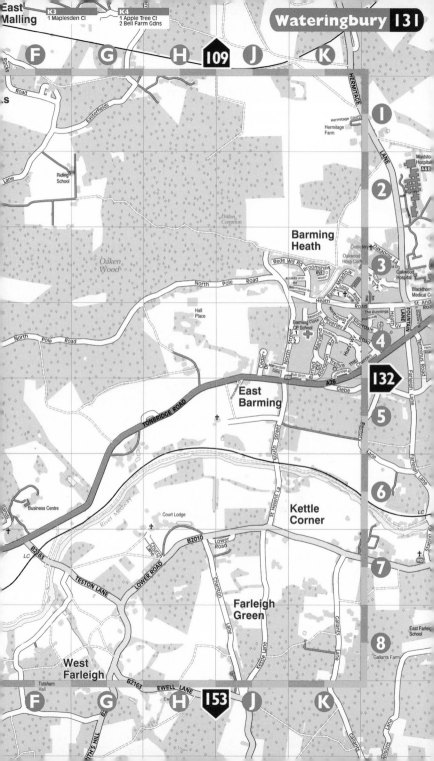

132

Barming
Station

Barming
Heath

131

East Farleigh

Dean
Street

154

1 grid square represents 500 metres

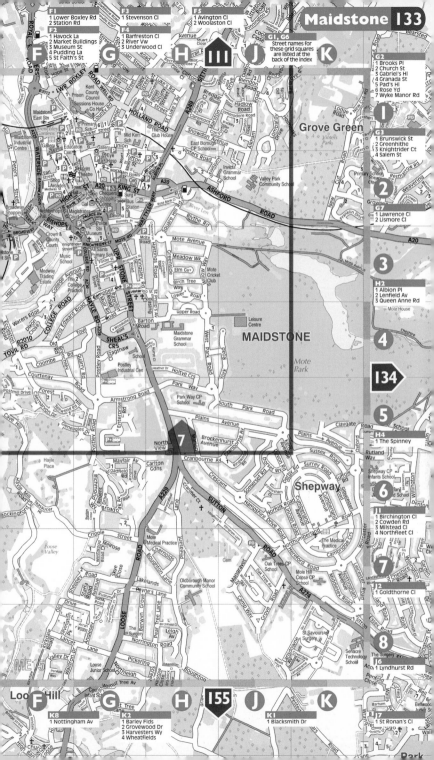

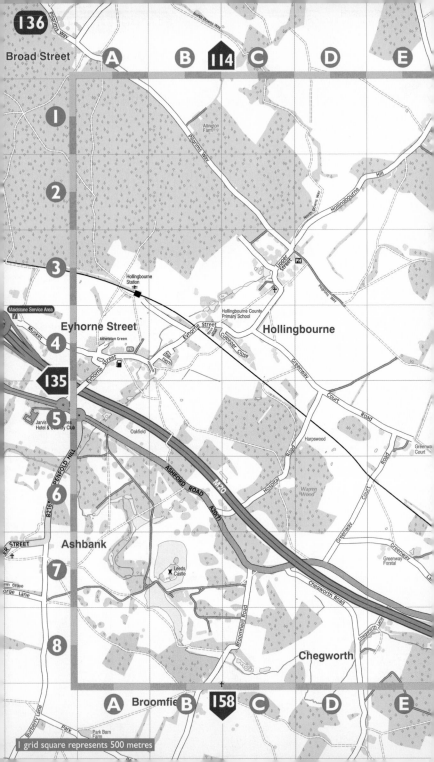

F

G

H

117

J

K

Timbold

Coa

Syndale
Bottom

Wichling

Old Lenham Road

Solomons
Temple

1

Temple Farm

Wichling
Wood

Filmer
Wood

2

ndown

Ashtown Road

Faversham Road

†

Lord's
Wood

Lady
Margaret
Manor

Greet

3

Maitlands
Farm

Payden Street

Oakenpole
Wood

4

Slade

5

Lone Barn Road

Payden
Street

Bunker's
Hill

Slade Road

6

Hurstwood

Tophill
Farm

Payden Street

Warren
Street

Stubblefield House

7

Warren Street

PH

Waterditch Lane

8

Great
Pivington
Farm

Hubbards Hill

Rayners Hill

Waterditch
Farm

North Downs Way

Highbourne
Park

F

G

H

161

J

K

ASHFORD ROAD

Road

A   B   **120**   C   D   E

1

Moorhouse Road

The High Chart

Surrey County
Kent County

Greenstead Way

Goodley Stock

2 Limpsfield Chart

Kent Hatch

Trevereux Hill

KENT HATCH ROAD

Greenstead Way

Kent Hatch

Crockhamhill Common

3

Trevereux

Vanguard Way

Froghole

B269

Froghole Lane

4

Oakden Lane

Vanguard Way

Crockham Hill

Crockham Hill C of E Primary School

PO

141

Swayne
Swaynesland

Stables Lane

Vanguard Way Pit

Hurst Farm

Dairy Lane

B269

MAIN ROAD

SPOUT LANE

5

Vanguard Way

B2026

Dennettsland Road

Crockham Grange

6

Guildables Wood

B2026

Redlands

Coakham Farm

Earlylands

B269

7

Stables Lane

Rushett

Pootings

8

Gaywood

Hole Lane

Vanguard Way

Batchelor's Farm

A   B   **164**   C   D   E

Troy Town

MAIN ROAD

Scamp

Homestead Road

Swan Lane Farm

Fairmead Road

Oakfield Road

1 grid square represents 500 metres

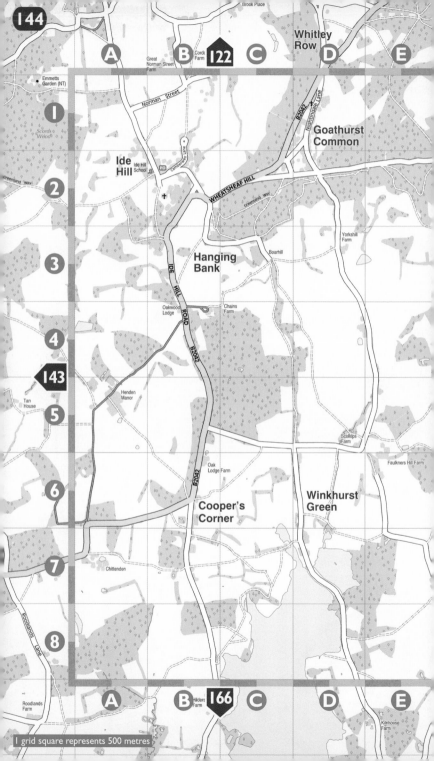

146

A **B** 124 **C** **D** **E**

ubbard's
Hill

1

Weald
Place

A21(T)   SEVENOAKS   BY-PASS

2

Panthurst
Farm

Riverhill House

Riverhill

River/Hill

Under

Romshed
Farm

Bank Lan

3

Weald CP
School

Windmill

The
Surgery
Pa[ ]oss
Farm

Morley's Road

Elses
Farm

Long Barn Road

Mount Pleasant Rd

4

Scabharbour Road

145

5

Fletcher's
Green

Oakhurst

Nizels Hotel
Golf & Leisure
Club

Nizels

Nizels   Lane

TONBRIDGE   BY-PASS   ROAD

LONDON ROAD   B245

A21(T)

6

's
en

Eggpie Lane

Mansers

7

Gaza
Trading
Est

Nizels Lane

Bourne
Place

LON

TONBRIDGE BY-PASS   A21(

8

Southwood

The
Priory

Tips
Cross

Philpots Lane

A **B** 168 **C** **D** **E**

Coppings Farm

Copp[ ] Road

Lower
Street Farm

Lower Street

1 grid square represents 500 metres

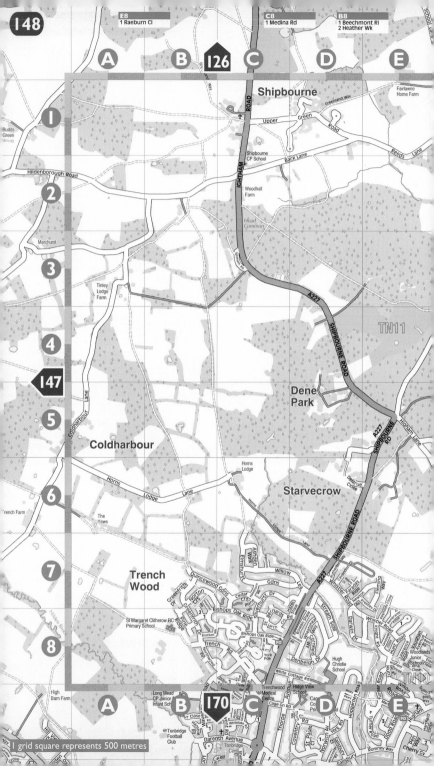

F1
1 Church St
2 Mill St

F2
1 Malthouse Hl

133

F
G
H
J
K

SUTTON

Loose Hill

I

F3
1 Herts Crs

Park Wood

2

H2
1 The Maltings

Loose

3

H3
1 Windmill Ct

Boughton Green

Boughton Monchelsea

HEATH ROAD B2163

Cock Street

4

156

5

Linton

6

East Hall

7

8

F
G
H
177
J
K

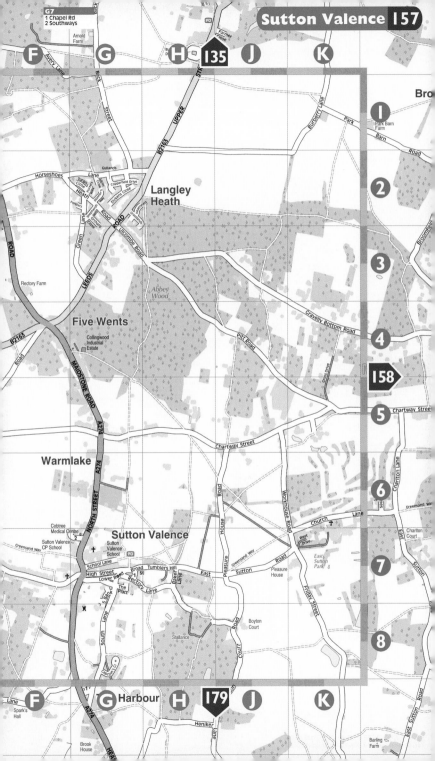

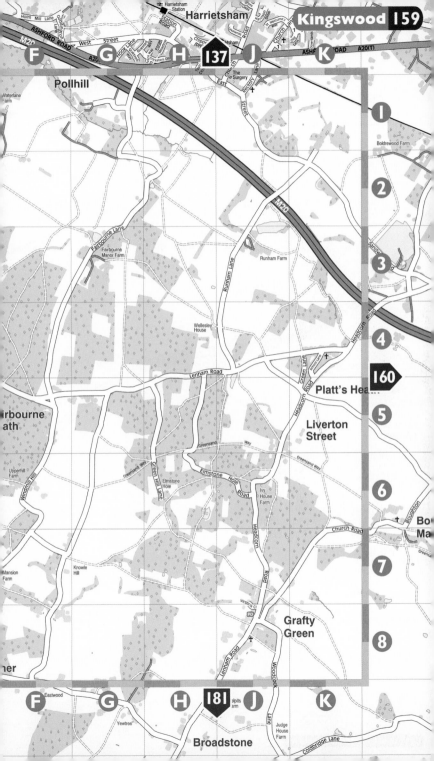

166

1
Roodlands
Farm

Hilders
Farm

Kilnhouse
Farm

2
Furnace House
Farm

Bough
Beech
Reservoir

Bough Beech
Sailing Club

Coles Farm

3
CLINTON LANE

Harborough

Waterlake

Somerden

Brasted
B2027

4
PH
The Close

**Bough
Beech**

Gravelpits

Somerden

How
Green

165

Hever Rd
Hever
Golf
Club

Hever

5
Hever Golf
Clubhouse

Mill
Farm

6

Chiddingstone

Somer
Green

7
x

Gilwyns

Chiddingstone
Church of England School

PH PO

†

8
Hever C of E
Primary Sc

Eden Valley Walk

**Hill
Hoath**

1 grid square represents 500 metres

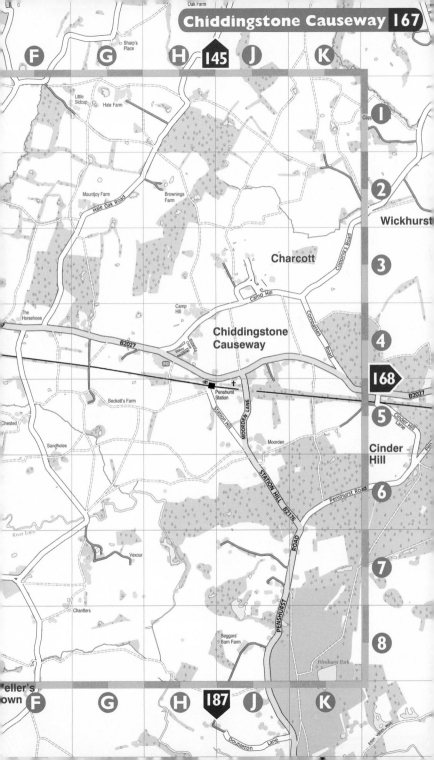

Oak Farm

F G H 145 J K

Sharp's Place

I

Little Sidcup
Hale Farm

2

Wickhurst

Mountjoy Farm
Brownings Farm

Hale Oak Road

Charcott

3

Camp Hill

Camp Hill

The Horseshoes

B2027

Chiddingstone
Causeway

4

Cobham's Road

Compasses Road

168

PO

B2027

5

Cinder Hill Lane

Penshurst
Station

Beckett's Farm

Chested

Station Hill

Moordex Lane

Moorden

Cinder
Hill

6

Penshurst Road

Eden

Sandholes

River Eden

Vexour

STATION HILL B2176

7

Chanlers

PENSHURST ROAD

8

Beggars'
Barn Farm

Penshurst Park

eller's
own F G H 187 J K

Doubleton Lane

Eden Valley Walk

River Beult

F **G** **H** 153 **J** **K**

Hunton Road

Benover

BENOVER ROAD

Reed Court Farm

I

Dairy Lane

Chainhurst

2

Dairy House

Jarmon's Farm

Den Farm

Den Lane

New Lodge House

3

Hunton Road

B2162

Mockbeggar

Spitzbrook

4

176

Bradenbury Farm

Haviker Street

Murzle Farm

5

Claygate Road

Green Lane

Collier Street

6

Brook Farm

B2162

7

Kings Lane

Spenny Farm

Longend Farm

Great Patter

8

Bockingfold

Spenny Lane

TN12

Turkey Farmhouse

F **G** Claygate **H** 195 **J** **K**

Sheephurst Lane

Little Cheveney Farm

Gravel Farmhouse

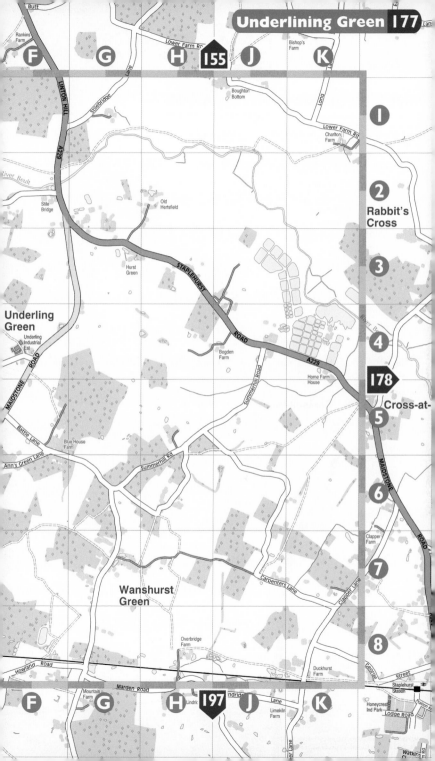

Butt

F   G   H **155** J   K

Rankins
Farm

Lower Farm Rd

Bishop's
Farm

Linton Hill

A229

Stilebridge Lane

Boughton
Bottom

1

Lower Farm Rd

Charlton
Farm

River Beult

Stile
Bridge

Old
Hertsfield

2

**Rabbit's
Cross**

3

Hurst
Green

STAPLEHURST

River B

4

**Underling
Green**

Underling
Industrial
Est

ROAD

MAIDSTONE ROAD

Bogden
Farm

Home Farm
House

A229

178 ▶

Cross-at-

5

Battle Lane

Blue House
Farm

Ann's Green Lane

Summerhill Road

Summerhill Rd

MAIDSTONE

6

Clapper
Farm

7

Carpenters Lane

Clapper Lane

**Wanshurst
Green**

ROAD

8

Overbridge
Farm

Howland Road

Mountain
Farm

Marden Road

Lindridge

Duckhurst
Farm

George   Street

Staplehurst
Station

F   G   H **197** ▼ J   K

Lindr

Lane

Limekiln
Farm

Honeycrest
Ind Park

Lodge Road

Watkins

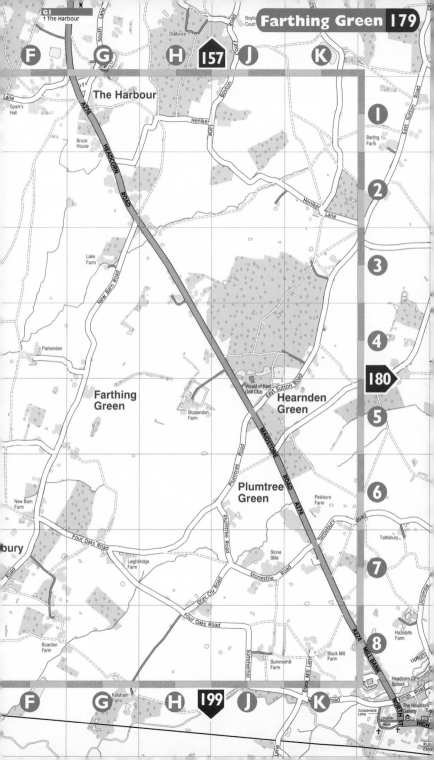

F   G   H   **161**   J   K

Brockton
Farm

Foxen
Farm

M20

Hurst
Wood

1

Coach   Rd

Southfield

Stonebridge Green

Stonebridge Green Road

Field

Mill   Rd

Iden   Lane

Stour Valley Walk

2

Junger
Hatch

Court Lodge
Farm

Clieland

The St

Stivers Rd

Egerton
CP
School

PO

Stevens Cl

Barnfield

Iden

3

Swallow Mill
Farm

Road

Old
School
Court

Elm
Hartnip
Valley

Stone

Stone Hill

Stone

Hill

Greensand Way

New   Road

Greenhill
Farm

Greenhill La

Plvington   Lane

Pivington
Mill

Stour Valley Walk

4

Chart
Court

Britcher
Farm

Egerton   Road

Northgoole   Lane

5

Greensand Way

Elvey
Farm

Egerton   Road

Munday
Farm

6

**Mundy
Bois**

PH

Mill Lane

Westfields

Pluckley

PO

The St

Sheerland

7

Greensand Way

Pluckley C of E
Primary School

Smarden Road

Stanton   Road

8

Pluckley Thorne

Giles
Farm

The Thorn
Estate

**Fir
Toll**

Malmains

The
Pinnock

Lambden   Road

F   G   H   **203**   J   K

Smarden Road

Rushbrook
Farm

GB
1 Prior's Wy

F G H 165 J K

Hever C of E
Primary School

I

Hever Station

Hever Warren

Eden Va

Hartfield Road

Brook Street
Farm

Pigdown

Pigdown
Lane

Hill House

2

Stick
Hill

3

Wilderness
Farm

Eden Hall
(Convent)

Falconhurst

Markbeech

PH

4

186

Cowden
Pound

Cow
Lane

Gilridge

Hartfield Road

Horshoe
Green

5

Edells

Polefields

Claydene

Pyle Gate
Farm

B2026

Wickens

6

Spode Lane

Cowden
Station

Blowers Hill

7

The
Paddocks

Moat Lane

Saxbys

The
Moat

M23

North Street

Leighton
Manor
Farm

Glover's
Hawes

B2026

Hartfield Road

8

Kent County
East Sussex County

Cowden

Cowden
Mead

Church Street

Holywych
House

F

Cowden
Mews

High Street

G H J K

Sussex House
Farm

Holywych
Farm

G1
1 Goldings

H1
1 The Greenways
2 Hornbeam Cl
3 Sycamore Gdns

I
1 Bullfinch Cl
2 Goldfinch Cl
3 Haywain Cl

F

G

H

173

J

K

I

2 Mile Oak

3

4

194

5

6 Brenchley

7

8

BADSELL ROAD

B2017

Mascalls

Mascall's

Mascalls Secondary School

Crittenden

Gedge's Hill

Gedges Farm

Crundalls Farm

Pratt's Lane

Crittenden Road

Chestnut Lane

Birch Close

Chestnut Lane

Maynard's Lane

Maidstone Road

Brenchley Road

Maycotts Lane

B2160

Oakfield Road

Matfield

Brenchley & Matfield C of E Primary School

Brenchley Road

The Lawns

High St

Holm Bank

The Noble Clinic

Broad Oak

Broad Oak Cl

Windmill Hill

Pixot Hill

Moatlands

Waterman's Lane

Biggenden

Mile Oak Road

Knowle

Chantler's Hill

Mascall's Court

Mascalls Court Lane

Mascall Court

Catts Place

Queen Street

Church Road

Green Lane

Hornspocken Road

Friars

Petteridge Lane

Porter's Close

Petteridge

Tibbs Court

Tibb's Court

Chillmill

Hartmill Lane

Kite Lane

Lane

Fairman's Lane

Cryals Road

Old Cryals

Cryals Lane

F

G

H

210

J

K

Battles Grange

Tong Road

Marie Place Road

Flightshott Farm

Court Lane

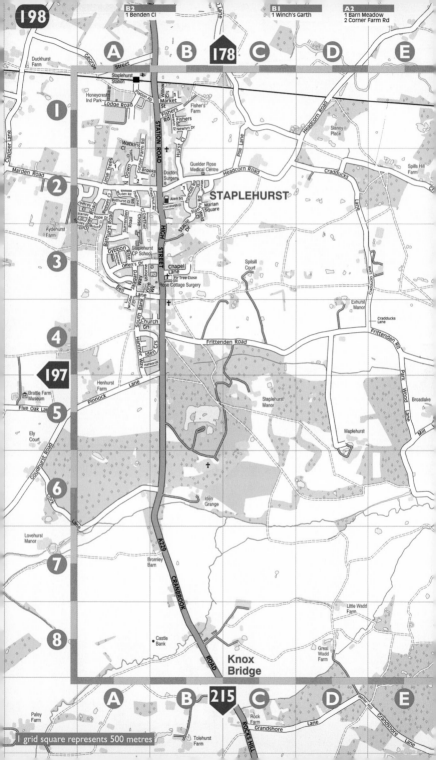

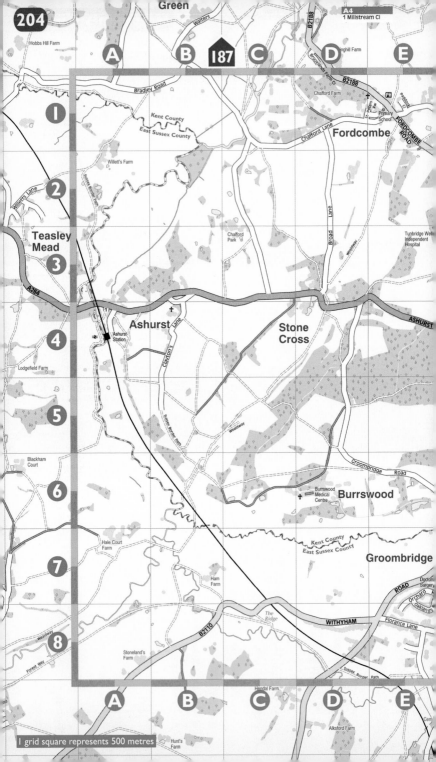

206

189

205

B2
1 Shirley Gdns
2 Vermont Rd

B1
1 Greenfield Cl

A3
1 Ironstones

A2
1 Burdett Rd
2 Gladstone Rd

A1
1 Parsonage Cl

1

C2
1 Rusthall Gra
2 Tristan Gdns

2

C5
1 Nottidge Rd

3

D5
1 Charlton's Wy
2 Rowan Tree Rd
3 Tudor Ct

4

5

D6
1 Eastlands Rd

6

E2
1 Hollin Cl
2 Holmhurst Cl

7

E3
1 Clanricarde Rd

8

E4
1 Linden Cl
2 Montacute Gdns
3 Nevill Ter

Lower Green

Rusthall

Denny Bottom

ROYAL TUNBR WELLS

Hungershall Park

Ramslye

10

Strawberry Hill

Bro

The Warren

Hargate Forest

A B C D E

E5
Street names for
this grid square are
listed at the back of
the index

E6
1 Broadmead Av
2 Devonshire Cl
3 Leicester Dr

E7
1 Harescroft

1 grid square represents 500 metres

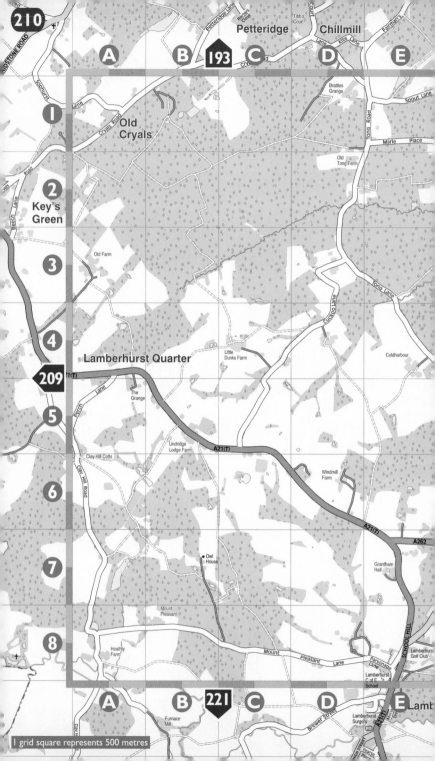

Horsmonden
CP School

Horsmonden **A** **B** 195 **C** **D** **E**

1

Goudhurst Road

Capel
Cross

2

Broad Ford

Grovehurst

Finchurst
Farm

B2079

Gore
Court

Swan
Farm

3

Lewes
Heath

Nevergood
Farm

Brick Kiln Lane

Share
Farm

Brandfold

Swan Lane

Cole Lane

4

Rectory
Park

Rectory Park Road

Small
bridge

Smallbridge

Lidwells
House

Bridge Road

Lidwells Lane

Trottenden
Farm

Blind Lane

Lovers Lane

Trowswell

NORTH ROAD

B2084

5

Lane

6

Schoondersen Road

Crowbourne
Farm

PO
HIGH ST
WEST ROAD
Back Lane

CLAYHILL
BALCOMBES HILL

Maypole

B2079
CHURCH ROAD
A262

Goudhurst and Kilndown
C of E Primary School

Beaman Close

Goudhurst

High Ridge
Mary Day's

Beaman Wy
Curpepp
Jenkins Rise

7

A262

STATION ROAD
A262

Blue Coat Lane

Ranters Lane

Peasley Lane

B2079

8

River Teise

Finchcocks

Pattenden
Farm

Smugley
Farm

A **B** 223 **C** **D** **E**

Trillinghurst
Farmhouse

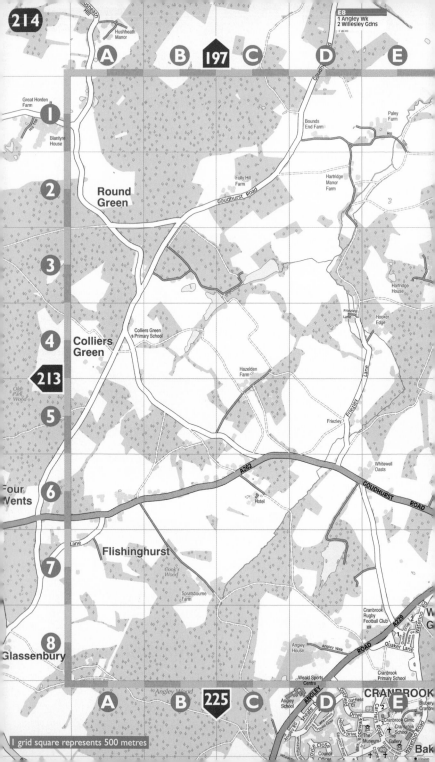

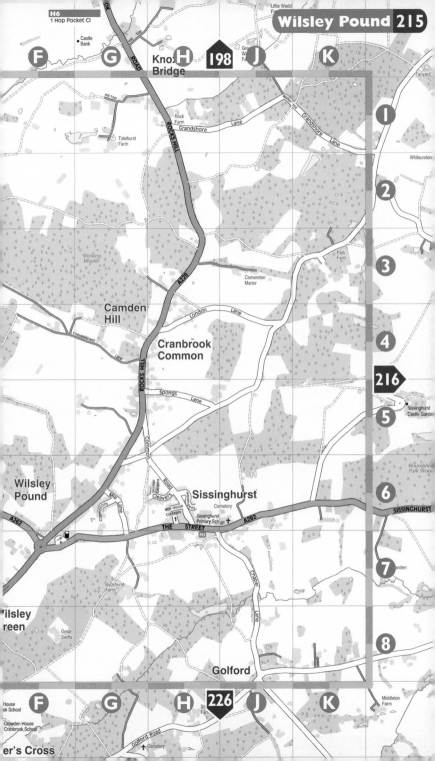

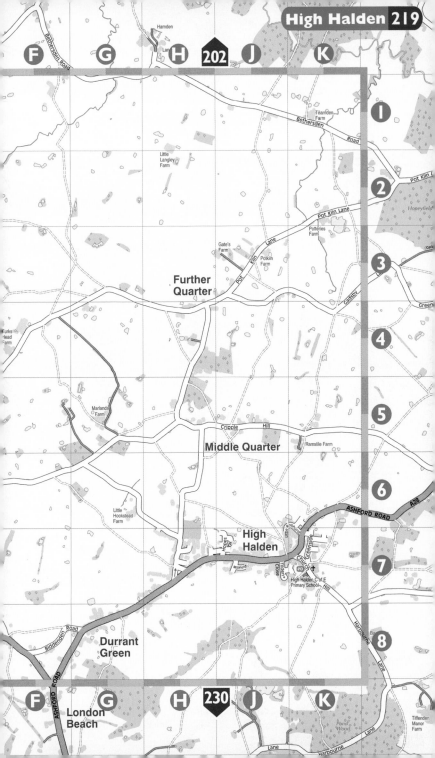

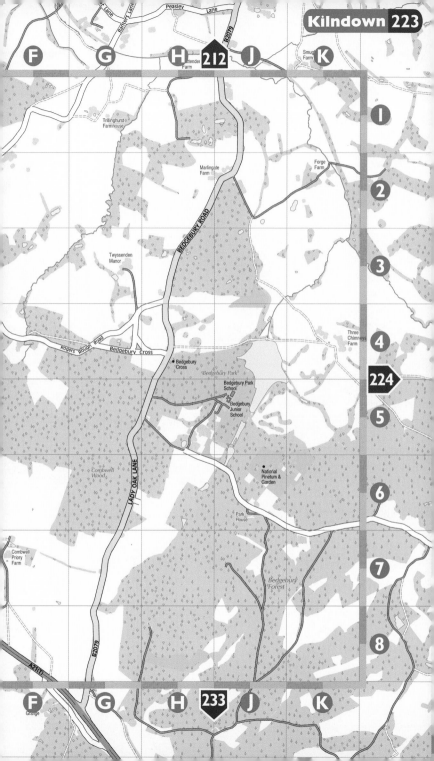

224

A   B   **213**   C   Glassen House   D   Glass E bury

Smugley Farm

I

B2085

Forge Farm

2

GLASSENBURY ROAD

Blackbush Wood

3

Furnace Farm

4   Three Chimneys Farm

223

Bis

5

6   Whitelimes

Louisa Lodge

Park Lane

7

8   Frith Farm   Trenley Farm

A   B   **234**   C   D   E

Tanyard Farm

I grid square represents 500 metres

F G H 216 J K

I
2
3
4
228
5
6
7
8

Middleton Farm

Chittenden Wood

Gaulston Wood

Cranbrook Golf Club

Hemsted Forest

Dockenden

Benenden Hospital

Wood Lane

Frith Lane

Green Lane

Admirals Walk

Goddard's Green

Pympne Manor

New Pond Road

Benenden Girls School

Mount Hall Farm

Mount Le Hoe

Walkhurst Road

Stepneyford La

Benenden

Hortons Close

PO

THE STREET

Fuggles Court

Rothermere Close

Walkhurst Farm

Larkspine Dell

Benenden C of E Primary School

B2086

BENENDEN

Pullin n 237

Beacon ll

Hole Park

Ramsden Farm

F G H 237 J K

228

Ⓐ Ⓑ **217** Ⓒ Ⓓ Ⓔ

Fosten
Green

Clapper
Hill

Cranbrook Road

Birchwood
Farm

Benenden Road

Little
Whatmans

Sandpit
Wood

1

2

The
Brogue

Mockbeggar

Lane

Wood
Lane

East End

3

Benenden
Hospital

Clevelands

Green

Lane

Hole

Lane

Tenterden Road

Shorts
Farm

Bishopsdale
Farm

4

Frogs

Pympne
Manor

227

5

Stephenford Lane

Halden Lane

Mount
Hall
Farm

Colebarn
Farm

Mount
Pleasant
Farm

6

Mount
Le Hoe

Halden
Place

7

Maplesden

8

Little
Halden

Hole
Park

Ⓐ Ⓑ **238** Ⓒ Ⓓ Ⓔ

Halden
Lane Farm

ROAD

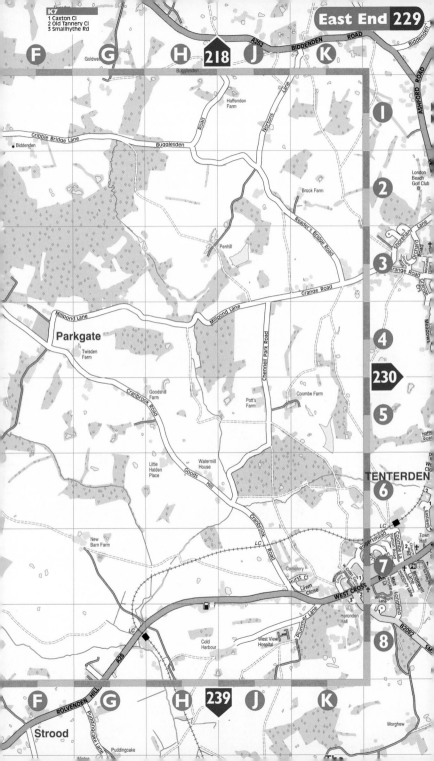

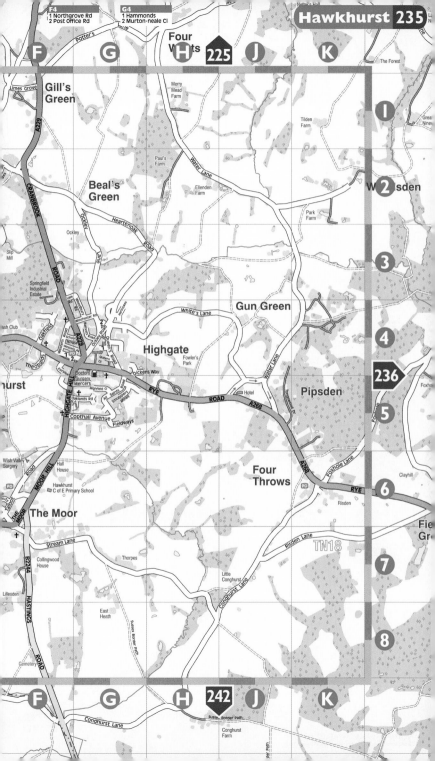

A   B   **226**   C   D   E

Netter's Hall Farm

Nineveh Lane

Little Nineveh

Babbes Farm

The Forst

1

Tilden Farm

Great Nineveh

Scullsgate House

Stream Farm

Coldharbour Road

Coldharbour Chapel L

2 Woodsden

Park Farm

Diprose

Sarnden

3

The Paper Mill

Hinksden Road

Eaglesden

Mill Street

4

235

Pipsden

5

Foxhole Lane

Foxhole

Sponden Lane

6 RYE ROAD

PD

Risden

Foxhole Lane

Clayhill

Beeches Farm

Sponden Lane

Sponden House

A268

7

TN18

Alderden Manor

8

Downgale

Field Green

A268

MEGRIMS HILL

QUEEN STREET

Sandhurst CP School

Back Road

QUEEN STREET

Burnt House Close

A   B   **243**   C Sandhurst   D   E

Iverdale Lane

Silve

F G H **229** J K

I
Morghew

The
Quarter

2
B
T

Strood

Puddingcake Lane
ROLVENDEN HILL

Winton
Farm

Puddingcake

Cold
Harb

West View
Hospital

LC

Lower
Woolwich

3
Morghew
Farm

Kent & East Sussex Railway

Kingsgate

4

240

5
ulleign

Friezingham
Farm

6

Hillgate
Farm

Lowden
Farm

Britcher
Farm

7

Lambsland
Farm

Maytham Road

Newmill Channel

8

LC

Maytham
Farm

Plastre Court

West Sussex Railway

F G H **246** J K

Potman's
Heath

Witt

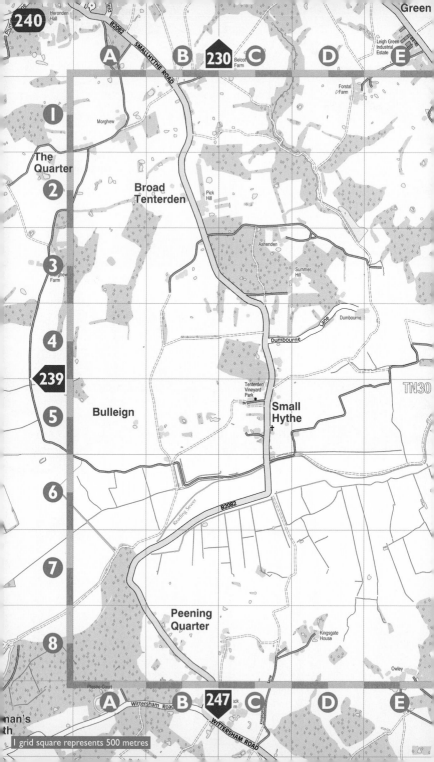

235

A B C D E

1 Merriments Farm

Conghurst Lane

Sussex Border Path

Conghurst Farm

Sussex Border Path

2 Brickhurst Wood

Northlands

3 B2244

Sussex Border Path

JUNCTION ROAD

4

High Wigsell

Neals

5 Climsett's Farm

Boarsney Farm

South Park

Elms Farm

Bourne Lane

B2244

6 Bourne Farm

New House

7 Haiselman's Farm

Rocks Hill

Park Farm

JUNCTION ROAD

8 Higham House

Moat Farm

A B C D E

B2244

1 grid square represents 500 metres

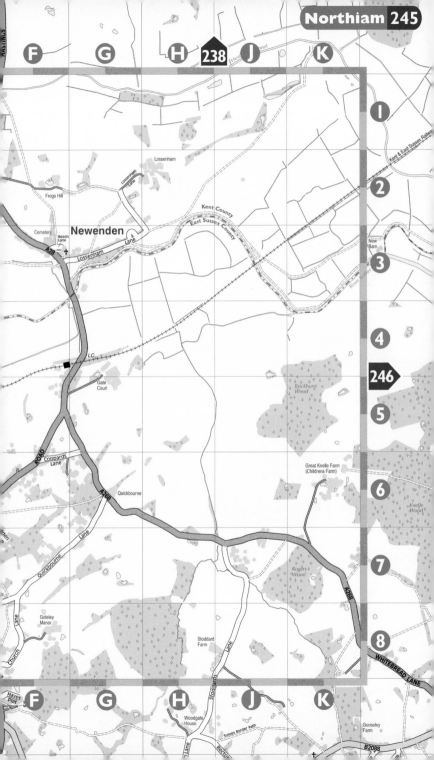

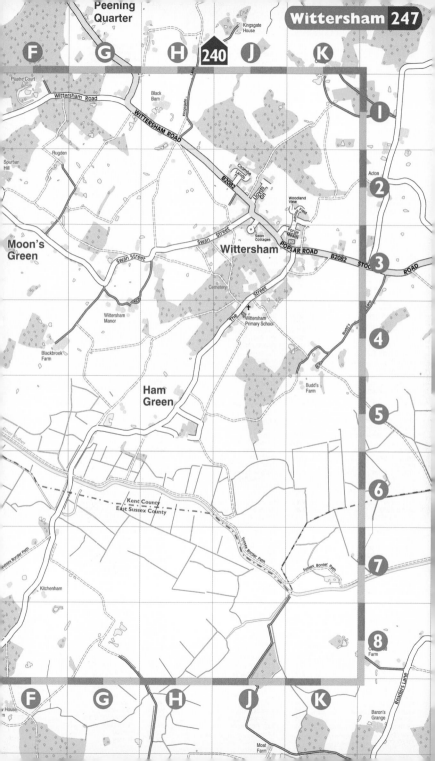

Abbey Gate	111 F3	
Addington	107 F4	
Allhallows	19 G7	
Allhallows-on-Sea	19 J4	
Allington	110 D6	
Aperfield	97 K4	
Ash	81 K1	
Ashbank	135 K7	
Ashurst	204 A4	
Aylesford	109 K3	
Badgers Mount	77 J4	
Baker's Cross	225 K11	
Bapchild	95 F3	
Barden Park	169 K5	
Barming Heath	131 K3	
Barnehurst	22 A2	
Barnes Cray	22 E3	
Barnes Street	172 C2	
Barnfield	183 J2	
Basted	127 F2	
Bayley's Hill	145 G2	
Beacon Hill	237 J1	
Beal's Green	235 G2	
Bean	43 G1	
Bearsted	134 D4	
Beltring	173 K2	
Benenden	227 F7	
Benover	175 F1	
Berner's Hill	232 E4	
Berry's Green	98 A3	
Bessels Green	123 F3	
Betsham	44 A2	
Bexon	116 B2	
Bicknor	115 G4	
Bidborough	189 H3	
Biddenden	217 H4	
Biddenden Green	202 B4	
Biggin Hill	97 F4	
Birchden	205 G8	
Birling	84 E8	
Bitchet Green	125 H5	
Blue Bell Hill	87 H5	
Bluetown	117 H5	
Bobbing	73 G7	
Bodiam	243 F6	
Borden	93 F4	
Borough Green	105 G6	
Borstal	2 B6	
Bottom Pond	116 D4	
Bough Beech	166 B4	
Boughton Green	155 G2	
Boughton Malherbe	160 A6	
Boughton Monchelsea	155 G3	
Bowmans	22 C6	
Boxley	111 K4	
Branbridges	151 K8	
Brasted	121 K3	
Brasted Chart	121 H7	
Breach	71 J6	
Bredgar	116 A1	
Bredhurst	89 J5	
Brenchley	194 A6	
Broad Ford	212 B2	
Broadham Green	140 A3	
Broadstone	181 H1	
Broad Street	50 D2	
Broad Street	113 K8	
Broad Tenterden	240 A2	
Broadwater Down	206 E6	
Brompton	4 B2	
Brook Street	170 A7	
Broomfield	158 A1	
Broom Hill	56 A4	
Broomhill Bank	189 G7	
Buckhurst	217 F1	
Bulleign	240 A5	
Burham	86 E5	
Burham Court	86 C5	
Burrswood	204 D6	
Cage Green	170 C2	
Camden Hill	215 G4	
Camden Park	11 E5	
Camer	63 K3	
Capel	172 B8	
Capel Cross	212 B1	
Capstone	68 E7	
Castle Hill	194 C5	
Cellarhill	95 K5	
Chainhurst	176 A2	
Chalk	28 D7	
Chalkwell	93 H2	
Chamber's Green	203 J2	
Charcott	167 J3	
Chart Corner	156 D5	
Chart Hill	156 D6	
Chart Sutton	178 C1	
The Chart	143 H1	
Chatham	3 F5	
Chattenden	49 K1	
Chegworth	136 D8	
Chelsfield	77 F1	
Chesley	91 K3	
Chestnut Street	92 D2	
Chevening	100 B6	
Chiddingstone	166 C6	
Chiddingstone Causeway	167 H4	
Chiddingstone Hoath	186 C4	
Childsbridge	102 D6	
Chillmill	193 J8	
Chipstead	122 E1	
Church Street	30 C5	
Cinder Hill	168 A5	
Clapper Hill	228 D1	
Claygate	149 F2	
Claygate	195 G1	
Claygate Cross	127 G3	
Clement Street	41 G4	
Cliffe	15 H8	
Cliffe Woods	31 H7	
Cobham	64 C1	
Cock Street	155 K4	
Coldblow	40 C2	
Cold Harbour	72 E8	
Coldharbour	148 A5	
Colliers Green	214 A4	
Collier Street	175 J6	
Colt's Hill	192 D2	
Comp	106 B8	
Congelow	152 C7	
Cooling	32 A1	
Cooling Street	31 J5	
Coomb Hill	64 B8	
Cooper's Corner	144 B6	
The Corner	195 F6	
Cousley Wood	220 E7	
Cowden	185 G8	
Coxheath	154 D3	
Cranbrook	225 K1	
Cranbrook Common	215 H4	
Crayford	22 D4	
Crit Hall	226 B7	
Crockenhill	58 A4	
Crockham Hill	142 A4	
Crockhurst Street	171 H8	
Cross-at-Hand	178 A5	
Cross Keys	8 B6	
Crouch	127 H2	
Crowdleham	103 H4	
Crowhurst	162 B3	
Cudham	98 D2	
Culverstone Green	83 F4	
Curteis' Corner	217 K3	
Curtisden Green	213 H1	
Cuxton	66 B4	
Dale Hill	232 D4	
Danaway	92 B4	
Darenth	42 B3	
Dartford	23 F6	
David Street	83 H1	
Dean Bottom	43 G8	
Deans Bottom	115 G1	
Deans Hill	92 C8	
Dean Street	132 D8	
Dene Park	148 D5	
Denny Bottom	206 C3	
Denton	28 B6	
Derry Downs	56 E3	
Detling	112 D5	
Dingleden	237 H3	
Ditton	109 G4	
Downe	74 E6	
The Down	221 H3	
Dryhill	122 D3	
Dungate	117 H3	
Dunk's Green	127 G8	
Dunn Street	89 H6	
Dunton Green	101 G6	
Durrant Green	219 G8	
East Barming	131 J5	
East End	200 E2	
East End	228 B3	
East Farleigh	132 B7	
East Hill	80 A4	
East Malling	109 F8	
East Malling Heath	130 C3	
East Peckham	151 H8	
Eccles	110 A1	
Edenbridge	164 D4	
Egerton	182 E3	
Egerton Forstal	182 D5	
Eyhorne Street	135 K4	
Eynsford	59 H6	
Fairbourne Heath	158 E5	
Fairseat	82 D7	
Fant	6 A4	
Farleigh Green	131 J8	
Farnborough	75 G1	
Farningham	59 K4	
Farthing Corner	90 B3	
Farthing Green	179 G5	
Fawkham Green	61 G3	
Fenn Street	33 H3	
Ferndale	11 E2	
Field Green	236 A7	
Fir Toll	183 J8	
Five Oak Green	172 C6	
Five Wents	157 G4	
Fleet Downs	24 A8	
Fletcher's Green	146 B5	
Flimwell	233 G3	
Flishinghurst	214 A7	
Foots Cray	38 C4	
Force Green	120 E3	
Fordcombe	204 D1	
Forstal	110 C4	
Fosten Green	228 B1	
Four Elms	165 G1	
Four Throws	235 J6	
Four Wents	213 K6	
Four Wents	225 H8	
Foxenden	63 K6	
French Street	143 F1	
Frindsbury	49 H6	
Friningham	113 H5	
Frinsted	116 C7	
Frittenden	199 H7	
Froghole	142 D3	
Further Quarter	219 H3	
Gadshill	48 B4	
Gillingham	5 E5	
Gill's Green	235 F5	
Glassenbury	213 K8	
Goathurst Common	144 D1	
Goddard's Green	227 H4	
Godden Green	125 F4	
Goddington	56 D7	
Golden Green	172 B3	
Golford	215 H8	
Goodley Stock	142 B3	
Goose Green	150 D4	
Goose Green	217 H6	
Goudhurst	212 E6	
Gover Hill	128 A8	
Grafty Green	159 J8	
Grain	21 H8	
Grange	51 J8	
Gravesend	27 K5	
Great Buckland	84 D3	
Great Cheveney	196 A5	
Greatness	102 D3	
Great Pattenden	176 A8	
Green Hill	134 D6	
Greenhithe	25 G4	
Green Street Green	43 F4	
Green Street Green	75 K3	
Greet	139 K3	
Grigg	180 E8	
Groombridge	204 D4	
Grove End	93 H7	
Grove Green	133 K1	
Grubb Street	43 G6	
Gun Green	235 J4	
Hadlow	150 B5	
Hadlow Stair	171 G2	
Haffenden Quarter	202 A7	
Hale	68 E6	
Hale Street	151 J7	
Halling	86 A1	
Hall's Green	145 J6	
Halstead	77 H7	
Ham Green	53 J8	
Ham Green	247 H5	
Ham Hill	85 K8	
Hamptons	149 H1	
Hanging Bank	144 B3	
Harbourland	111 K5	
The Harbour	179 G1	
Hareplain	217 F3	
Harman's Corner	93 G4	
Harrietsham	137 H8	
Hartley	62 A2	
Hartley	225 F4	

Hartley Green 61 K2	Lamberhurst 221 K1	Mowshurst 164 E2
Hartlip 91 G1	Lamberhurst Quarter 210 A4	Mundy Bois 182 D6
Harvel 83 K3	Lamb's Cross 156 B8	Mundy Bois 183 F6
Haviker Street 175 J5	Lane End 42 C3	Murston 94 D2
Hawkenbury 11 F5	Langley 156 E2	Nash 74 A2
Hawkenbury 178 E7	Langley Heath 157 H2	Nash Street 45 H7
Hawkhurst 234 E5	Langton Green 205 J2	Nettlestead 130 A6
Hawley 41 H3	Larkfield 108 E4	Nettlestead Green 151 K4
Haxted 163 K6	Leadingcross Green 160 C3	New Ash Green 62 E1
Hazel Street 114 E3	Leaves Green 74 C6	New Barn 44 C7
Hazel Street 211 H3	Leeds 135 J7	Newenden 245 G3
Hazelwood 75 H6	Leigh 168 D4	New House 27 F8
Headcorn 180 B8	Leigh Green 230 E7	New Hythe 109 F2
Hearnden Green 179 J5	Lenham 160 D1	Newington 72 B8
Hearts Delight 93 G5	Lenham Forstal 161 H5	New Street 82 E1
Heath Side 22 C8	Lenham Heath 161 H6	New Town 23 J5
Heaverham 103 J4	Lett's Green 99 F3	New Town 65 K8
Hempstead 89 F1	Leybourne 108 C3	New Town 107 K5
Henhurst 46 B6	Lidsing 89 F5	Noah's Arks 102 E6
Henley Street 64 C3	Limpsfield 118 D6	Noke Street 49 H2
Henwood Green 192 B8	Limpsfield Chart 141 K2	North Cray 39 H1
Herne Pound 129 G4	Limpsfield Common 141 F1	Northfleet 26 D4
Hever 165 J8	Lingfield Common 162 B8	Northfleet Green 44 D3
Hextable 40 D5	Linkhill 244 B3	North Halling 65 K7
Higham 48 B2	Linton 155 F6	Northiam 244 E8
Higham Wood 149 F8	Little Bayham 220 B2	North Street 34 A3
High Brooms 190 C6	Little Cheveney Fm 195 J2	Oad Street 92 D5
Highgate 235 G4	Little Mill 173 F1	Oakhurst 146 E4
High Halden 219 J7	Little Pattenden 176 C6	Offham 107 F6
High Halstow 33 F3	Little Preston 110 A5	Oldbury 104 B8
Highsted 94 A7	Liverton Street 159 K5	Old Cryals 210 A1
High Street 234 D4	Livesey Street 130 E4	Orpington 56 A7
Hildenborough 147 J8	London Beach 230 A1	Otford 101 J4
Hilden Park 169 J2	Longfield 44 A8	Otham 134 C7
Hill Green 91 F5	Longfield Hill 62 E1	Otham Hole 134 E8
Hill Hoath 166 D8	Longford 101 F7	Otterham Quay 71 F4
Hill Park 120 B2	Loose 155 F2	Oxted 118 B8
Hoath Corner 186 D3	Loose Hill 155 F1	Paddlesworth 85 C5
Hockenden 39 J8	Lords Wood 88 D4	Paddock Wood 173 K8
Hodsoll Street 82 D4	Lower Bitchet 125 G5	Pains Hill 141 G2
Holborough 85 K4	Lower Bush 65 J3	Palmer's Green 194 B6
Holland 140 E4	Lower Cousley Wood 221 G6	Parker's Green 149 G8
Hollingbourne 136 C4	Lower Cox Street 90 A8	Parkgate 229 F4
Hollybushes 117 G6	Lower Green 191 K6	Park Wood 89 K3
Holt Hill 109 H6	Lower Green 206 B1	Park Wood 156 A2
Hook Green 40 C2	Lower Halstow 72 B3	Parrock Farm 46 A1
Hook Green 44 A4	Lower Hartlip 91 H2	Payden Street 139 J2
Hook Green 63 H3	Lower Haysden 169 J6	Pearson's Green 194 C3
Hook Green 221 F2	Lower Higham 30 C8	Peckham Bush 151 F6
Hoo St Werburgh 32 D8	Lower Rainham 70 B3	Peening Quarter 240 B8
Horns Green 98 E4	Lower Stoke 35 F1	Pell Green 220 D7
Horn Street 85 H8	Lower Twydall 69 K1	Pembles Cross 182 C3
Horsalls 137 K4	Lower Upnor 50 A3	Pembury 191 J8
Horshoe Green 185 K5	Luddesdown 64 C5	Penenden Heath 111 J7
Horsmonden 195 F8	Lunsford 108 C2	Penshurst 187 K2
Horton Kirby 60 C1	Luton 68 C5	Perry Street 27 G6
Hosey Hill 120 E7	Luxted 98 A1	Petteridge 193 H8
How Green 165 K4	Lynsted 95 H8	Pettings 82 C3
Howt Green 73 J5	Mabledon 169 K8	Pipsden 235 K5
Hubbard's Hill 145 K1	Maidstone 7 F5	Pittswood 149 G6
Hucking 114 C5	Maltman's Hill 202 E3	Pizien Well 129 K7
Hulberry 58 E6	Maplescombe 80 A1	Platt 105 J7
Hungershall Park 10 A5	Marden 196 C1	Platt's Heath 159 K5
Hunton 153 J6	Marden Beech 196 B3	Plaxtol 127 F6
Hurst Green 140 C3	Marden Thorn 197 G4	Pluckley 183 J7
Ide Hill 144 A2	Markbeech 185 K4	Pluckley Thorne 183 G8
Iden Green 213 H6	Marlpit Hill 164 B2	Plumtree Green 179 J6
Iden Green 237 F2	Marsh Green 184 B1	Pollhill 159 F1
Ightham 126 D1	Matfield 193 G6	Pootings 142 E7
Ightham Common 126 A3	Maypole 22 B7	Potman's Heath 246 D1
Istead Rise 45 F5	Maypole 77 G2	Potter's Forstal 182 B4
Ivy Hatch 126 B4	Medhurst Row 165 H4	Poundsbridge 188 B2
Iwade 73 J2	Meopham 63 G6	Poverest 56 B1
Kemsing 102 D4	Meopham Green 63 H7	Powder Mills 169 J3
Kemsley Street 89 K5	Meopham Station 63 J2	Pratling Street 110 B2
Kent Street 129 H4	Meresborough 90 B1	Pratt's Bottom 76 C5
Kettle Corner 131 K6	Mereworth 128 E6	Priestwood 83 J1
Kevingtown 57 G3	Merle Common 140 E7	Priestwood Green 83 K1
Keycol 72 D8	Middle Quarter 219 H5	Printstile 188 E3
Key's Green 209 K2	Middle Stoke 35 F2	Puddledock 40 A4
Key Street 93 F1	Milebush 176 E6	Puddledock 143 G4
Kilndown 222 E4	Mile Oak 194 A2	Pullington 237 H1
Kingsdown 117 K2	Millhall 109 G4	Purfleet 12 E6
Kings Farm 45 K1	Mill Street 108 C7	Pye Corner 158 E8
Kingswood 158 C4	Milstead 116 E4	The Quarter 202 B1
Kipping's Cross 209 H2	Milton 28 A5	The Quarter 239 K2
Kippington 8 C5	Milton Regis 93 H1	Queen Street 174 B6
Kit's Coty 87 H6	Mockbeggar 49 F1	Rabbit's Cross 178 A2
Knatts Valley 80 D5	Modest Corner 189 J4	Radfield 95 H4
Knockhall 25 G4	Monks Hill 201 G7	Rainham 70 D7
Knockholt 99 G4	Moon's Green 247 F3	Ramsden 56 D5
Knockmill 80 D7	Moorhouse Bank 120 A7	Ramslye 206 C5
Knox Bridge 198 C8	Moor Street 70 E7	Reading Street 241 J4
Laddingford 174 C1	The Moor 235 F6	Red Hill 130 D5

Ridley 82 C2
Ringlestone 110 D7
Ringlestone 137 K2
Riseden 222 E1
Riverhead 123 F1
Riverview Park 46 D2
Robhurst 231 J4
Rochester 2 B2
The Rocks 130 E1
Rodmersham 94 E6
Rodmersham Green 94 C7
Rolvenden 238 D2
Rolvenden Layne 238 E4
Romford 192 B7
Romney Street 79 J7
Rooks Hill 125 C7
Roseacre 134 C2
Rosherville 27 C4
Roughway 127 H8
Round Green 214 A2
Round Street 64 A1
Royal British Legion Village . 109 K6
Royal Tunbridge Wells 10 B4
Rushmore Hill 76 D8
Rusthall 206 B2
Ruxley 39 F4
Ryarsh 107 J2
St John's 8 C1
St John's 10 B1
St Leonard's Street 107 J7
St Mary Cray 56 D2
St Mary's Hoo 17 K8
St Michaels 230 B2
St Paul's Cray 38 B7
Saint's Hill 187 K6
Salmans 187 G3
Sandhurst 243 H1
Sandhurst Cross 243 F2
Sandling 111 F5
Sandown Park 191 F8
Sandway 160 B3
Scragged Oak 90 A7
Seacox Heath 233 J4
Seal 102 E8
Sevenoaks 9 F3
Sevenoaks Common 123 J8
Sevenoaks Weald 145 J3
Sharnal Street 33 H5
Shepway 133 K6
Sherwood Park 190 E8
Shipbourne 148 C1
Shoreham 78 B6
Shorne 47 H3
Shorne Ridgeway 47 G5
Sidcup 38 C2
Silver Street 92 E8
Singlewell 45 K4
Sinkhurst Green 199 C5
Sissinghurst 215 H6
Sittingbourne 94 B4
Slade Green 22 D1
Small Hythe 240 C5
Smarden 202 A5
Smarden Bell 201 J4
Smart's Hill 187 H6
Snipeshill 94 D3
Snodland 86 A7
Sole Street 63 K2
Southborough 190 A5
South Darenth 42 C6

Southfleet 44 C4
South Green 114 E1
South Street 83 F2
South Street 91 G7
South Street 97 K6
Speed Gate 60 E6
Speldhurst 188 E7
Spitals Cross 164 C3
Standen 217 K1
Standen Street 237 F5
Stanstead 81 K6
Staplehurst 198 B2
Starvecrow 148 C6
Stede Quarter 218 D5
Stick Hill 185 H3
Stiff Street 92 E7
Stockbury 91 H6
Stockland Green 189 G6
Stocks Green 169 F2
Stoke 34 D3
Stone 24 E4
Stonebridge Green 183 G1
Stone Cross 204 C4
Stonecrouch 222 C7
Stonehill Green 39 K4
Stone Street 125 J4
Stonewood 43 J1
Strawberry Hill 206 C6
Strood 48 E7
Strood 239 F1
Styants Bottom 103 K8
Sundridge 122 B3
Sutton at Hone 41 K5
Sutton Valence 157 G7
Swanley 40 D8
Swanley Village 40 D7
Swanscombe 25 J5
Swanton Street 115 K3
Swift's Green 201 J1
Tatsfield 97 H7
Temple Hill 23 G3
Tenterden 230 A6
Teston 130 E7
Teynham 95 K3
Thong 46 D4
Three Chimneys 216 E5
Three Leg Cross 232 B3
Thurnham 112 E6
Ticehurst 232 C4
Timberden Bottom 78 B5
Titsey 119 G4
Tonbridge 170 C5
Tong 180 A4
Tovil 6 B5
Toy's Hill 143 J3
Trench Wood 148 A7
Trottiscliffe 106 C1
Troy Town 2 B4
Troy Town 163 K1
Tubslake 225 F6
Tudeley 171 J7
Tudeley Hale 171 J5
Tunbridge Hill 34 A5
Tunstall 93 J6
Turner's Green 220 A8
Twitton 101 G3
Twydall 69 J4
Ulcombe 158 C7
Underlining Green 177 F4
Underriver 146 E1

Union Street 233 F3
Upchurch 71 J2
Upper Bush 65 J4
Upper Halling 85 G1
Upper Hayesden 169 F8
Upper Rodmersham 94 D8
Upper Upnor 49 K5
Vigo Village 83 G6
Wainscott 49 H4
Walderslade 88 A3
Walter's Green 187 G7
Wanshurst Green 177 G7
Ware Street 134 D1
Warmlake 157 F6
Warren Street 139 K7
Wateringbury 130 B6
Waterman Quarter 200 B4
Waterside 162 D7
Wayfield 68 C7
Weavering Street 134 B2
Weller's Town 186 E1
Well Hill 77 J1
Well Street 108 C8
West Court 28 B8
West Cross 238 B2
Wested Fm 58 B4
West End 117 K7
Westerham 120 D6
West Farleigh 131 F8
Westfield Sole 88 D7
West Kingsdown 80 D4
West Malling 107 K7
West Peckham 128 D8
West Street 31 F1
West Street 138 E5
Westwood 43 H5
West Yoke 61 J7
Wetham Green 71 J1
Whetsted 173 G5
White Oak 40 B7
White Post 187 F7
Whitley Row 122 D8
Wichling 139 J1
Wick Hill 200 D6
Wickhurst 168 A2
Wierton 156 B6
Wigmore 89 K2
Wildernesse 124 C1
Willington 134 B5
Wilmington 40 E2
Wilsley Green 214 E8
Wilsley Pound 215 F6
Winchet Hill 196 B8
Windmill Hill 71 F3
Winkhurst Green 144 D6
Wissenden 203 F7
Wittersham 247 J3
Woodlands 80 B8
Woodsden 236 A2
Wood's Green 220 B6
Woodside Green 138 E6
Woodstock 93 K8
Worms Hill 213 G2
Wormshill 116 A7
Wouldham 86 B1
Wrotham 105 G3
Wrotham Heath 106 A5
Yalding 152 E5
Yelsted 90 D5
Yopps Green 126 E5

USING THE STREET INDEX

Street names are listed alphabetically. Each street name is followed by its postal town or area locality, the Postcode
District, the page number, and the reference to the square in which the name is found.

Example: **Acorn Wharf Rd** *ROCH* ME1...................**2** C2 🔟

Some entries are followed by a number in a blue box. This number indicates the location of the street within the
referenced grid square. The full street name is listed at the side of the map page.

GENERAL ABBREVIATIONS

ACC	ACCESS	
ALY	ALLEY	
AP	APPROACH	
AR	ARCADE	
ASS	ASSOCIATION	
AV	AVENUE	
BCH	BEACH	
BLDS	BUILDINGS	
BND	BEND	
BNK	BANK	
BR	BRIDGE	
BRK	BROOK	
BTM	BOTTOM	
BUS	BUSINESS	
BVD	BOULEVARD	
BY	BYPASS	
CATH	CATHEDRAL	
CEM	CEMETERY	
CEN	CENTRE	
CFT	CROFT	
CH	CHURCH	
CHA	CHASE	
CHYD	CHURCHYARD	
CIR	CIRCLE	
CIRC	CIRCUS	
CL	CLOSE	
CLFS	CLIFFS	
CMP	CAMP	
CNR	CORNER	
CO	COUNTY	
COLL	COLLEGE	
COM	COMMON	
COMM	COMMISSION	
CON	CONVENT	
COT	COTTAGE	
COTS	COTTAGES	
CP	CAPE	
CPS	COPSE	
CR	CREEK	
CREM	CREMATORIUM	
CRS	CRESCENT	
CSWY	CAUSEWAY	
CT	COURT	
CTRL	CENTRAL	
CTS	COURTS	
CTYD	COURTYARD	
CUTT	CUTTINGS	
CV	COVE	
CYN	CANYON	
DEPT	DEPARTMENT	
DL	DALE	
DM	DAM	
DR	DRIVE	
DRO	DROVE	
DRY	DRIVEWAY	
DWGS	DWELLINGS	
E	EAST	
EMB	EMBANKMENT	
EMBY	EMBASSY	
ESP	ESPLANADE	
EST	ESTATE	
EX	EXCHANGE	
EXPY	EXPRESSWAY	
EXT	EXTENSION	
F/O	FLYOVER	
FC	FOOTBALL CLUB	
FK	FORK	
FLD	FIELD	
FLDS	FIELDS	
FLS	FALLS	
FLS	FLATS	
FM	FARM	
FT	FORT	
FWY	FREEWAY	
FY	FERRY	
GA	GATE	
GAL	GALLERY	
GDN	GARDEN	
GDNS	GARDENS	
GLD	GLADE	
GLN	GLEN	
GN	GREEN	
GND	GROUND	
GRA	GRANGE	
GRG	GARAGE	
GT	GREAT	
GTWY	GATEWAY	
GV	GROVE	
HGR	HIGHER	
HL	HILL	
HLS	HILLS	
HO	HOUSE	
HOL	HOLLOW	
HOSP	HOSPITAL	
HRB	HARBOUR	
HTH	HEATH	
HTS	HEIGHTS	
HVN	HAVEN	
HWY	HIGHWAY	
IMP	IMPERIAL	
IN	INLET	
IND EST	INDUSTRIAL ESTATE	
INF	INFIRMARY	
INFO	INFORMATION	
INT	INTERCHANGE	
IS	ISLAND	
JCT	JUNCTION	
JTY	JETTY	
KG	KING	
KNL	KNOLL	
L	LAKE	
LA	LANE	
LDG	LODGE	
LGT	LIGHT	
LK	LOCK	
LKS	LAKES	
LNDG	LANDING	
LTL	LITTLE	
LWR	LOWER	
MAG	MAGISTRATE	
MAN	MANSIONS	
MD	MEAD	
MDW	MEADOWS	
MEM	MEMORIAL	
MKT	MARKET	
MKTS	MARKETS	
ML	MALL	
ML	MILL	
MNR	MANOR	
MS	MEWS	
MSN	MISSION	
MT	MOUNT	
MTN	MOUNTAIN	
MTS	MOUNTAINS	
MUS	MUSEUM	
MWY	MOTORWAY	
N	NORTH	
NE	NORTH EAST	
NW	NORTH WEST	
O/P	OVERPASS	
OFF	OFFICE	
ORCH	ORCHARD	
OV	OVAL	
PAL	PALACE	
PAS	PASSAGE	
PAV	PAVILION	
PDE	PARADE	
PH	PUBLIC HOUSE	
PK	PARK	
PKWY	PARKWAY	
PL	PLACE	
PLN	PLAIN	
PLNS	PLAINS	
PLZ	PLAZA	
POL	POLICE STATION	
PR	PRINCE	
PREC	PRECINCT	
PREP	PREPARATORY	
PRIM	PRIMARY	
PROM	PROMENADE	
PRS	PRINCESS	
PRT	PORT	
PT	POINT	
PTH	PATH	
PZ	PIAZZA	
QD	QUADRANT	
QU	QUEEN	
QY	QUAY	
R	RIVER	
RBT	ROUNDABOUT	
RD	ROAD	
RDG	RIDGE	
REP	REPUBLIC	
RES	RESERVOIR	
RFC	RUGBY FOOTBALL CLUB	
RI	RISE	
RP	RAMP	
RW	ROW	
S	SOUTH	
SCH	SCHOOL	
SE	SOUTH EAST	
SER	SERVICE AREA	
SH	SHORE	
SHOP	SHOPPING	
SKWY	SKYWAY	
SMT	SUMMIT	
SOC	SOCIETY	
SP	SPUR	
SPR	SPRING	
SQ	SQUARE	
ST	STREET	
STN	STATION	
STR	STREAM	
STRD	STRAND	
SW	SOUTH WEST	
TDG	TRADING	
TER	TERRACE	
THWY	THROUGHWAY	
TNL	TUNNEL	
TOLL	TOLLWAY	
TPK	TURNPIKE	
TR	TRACK	
TRL	TRAIL	
TWR	TOWER	
U/P	UNDERPASS	
UNI	UNIVERSITY	
UPR	UPPER	
V	VALE	
VA	VALLEY	
VIAD	VIADUCT	
VIL	VILLA	
VIS	VISTA	
VLG	VILLAGE	
VLS	VILLAS	
VW	VIEW	
W	WEST	
WD	WOOD	
WHF	WHARF	
WK	WALK	
WKS	WALKS	
WLS	WELLS	
WY	WAY	
YD	YARD	
YHA	YOUTH HOSTEL	

POSTCODE TOWNS AND AREA ABBREVIATIONS

BFN/LL	Blackfen/Longlands
BGR/WK	Borough Green/West Kingsdown
BH/WHM	Biggin Hill/Westerham
BUR/ETCH	Burwash/Etchingham
BXLY	Bexley
BXLYHN	Bexleyheath north
CHAT	Chatham
CHST	Chislehurst
CRBK	Cranbrook
CTHM	Caterham
DART	Dartford
DIT/AY	Ditton/Aylesford
E/WMAL	East & West Malling
EDEN	Edenbridge
EGRIN	East Grinstead
ERITH	Erith
EYN	Eynsford
GDST	Godstone
GILL	Gillingham
GRH	Greenhithe
GVE	Gravesend east
GVW	Gravesend west
HART	Hartley
HAWK	Hawkhurst
HAYES	Hayes
HDCN	Headcorn
HOO/HM	Hoo St Werburgh/Higham
HRTF	Hartfield
LING	Lingfield
MAID/BEAR	Maidstone/Bearsted
MAID/SHEP	Maidstone/Shepway
MAIDW	Maidstone west
MEO	Meopham
ORP	Orpington
OXTED	Oxted
PUR	Purfleet

QBOR ....Queenborough
RAIN ....Rainham (Gt Lon)
RASHW ....Rural Ashford west
RBTBR ....Robertsbridge
RDART ....Rural Dartford
RHAM ....Rainham (Kent)
RMAID ....Rural Maidstone
ROCH ....Rochester
RRTW ....Rural Royal Tunbridge Wells
RSEV ....Rural Sevenoaks
RSIT ....Rural Sittingbourne
RTON ....Rural Tonbridge

RTW ....Royal Tunbridge Wells
RTWE/PEM ....Royal Tunbridge Wells
                              east/Pembury
RYE ....Rye
SCUP ....Sidcup
SEV ....Sevenoaks
SIT ....Sittingbourne
SNOD ....Snodland
SOCK/AV ....South Ockendon/Aveley
STH/RUST ....Southborough/Rusthall
STMC/STPC ......St Mary Cray/St Paul's Cray
STPH/PW ....Staplehurst/Paddock Wood

STRD ....Strood
SWCM ....Swanscombe
SWLY ....Swanley
TENT ....Tenterden
TIL ....Tilbury
TON ....Tonbridge
TONN ....Tonbridge north
WADH ....Wadhurst
WALD ....Walderslade
WARL ....Warlingham
WBY/YAL ....Wateringbury/Yalding
WTHK ....West Thurrock

A

Abbey Rd *GRH* DA9 .... 25 H4	**STMC/STPC** BR5 .... 56 C3
GVE DA12 .... 28 B7	**SWCM** DA10 .... 26 A5
RHAM ME8 .... 69 H4	**TON** TN9 .... 170 B5
STRD ME2 .... 48 E6	**Albert St** *MAID/BEAR* ME14 .... 6 C1
Abbey Wood Rd *E/WMAL* ME19 ... 129 J1	**Albion Pl** *MAID/BEAR* ME14 .... 7 E3
Abbots Court Rd *HOO/HM* ME3 .... 51 G2	**Albion Rd** *GVE* DA12 .... 27 K6
Abbots Fld *MAIDW* ME16 .... 132 B4	*RTW* TN1 .... 11 D2
Abbott Rd *BGR/WK* TN15 .... 105 F7	*STPH/PW* TN12 .... 196 D1
Abbotts Cl *ROCH* ME1 .... 2 B5	*WALD* ME5 .... 88 C4
SWLY BR8 .... 58 D1	**Albion Ter** *GVE* DA12 .... 27 K5
Abigail Crs *WALD* ME5 .... 88 B5	**Albion Wy** *EDEN* TN8 .... 164 C2
Abingdon Rd *MAIDW* ME16 .... 131 K4	**Albury Cl** *WALD* ME5 .... 88 E4
Abingdon Wy *ORP* BR6 .... 56 C8	**Alder Cl** *RTWE/PEM* TN2 .... 190 C5
Abinger Dr *WALD* ME5 .... 88 C4	**Aldershot Rd** *WALD* ME5 .... 68 B7
Acacia Rd *DART* DA2 .... 23 F7	**Alders Meadow** *TON* TN9 .... 169 K4
GRH DA9 .... 24 D5	**Alders Rd** *RTON* TN11 .... 172 A8
Academy Dr *GILL* ME7 .... 69 G6	**The Alders** *WBY/YAL* ME18.......... 129 F7
Acer Av *RTWE/PEM* TN2 .... 207 H6	**Alder Wy** *SWLY* BR8 .... 40 A7
Acer Rd *BH/WHM* TN16 .... 97 H3	**Aldington Cl** *WALD* ME5 .... 88 C1
Achilles Rd *WALD* ME5 .... 88 D4	**Aldington La** *MAID/BEAR* ME14 .... 113 F6
Acorn Cl *STPH/PW* TN12 .... 172 D5	**Aldington Rd** *MAID/BEAR* ME14 .... 134 D2
Acorn Gv *DIT/AY* ME20 .... 109 H6	**Aldon Cl** *MAID/BEAR* ME14........... 7 F1
Acorn Pl *MAID/SHEP* ME15 .... 134 A8	**Aldon La** *E/WMAL* ME19 .... 106 D6
Acorn Rd *GILL* ME7 .... 5 F4	**Alen Sq** *STPH/PW* TN12 .... 198 B2
The Acorns *HDCN* TN27 .... 201 K5	**Alexander Dr** *SIT* ME10 .... 73 K7
SEV TN13 .... 8 C2	**Alexandra Av** *GILL* ME7 .... 5 E4
Acorn Wharf Rd *ROCH* ME1 .... 2 C2	*SWLY* BR8 .... 40 B7
Acott Flds *WBY/YAL* ME18 .... 152 D5	**Alexandra Gln** *WALD* ME5 .... 88 B5
Acre Cl *CHAT* ME4 .... 67 K5	**Alexandra Rd** *BH/WHM* TN16 .... 97 F6
Acre Gv *STRD* ME2.......................... 85 K2	*CHAT* ME4 .... 4 B6
Acres Ri *WADH* TN5 .... 232 C5	*GVE* DA12 .... 28 B6
Acton La *TENT* TN30 .... 241 G8	*TIL* RM18 .... 27 G1
Adam Cl *RMAID* ME17 .... 154 D3	*TON* TN9 .... 170 B6
Adams Cl *TENT* TN30 .... 230 B5	**Alexandra St** *MAID/BEAR* ME14 .... 6 C1
Addington La *E/WMAL* ME19 .... 106 C2	**Alfred Cl** *CHAT* ME4 .... 4 A6
Addington Rd *SIT* ME10 .... 93 K3	**Alfred Pl** *GVW* DA11 .... 13 D2
Addison Cl *MAIDW* ME16 .... 108 D5	**Alfred Rd** *GVW* DA11 .... 27 J8
Addlestead Rd *STPH/PW* TN12 ... 151 G8	*RDART* DA2 .... 41 J2
Adelaide Dr *SIT* ME10 .... 93 H2	*SOCK/AV* RM15 .... 13 G1
Adelaide Rd *GILL* ME7 .... 4 C4	**Alkerden La** *GRH* DA9 .... 25 H5
The Adelaide *HOO/HM* ME3 .... 30 B8	**Alkham Rd** *MAID/BEAR* ME14 .... 7 F2
Adisham Dr *MAIDW* ME16 .... 110 B7	**Allan Cl** *STH/RUST* TN4 .... 206 B2
Admers Wy *MEO* DA13 .... 83 J6	**Allandale Pl** *ORP* BR6 .... 56 E7
Admiral Cl *STMC/STPC* BR5 .... 56 E1	**Allandale Rd** *RTWE/PEM* TN2 ...... 11 F1
GRH DA9 .... 25 G4	**Allard Cl** *STMC/STPC* BR5 .... 56 C1
TENT TN30 .... 230 C5	**Allenby Rd** *BH/WHM* TN16........... 97 J4
Admiralty Rd *STRD* ME2 .... 50 A5	**Allen Cl** *WALD* ME5 .... 68 D8
Admiralty Ter *STRD* ME2 .... 50 A5	**Allendale Cl** *RDART* DA2 .... 24 C7
Admiral Wy *WBY/YAL* ME18......... 129 J5	**Allens La** *BGR/WK* TN15 .... 127 G7
Afghan Rd *CHAT* ME4 .... 3 E4	**Allen St** *MAID/BEAR* ME14 .... 7 D2
Aintree Cl *GVE* DA12 .... 45 J1	**Allhallows Rd** *HOO/HM* ME3 .... 35 F1
Aintree Rd *WALD* ME5 .... 88 D5	**Alliance Wy** *STPH/PW* TN12 .... 173 H8
Airedale Cl *RDART* DA2 .... 24 B7	*TONN* TN10 .... 171 C1
Aisher Wy *SEV* TN13 .... 101 G8	**Allington Gdns** *WBY/YAL* ME18...... 130 B7
Ajax Rd *ROCH* ME1 .... 67 H7	**Allington Rd** *RHAM* ME8................ 69 H3
Alamein Av *WALD* ME5 .... 68 A7	*STPH/PW* TN12 .... 173 H7
Alamein Gdns *RDART* DA2 .... 24 C6	**Allington Wy** *MAIDW* ME16 .... 110 B8
Alamein Rd *SWCM* DA10 .... 25 J5	**Allison Av** *GILL* ME7 .... 69 F5
Alanbrooke *GVE* DA12 .... 27 K6	**Allnutt Mill Cl** *MAID/SHEP* ME15 .... 6 B5
Alan Cl *DART* DA1........................... 23 F3	**Allotment La** *SEV* TN13 .... 9 E1
Alban Crs *EYN* DA4 .... 59 K5	**All Saints Cl** *SWCM* DA10 .... 26 A4
Albany Cl *TON* TN9 .... 170 D7	**All Saints' Rd** *GVW* DA11 .... 27 G7
Albany Hl *RTWE/PEM* TN2 .... 11 E2	*HAWK* TN18 .... 235 H5
Albany Rd *CHAT* ME4 .... 4 B6	*SIT* ME10 .... 94 D2
GILL ME7 .... 5 D4	*STH/RUST* TN4 .... 10 C1
ROCH ME1 .... 2 C4	**Allsworth Cl** *RSIT* ME9 .... 72 A8
SIT ME10 .... 93 K3	**Alma Pl** *STRD* ME2 .... 2 A1
Albany St *MAID/BEAR* ME14 .... 7 E2	**Alma Rd** *DIT/AY* ME20 .... 86 E8
Albany Ter *CHAT* ME4 .... 3 E4	*E/WMAL* ME19 .... 107 J6
Albatross Av *STRD* ME2 .... 48 B8	*SCUP* DA14 .... 38 B1
Albemarle Rd *WALD* ME5 .... 88 D4	*STMC/STPC* BR5 .... 56 E6
Albert Dr *MAID/SHEP* ME15 .... 154 B2	*SWCM* DA10 .... 25 K4
Albert Murray Cl *GVE* DA12 .... 27 K6	**Almond Dr** *SWLY* BR8 .... 40 A3
Albert Pl *STRD* ME2 .... 2 B1	**Almond Gv** *GILL* ME7 .... 89 H2
Albert Rd *CHAT* ME4 .... 4 A5	**Almond Rd** *RDART* DA2 .... 24 B6
GILL ME7 .... 5 D4	**The Almonds** *MAID/BEAR* ME14 .... 134 C2
ORP BR6 .... 76 B1	**Almon Pl** *ROCH* ME1 .... 3 D3
RDART DA2 .... 41 F1	**Alpha Cl** *HOO/HM* ME3 .... 34 A7
ROCH ME1 .... 2 C5	**Amanda Cl** *WALD* ME5 .... 87 K3
	Amber La *RMAID* ME17 .... 156 C5
	Amberleaze Dr *RTWE/PEM* TN2 .... 191 K8
	Amberley Cl *ORP* BR6 .... 76 A1
Amberley Ct *SCUP* DA14 .... 38 D3	**Ambleside** *SIT* ME10 .... 94 D3
Ambley Gn *GILL* ME7 .... 69 H6	**Ambley Rd** *GILL* ME7 .... 69 H5
Ambrose Cl *DART* DA1 .... 22 C3	*ORP* BR6 .... 56 A7
Ambrose Hl *WALD* ME5.................... 4 C6	**Ames Av** *MAID/BEAR* ME14 .... 134 C2
Ames Rd *SWCM* DA10 .... 25 K5	**Amethyst Av** *WALD* ME5 .... 67 K8
Amherst Cl *MAIDW* ME16 .... 6 A3	*STMC/STPC* BR5 .... 56 B1
Amherst Hl *SEV* TN13 .... 8 A1	**Amherst Redoubt** *GILL* ME7 .... 4 A3
Amherst Rd *ROCH* ME1 .... 3 D5	*SEV* TN13 .... 9 D1
STH/RUST TN4 .... 10 C2	**Amhurst Bank Rd**
RTWE/PEM TN2 .... 192 A3	**Ampleforth Cl** *ORP* BR6 .... 56 D8
Amsbury Rd *MAID/SHEP* ME15 .... 154 A4	**Amy Rd** *OXTED* RH8 .... 118 C8
Anchorage Cl *HOO/HM* ME3 .... 35 F3	**Anchor Bvd** *GRH* DA9 .... 24 B3
Anchor Rd *ROCH* ME1 .... 67 H5	**Andrew Broughton Wy**
MAID/BEAR ME14 .... 7 E3	**Andrew Cl** *DART* DA1 .... 22 A4
Andrew Rd *STH/RUST* TN4 .... 190 C6	**Andrews Cl** *RTWE/PEM* TN2 .... 11 F2
STMC/STPC BR5 .... 38 E3	**Anerley Cl** *MAIDW* ME16 .... 110 D7
Angel La *TON* TN9 .... 170 B5	**Anglesea Pl** *GVE* DA12 .... 27 J5
GVW DA11 .... 27 J5	**Anglesea Rd** *STMC/STPC* BR5 ...... 56 D3
Anglesey Av *MAID/SHEP* ME15 .... 133 G8	**Anglesey Cl** *WALD* ME5 .... 68 C7
Angley Ct *STPH/PW* TN12 .... 211 K1	**Angley Rd** *CRBK* TN17 .... 225 J1
Angley Wk *CRBK* TN17 .... 214 E8	**Anne of Cleves Rd** *DART* DA1 .... 23 C4
Annetts Hall *BGR/WK* TN15 .... 105 G6	**Annie Rd** *SNOD* ME6 .... 85 J8
Ansell Av *CHAT* ME4 .... 4 A6	**Anselm Cl** *SIT* ME10 .... 93 K2
Anson Av *E/WMAL* ME19 .... 129 H3	**Anson Cl** *WALD* ME5 .... 68 D8
Anthony Cl *SEV* TN13 .... 101 G8	**Anthonys La** *SWLY* BR8 .... 40 D6
Anthonys Wy *STRD* ME2 .... 49 K6	**Aperfield Rd** *BH/WHM* TN16 .... 97 J4
Appleby Cl *ROCH* ME1.................... 67 J7	**Apple Cl** *SNOD* ME6........................ 85 J8
Apple Ct *STPH/PW* TN12 .... 173 H8	**Applecross Cl** *ROCH* ME1 .... 2 B4
Appledore Rd *RHAM* ME8 .... 69 H3	*TENT* TN30 .... 230 C7
Applegarth Dr *DART* DA1 .... 23 H8	**Apple Orch** *SWLY* BR8 .... 58 A1
Appleshaw Cl *GVW* DA11 .... 45 H3	**Appleton Dr** *RDART* DA2 .... 40 E1
Appletons *RTON* TN15 .... 150 B6	**Apple Tree Cl** *MAIDW* ME16 .... 131 K4
Apple Tree La *RTWE/PEM* TN2 ...... 190 D6	**Approach Rd** *WARL* CR6................ 119 F1
The Approach *ORP* BR6 .... 56 A6	**April Cl** *ORP* BR6 .... 76 A1
Apsley St *STH/RUST* TN4 .... 206 C2	**Arbrook Cl** *STMC/STPC* BR5.......... 38 B8
Arcadia Rd *MEO* DA13 .... 45 C6	**Archer Rd** *STMC/STPC* BR5 .... 56 B3
	WALD ME5 .... 68 C8
Archer Wy *SWLY* BR8 .... 40 C8	**Archery Cl** *HOO/HM* ME3 .... 31 G7
Ardenlee Dr *MAID/BEAR* ME14 ...... 7 E2	**Arden St** *GILL* ME7 .... 4 C2
Arethusa Rd *ROCH* ME1 .... 67 H6	**Argles Cl** *GRH* DA9 .... 25 F4
Argyle Cl *ROCH* ME1 .... 67 J7	**Argyle Rd** *SEV* TN13 .... 9 D1
STH/RUST TN4 .... 190 A4	**Ariel Cl** *GVE* DA12.......................... 46 C2

Arkwright Rd TIL RM18 ...... 27 H1
Arlott Cl MAID/BEAR ME14 ...... 6 C1
Armada Wy CHAT ME4 ...... 3 F5
Armor Rd PUR RM19 ...... 13 H4
Armoury Dr GVE DA12 ...... 27 K6
Armstrong Cl RSEV TN14 ...... 100 D2
Armstrong Rd MAID/SHEP ME15 ...... 7 D6
Armytage Cl HOO/HM ME3 ...... 51 F2
Arne Cl TONN TN10 ...... 148 E8
Arne Gv ORP BR6 ...... 56 A7
Arnhem Av MEO DA13 ...... 13 C1
Arnhem Dr WALD ME5 ...... 68 A7
Arnold Av MEO DA13 ...... 63 J6
Arnolde Cl STRD ME2 ...... 3 E1
Arnold Rd GVE DA12 ...... 27 K8
Arnolds La RDART DA2 ...... 41 K4
Arran Rd MAID/SHEP ME15 ...... 133 G8
Artemis Cl GVE DA12 ...... 28 B6
Arterial Road Purfleet PUR RM19 ...... 13 G4
Arterial Road West Thurrock
  WTHK RM20 ...... 13 K3
Arthur Rd BH/WHM TN16 ...... 97 G2
  RHAM ME8 ...... 70 B6
  ROCH ME1 ...... 3 D5
Arthur St GVW DA11 ...... 27 H6
  SIT ME10 ...... 93 K2
Artillery Rw GVE DA12 ...... 27 K6
Arundel Av SIT ME10 ...... 93 K5
Arundel Cl TON TN9 ...... 170 A6
  WALD ME5 ...... 88 E5
Arundel Dr ORP BR6 ...... 76 C1
Arundel Rd DART DA1 ...... 23 F3
  RTW TN1 ...... 11 D5
Arundel Wy MAID/BEAR ME14 ...... 6 C1
  WALD ME5 ...... 88 D4
Ascot Cl BGR/WK TN15 ...... 105 H7
  WALD ME5 ...... 88 D4
Ascot Rd GVW DA11 ...... 45 J1
  STMC/STPC BR5 ...... 56 A1
Ashbee Cl SNOD ME6 ...... 85 K7
Ashburnham Rd
  MAID/BEAR ME14 ...... 111 H6
  TONN TN10 ...... 170 C3
Ashby Cl STRD ME2 ...... 85 K2
Ashby's Cl EDEN TN8 ...... 164 D6
Ash Cl DIT/AY ME20 ...... 109 J5
  EDEN TN8 ...... 164 B5
  RHAM ME8 ...... 69 J3
  RTWE/PEM TN2 ...... 207 J6
  SCUP DA14 ...... 38 C1
  SWLY BR8 ...... 39 K7
  WALD ME5 ...... 68 D5
Ashcombe Dr EDEN TN8 ...... 164 B2
Ash Crs HOO/HM ME3 ...... 48 A3
Ashcroft Rd STPH/PW TN12 ...... 193 H1
Ashden Wk TONN TN10 ...... 148 C7
Ashdown Cl MAIDW ME16 ...... 10 B3
  STH/RUST TN4
Ashdown Rd RSIT ME9 ...... 139 F3
Ashenden HDCN TN27 ...... 201 K4
Ashenden Cl STRD ME2 ...... 49 H4
Ashenden Wk RTWE/PEM TN2 ...... 190 E6
Ashen Dr DART DA1 ...... 22 D5
Ashen Grove Rd EYN DA4 ...... 80 A5
Asher Reeds RRTW TN3 ...... 205 K2
Ashes La RTON TN11 ...... 149 H6
Ashford Dr RMAID ME17 ...... 158 B4
Ashford Rd MAID/BEAR ME14 ...... 7 E3
  MAID/BEAR ME14 ...... 135 C3
  RASHW TN26 ...... 219 K6
  RMAID ME17 ...... 136 B6
  RMAID ME17 ...... 161 F1
  TENT TN30 ...... 230 B6
  TENT TN30 ...... 230 A1
Ash Gv MAIDW ME16 ...... 110 C8
Ashgrove Rd SEV TN13 ...... 8 C6
  SEV TN13 ...... 123 K7
Ashington Cl SIT ME10 ...... 93 H1
Ash Keys MEO DA13 ...... 83 J6
Ash La BGR/WK TN15 ...... 95 K6
Ashleigh Cl MEO DA13 ...... 83 C5
Ashleigh Gdns HDCN TN27 ...... 180 B8
Ashley Cl SEV TN13 ...... 9 D3
Ashley Gdns ORP BR6 ...... 75 K1
  STH/RUST TN4 ...... 206 B1
Ashley Park Cl STH/RUST TN4 ...... 206 B1
Ashley Rd RHAM ME8 ...... 69 K4
  RTON TN11 ...... 169 J1
  SEV TN13 ...... 9 D3
Ashmead Cl WALD ME5 ...... 88 D3
Ashmore Gdns GVW DA11 ...... 44 E1
Ashmore La HAYES BR2 ...... 74 B6
Ash Platt Rd BGR/WK TN15 ...... 102 C8
Ash Rd BGR/WK TN15 ...... 61 J8
  BH/WHM TN16 ...... 120 D4
  DART DA1 ...... 23 G7
  GVE DA12 ...... 45 K2
  HART DA3 ...... 43 K8
  HART DA3 ...... 61 K7
  ORP BR6 ...... 76 B3
  RDART DA2 ...... 41 J2
  STRD ME2 ...... 48 E8
Ashtead Dr RSIT ME9 ...... 94 E4
Ashton Wy E/WMAL ME19 ...... 108 A8
Ash Tree Cl BGR/WK TN15 ...... 80 E4
Ash Tree Dr BGR/WK TN15 ...... 80 E4

Ash Tree La WALD ME5 ...... 5 D6
Ashurst Cl DART DA1 ...... 22 C2
Ashurst Rd MAID/BEAR ME14 ...... 7 F2
  RRTW TN3 ...... 204 E4
Ashwood Cl HOO/HM ME3 ...... 31 H7
Aspdin Rd GVW DA11 ...... 44 E1
Aspen Cl ORP BR6 ...... 76 B1
  SWLY BR8 ...... 40 A6
Aspen Wy RTWE/PEM TN2 ...... 190 C5
Aspian Dr RMAID ME17 ...... 154 D4
Asquith Rd RHAM ME8 ...... 69 K8
Aster Rd HOO/HM ME3 ...... 51 F3
Astley St MAID/BEAR ME14 ...... 7 D3
Aston Cl SCUP DA14 ...... 38 B1
  WALD ME5 ...... 88 B4
Astor Rd BGR/WK TN15 ...... 80 D2
Astra Dr GVE DA12 ...... 46 B3
Athelstan Gn RMAID ME17 ...... 136 A4
Athelstan Rd CHAT ME4 ...... 3 F6
Athelstan Wy STMC/STPC BR5 ...... 38 B6
Atkinson Cl ORP BR6 ...... 76 B1
Atlas Rd DART DA1 ...... 23 J2
Atterbury Cl BH/WHM TN16 ...... 120 C5
Attlee Dr DART DA1 ...... 23 K4
Attlee Wy SIT ME10 ...... 73 K7
Attwaters La HAWK TN18 ...... 225 J8
Auckland Cl TIL RM18 ...... 27 H1
Auckland Dr SIT ME10 ...... 93 H3
Auckland Rd RTW TN1 ...... 11 E1
Auden Rd DIT/AY ME20 ...... 108 E2
Audley Av GILL ME7 ...... 69 F5
  TON TN9 ...... 169 K4
Audley Cl MAIDW ME16 ...... 132 B1
Audley Ri TON TN9 ...... 169 K5
Auger Cl RSIT ME9 ...... 91 H1
Augusta Cl GILL ME7 ...... 4 C1
Augustine Rd GVE DA12 ...... 27 K6
  STMC/STPC BR5 ...... 38 E8
Austen Cl CRH DA9 ...... 25 H5
  TIL RM18 ...... 27 K1
Austen Wy DIT/AY ME20 ...... 108 D2
Austin Cl GILL ME7 ...... 5 E6
Austin Rd GVW DA11 ...... 27 G7
  STMC/STPC BR5 ...... 56 B3
Austral Cl BFN/LL DA15 ...... 38 A1
Autumn Gld MAID/BEAR ME14 ...... 88 E6
Avalon Cl ORP BR6 ...... 56 E6
Avalon Rd ORP BR6 ...... 56 E6
Avards Cl HAWK TN18 ...... 234 E6
Aveling Cl HOO/HM ME3 ...... 32 E8
Aveling Ri TON TN9 ...... 169 K5
Avebury Av TON TN9 ...... 170 B5
Avenue Cl HOO/HM ME3 ...... 32 E8
Avenue La Puy TON TN9 ...... 170 C5
Avenue of Remembrance
  SIT ME10 ...... 94 A3
Avenue Rd BH/WHM TN16 ...... 97 J7
  SEV TN13 ...... 9 E3
The Avenue BGR/WK TN15 ...... 105 G6
  BH/WHM TN16 ...... 119 K1
  DIT/AY ME20 ...... 109 J5
  GVW DA11 ...... 27 H7
  ORP BR6 ...... 56 A6
  STMC/STPC BR5 ...... 38 C5
  TON TN9 ...... 170 B4
Averenches Rd MAID/BEAR ME14 ...... 134 B1
Avery Cl HOO/HM ME3 ...... 19 G6
  MAID/SHEP ME15 ...... 6 C6
Avery La MAID/SHEP ME15 ...... 134 E8
Avery Wy HOO/HM ME3 ...... 19 G6
Aviemore Gdns MAID/BEAR ME14 ...... 134 B2
Avington Cl MAID/SHEP ME15 ...... 6 C6
Avon Cl GVE DA12 ...... 28 A8
  TONN TN10 ...... 170 C1
Avondale Rd GILL ME7 ...... 5 D3
Avonmouth Rd DART DA1 ...... 23 G4
Avon St RTW TN1 ...... 11 E5
Axtaine Rd STMC/STPC BR5 ...... 56 E4
Axtane Cl EYN DA4 ...... 42 B7
Ayelands HART DA3 ...... 61 K6
Ayelands La HART DA3 ...... 61 K7
Aylesford Crs RHAM ME8 ...... 69 H3
Aylesware La HDCN TN27 ...... 200 C6
Aynscombe Angle ORP BR6 ...... 56 B4
Azalea Dr SWLY BR8 ...... 58 A1

B

Babb's La CRBK TN17 ...... 226 C8
Babylon La RMAID ME17 ...... 178 D3
  STPH/PW TN12 ...... 178 E5
Backfields ROCH ME1 ...... 2 B4
Back La BGR/WK TN15 ...... 124 E3
  BGR/WK TN15 ...... 126 C3
  CRBK TN17 ...... 212 D6
  PUR RM19 ...... 13 J4
  RMAID ME17 ...... 155 K4
  RSEV TN14 ...... 122 D7
  RTON TN11 ...... 148 C2
  SEV TN13 ...... 123 F3
  STPH/PW TN12 ...... 194 E8
Back Rd HAWK TN18 ...... 243 J1
  SCUP DA14 ...... 38 B2
Back St RMAID ME17 ...... 135 G8

Baden Powell Rd SEV TN13 ...... 8 A1
Baden Rd GILL ME7 ...... 5 D1
Bader Crs WALD ME5 ...... 68 B7
Bader Wk GVW DA11 ...... 45 F1
Badger Rd WALD ME5 ...... 88 D5
Badgers Copse ORP BR6 ...... 56 A6
Badgers Holt RTWE/PEM TN2 ...... 207 K1
Badgers Ri RSEV TN14 ...... 77 H5
Badgers Rd RSEV TN14 ...... 77 J5
Badsell Rd STPH/PW TN12 ...... 172 D7
Baffin Cl CHAT ME4 ...... 3 F6
Bailey Cl PUR RM19 ...... 13 H4
Bailey Dr GILL ME7 ...... 69 H6
Baker Cl RSIT ME9 ...... 95 K5
Baker Hill Cl GVW DA11 ...... 45 G2
Baker La HDCN TN27 ...... 180 D7
  RMAID ME17 ...... 157 H7
Baker Ms ORP BR6 ...... 76 A2
Bakers Av BGR/WK TN15 ...... 80 D3
Bakers Cross CRBK TN17 ...... 225 K2
Baker St ROCH ME1 ...... 2 C5
  ROCH ME1 ...... 86 E5
Baker's Wk ROCH ME1 ...... 2 C2
Balaclava La WADH TN5 ...... 220 B7
Balcombes Hl CRBK TN17 ...... 212 D6
Baldwyn's Pk BXLY DA5 ...... 22 A8
Baldwyn's Rd BXLY DA5 ...... 22 A8
Balfour Rd CHAT ME4 ...... 67 K5
Ballard Cl STPH/PW TN12 ...... 176 D8
Ballards La OXTED RH8 ...... 119 G8
Ballard Wy STPH/PW TN12 ...... 173 K7
Ballens Rd WALD ME5 ...... 88 D5
Balmer Cl RHAM ME8 ...... 70 A7
Balmoral Rd EYN DA4 ...... 81 K5
  GILL ME7 ...... 5 D3
Baltic Rd TON TN9 ...... 170 B7
Banbury Vls MEO DA13 ...... 44 A4
Banckside HART DA3 ...... 61 K1
Bancroft Gdns ORP BR6 ...... 56 A5
Bancroft Rd BGR/WK TN15 ...... 105 F5
Bangor Rd STRD ME2 ...... 48 C8
Bankfields HDCN TN27 ...... 200 A1
Bankfield Wy CRBK TN17 ...... 212 C7
Bank La BGR/WK TN15 ...... 146 E3
Bankside GVW DA11 ...... 26 D5
  SEV TN13 ...... 101 F8
  WALD ME5 ...... 68 C8
Bankside Cl BH/WHM TN16 ...... 97 G5
  RDART DA2 ...... 40 A2
Banks Rd STRD ME2 ...... 49 H6
Bank St CHAT ME4 ...... 4 B5
  CRBK TN17 ...... 225 J1
  GVE DA12 ...... 27 J5
  MAID/SHEP ME15 ...... 6 C5
  TON TN9 ...... 170 B4
Banky Fields Cl RHAM ME8 ...... 70 E5
Banky Meadow MAIDW ME16 ...... 131 K3
Banner Cl PUR RM19 ...... 13 H4
Banner Farm Rd RTWE/PEM TN2 ...... 11 D5
Banning St STRD ME2 ...... 49 F6
Bannister Gdns STMC/STPC BR5 ...... 38 D8
Bannister Hl RSIT ME9 ...... 93 G4
Bannister Rd MAID/BEAR ME14 ...... 111 K2
Bapchild Pl STMC/STPC BR5 ...... 56 D1
Barberry Av WALD ME5 ...... 87 J1
Barchester Wy TONN TN10 ...... 149 F8
Barclay Av TONN TN10 ...... 171 F2
Barclay Wy WTHK RM20 ...... 19 K3
Barcombe Cl CHST BR7 ...... 38 B8
Bardell Ter ROCH ME1 ...... 3 D3
Barden Park Rd TON TN9 ...... 170 A5
Barden Rd RRTW TN3 ...... 188 D4
  TON TN9 ...... 170 A5
Bardsley Cl STPH/PW TN12 ...... 151 J7
Barfield EYN DA4 ...... 42 A6
Barfleur Mnr GILL ME7 ...... 4 A2
Barfreston Cl MAID/SHEP ME15 ...... 6 C5
Bargrove Rd MAID/BEAR ME14 ...... 133 K1
Barham Cl GVE DA12 ...... 28 C7
  MAID/SHEP ME15 ...... 156 A1
Barham Rd DART DA1 ...... 23 K6
Barham's Mill Rd HDCN TN27 ...... 182 B4
Barker Rd MAIDW ME16 ...... 6 C4
Barkers Ct SIT ME10 ...... 93 J2
Bark Hart Rd ORP BR6 ...... 56 C5
Barkis Cl ROCH ME1 ...... 67 J7
Barleycorn E/WMAL ME19 ...... 108 C5
Barleycorn Dr RHAM ME8 ...... 70 B8
Barleyfds MAID/BEAR ME14 ...... 133 K2
Barleymow Cl WALD ME5 ...... 68 D8
Barling Cl WALD ME5 ...... 87 H5
Barlow Cl RHAM ME8 ...... 90 B1
Barming Rd E/WMAL ME19 ...... 130 D4
Barnaby Ter ROCH ME1 ...... 3 D2
Barn Cl RSIT ME9 ...... 93 F4
Barncroft Cl MAID/BEAR ME14 ...... 134 B2
Barncroft Dr GILL ME7 ...... 89 G2
Barned Ct MAIDW ME16 ...... 131 K5
Barn End Dr RDART DA2 ...... 41 F2
Barn End La SWLY BR8 ...... 41 F4
Barnes Cray Rd DART DA1 ...... 22 D3
Barnesdale Crs STMC/STPC BR5 ...... 56 B3
Barnes La RMAID ME17 ...... 154 D6
Barnes Wk STPH/PW TN12 ...... 196 D1
Barnett Cl ERITH DA8 ...... 22 C1

Barnetts Cl RTWE/PEM TN2 ...... 190 C5
Barnetts Rd RTON TN11 ...... 168 E4
Barnett's Shaw OXTED RH8 ...... 118 B6
Barnetts Wy STH/RUST TN4 ...... 190 C5
Barnfield GVW DA11 ...... 27 H8
 RTWE/PEM TN2 ...... 206 E7
 TENT TN30 ...... 230 B4
 WALD ME5 ...... 68 B6
Barnfield Cl GRH DA9 ...... 24 E5
 HART DA3 ...... 44 E8
 SWLY BR8 ...... 57 K4 □
Barnfield Crs RSEV TN14 ...... 102 C4
Barnfield Rd BH/WHM TN16 ...... 97 H7
 SEV TN13 ...... 123 F2
 STMC/STPC BR5 ...... 38 E8
Barnfield Wy OXTED RH8 ...... 140 E4
Barn Hi MAID/SHEP ME15 ...... 153 J4
Barnhurst Rd MAID/BEAR ME14 ...... 111 G6
Barn Meadow STPH/PW TN12 ...... 198 A2 □
 STRD ME2 ...... 85 H2
Barnsole Rd GILL ME7 ...... 5 E4
Barnwell Rd DART DA1 ...... 23 J2
Barnwood Cl ROCH ME1 ...... 67 G6 □
Baron Cl GILL ME7 ...... 5 E4
 MAID/BEAR ME14 ...... 134 B1 □
Barrack Rd CHAT ME4 ...... 50 C6
Barrack Rw GVW DA11 ...... 27 H5 □
Barrel Arch Cl STPH/PW TN12 ...... 176 C8 □
Barretts Rd HAWK TN18 ...... 235 G4
 SEV TN13 ...... 101 F7
Barrie Dr DIT/AY ME20 ...... 108 D2 □
Barrier Rd CHAT ME4 ...... 3 F3
Barrington Cl WALD ME5 ...... 88 A1
Barrowfields WALD ME5 ...... 88 E5
Barrow Green Rd OXTED RH8 ...... 118 A8
Barrow Gv SIT ME10 ...... 93 J3
Barrow La RRTW TN3 ...... 205 J5
Barr Rd GVE DA12 ...... 28 C8
Bartholomew Wy SWLY BR8 ...... 40 B8
Bartlett Cl WALD ME5 ...... 88 D5
Bartlett Rd BH/WHM TN16 ...... 120 C5 □
 GVW DA11 ...... 27 H7
Bartley Mill Rd RRTW TN3 ...... 220 A2
Barton Rd EYN DA4 ...... 42 A6
 MAID/BEAR ME15 ...... 7 D5
 SCUP DA14 ...... 39 F4
 STRD ME2 ...... 2 A1
Bashford Barn La RSIT ME9 ...... 116 A3
Basi Cl STRD ME2 ...... 49 H5
Basing Cl MAID/SHEP ME15 ...... 7 H4
Basmere Cl MAID/BEAR ME14 ...... 7 F1 □
Bassett Rd SIT ME10 ...... 93 J2
Bassetts La EDEN TN8 ...... 186 E7
Basted La BGR/WK TN15 ...... 104 C8
 BGR/WK TN15 ...... 127 G2
Batchelors RTWE/PEM TN2 ...... 192 A6 □
Batchelor St CHAT ME4 ...... 4 A4
Batchwood Gn STMC/STPC BR5 ...... 56 B1
Bates Cl DIT/AY ME20 ...... 108 E3
Bates Hi BGR/WK TN15 ...... 126 C1
Bath Hard ROCH ME1 ...... 5 D4
Bath Rd DART DA1 ...... 22 E6
Bath St GVW DA11 ...... 27 J5 □
Bathurst Cl RTWE/PEM TN2 ...... 198 A2
Bathurst Rd STPH/PW TN12 ...... 198 A3
Baton Cl PUR RM19 ...... 13 H4
Batteries Rd RSIT ME9 ...... 95 J6
Battlefields BGR/WK TN15 ...... 105 F3
Battle La STPH/PW TN12 ...... 177 F5
Battlesmere Rd HOO/HM ME3 ...... 31 G6
Battle St GVE DA12 ...... 46 C8
Batt's Rd GVE DA12 ...... 64 D2
Baugh Rd SCUP DA14 ...... 38 D3
Bay Cl HOO/HM ME3 ...... 51 F3 □
Bayford Rd SIT ME10 ...... 94 B3
Bayhall Rd RTWE/PEM TN2 ...... 11 F4
Bayham Rd RTWE/PEM TN2 ...... 207 F6
 SEV TN13 ...... 123 F1
Bayley's HI RSEV TN14 ...... 145 G3
Bayly Rd DART DA1 ...... 23 K5
Bay Manor La WTHK RM20 ...... 13 K6
Bayswater Dr RMAID ME17 ...... 90 B2
Baywell DIT/AY ME20 ...... 108 C5
 E/WMAL ME19 ...... 108 C4
Bazes Shaw HART DA3 ...... 62 A6
Beacon Cl RHAM ME8 ...... 70 A7
Beacon Dr RDART DA2 ...... 43 H1
Beaconfields SEV TN13 ...... 8 B5
Beacon HI PUR RM19 ...... 13 F5
 WALD ME5 ...... 5 D6
Beacon Hill La HOO/HM ME3 ...... 50 A2
Beacon Oak Rd TENT TN30 ...... 230 B6
Beacon Ri SEV TN13 ...... 8 C5
Beacon Rd RMAID ME17 ...... 160 C1
 WALD ME5 ...... 4 C6
Beaconsfield Av GILL ME7 ...... 5 D3
Beaconsfield Rd BXLY DA5 ...... 22 B8
 CHAT ME4 ...... 3 F6
 MAID/SHEP ME15 ...... 6 B5 □
 SIT ME10 ...... 94 D3
The Beacons RMAID ME17 ...... 154 C4 □
Beacles La OXTED RH8 ...... 140 B1
Beagles Cl STMC/STPC BR5 ...... 56 E6
Beagles Wood Rd
 RTWE/PEM TN2 ...... 192 A7 □

Beales La RYE TN31 ...... 244 E8
Beaman Cl CRBK TN17 ...... 212 E6
Beamish Rd STMC/STPC BR5 ...... 56 D4
The Beams MAID/SHEP ME15 ...... 134 A5
Bean La RDART DA2 ...... 25 G8
 RDART DA2 ...... 43 G1
Bean Rd GRH DA9 ...... 25 G5
Bearsted Cl RHAM ME8 ...... 69 J3
Bearsted Rd MAID/BEAR ME14 ...... 111 J2
Beaton Cl RHAM ME8 ...... 25 G3
Beatrice Gdns GVW DA11 ...... 27 F8
Beatrice Rd OXTED RH8 ...... 118 C7
Beatty Av GILL ME7 ...... 5 F5
Beatty Rd ROCH ME1 ...... 67 J6
Beaufighter Rd E/WMAL ME19 ...... 129 G3
Beaufort Rd STRD ME2 ...... 48 D6
Beaufort Wk MAID/SHEP ME15 ...... 156 A2
Beaulieu Ri ROCH ME1 ...... 67 J5
Beaulieu Rd TONN TN10 ...... 117 J3
Beaumont Dr GVW DA11 ...... 27 F6
Beaumont Rd GVW DA11 ...... 27 F6
 MAIDW ME16 ...... 132 A4
Beau Nash Wy RTWE/PEM TN2 ...... 11 D6 □
Beauworth Pk MAID/SHEP ME15 ...... 134 A6
Beaver Rd MAIDW ME16 ...... 110 B7
Beblets Cl ORP BR6 ...... 76 A1
Beckenham Dr MAIDW ME16 ...... 110 D7
Becket Ct HDCN TN27 ...... 200 B1
Beckets Fld RTON TN11 ...... 187 J3
Becketts Cl ORP BR6 ...... 76 A1
Beckley Cl GVE DA12 ...... 28 E8 □
Beckley Ms WALD ME5 ...... 88 A1
Beckman Cl RSEV TN14 ...... 100 E2
Becksbourne Cl
 MAID/BEAR ME14 ...... 111 G6 □
Becks Rd SCUP DA14 ...... 38 B1
Beddington Gn STMC/STPC BR5 ...... 38 A6
Beddlestead La WARL CR6 ...... 96 D5
Beddow Wy DIT/AY ME20 ...... 110 B4
Bedens Rd SCUP DA14 ...... 39 F4
Bedford Av RHAM ME8 ...... 70 A5
Bedford Pl MAIDW ME16 ...... 6 B3
Bedford Rd DART DA1 ...... 23 K6
 GVW DA11 ...... 27 G8
 ORP BR6 ...... 56 C6
 STH/RUST TN4 ...... 190 A5
Bedgebury Cl MAID/BEAR ME14 ...... 7 F1
 ROCH ME1 ...... 67 J2
Bedgebury Cross CRBK TN17 ...... 223 G4
Bedgebury Rd CRBK TN17 ...... 223 H3
Bedlam La WARL CR6 ...... 201 C1
Bedson Wk RHAM ME8 ...... 70 E5 □
Bedwin Cl ROCH ME1 ...... 67 J7
Beecham Rd TONN TN10 ...... 148 E8
Beech Av BH/WHM TN16 ...... 97 H6
 SWLY BR8 ...... 58 C1
Beech Dr MAIDW ME16 ...... 132 C1
Beechen Bank Rd WALD ME5 ...... 88 B3
Beechenlea La SWLY BR8 ...... 58 D1
The Beeches DIT/AY ME20 ...... 109 J5
 MEO DA13 ...... 64 A1
 TIL RM18 ...... 13 G1
 WALD ME5 ...... 88 B2 □
Beech Farm Rd WARL CR6 ...... 96 B7
Beech Gv HOO/HM ME3 ...... 48 A3
 SOCK/AV RM15 ...... 13 G2
Beech Hurst RTWE/PEM TN2 ...... 191 K7 □
Beech Hurst Cl MAID/SHEP ME15 ...... 7 F5
Beeching Rd WALD ME5 ...... 88 C3 □
Beechings Gn RHAM ME8 ...... 69 K3
Beechings Wy RHAM ME8 ...... 69 H2
Beechin Wood La BGR/WK TN15 ...... 127 J1
Beechlands Cl HART DA3 ...... 62 B2
Beech La HAWK TN18 ...... 245 F3
 STPH/PW TN12 ...... 209 K3
Beechmont Ri TONN TN10 ...... 148 B8 □
Beechmont Rd SEV TN13 ...... 123 K8
Beechmore Dr WALD ME5 ...... 88 B4 □
Beech Rd BH/WHM TN16 ...... 97 H6
 DART DA1 ...... 23 G7
 E/WMAL ME19 ...... 129 K2
 HOO/HM ME3 ...... 51 F3 □
 ORP BR6 ...... 76 B3
 SEV TN13 ...... 9 D4
 STPH/PW TN12 ...... 195 K3
 STRD ME2 ...... 48 B8
 WBY/YAL ME18 ...... 129 F4
Beech St RTW TN1 ...... 11 D2
Beech Wk DART DA1 ...... 22 D3
 SIT ME10 ...... 73 K8
 WALD ME5 ...... 5 D6
Beechwood Dr MEO DA13 ...... 83 H5
Beechwood Gdns MEO DA13 ...... 83 H5
Beechwood Ms RTWE/PEM TN2 ...... 207 K2
Beechwood Rd MAIDW ME16 ...... 131 K3
Beechy Lees Rd RSEV TN14 ...... 102 B4
Beesfield La EYN DA4 ...... 59 K5
Beggars La BH/WHM TN16 ...... 120 D4
Begonia Av RHAM ME8 ...... 69 K4
Beke Rd RHAM ME8 ...... 90 A2
Beldam Haw RSEV TN14 ...... 77 H6
Belfield Rd RTWE/PEM TN2 ...... 191 K8
Belgrave Rd STMC/STPC BR5 ...... 56 D1
Belgrave Rd RTW TN1 ...... 10 C3 □

Belgrave St DIT/AY ME20 ...... 86 B3
Bell Cl GRH DA9 ...... 24 E4
Bell Crs ROCH ME1 ...... 86 E6
Bellefield Rd STMC/STPC BR5 ...... 56 C2
Belle Friday Cl RSIT ME9 ...... 95 K4
Belle Vue Rd ORP BR6 ...... 75 F5
Bell Farm Gdns MAIDW ME16 ...... 131 K4 □
Bell Gdns STMC/STPC BR5 ...... 56 D2
Bellgrove Ct WALD ME5 ...... 88 B6 □
Bellingham Wy DIT/AY ME20 ...... 109 F3
Bell La DIT/AY ME20 ...... 109 F4
 HDCN TN27 ...... 200 D2
 MAID/BEAR ME14 ...... 88 B7
 MAID/BEAR ME14 ...... 134 C1
 ROCH ME1 ...... 86 E6
 STPH/PW TN12 ...... 188 A3
Bellman Av GVE DA12 ...... 28 B7
Bellmeadow MAID/SHEP ME15 ...... 134 A8
Bell Rd MAID/SHEP ME15 ...... 156 A1
 SIT ME10 ...... 93 K4
Bells Farm Rd STPH/PW TN12 ...... 151 F5
Bell's La HOO/HM ME3 ...... 32 E7
Bell Wy RMAID ME17 ...... 158 C4
Bellwood Ct HOO/HM ME3 ...... 33 K3
Belmont Cl MAIDW ME16 ...... 131 K4
Belmont Rd GILL ME7 ...... 4 C4
 SIT ME10 ...... 93 K3
Belnor Av RSIT ME9 ...... 72 D5
Beltana Dr GVE DA12 ...... 46 B2
Belton Rd SCUP DA14 ...... 38 B2
Beltring Rd STH/RUST TN4 ...... 10 C1
 STPH/PW TN12 ...... 173 K2
Belvedere Cl GVE DA12 ...... 27 K7 □
Belvedere Rd BH/WHM TN16 ...... 97 K5
Benden Cl STPH/PW TN12 ...... 198 B2 □
Bendon Wy RHAM ME8 ...... 70 A6
Benedict Cl STRD ME2 ...... 86 A2 □
Benenden Rd CRBK TN17 ...... 237 H1
 HDCN TN27 ...... 228 C2
 STRD ME2 ...... 49 H4
Benhall Mill Rd RTWE/PEM TN2 ...... 207 H6
Bennetts Av BGR/WK TN15 ...... 81 H7
Bennett Wy RDART DA2 ...... 42 C2
Benover Rd WBY/YAL ME18 ...... 152 D6
 WBY/YAL ME18 ...... 175 F1
Bensted Cl MAID/SHEP ME15 ...... 153 H6
Bentham Hi RRTW TN3 ...... 189 H5
Bentley Cl HART DA3 ...... 44 D8
 WALD ME5 ...... 88 E4 □
Bentley's Meadow BGR/WK TN15 ...... 102 E3
Bentley St GVE DA12 ...... 27 K5
Bentlif Cl MAIDW ME16 ...... 6 A2
Berber Rd STRD ME2 ...... 49 G6
Berengrave La RHAM ME8 ...... 70 B5
Berens Rd STMC/STPC BR5 ...... 56 D2
Berens Wy CHST BR7 ...... 56 A1
Beresford Av CHAT ME4 ...... 3 E6
Beresford Rd CRBK TN17 ...... 212 E6
 DIT/AY ME20 ...... 87 H7
 GILL ME7 ...... 5 D4
 GVW DA11 ...... 27 F6
Beresfords Hl RMAID ME17 ...... 155 H2
Berkeley Cl ROCH ME1 ...... 67 J6
 RTWE/PEM TN2 ...... 192 A7
Berkeley Ct SIT ME10 ...... 93 J3
Berkeley Crs DART DA1 ...... 23 J7
Berkeley Rd RTW TN1 ...... 10 C5 □
Berkley Rd GVE DA12 ...... 27 J5 □
Berkshire Cl WALD ME5 ...... 68 D6
Bermuda Rd TIL RM18 ...... 27 H1
Bernard St GVE DA12 ...... 27 J5
Berrylands HART DA3 ...... 62 B3
 ORP BR6 ...... 56 D7
Berry Rd HOO/HM ME3 ...... 51 F3 □
Berry's Green Rd BH/WHM TN16 ...... 98 B3
Berry's HI BH/WHM TN16 ...... 98 B2
Berry St SIT ME10 ...... 94 A2
Berwick Wy RSEV TN14 ...... 101 K8
Berwyn Cv MAID/SHEP ME15 ...... 133 G8
Bessels Green Rd SEV TN13 ...... 123 F2
Bessels Meadow SEV TN13 ...... 123 F3
Best St CHAT ME4 ...... 3 F4
Beta Rd HOO/HM ME3 ...... 34 A7
Betenson Av SEV TN13 ...... 8 B1
Bethel Rd SEV TN13 ...... 9 E2
Bethersden Rd HDCN TN27 ...... 201 K6
 RASHW TN26 ...... 219 K1
Betjeman Cl DIT/AY ME20 ...... 108 D3
Betsham Rd MAID/SHEP ME15 ...... 134 B8 □
 MEO DA13 ...... 43 J3
 SWCM DA10 ...... 25 K6
Bettescombe Rd RHAM ME8 ...... 70 A7
Beulah Rd RTW TN1 ...... 11 E3
Beult Meadow HDCN TN27 ...... 202 A5
Beult Rd DART DA1 ...... 24 B3
Bevan Pl SWLY BR8 ...... 58 C1 □
Bevans Cl GRH DA9 ...... 25 H5 □
Beverley Cl RHAM ME8 ...... 70 C6
Beverley Crs TON TN9 ...... 157 H6
Beverley Rd MAIDW ME16 ...... 131 K4
Bevis Cl RDART DA2 ...... 24 B6
Bewl Bridge Cl WADH TN5 ...... 233 F3
Bewlbridge La RRTW TN3 ...... 222 A5
Bewley La BGR/WK TN15 ...... 126 C4
Bexley Cl DART DA1 ...... 22 B4

Bexley La DART DA1 .... 22 B4
  SCUP DA14 .... 38 D2
Bexon La RSIT ME9 .... 116 C2
Bickley Rd TON TN9 .... 170 B6 🔽
Bickmore Wy SCUP DA14 .... 170 C3
Bicknor La RSIT ME9 .... 115 G3
Bicknor Rd MAID/SHEP ME15 .... 156 B2
Bidborough Rdg STH/RUST TN4 ..... 189 H2
Biddenden CI MAID/BEAR ME15 ..... 134 B3
Biddenden La HDCN TN27 .... 200 C1
Biddenden Rd HDCN TN27 .... 200 C4
  HDCN TN27 .... 201 J6
  HDCN TN27 .... 218 E8
  RASHW TN26 .... 219 F8
Biddenden Wy MEO DA13 .... 45 F6
Bilberry CI MAID/BEAR ME14 .... 134 A1 🔽
Billet HI BGR/WK TN15 .... 61 H8
Billings HART DA3 .... 62 A3
Bill Street Rd STRD ME2 .... 49 H6
Bilsington CI WALD ME5 .... 88 C1
Binbury La MAID/BEAR ME14 .... 113 H2
The Bines STPH/PW TN12 .... 193 J1
Bingham Rd STRD ME2 .... 49 H5
Bingley CI SNOD ME6 .... 85 J6
Bingley Rd ROCH ME1 .... 3 E4
Binland Gv WALD ME5 .... 87 J1
Binnacle Rd ROCH ME1 .... 67 H6
Binney Rd HOO/HM ME3 .... 19 C6
Birch CI EYN DA4 .... 59 C7
  HART DA3 .... 44 D7
  RTON TN11 .... 169 H2
  RTWE/PEM TN2 .... 190 D7
  SEV TN13 .... 153 D2
  STPH/PW TN12 .... 193 F5
Birch Crs DIT/AY ME20 .... 109 H6
Birch Dr WALD ME5 .... 88 C5
The Birches SWLY BR8 .... 39 H7
  TON TN9 .... 170 B7 🔽
Birchetts Av RRTW TN3 .... 205 H3 🔽
Birchfield CI MAID/SHEP ME15 ...... 133 H8
Birchfields WALD ME5 .... 88 B3
Birch Gv GILL ME7 .... 89 H1
Birchin Cross Rd RSEV TN14 .... 102 C2
Birchington CI MAID/BEAR ME14 .... 7 F2 🔽
Bircholt Rd MAID/SHEP ME15 .... 156 B2
Birch PI GRH DA9 .... 24 D5
Birch Rd HOO/HM ME3 .... 51 F3
  STPH/PW TN12 .... 173 J8
Birch Tree Wy MAID/SHEP ME15 ..... 7 E4
Birchway BGR/WK TN15 .... 80 C3 🔽
Birch Wy RTWE/PEM TN2 .... 190 D7
Birchwood Av SCUP DA14 .... 38 C1
  STH/RUST TN4 .... 189 J3
Birchwood Dr RDART DA2 .... 40 B2
Birchwood La RSEV TN14 .... 100 B2
Birchwood Park Av SWLY BR8 .... 39 K6
Birchwood Rd MAIDW ME16 .... 132 C1
  RDART DA2 .... 39 K5
Bird House La ORP BR6 .... 98 A1
Bird In Hand St RRTW TN3 .... 205 F6 🔽
Birkbeck Rd SCUP DA14 .... 38 B1
Birken Rd RTWE/PEM TN2 .... 11 F1
Birkhall CI RTWE/PEM TN2 .... 88 B1
Birling Av MAID/BEAR ME14 .... 134 C2
  RHAM ME8 .... 70 A5
Birling CI MAID/BEAR ME14 .... 134 B2
Birling Dr RTWE/PEM TN2 .... 207 F6
Birling HI MEO DA13 .... 84 D5
Birling Pk E/WMAL ME19 .... 108 A1
Birling Park Av RTWE/PEM TN2 ..... 207 G6
Birling Rd E/WMAL ME19 .... 107 J2
  RTWE/PEM TN2 .... 207 G6
  SNOD ME6 .... 85 J7
Birling Road Rookery HI
  SNOD ME6 .... 85 J7
Birnam Sq MAIDW ME16 .... 6 B3 🔽
Birtrick Dr MEO DA13 .... 63 C2
Bishop Butt CI ORP BR6 .... 56 A7 🔽
Bishop La RSIT ME9 .... 71 H3
Bishops CI WBY/YAL ME18 .... 130 A8
Bishops Ct GRH DA9 .... 24 D4
Bishop's Down
  STH/RUST TN4 .... 10 A4
Bishop's Down Park Rd
  STH/RUST TN4 .... 10 A3
Bishop's Down Rd
  STH/RUST TN4 .... 10 A4
Bishops La CRBK TN17 .... 224 E4
  MAID/SHEP ME15 .... 153 H7
Bishops Ms TON TN9 .... 170 C6 🔽
Bishops Oak Ride TONN TN10 .... 148 B8
Bishops Wk ROCH ME1 .... 2 C3
Bishops Wy MAIDW ME16 .... 6 C3
Blackberry Fld STMC/STPC BR5 .... 38 B6 🔽
Blackberry Wy STPH/PW TN12 ...... 173 J8
Black Eagle CI BH/WHM TN16 .... 120 C6
Blackhall La BGR/WK TN15 .... 124 C2
Black Horse Ms BGR/WK TN15 ...... 105 C8
Black Horse Rd SCUP DA14 .... 38 B2 🔽
Blackhurst La RTWE/PEM TN2 .... 191 G7
Blacklands E/WMAL ME19 .... 108 D6
Blacklands Dr E/WMAL ME19 .... 108 D6
Blackman CI HOO/HM ME3 .... 32 E7
Blackmans CI DART DA1 .... 23 F7 🔽
Blackman's La RTON TN11 .... 149 K7
Blackmanstone Wy DIT/AY ME20 ... 110 B7

Blackmead SEV TN13 .... 101 G8
Black Mill La HDCN TN27 .... 199 K1
Blackness La HAYES BR2 .... 74 C4
Black Rock Gdns GILL ME7 .... 89 J2 🔽
Blacksmith Dr
  MAID/BEAR ME14 .... 133 K1 🔽
Blacksmiths CI MAID/SHEP ME15 ... 56 D2
Blacksole La BGR/WK TN15 .... 105 F3
Blacksole Rd BGR/WK TN15 .... 105 F3 🔽
Blackthorn Av RTWE/PEM TN2 ...... 190 C5
  WALD ME5 .... 88 B3
Blackthorn CI BGR/WK TN15 .... 80 C4 🔽
Blackthorn Dr DIT/AY ME20 .... 109 F4
Blackthorne Rd RHAM ME8 .... 70 D6
Blackthorn Rd BH/WHM TN16 .... 97 J3 🔽
Blair Dr SEV TN13 .... 9 D2
Blake Dr DIT/AY ME20 .... 108 D2
Blake Gdns DART DA1 .... 23 J3
Blakeney CI MAID/BEAR ME14 ...... 134 D2
Blaker Av ROCH ME1 .... 67 K5
Blake Wy RTWE/PEM TN2 .... 190 D7
Blandford Gdns SIT ME10 .... 93 K5
Blatchford CI E/WMAL ME19 .... 108 D5 🔽
Blatchington Rd RTW TN1 .... 10 C6
Bleakwood Rd WALD ME5 .... 88 A1
Blean Rd RHAM ME8 .... 69 K4
Blendon Rd MAID/BEAR ME14 .... 7 F2
Blenheim Av CHAT ME4 .... 3 E6
Blenheim CI DART DA1 .... 25 F5
  MAID/SHEP ME15 .... 134 B3
  MEO DA13 .... 63 J6 🔽
Blenheim Gdns SOCK/AV RM15 ..... 13 F1
Blenheim Gv CI CVE DA12 .... 27 K6 🔽
Blenheim Rd DART DA1 .... 25 F5
  E/WMAL ME19 .... 129 H3
  ORP BR6 .... 56 D6
Blenheim Wy WADH TN5 .... 233 G3
Bligh Rd GVW DA11 .... 27 H5
Bligh's Rd SEV TN13 .... 9 D4
Bligh Wy STRD ME2 .... 48 B8
Blind La CRBK TN17 .... 212 D5
  GILL ME7 .... 89 G5
Blind Mary's La RSIT ME9 .... 115 J2
Bliss Wy TONN TN10 .... 170 E1
Blockmakers Ct CHAT ME4 .... 68 C5
Bloors La RHAM ME8 .... 70 A5
Bloors Wharf Rd GILL ME7 .... 70 B2
Blowers Grove Wd GILL ME7 .... 89 J3
Blowers HI EDEN TN8 .... 185 K6
Bluebell CI GILL ME7 .... 5 F2
Bluebell Wks STPH/PW TN12 .... 173 J8
Blueberry La RSEV TN14 .... 99 J3
Blue Boar La ROCH ME1 .... 3 J5
Blue Coat La CRBK TN17 .... 212 B7
Bluehouse Gdns OXTED RH8 .... 118 E7
Bluehouse La OXTED RH8 .... 118 C7
Bluett St MAID/BEAR ME14 .... 7 D2
Bluewater Pkwy GRH DA9 .... 24 E6
Blunden La WBY/YAL ME18 .... 152 E5
Blythe HI STMC/STPC BR5 .... 38 A4
Blythe Rd MAID/SHEP ME15 .... 7 E3
Boakes Meadow RSEV TN14 .... 78 C6
Boarders La WADH TN5 .... 232 A3
Boarley La MAID/BEAR ME14 .... 111 F5
Bobbing HI RSIT ME9 .... 93 F1
Bockingford La MAID/SHEP ME15 .. 132 E6
Bodiam CI RHAM ME8 .... 69 K4
Bodiam Rd HAWK TN18 .... 243 G4
Bodle Av SWCM DA10 .... 25 K5
Bodmin CI STMC/STPC BR5 .... 56 D5
Bodsham Crs MAID/SHEP ME15 .... 134 D3
Bogle Rd RSIT ME9 .... 95 K7
Boley HI ROCH ME1 .... 2 C2
Boleyn Rd RSEV TN14 .... 102 C4
Boleyn Wy SWCM DA10 .... 25 K6
Bolner CI WALD ME5 .... 88 A4
Bombers La BH/WHM TN16 .... 98 D7
Bonaventure Ct GVE DA12 .... 46 C2
Bond CI RSEV TN14 .... 99 K2
Bondfield CI STH/RUST TN4 .... 190 A5
Bondfield Rd E/WMAL ME19 .... 108 D6
Bond Rd RHAM ME8 .... 90 B2
Boneashe La BGR/WK TN15 .... 105 K8
Bonflower La RMAID ME17 .... 154 C7
Bonham Dr SIT ME10 .... 94 B1
Bonney Wy SWLY BR8 .... 40 B7
Bonnington Rd MAID/BEAR ME14 .... 7 F1
Bootham CI STRD ME2 .... 66 C2
Booth Rd CHAT ME4 .... 3 F6
Borden La RSIT ME9 .... 93 G4
Bordyke TON TN9 .... 170 C4
Borkwood Pk ORP BR6 .... 56 A8
Borland CI GRH DA9 .... 25 F4 🔽
Borough Green Rd BGR/WK TN15 .. 104 D8
Borough Rd BH/WHM TN16 .... 97 H8
  GILL ME7 .... 5 D4
Borstal Rd ROCH ME1 .... 2 B5
Borstal St ROCH ME1 .... 2 A6
Bostall Rd STMC/STPC BR5 .... 38 C5
Boston Gdns RHAM ME8 .... 69 K5
Boston Rd WALD ME5 .... 88 C4
Bosville Dr SEV TN13 .... 8 C1
Bosville Rd SEV TN13 .... 8 C2
Boswell CI STMC/STPC BR5 .... 56 D3 🔽
Botany TON TN9 .... 170 C5

Botany Wy PUR RM19 .... 13 F5
Botsom La BGR/WK TN15 .... 80 B2
Bottlescrew HI RMAID ME17 .... 155 H2
Bottles La RSIT ME9 .... 117 G1
Bottom Pond Rd RSIT ME9 .... 116 E2
Bott Rd RDART DA2 .... 41 J2
Boucher Dr GVW DA11 .... 45 G1
Boughton La MAID/SHEP ME15 ..... 133 H7
Boughton Rd RMAID ME17 .... 160 B5
Boulthurst Wy OXTED RH8 .... 140 E3
Boundary Rd ROCH ME1 .... 1 G3
  RTWE/PEM TN2 .... 11 F6
The Boundary RRTW TN3 .... 206 A3
Bounds Oak Wy STH/RUST TN4 .... 189 J3
The Bounds DIT/AY ME20 .... 109 J3
Bourne CI TON TN9 .... 170 D3
Bourne Grange La RTON TN11 ...... 149 K6
Bourne Gv SIT ME10 .... 93 H1
Bourne La BGR/WK TN15 .... 127 F4
  RBTBR TN32 .... 242 A6
  TON TN9 .... 170 C3
Bourne Pk RTON TN11 .... 172 B1
Bourne Rd RTON TN11 .... 28 C8
Bourne V BGR/WK TN15 .... 127 G6
Bourne Wy SWLY BR8 .... 39 K8
Bournewood CI MAID/SHEP ME15 . 134 B5
Bournewood Rd STMC/STPC BR5 .. 56 C4
Bournville Av CHAT ME4 .... 68 A5
Bow Arrow La DART DA1 .... 23 K5
  RDART DA2 .... 24 A5
Bowen Rd STH/RUST TN4 .... 206 A1
Bower CI MAIDW ME16 .... 6 B3
Bowerland La LING RH7 .... 162 B6
Bower La EYN DA4 .... 59 H7
  EYN DA4 .... 79 K3
  MAIDW ME16 .... 6 B3
Bower Mount Rd MAIDW ME16 .... 6 A4
Bower PI MAIDW ME16 .... 6 B3
Bower Rd SWLY BR8 .... 40 D5
Bowers Av GVW DA11 .... 45 G2
Bowers Rd RSEV TN14 .... 78 C6
Bower St MAIDW ME16 .... 6 B3
Bowesden La GVE DA12 .... 47 J5
  STRD ME2 .... 47 J6
Bowes Rd STRD ME2 .... 49 G6
Bowes Wd HART DA3 .... 62 A7
Bow HI WBY/YAL ME18 .... 152 C1
Bowley La RMAID ME17 .... 160 E8
Bowls PI STPH/PW TN12 .... 173 J7 🔽
Bowman Cl WALD ME5 .... 88 D1
Bowmans Rd DART DA1 .... 22 C6
Bown CI TIL RM18 .... 27 J1
Bow Rd WBY/YAL ME18 .... 130 C7
Bow Ter WBY/YAL ME18 .... 130 C7
Bowzell Rd RSEV TN14 .... 145 H4
Boxley CI MAID/BEAR ME14 .... 111 H6
Boxley Rd MAID/BEAR ME14 .... 7 D1
  MAID/BEAR ME14 .... 88 D7
  WALD ME5 .... 88 C5
Boxted La RSIT ME9 .... 71 K5
Boyces St RSIT ME9 .... 72 C8
Boy Court La HDCN TN27 .... 180 C5
Boyne Pk STH/RUST TN4 .... 10 B3
Boyton Court Rd RMAID ME17 ..... 179 J1
Brabourne Av RHAM ME8 .... 69 K2
Bracken Cl RTWE/PEM TN2 .... 207 K1 🔽
Brackendene BXLY DA5 .... 40 B2
Bracken HI WALD ME5 .... 88 B5
Bracken Lea WALD ME5 .... 68 C3
Bracken Rd RTWE/PEM TN2 .... 207 K1
The Brackens ORP BR6 .... 76 B1
Bracken Wk TONN TN10 .... 148 B8
Brackley CI MAID/BEAR ME14 .... 7 F2
Brackwood CI RHAM ME8 .... 90 A1 🔽
Bracondale Av MEO DA13 .... 45 G6 🔽
Bradbourne La DIT/AY ME20 .... 109 F5
Bradbourne Park Rd SEV TN13 .... 8 C2
Bradbourne Pkwy DIT/AY ME20 ... 108 E5
Bradbourne Rd SEV TN13 .... 9 D1
Bradbourne Vale Rd SEV TN13 .... 8 B1
Braddick CI MAID/SHEP ME15 ...... 155 H1
Bradfields Av WALD ME5 .... 68 A8
Bradfields Av West WALD ME5 ...... 88 A1
Bradford St TON TN9 .... 170 B5 🔽
Bradley Dr SIT ME10 .... 93 K4
Bradley Rd RRTW TN3 .... 204 A1
  STRD ME2 .... 85 H1
Bradshaw CI RSIT ME9 .... 71 H3
Braeside Av SEV TN13 .... 8 B3
Braeside CI SEV TN13 .... 8 B2
The Braes HOO/HM ME3 .... 48 B3
Brake Av WALD ME5 .... 87 K1
Brakefield Rd MEO DA13 .... 44 C4
Brakes PI BGR/WK TN15 .... 80 D2
Bramber Av RDART DA2 .... 23 H1
Bramble Bank MEO DA13 .... 83 G7 🔽
Bramble CI MAIDW ME16 .... 132 B3
  RTON TN11 .... 169 K2
Brambledown HART DA3 .... 62 A1
  WALD ME5 .... 68 C6
Bramblefield CI HART DA3 .... 43 J8
Bramblefield La SIT ME10 .... 73 K5
Bramble La SEV TN13 .... 123 K7
Bramble Reed La STPH/PW TN12 .. 192 D7
Brambletree Crs ROCH ME1 .... 66 E4

Bramley Cl *MEO* DA13 .... **45** G5 ◻
RHAM ME8 .... **70** E6 ◻
SWLY BR8 .... **58** B1
Bramley Ct *STPH/PW* TN12 .... **176** B8
Bramley Crs *MAID/SHEP* ME15 .... **134** B3
Bramley Dr *CRBK* TN17 .... **225** K2
Bramley Gdns *RMAID* ME17 .... **154** D3
STPH/PW TN12 .... **173** G7
Bramley Pl *DART* DA1 .... **22** D3
Bramley Ri *STRD* ME2 .... **48** D6
Bramley Rd *SNOD* ME6 .... **85** K6
STPH/PW TN12 .... **193** H8 ◻
Bramleys *HDCN* TN27 .... **200** B1 ◻
Bramley Wy *WBY/YAL* ME18 .... **129** J4
Bramshott Cl *MAIDW* ME16 .... **110** C8 ◻
Branbridges Rd *STPH/PW* TN12 ..... **173** K1
Brandon Rd *DART* DA1 .... **23** K6
Brandon St *GVW* DA11 .... **27** J6
Brands Hatch Rd *BGR/WK* TN15 ..... **61** F7
Bransell Cl *SWLY* BR8 .... **57** K3
Bransgore Cl *RHAM* ME8 .... **70** A7
Brantingham Cl *TON* TN9 .... **169** K7 ◻
Branton Rd *GRH* DA9 .... **24** E5
Brantwood Wy *STMC/STPC* BR5 ..... **38** D8
Brasenose Rd *GILL* ME7 .... **5** E5
Brassey Dr *DIT/AY* ME20 .... **109** H6
Brassey Hl *OXTED* RH8 .... **118** E8
OXTED RH8 .... **140** E1
Brassey Rd *OXTED* RH8 .... **118** E8
Brasted Cl *STRD* ME2 .... **49** F5
Brasted Hl *RSEV* TN14 .... **99** G7
Brasted Hill Rd *BH/WHM* TN16 ..... **121** J1
Brasted La *RSEV* TN14 .... **99** G6
Brasted Rd *BH/WHM* TN16 .... **120** E5
Brattle Wd *SEV* TN13 .... **124** A8
Braunstone Dr *MAIDW* ME16 .... **110** D7
Bray Gdns *MAID/SHEP* ME15 .... **155** F1
Breach La *RSIT* ME9 .... **71** J6
Breach Rd *WTHK* RM20 .... **13** K6
Breakneck Hl *GRH* DA9 .... **25** G4
Breakspears Dr *STMC/STPC* BR5 ..... **38** B6
Bredgar Cl *MAID/BEAR* ME14 .... **7** E2
Bredgar Rd *RHAM* ME8 .... **69** H2
Bredhurst Rd *RHAM* ME8 .... **89** J3
Breedon Av *STH/RUST* TN4 .... **189** K5 ◻
Bremner Cl *SWLY* BR8 .... **58** D1 ◻
Brenchley Av *GVW* DA11 .... **45** J3
Brenchley Cl *ROCH* ME1 .... **3** D6
Brenchley Rd *MAID/SHEP* ME15 .... **6** C5
RHAM ME8 .... **69** J4
SIT ME10 .... **94** A4
STPH/PW TN12 .... **195** G5
STPH/PW TN12 .... **211** J1
Brendon Av *WALD* ME5 .... **88** B2
Brendon Rd *RTWE/PEM* TN2 .... **11** F2 ◻
Brennan Rd *TIL* RM18 .... **27** J1
Brent Cl *RDART* DA2 .... **24** A5
WALD ME5 .... **87** K1
Brentfield Cl *WALD* ME5 .... **88** C1
Brentlands Dr *DART* DA1 .... **23** K7
Brent La *DART* DA1 .... **23** J6
The Brent *DART* DA1 .... **24** A6
Brent Wy *DART* DA1 .... **24** A5
Brenzett Cl *WALD* ME5 .... **88** C1
Bretland Rd *STH/RUST* TN4 .... **206** C2
Breton Rd *ROCH* ME1 .... **2** C6
Brevet Cl *PUR* RM19 .... **13** H4
Brewer Cl *HOO/HM* ME3 .... **31** G7
Brewers Fld *RDART* DA2 .... **41** F2
Brewers Rd *GVE* DA12 .... **47** F6
Brewer St *MAID/BEAR* ME14 .... **7** D2
RRTW TN3 .... **221** J1
Brewery Rd *SIT* ME10 .... **73** K8
Brewhouse Yd *GVE* DA12 .... **27** J5 ◻
Brian Crs *STH/RUST* TN4 .... **190** B6
Briar Cl *DIT/AY* ME20 .... **108** E4
Briar Dl *HOO/HM* ME3 .... **48** A3
Briar Flds *MAID/BEAR* ME14 .... **134** A1
Briar Rd *BXLY* DA5 .... **40** A1
The Briars *BGR/WK* TN15 .... **80** C2
Briars Wy *HART* DA3 .... **62** B3
Briarswood Wy *ORP* BR6 .... **76** A1
Briar Wk *TONN* TN10 .... **148** C8
Briary Ct *SCUP* DA14 .... **38** C3
Brice Rd *HOO/HM* ME3 .... **48** A3
Brickenden Rd *CRBK* TN17 .... **225** K2
Brickfields *E/WMAL* ME19 .... **107** K5
RTWE/PEM TN2 .... **192** A6
Brick Field Vw *STRD* ME2 .... **49** H5
Brick Kiln La *OXTED* RH8 .... **141** G1
RMAID ME17 .... **180** B1
STPH/PW TN12 .... **211** K5
Brickworks Cl *TON* TN9 .... **170** A7
Bridewell La *TENT* TN30 .... **230** A7
Bridge Cl *GRH* DA9 .... **24** C2
TON TN9 .... **170** C6
Bridge Mill Wy *MAID/SHEP* ME15 .... **6** A5
Bridge Rd *GILL* ME7 .... **4** C1
ROCH ME1 .... **2** C6
STMC/STPC BR5 .... **56** C3
Bridges Dr *DART* DA1 .... **24** A4
Bridge St *MAID/SHEP* ME15 .... **155** F1
Bridgewater Pl *E/WMAL* ME19 ..... **108** C4
Bridlington Cl *BH/WHM* TN16 .... **97** F6

Brier Cl *WALD* ME5 .... **68** D6
Brier Rd *SIT* ME10 .... **93** F1
Brightlands *GVW* DA11 .... **45** F2 ◻
Bright Rdg *STH/RUST* TN4 .... **189** J6
Bright Rd *CHAT* ME4 .... **4** B6
Brimfield Rd *PUR* RM19 .... **13** H4
The Brimp *HOO/HM* ME3 .... **19** C5
Brimstone Cl *ORP* BR6 .... **76** D3
Brimstone Hl *MEO* DA13 .... **63** K6
Brindle's Fld *TON* TN9 .... **169** K7
Brindle Wy *WALD* ME5 .... **88** D5
Brionne Gdns *TON* TN9 .... **170** D6
Brisbane Av *SIT* ME10 .... **93** H2
Brisbane Rd *CHAT* ME4 .... **4** A5
Brishing Cl *MAID/SHEP* ME15 .... **156** A1 ◻
Brishing La *MAID/SHEP* ME15 .... **156** A1
RMAID ME17 .... **155** K3
Brishing Rd *RMAID* ME17 .... **156** A2
Brissenden Cl *STRD* ME2 .... **50** B3
Bristol Cl *STRD* ME2 .... **66** C1
Bristol La *GVE* DA12 .... **46** A1
Britannia Cl *SIT* ME10 .... **93** K2 ◻
STRD ME2 .... **85** K2 ◻
Britannia Dr *GVE* DA12 .... **46** C3
Brittains La *SEV* TN13 .... **8** B3
Britten Cl *TON* TN10 .... **149** F8
Britton St *GILL* ME7 .... **4** B3
Broadcloth *CRBK* TN17 .... **225** K3
Broadcroft *RTWE/PEM* TN2 .... **206** D5
Broad Ditch Rd *MEO* DA13 .... **44** D5
Broader La *MAID/BEAR* ME14 .... **112** D4
Broad Gv *MAID/SHEP* ME15 .... **133** G6
Broad Ov *RTWE/PEM* TN2 .... **10** C5 ◻
Broadham Green Rd *OXTED* RH8 ... **140** D4
Broadham Pl *OXTED* RH8 .... **140** B3
Broadlands Dr *WALD* ME5 .... **88** C2
Broad La *RDART* DA2 .... **40** E2
RRTW TN3 .... **204** D3
Broadmead *RTWE/PEM* TN2 .... **206** D6
Broadmead Av *RTWE/PEM* TN2 .... **206** E6 ◻
Broadoak *E/WMAL* ME19 .... **108** D4 ◻
Broad Oak *RRTW* TN3 .... **204** E8
STPH/PW TN12 .... **194** A6
Broadoak Av *MAID/SHEP* ME15 ..... **133** G6
Broadoak Cl *RDART* DA2 .... **41** K4
Broad Oak Cl *RTWE/PEM* TN2 .... **10** B7
STMC/STPC BR5 .... **38** B7
STPH/PW TN12 .... **194** A6
Broad Rd *RSIT* ME9 .... **93** J7
Broad Rd *SWCM* DA10 .... **25** K5
Broad St *RMAID* ME17 .... **157** G7
Broad Street Hl *RMAID* ME17 .... **114** B7
Broadview Av *RHAM* ME8 .... **70** B6
Broad Wk *BGR/WK* TN15 .... **124** C7
ORP BR6 .... **56** E7
Broadwater Down
RTWE/PEM TN2 .... **206** E6
Broadwater La *RTWE/PEM* TN2 ...... **10** B6
Broadwater Ri *RTWE/PEM* TN2 ...... **10** B6
Broadwater Rd *E/WMAL* ME19 ..... **108** B8
Broadway *MAIDW* ME16 .... **6** C4
RHAM ME8 .... **69** H4
TIL RM18 .... **27** G1 ◻
The Broadway *RRTW* TN3 .... **221** K1
Broadway *GVW* DA11 .... **45** J3 ◻
Broadwood Rd *HOO/HM* ME3 .... **50** A2
Brockenhurst Av *MAID/SHEP* ME15 .. **7** E6
Brockenhurst Cl *RHAM* ME8 .... **69** K7
Brockway *BGR/WK* TN15 .... **105** G8
Brockwell Cl *STMC/STPC* BR5 .... **56** A2
Brogden Crs *RMAID* ME17 .... **135** H7
Broke Farm Dr *ORP* BR6 .... **76** D4
Brokes Wy *STH/RUST* TN4 .... **190** C5
Bromford Cl *OXTED* RH8 .... **140** E4
Bromley Cl *WALD* ME5 .... **88** C2
Brompton Farm Rd *STRD* ME2 .... **48** E5
Brompton Hl *CHAT* ME4 .... **3** F2
Brompton La *STRD* ME2 .... **49** F6
Brompton Rd *GILL* ME7 .... **4** B2
Bronington Cl *WALD* ME5 .... **88** B1
Bronte Cl *DIT/AY* ME20 .... **108** D3
TIL RM18 .... **27** K1 ◻
Bronte Gv *DART* DA1 .... **23** J3
Bronte Vw *GVE* DA12 .... **27** K1 ◻
Brook *CHAT* ME4 .... **4** A4
Brookbank *MAID/BEAR* ME14 .... **111** G6
Brooke Dr *GVE* DA12 .... **28** E7
Brookes Pl *RSIT* ME9 .... **72** A8
Brookfield *RSEV* TN14 .... **102** C4
Brookfield Av *DIT/AY* ME20 .... **108** E2
Brookfields *RTON* TN11 .... **150** A5
Brook Hl *OXTED* RH8 .... **140** A1
Brookhurst Gdns *STH/RUST* TN4 .. **189** J3
Brooklands *DART* DA1 .... **23** H7
HDCN TN27 .... **180** A8
RTWE/PEM TN2 .... **190** D7 ◻
Brooklands Farm Cl *RRTW* TN3 .... **187** J8
Brooklands Rd *DIT/AY* ME20 .... **108** E3
Brook La *BGR/WK* TN15 .... **127** G6
SNOD ME6 .... **85** K8
TON TN9 .... **170** D6
Brooklyn Paddock *GILL* ME7 .... **5** D2 ◻
Brookmead *RTON* TN11 .... **169** J2
Brookmead Cl *ORP* BR6 .... **56** C4 ◻
Brookmead Rd *HOO/HM* ME3 .... **31** G7

Brookmead Wy *ORP* BR6 .... **56** C3
Brook Rd *DIT/AY* ME20 .... **108** C2
GVW DA11 .... **27** F7
RTWE/PEM TN2 .... **190** C7
SWLY BR8 .... **40** A8
Brooks Cl *STPH/PW* TN12 .... **198** A2
Brookside *CRBK* TN17 .... **225** K2
HOO/HM ME3 .... **51** F1
ORP BR6 .... **56** A4
Brookside Rd *MEO* DA13 .... **45** G5
Brooks Pl *MAID/BEAR* ME14 .... **7** D3 ◻
Brook St *RASHW* TN26 .... **231** J6
SNOD ME6 .... **86** A6
TON TN9 .... **169** K6
Broom Av *STMC/STPC* BR5 .... **38** C7
Broom Bank *WARL* CR6 .... **96** A6
Broomcroft Rd *RHAM* ME8 .... **70** C4
Broome Pl *SOCK/AV* RM15 .... **13** H1 ◻
Broomes Ct *RMAID* ME17 .... **158** A6
Broomfield Rd *RMAID* ME17 .... **158** A3
SEV TN13 .... **8** B1
SWCM DA10 .... **25** K5
Broomfields *HART* DA3 .... **61** K2
Broomhill Park Rd *STH/RUST* TN4 . **189** J6
Broomhill Rd *DART* DA1 .... **22** E5
ORP BR6 .... **56** B4
RRTW TN3 .... **189** H8
Broom Hill Rd *STRD* ME2 .... **48** E6
Broomlands La *OXTED* RH8 .... **119** J6
Broom La *RRTW* TN3 .... **205** J5
Broom Pk *RRTW* TN3 .... **205** H3
Broom Rd *SIT* ME10 .... **94** D1
Broomshaw Rd *MAIDW* ME16 .... **131** K3
Broomwood Cl *BXLY* DA5 .... **22** A8
Broomwood Rd *STMC/STPC* BR5 .... **38** C7
Brow Cl *STMC/STPC* BR5 .... **56** E4
Brow Crs *STMC/STPC* BR5 .... **56** D5
Browndens Rd *STRD* ME2 .... **85** H3
Brownelow Copse *WALD* ME5 .... **88** B5
Brownhill Cl *WALD* ME5 .... **88** B2
Browning Cl *DIT/AY* ME20 .... **108** D2 ◻
Browning Rd *DART* DA1 .... **23** J3
Brownings *EDEN* TN8 .... **164** C2
Brownings Orch *RSIT* ME9 .... **94** B7
Brown Rd *GVE* DA12 .... **28** B8
Brown St *RHAM* ME8 .... **70** B5
Broxbourne Rd *ORP* BR6 .... **56** A5
Bruce Gv *ORP* BR6 .... **56** B5
The Brucks *WBY/YAL* ME18 .... **130** C7
Brunel Cl *TIL* RM18 .... **27** J1
Brunel Wy *CHAT* ME4 .... **4** A3
Brunswick St *MAID/SHEP* ME15 ...... **7** D4 ◻
Brunswick St East
MAID/SHEP ME15 .... **7** D4
Brunswick Wk *GVE* DA12 .... **28** A5 ◻
Bryanston Rd *TIL* RM18 .... **27** K1
Bryant Cl *WBY/YAL* ME18 .... **130** B3
Bryant Rd *STRD* ME2 .... **49** F6
Bryant St *CHAT* ME4 .... **3** F5
Bubblestone Rd *RSEV* TN14 .... **101** K3
Bubhurst La *CRBK* TN17 .... **199** K7
Buchanan Cl *SOCK/AV* RM15 .... **13** G1 ◻
Buckham Thorns Rd
BH/WHM TN16 .... **120** C5
Buckhole Farm Rd *HOO/HM* ME3 ... **32** D2
Buckhurst La *SEV* TN13 .... **9** E4
Buckhurst Rd *BH/WHM* TN16 .... **98** B7
Buckingham Rd *GILL* ME7 .... **5** D3 ◻
GVW DA11 .... **26** E6 ◻
RTW TN1 .... **11** D5
Buckingham Rw
MAID/SHEP ME15 .... **134** A7
Buckland Cl *WALD* ME5 .... **88** B4 ◻
Buckland Hl *MAIDW* ME16 .... **6** A2
Buckland La *MAIDW* ME16 .... **6** A1
Buckland Rd *HOO/HM* ME3 .... **30** E7
MAIDW ME16 .... **6** B3
MEO DA13 .... **64** D7
Bucklers Cl *RTWE/PEM* TN2 .... **11** E4 ◻
Buckley Cl *DART* DA1 .... **22** C1
Bucks Cross Rd *GVW* DA11 .... **45** G1
ORP BR6 .... **77** F1
Budd's La *TENT* TN30 .... **247** K4
Budgin's Hl *ORP* BR6 .... **76** C7
Bugglesden Rd *HDCN* TN27 .... **229** H1
Bulldog Rd *WALD* ME5 .... **88** C4
Buller Rd *CHAT* ME4 .... **3** F6
Bullers Cl *SCUP* DA14 .... **39** F3
Bull Flds *SNOD* ME6 .... **85** K6
Bullfinch Cl *SEV* TN13 .... **123** F1
STPH/PW TN12 .... **193** J1 ◻
Bullfinch Dene *SEV* TN13 .... **123** F1
Bullfinch La *SEV* TN13 .... **8** A1
Bull Hl *RMAID* ME17 .... **116** D5
Bullingstone La *RRTW* TN3 .... **188** D7
Bullingstone Cl *STPH/PW* TN12 .... **173** G8
Bullivant Cl *GRH* DA9 .... **25** F4
Bull La *BGR/WK* TN15 .... **105** G3
DIT/AY ME20 .... **87** F8
DIT/AY ME20 .... **109** K3
HOO/HM ME3 .... **30** C7
RSIT ME9 .... **91** H5
Bull Orch *MAIDW* ME16 .... **131** K4
Bull Rd *E/WMAL* ME19 .... **108** A1
Bulls Pl *RTWE/PEM* TN2 .... **191** K8

Bulrush Cl *WALD* ME5 .... 88 A3
Bumbles Cl *ROCH* ME1 .... 67 J6
Bunkers Hl *SCUP* DA14 .... 39 G1
Bunters Hill Rd *HOO/HM* ME3 .... 49 F1
Burberry La *RMAID* ME17 .... 157 K1
The Burdens *HDCN* TN27 .... 200 D1
Burdett Av *GVE* DA12 .... 47 H2
Burdett Rd *SCUP* DA14 .... 39 F3
Burdett Rd *STH/RUST* TN4 .... 206 A2 ⬛
Burgate Cl *DART* DA1 .... 22 C2
Burgess Hall Dr *RMAID* ME17 .... 135 H8
Burgess Rd *STRD* ME2 .... 2 B1 ⬛
Burghclere Dr *MAID* ME16 .... 132 B4 ⬛
Burghfield Rd *MEO* DA13 .... 45 G5
Burham Rd *ROCH* ME1 .... 66 D7
Burial Ground La *MAID/SHEP* ME15... 6 B6
Burleigh Cl *STRD* ME2 .... 48 D6 ⬛
Burleigh Rd *MAID/BEAR* ME14 ...... 111 F5
Burley Rd *SIT* ME10 .... 93 K2
Burlings La *RSEV* TN14 .... 99 F4
Burman Rd *RDART* DA2 .... 24 B6
Burmarsh Cl *RMAID* ME8 .... 88 C1
Burma Wy *WALD* ME5 .... 68 A8
Burnaby Rd *GVW* DA11 .... 27 F6
Burnett Rd *ERITH* DA8 .... 12 B6
Burnham Cl *SIT* ME10 .... 73 K6
Burnham Crs *DART* DA1 .... 23 F3
Burnham Rd *DART* DA1 .... 23 C4
Burnham Wk *RHAM* ME8 .... 90 B3
Burnley Rd *WTHK* RM20 .... 13 K8
Burns Crs *TON* TN9 .... 170 A7
Burn's Rd *GILL* ME7 .... 4 C1
  MAIDW ME16 .... 132 C4
  STRD ME2 .... 49 H4
Burnt House Cl *HAWK* TN18 .... 243 K1
Burnthouse La *HDCN* TN27 .... 201 H5
Burnt House La *RDART* DA2 .... 201 H5
  RRTW TN3 .... 205 J1
Burnt Oak Ter *GILL* ME7 .... 4 C2
Burntwick Dr *RSIT* ME9 .... 72 K1
Burntwood Gv *SEV* TN13 .... 9 D6
Burntwood Rd *SEV* TN13 .... 123 K7
Burrfield Dr *STMC/STPC* BR5 .... 56 E2
Burrows La *HOO/HM* ME3 .... 35 F3
The Burrs *SIT* ME10 .... 94 A3 ⬛
Burslem Rd *RTWE/PEM* TN2 .... 190 E8
Burston Rd *RMAID* ME17 .... 154 B4
Burton Cl *HOO/HM* ME3 .... 49 H3
Burwash Cl *STMC/STPC* BR5 .... 56 D2 ⬛
Busbridge Rd *MAID/SHEP* ME15.... 154 E1 ⬛
  SNOD ME6 .... 85 H7
Bush Cl *RSIT* ME9 .... 115 K1
Bushey Cft *OXTED* RH8 .... 140 E1
Bushmeadow Rd *RHAM* ME8 .... 70 C4
Bush Rd *STPH/PW* TN12 .... 151 C6
  STRD ME2 .... 66 A4
Bush Rw *DIT/AY* ME20 .... 110 A4
Bushy Gill *RRTW* TN3 .... 205 K3
Bushy Gv *RMAID* ME17 .... 158 B4
Busty La *BGR/WK* TN15 .... 104 D8
Butcher Cl *STPH/PW* TN12 .... 198 A3
Butchers La *BGR/WK* TN15 .... 61 J6
  WBY/YAL ME18 .... 129 F5
Butchers Yd *ORP* BR6 .... 75 F6
Buttercup Cl *STPH/PW* TN12 .... 193 J1
Butterfly Av *DART* DA1 .... 23 J8
Buttermere Cl *GILL* ME7 .... 5 F3
Butt Green La *RMAID* ME17 .... 155 F8
Butt Haw Cl *HOO/HM* ME3 .... 51 F1
Button Dr *HOO/HM* ME3 .... 35 F3
Button Rd *MAID/SHEP* ME15 .... 134 D4 ⬛
Button St *SWLY* BR8 .... 59 F1
Butts La *WADH* TN5 .... 220 E7
The Butts *RSEV* TN14 .... 101 K4
  SIT ME10 .... 94 A3 ⬛
Buttway La *HOO/HM* ME3 .... 15 F8
Buxton Cl *MAID/SHEP* ME15 .... 133 C6
  WALD ME5 .... 88 E5
Byng Rd *STH/RUST* TN4 .... 10 A2
Byrneside *RTON* TN11 .... 169 J2
Byron Rd *DART* DA1 .... 24 A3
  GILL ME7 .... 4 C5
  MAID/BEAR ME14 .... 111 H7
Bythorne Rd *RHAM* ME8 .... 70 E5 ⬛

Calder Rd *MAID/BEAR* ME14 .... 110 E7
Calderwood *GVE* DA12 .... 46 B4
Caldew Av *RHAM* ME8 .... 69 K5
Caldew Gv *SIT* ME10 .... 94 B3
Calehill Cl *MAID/BEAR* ME14 .... 7 F1
Caley Rd *RTWE/PEM* TN2 .... 190 D6
Calfstock La *EYN* DA4 .... 59 H1
Caliph Cl *GVE* DA12 .... 46 C1
Callaways La *RSIT* ME9 .... 72 A3
Calverley Ct *RTWE/PEM* TN2 .... 11 E4 ⬛
Calverley Pk *RTWE/PEM* TN2 .... 11 D4
Calverley Park Crs
  RTWE/PEM TN2 .... 11 D4 ⬛
Calverley Park Gdns *RTW* TN1 ..... 11 D4
Calverley Rd *RTW* TN1 .... 11 D3 ⬛
  RTWE/PEM TN2 .... 11 D3
Calverts St *RTW* TN1 .... 11 D3 ⬛
Calvin Cl *STMC/STPC* BR5 .... 38 E3
Camberwell La *RSEV* TN14 .... 144 B2
Camborne Rd *SCUP* DA14 .... 38 D1
Cambray Rd *ORP* BR6 .... 56 A4
Cambria Av *ROCH* ME1 .... 66 E4
Cambria Crs *GVE* DA12 .... 46 B2
Cambrian Gv *GVW* DA11 .... 27 H6
Cambrian Rd *STH/RUST* TN4 .... 190 D6
Cambridge Crs *MAID/SHEP* ME15... 133 K7 ⬛
Cambridge Gdns
  RTWE/PEM TN2 .... 11 D5 ⬛
Cambridge Rd *RHAM* ME8 .... 69 K8
  SIT ME10 .... 94 C4
  STRD ME2 .... 49 F6
Cambridge St *RTWE/PEM* TN2 ...... 11 E4 ⬛
Cambridge Ter *CHAT* ME4 .... 3 F4 ⬛
  STH/RUST TN4 .... 10 C1 ⬛
Camden Av *RTWE/PEM* TN2 .... 191 J8
Camden Cl *GVW* DA11 .... 26 D7
  WALD ME5 .... 88 C1
Camden Hl *RTWE/PEM* TN2 .... 11 D4 ⬛
  RTWE/PEM TN2 .... 11 E5 ⬛
Camden Pk *RTWE/PEM* TN2 .... 11 D4 ⬛
  RTWE/PEM TN2 .... 11 F5 ⬛
Camden Rd *GILL* ME7 .... 5 D1 ⬛
  RTW TN1 .... 11 D3
  SEV TN13 .... 9 D1
Camden St *MAID/BEAR* ME14 .... 7 D2 ⬛
Camellia Cl *RHAM* ME8 .... 70 A7
Camelot Cl *BH/WHM* TN16 .... 97 G3 ⬛
Cameron Cl *BXLY* DA5 .... 40 A1
  WALD ME5 .... 68 C6 ⬛
Camer Park Rd *MEO* DA13 .... 63 J4
Camer Rd *MEO* DA13 .... 63 K3
Camer St *MEO* DA13 .... 63 K3
Campbell Rd *GVW* DA11 .... 27 G7
  MAID/SHEP ME15 .... 133 J7
  STH/RUST TN4 .... 10 C1 ⬛
Camp Hl *RTON* TN11 .... 167 J3
Campion Cl *GVW* DA11 .... 45 F2 ⬛
  WALD ME5 .... 87 K3
Campion Crs *CRBK* TN17 .... 225 F4
Campleshon Rd *RHAM* ME8............. 90 A1
Campus Wy *GILL* ME7 .... 69 H6
Camp Wy *MAID/SHEP* ME15 .... 133 J7
Canada Farm Rd *EYN* DA4 .... 61 G2
Canadian Av *GILL* ME7 .... 5 E4
Canal Basin *GVE* DA12 .... 28 A5
Canal Rd *GVE* DA12 .... 28 A5
  HOO/HM ME3 .... 30 A6
  STRD ME2 .... 2 B1
Canberra Gdns *SIT* ME10 .... 93 H7
Canberra Sq *TIL* RM18 .... 27 H1 ⬛
Canbury Pth *STMC/STPC* BR5 .... 56 B1
Canning St *MAID/BEAR* ME14 .... 7 D1
Cannon La *TON* TN9 .... 170 D4
Canon Cl *ROCH* ME1 .... 66 E2
Canon La *WBY/YAL* ME18 .... 130 A5
Canterbury Ct *DART* DA1 .... 23 K6
Canterbury Crs *TONN* TN10 .... 170 D1 ⬛
Canterbury La *RHAM* ME8 .... 71 F5
Canterbury Rd *GVE* DA12 .... 192 A8 ⬛
  RTWE/PEM TN2 .... 192 A8 ⬛
  SIT ME10 .... 94 C3
Canterbury St *GILL* ME7 .... 4 C3
Canterbury Wy *DART* DA1 .... 24 B3
  WTHK RM20 .... 13 J7
Capel Cl *RHAM* ME8 .... 89 K1
Capell Cl *RMAID* ME17 .... 154 C3
Capel Pl *RDART* DA2 .... 41 F2
Capel Rd *SIT* ME10 .... 93 K4
Capstan Cl *GRH* DA9 .... 24 B3
Capstone Rd *GILL* ME7 .... 69 F7
  WALD ME5 .... 68 C5
Captain's Cl *RMAID* ME17 .... 157 G8
The Caravan Site *SOCK/AV* RM15... 13 H3
Cardens Rd *HOO/HM* ME3 .... 31 G6
Cardinal Cl *TON* TN9 .... 170 D1
Cardinal Cl *SIT* ME10 .... 73 K7
Carey's Fld *SEV* TN13 .... 101 G7 ⬛
Caring La *RMAID* ME17 .... 135 G4
Caring Rd *MAID/SHEP* ME15 .... 135 F5
Carisbrooke Dr *MAIDW* ME16 .... 6 A2
Carisbrooke Rd *STRD* ME2 .... 48 D6
Carleton Pl *EYN* DA4 .... 60 B1
Carleton Rd *DART* DA1 .... 23 K6
Carlisle Rd *DART* DA1 .... 23 K5

Carlton Av *GILL* ME7 .... 5 E4
  GRH DA9 .... 24 D5
Carlton Crs *RTWE/PEM* TN2 .... 11 E3 ⬛
  WALD ME5 .... 68 E6
Carlton Gdns *MAID/SHEP* ME15 ... 133 H6
Carlton Rd *RTWE/PEM* TN2 .... 11 E3 ⬛
  SCUP DA14 .... 38 A3
Carmelite Wy *HART* DA3 .... 62 A2
Carnation Cl *E/WMAL* ME19 .... 108 E5 ⬛
Carnation Crs *E/WMAL* ME19 .... 108 D6
Carnation Rd *STRD* ME2 .... 48 C7
Caroline Crs *MAIDW* ME16 .... 110 D7
Carousel Dr *ORP* BR6 .... 56 B7
Carpeaux Cl *CHAT* ME4 .... 3 K4 ⬛
Carpenters Cl *ROCH* ME1 .... 3 E6
Carpenters La *RTON* TN11 .... 149 K3 ⬛
  STPH/PW TN12 .... 177 J7
Carpinus Cl *WALD* ME5 .... 88 C5
The Carriageway *RSEV* TN14 .... 121 K3
Carrick Dr *SEV* TN13 .... 9 D2
Carriers Rd *CRBK* TN17 .... 225 K1
Carrington Cl *GILL* ME7 .... 5 F2
Carrington Rd *DART* DA1 .... 23 J3
Carroll Cl *STRD* ME2 .... 85 K2 ⬛
Carroll Gdns *DIT/AY* ME20 .... 108 C3
Carsington Gdns *DART* DA1 .... 23 G8
Cartel Cl *PUR* RM19 .... 13 H4
Carter's Hl *BGR/WK* TN15 .... 147 F1
Carter's Hill La *MEO* DA13 .... 83 G4
Carton Cl *ROCH* ME1 .... 3 D6
Carton Rd *HOO/HM* ME3 .... 48 A3
Carville Av *STH/RUST* TN4 .... 189 K5
Carvoran Wy *RHAM* ME8 .... 89 K1
Cascade Cl *STMC/STPC* BR5 .... 38 B8
Casine Cl *SWLY* BR8 .... 40 C6
Castle Av *ROCH* ME1 .... 2 C4
Castle Dene *MAID/BEAR* ME14 ..... 110 E6
Castle Farm Rd *RSEV* TN14 .... 78 C4
Castlefields *MEO* DA13 .... 45 G6
Castle Hl *HART* DA3 .... 61 J2
  MAID/BEAR ME14 .... 113 F5
  ROCH ME1 .... 2 C2
  RTON TN11 .... 191 F1
Castle Hurst *RBTBR* TN32 .... 242 C6
Castle La *GVE* DA12 .... 28 E8
Castlemaine Av *GILL* ME7 .... 5 E2
Castle Rd *CHAT* ME4 .... 4 A6
  EYN DA4 .... 78 E2
  MAIDW ME16 .... 110 D6
  SIT ME10 .... 94 C1
  STH/RUST TN4 .... 10 B4
  SWCM DA10 .... 26 A5
Castle St *GRH* DA9 .... 25 F4
  ROCH ME1 .... 86 B2 ⬛
  RTW TN1 .... 10 C5 ⬛
  STH/RUST TN4 .... 189 K4
  STRD ME2 .... 49 K5
  SWCM DA10 .... 26 A5
  TON TN9 .... 170 C4 ⬛
Castle View Rd *STRD* ME2 .... 48 C7 ⬛
Castle Wy *DIT/AY* ME20 .... 108 C1
  E/WMAL ME19 .... 108 C3
Caterfield La *LING* RH7 .... 162 D4
Catherine Cl *MAIDW* ME16 .... 132 A3 ⬛
Catherine Pl *RTW* TN1 .... 11 D4 ⬛
Catherine St *ROCH* ME1 .... 3 D5
Catkin Cl *WALD* ME5 .... 88 A5
Catlyn Cl *E/WMAL* ME19 .... 108 C3
Catterick Rd *MAID* ME15 .... 88 E4
Causeway Br *SOCK/AV* RM15 .... 13 J3
Causton Rd *CRBK* TN17 .... 225 J1
Cave Hl *MAID/SHEP* ME15 .... 6 C6
Cavell Crs *DART* DA1 .... 23 K3
Cavell Wy *SIT* ME10 .... 93 J1
Cavendish Av *GILL* ME7 .... 5 F3
  SEV TN13 .... 8 C1
Cavendish Cl *TONN* TN10 .... 148 D7
Cavendish Dr *RTWE/PEM* TN2 ...... 11 D5 ⬛
Cavendish Rd *ROCH* ME1 .... 3 D5
Cavendish Sq *HART* DA3 .... 43 J8
Cavendish Wy *MAID/SHEP* ME15 ... 134 C3 ⬛
Caversham Rd *RHAM* ME8 .... 70 C5 ⬛
Caxton Cl *HART* DA3 .... 62 A1
  TENT TN30 .... 229 K7 ⬛
  RTON TN11 .... 150 A6
Caxton La *OXTED* RH8 .... 141 J2
  RTON TN11 .... 150 A6
Cayser Dr *RMAID* ME17 .... 158 C4
Cazeneuve St *ROCH* ME1 .... 2 C3 ⬛
Cecil Av *RHAM* ME8 .... 69 H4
  STRD ME2 .... 49 G6
Cecil Rd *GVW* DA11 .... 27 G7
  ROCH ME1 .... 2 C5
Cedar Av *GVE* DA12 .... 45 K2
Cedar Cl *DIT/AY* ME20 .... 109 H6
  MEO DA13 .... 63 H3 ⬛
  SIT ME10 .... 94 C4 ⬛
  SWLY BR8 .... 39 K7
Cedar Crs *TONN* TN10 .... 148 C7
Cedar Dr *EDEN* TN8 .... 164 B4
  EYN DA4 .... 42 A7
  MAIDW ME16 .... 131 J4
Cedar Gv *GILL* ME7 .... 89 H1
Cedar Rdg *RTWE/PEM* TN2 .... 11 F1
Cedar Rd *DART* DA1 .... 23 G7

HOO/HM ME3 .... 51 F3
STRD ME2 .... 48 E8
The Cedars *STPH/PW* TN12 .... 173 J7
Cedar Terrace Rd *SEV* TN13 ...... 9 E2
Celestine Cl *WALD* ME5 .... 88 B5
Cellar Hl *RSIT* ME9 .... 95 K6
Cemetery La *RTON* TN11 ...... 150 C6
Cemetery Rd *SNOD* ME6 .... 85 J5
STRD ME2 .... 85 K2
Centenary Walk - Maidstone
DIT/AY ME20 .... 87 F8
MAID/BEAR ME14 .... 6 B1
MAID/BEAR ME14 .... 110 E1
MAID/BEAR ME14 .... 111 H2
Centenary Walk - Rochester
ROCH ME1 .... 2 A5
Central Av *GVE* DA12 .... 27 J8
SIT ME10 .... 94 A3
SOCK/AV RM15 .... 13 G2
WTHK RM20 .... 13 K5
Central Park Gdns *ROCH* ME1 ...... 3 E6
Central Rd *DART* DA1 .... 23 H4
DIT/AY ME20 .... 109 F2
STRD ME2 .... 2 A1
Central Ter *HOO/HM* ME3 .... 32 A8
Central Wy *OXTED* RH8 .... 118 B6
Centre Rd *HART* DA3 .... 61 K7
Centurion Cl *GILL* ME7 .... 69 G5
Centurion Wy *PUR* RM19 .... 12 D3
Century Rd *RHAM* ME8 .... 70 A6
Cerne Rd *GVE* DA12 .... 46 B2
Cervia Wy *GVE* DA12 .... 46 C1
Chada Av *GILL* ME7 .... 5 E5
Chadwick Cl *GVW* DA11 .... 27 F8
Chaffe's La *RSIT* ME9 .... 71 H4
Chaffinch Cl *WALD* ME5 .... 88 B7
Chaffinch Wy *STPH/PW* TN12 .... 193 H1
Chafford La *RRTW* TN3 .... 204 D1
Chalet Cl *RDART* DA2 .... 40 A2
Chalfont Dr *RHAM* ME8 .... 70 A8
Chalice Wy *GRH* DA9 .... 24 D4
Chalk Av *TENT* TN30 .... 230 B4
Chalkenden Av *RHAM* ME8 .... 69 H4
Chalket La *RTWE/PEM* TN2 ...... 208 D1
Chalk La *OXTED* RH8 .... 213 K7
Chalk Pit Av *STMC/STPC* BR5.... 38 C8
Chalk Pit Hl *CHAT* ME4 .... 4 A5
Chalkpit Wd *OXTED* RH8 .... 118 B6
Chalk Rd *GVE* DA12 .... 28 D7
HOO/HM ME3 .... 30 B8
Chalkways *RSEV* TN14 .... 102 C3
Chalkwell Rd *SIT* ME10 .... 93 J2
Chalky Bank *GVW* DA11 .... 45 H3
Chalky Bank Rd *RHAM* ME8 ...... 70 C4
Chalky Rd *RSIT* ME9 .... 91 F8
Challenge Cl *GVE* DA12 .... 46 C2
Challenger Cl *SIT* ME10 .... 73 K7
STPH/PW TN12 .... 175 H8
Challock Cl *BH/WHM* TN16 ...... 96 C1
Chamberlain Av *MAIDW* ME16 .... 132 B4
Chamberlain Ct *RHAM* ME8 ...... 89 J1
Chamberlain Rd *CHAT* ME4 ...... 4 B6
Chambers Cl *GRH* DA9 .... 24 E4
Chancel Cl *BGR/WK* TN15 .... 80 D3
Chancery La *MAID/SHEP* ME15 .... 7 E3
Chancery Rd *HOO/HM* ME3 ...... 31 G1
Chandler's Hl *MEO* DA13 .... 63 K8
MEO DA13 .... 83 K1
Chandler's Rd *MEO* DA13 .... 83 K1
Chandos Rd *RTW* TN1 .... 11 E2
Chantler's Hl *STPH/PW* TN12...... 193 H3
Chantry Av *HART* DA3 .... 61 K3
Chantry Pl *STPH/PW* TN12........ 196 C1
Chantry Rd *STPH/PW* TN12 ...... 196 C1
Chapel Cl *DART* DA1 .... 22 B4
E/WMAL ME19 .... 107 H1
Chapel Fld *RYE* TN31 .... 244 D7
Chapel Hl *DART* DA1 .... 22 B3
Chapel La *CRBK* TN17 .... 215 J7
CRBK TN17 .... 236 C1
GILL ME7 .... 89 H2
GILL ME7 .... 89 H4
HDCN TN27 .... 182 B3
MAID/BEAR ME14 .... 134 C1
STPH/PW TN12 .... 198 B3
STRD ME2 .... 85 F2
Chapel Rd *HOO/HM* ME3 .... 37 F1
OXTED RH8 .... 141 G1
RMAID ME17 .... 157 G7
SNOD ME6 .... 85 K6
Chapel Rw *BGR/WK* TN15 ...... 104 C8
HOO/HM ME3 .... 35 F2
Chapel St *E/WMAL* ME19 ...... 107 H2
E/WMAL ME19 .... 108 E8
Chapel Wd *HART* DA3 .... 61 K6
Chapel Wood Rd *HART* DA3...... 61 K6
Chaplin Cl *HOO/HM* ME3 .... 49 H3
Chaplin Dr *HDCN* TN27 .... 200 B1
Chapman Av *MAID/SHEP* ME15 .. 134 B5
Chapman's Hl *BGR/WK* TN15...... 85 F2
Chapman's La *STMC/STPC* BR5.... 38 E7
SWLY BR8 .... 39 H7
Chapmans Rd *RSEV* TN14 ...... 122 A3

Chapman Wy *E/WMAL* ME19 ...... 108 D6
RTWE/PEM TN2 .... 190 C6
Chappell Wy *SIT* ME10 .... 73 J8
Chapter Rd *STRD* ME2 .... 48 E7
Charing Cl *ORP* BR6 .... 56 A8
Charing Rd *RHAM* ME8 .... 69 J3
Chariot Wy *STRD* ME2 .... 66 D3
Charlbury Cl *MAIDW* ME16........ 132 C3
Charles Cl *SCUP* DA14 .... 38 C2
SNOD ME6 .... 85 K6
Charles Dickens Av *STRD* ME2 .... 48 B4
Charles Dr *STRD* ME2 .... 66 A3
Charlesford Av *RMAID* ME17 .... 158 B3
Charles Rd *RSEV* TN14 .... 77 J5
Charles St *CHAT* ME4 .... 3 E5
GRH DA9 .... 24 E4
MAIDW ME16 .... 6 B4
STH/RUST TN4 .... 190 A6
STRD ME2 .... 2 A1
Charlock Cl *MAIDW* ME16 ...... 110 D6
Charlotte Cl *WALD* ME5 .... 68 C8
Charlotte Dr *RHAM* ME8.......... 69 K5
Charlotte St *SIT* ME10.......... 93 K1
Charlton Dr *BH/WHM* TN16 ...... 97 H4
Charlton La *MAID/SHEP* ME15.... 131 H7
RMAID ME17 .... 158 A6
Charlton St *MAIDW* ME16........ 132 C4
Charlton's Wy *STH/RUST* TN4 .... 10 A6
Charnwood La *ORP* BR6 .... 76 C5
The Charne *RSEV* TN14.......... 101 J4
Charnock Rd *SWLY* BR8 .... 58 B1
Charterhouse Dr *SEV* TN13........ 8 C2
Charterhouse Rd *ORP* BR6 ...... 56 B7
Charter St *CHAT* ME4 .... 3 F6
GILL ME7 .... 4 C1
Chart Hill Rd *RMAID* ME17 ...... 156 C8
Chart La *RBH/WHM* TN16........ 121 J4
Chart Pl *RHAM* ME8.............. 89 K3
Chart Rd *RMAID* ME17 .... 156 E7
Chart Vw *BGR/WK* TN15.......... 102 E4
Chartway *BGR/WK* TN15 .... 9 E3
Chartway St *RMAID* ME17 ...... 157 H5
Chartwell Cl *STRD* ME2.......... 49 G5
Chartwell Dr *ORP* BR6 .... 75 J1
Chartwell Gv *SIT* ME10 .... 93 H3
Chase Sq *GVE* DA12 .... 27 J5
The Chase *ORP* BR6 .... 76 B6
RHAM ME8 .... 69 H4
ROCH ME1 .... 3 D6
RSEV TN14.......... 102 C3
TONN TN10 .... 170 C1
Chastilian Rd *DART* DA1 .... 22 D6
Chatfield Wy *DIT/AY* ME20........ 109 F5
Chatham Gv *CHAT* ME4 .... 68 A5
Chatham Hl *CHAT* ME4 .... 4 B5
Chatham Hill Rd *RSEV* TN14 .... 102 A8
Chatham Rd *DIT/AY* ME20 ...... 87 J8
MAID/BEAR ME14........ 110 C2
WALD ME5 .... 87 J5
Chatsworth Dr *SIT* ME10 .... 93 G1
STRD ME2 .... 49 G5
Chatsworth Rd *DART* DA1 ...... 23 F3
GILL ME7 .... 4 C2
Chattenden Ct *MAID/BEAR* ME14.. 111 H7
Chattenden La *HOO/HM* ME3 .... 50 A2
Chaucer Cl *STRD* ME2 .... 49 K6
TIL RM18 .... 27 K1
Chaucer Gdns *TON* TN9 .... 169 K7
Chaucer Pk *DART* DA1.......... 23 J6
Chaucer Rd *GILL* ME7 .... 4 C5
GVW DA11 .... 44 E1
SIT ME10 .... 93 J3
Chaucer Wy *DART* DA1.......... 23 K3
DIT/AY ME20 .... 108 D3
Chave Rd *DART* DA1.............. 41 H1
Cheeselands *HDCN* TN27 ...... 217 J4
Chegwell Dr *WALD* ME5 .... 88 C2
Chegworth Gdns *SIT* ME10 ...... 93 K5
Chegworth La *RMAID* ME17 .... 136 D8
Chegworth Rd *RMAID* ME17 .... 136 D7
Chellows La *LING* RH7.......... 162 D4
Chelmar Rd *CHAT* ME4 .... 4 B4
Chelmsford Rd *STRD* ME2 ...... 48 C8
Chelsfield Hl *ORP* BR6 .... 76 D4
Chelsfield La *ORP* BR6 .... 56 E8
ORP BR6 .... 77 H3
RSEV TN14.......... 77 K4
STMC/STPC BR5.......... 56 E4
Chelsfield Rd *STMC/STPC* BR5.... 56 D3
Chelsham Court Rd *WARL* CR6 .. 96 B5
Cheltenham Cl *GVE* DA12........ 45 F7
MAID/SHEP ME15 .... 134 B8
Cheltenham Rd *ORP* BR6........ 56 B7
Cheney Cl *RHAM* ME8 .... 90 A1
Cheney Hl *RSIT* ME9 .... 117 G2
Chenies Cl *RTWE/PEM* TN2 .... 207 H3
The Chenies *RDART* DA2.......... 40 B2
Chennell Park Rd *TENT* TN30 .. 229 J5
Chequers Cl *MEO* DA13 .... 45 F7
STMC/STPC BR5.......... 56 A1
WALD ME5 .... 88 B5
Chequers Ct *STRD* ME2.......... 49 F5
Cherbourg Crs *WALD* ME5 ...... 68 A7
Cheriton Rd *RHAM* ME8 .... 70 A7
Cheriton Wy *MAIDW* ME16 ...... 110 C7

The Cherries *MAIDW* ME16 .... 131 K4
Cherry Amber Cl *RHAM* ME8 .... 70 C6 ▣
Cherry Av *SWLY* BR8 .... 40 A8
Cherry Cl *SIT* ME10 .... 73 J8
Cherry Flds *SIT* ME10 .... 93 F1
Cherry Gdns *RSIT* ME9 .... 95 K6
Cherry Gv *TONN* TN10 .... 170 E1
Cherry Orch *DIT/AY* ME20 ...... 109 G6
TENT TN30 .... 230 A8 ▣
Cherry Orchard Cl
STMC/STPC BR5.......... 56 D2
The Cherry Orch *RTON* TN11 .... 150 A5
Cherry Orchard Wy *MAIDW* ME16 .. 132 B3
Cherry Rd *HOO/HM* ME3 .... 51 F3 ▣
Cherry Tree Gv *EYN* DA4 .... 80 A5
Cherry Tree La *RDART* DA2 ...... 40 C1
Cherry Tree Rd *RHAM* ME8 ...... 70 C6
RTWE/PEM TN2 .... 70 C6
Cherry Trees *HART* DA3 .... 62 A3
Cherrywood Dr *GVW* DA11 ...... 45 F2
Chervilles *MAIDW* ME16 .... 132 A4
Cherwell Cl *TONN* TN10 .... 170 B2
Chesham Dr *RHAM* ME8 .... 70 B8
Cheshire Rd *MAID/SHEP* ME15 .. 134 A4
Cheshunt Cl *MEO* DA13 .... 63 H3
Chessenden La *HDCN* TN27 .... 202 A5
Chester Av *RTWE/PEM* TN2 ...... 11 F5
Chester Cl *STRD* ME2 .... 48 C8
Chesterfield Cl *STMC/STPC* BR5 .. 56 E1
Chesterfield Dr *DART* DA1 ...... 22 E4
SEV TN13 .... 123 F1
Chester Rd *GILL* ME7 .... 5 D6
Chesterton Rd *DIT/AY* ME20 .... 108 D2
HOO/HM ME3 .... 31 G1 ▣
Chestfield Cl *RHAM* ME8 .... 70 B4 ▣
Chestnut Av *BH/WHM* TN16 .... 119 H1
GRH DA9 .... 24 E6
STH/RUST TN4 .... 190 A6
STPH/PW TN12 .... 198 A2
WALD ME5 .... 87 K3
Chestnut Cl *CRBK* TN17 .... 199 G8
E/WMAL ME19 .... 129 J4
EDEN TN8 .... 164 B4 ▣
GVW DA11 .... 27 G5 ▣
ORP BR6 .... 76 B1
RMAID ME17 .... 158 D3
STH/RUST TN4 .... 190 B6
TENT TN30 .... 230 B5
Chestnut Copse *OXTED* RH8 .... 141 F4
Chestnut Dr *RMAID* ME17 ...... 154 B3
RMAID ME17 .... 158 B4
Chestnut Gv *RDART* DA2 .... 40 A3
Chestnut La *MEO* DA13 .... 83 J6
SEV TN13 .... 9 D3
STPH/PW TN12 .... 193 G5
Chestnut Rd *DART* DA1 .... 23 G7
STRD ME2 .... 48 B8
The Chestnuts *E/WMAL* ME19 .. 106 E3
HAWK TN18 .... 234 E6
Chestnut St *RSIT* ME9 .... 92 D2
Chestnut Wk *BGR/WK* TN15 .... 124 D7
TON TN9 .... 169 K4 ▣
Chestnut Wood La *RSIT* ME9 .... 92 D2
Cheswick Cl *DART* DA1 .... 22 C3
Chetney Cl *STRD* ME2 .... 48 B7
Chevening Cl *WALD* ME5 .... 88 B1
Chevening La *RSEV* TN14 ...... 100 A3
Chevening Rd *RSEV* TN14 ...... 100 B6
The Chevenings *SCUP* DA14 .... 38 C1
Cheviot Cl *BXLYHN* DA7.......... 22 B1
TON TN9 .... 170 C2
Cheviot Gdns *MAID/SHEP* ME15 .. 134 C5
Cheyne Wk *MEO* DA13.......... 63 H6
Chicago Av *GILL* ME7 .... 5 E3
Chichele Rd *OXTED* RH8 .... 118 C7
Chichester Cl *RHAM* ME8 ...... 70 D6
SOCK/AV RM15 .... 13 C1
Chichester Dr *SEV* TN13........ 123 J4
Chichester Ri *GVE* DA12 .... 46 A2
Chichester Rd *GRH* DA9 .... 24 E4
TON TN9 .... 170 A6
Chickenden La *STPH/PW* TN12 .. 198 A4
Chickfield Gdns *WALD* ME5 ...... 4 C6 ▣
Chicks La *CRBK* TN17 .... 222 E4
Chiddingstone Cl
MAID/SHEP ME15 .... 134 B8 ▣
Chidley Cross Rd *STPH/PW* TN12 .. 151 G8
Chieftain Cl *GILL* ME7 .... 69 J5
Chieftan Dr *PUR* RM19 .... 12 E4
Chieveley Dr *RTWE/PEM* TN2 .. 11 E6
Chiffinch Gdns *GVW* DA11 ...... 45 F1
Childsbridge La *RSEV* TN14 .... 102 C5
Childsbridge Wy *BGR/WK* TN15 .. 102 D7
Childs Crs *SWCM* DA10 .... 25 J5
Childscroft Rd *RHAM* ME8 ...... 70 C4
Childs Wy *BGR/WK* TN15 ...... 105 F3
Chilham Cl *CHAT* ME4 .... 3 E5 ▣
Chilham Rd *MAIDW* ME16 ...... 110 C7
RHAM ME8 .... 69 H5
Chillington St *MAID/BEAR* ME14.... 6 C1
Chilliwack Rd *HOO/HM* ME3 .... 50 A1
Chilston Cl *STH/RUST* TN4 ...... 10 C2
Chilston Rd *RMAID* ME17 ...... 160 D1
STH/RUST TN4 .... 10 C2
Chiltern Cl *MAID/SHEP* ME15.... 134 B5

Chiltern Rd *GVW* DA11 .... 45 F1
Chiltern Wy *TON* TN9 .... 170 C2
Chilton Av *SIT* ME10 .... 94 B3
Chilton Ct *RHAM* ME8 .... 70 B5
Chilton Dr *HOO/HM* ME3 .... 48 A3
Chippendale CI *WALD* ME5 .... 88 A5
Chippendayle Dr *RMAID* ME17 .... 137 H8
Chipperfield Rd *STMC/STPC* BR5 ...... 38 B7
Chipstead CI *MAIDW* ME16................. 6 A1
Chipstead La *SEV* TN13...................... 123 F1
Chipstead Pk *SEV* TN13 .... 123 F1
Chipstead Park CI *SEV* TN13 .... 123 F1
Chipstead Rd *RHAM* ME8 .... 90 A2
Chislehurst CI *MAID/SHEP* ME15 .. 134 B8
Chislehurst Rd *ORP* BR6...................... 56 B4
  SCUP DA14 .... 38 B3
  .... 38 B3
Chorleywood Crs *STMC/STPC* BR5 .... 38 A7
Christchurch Rd *BFN/LL* DA15 ...... 38 A2
  DART DA1 .... 23 F6
Christ Church Rd *GVE* DA12 .... 27 K6
Christian Fields Av *GVE* DA12 .... 45 K2
Christie CI *WALD* ME5 .... 68 C8
Christie Dr *DIT/AY* DA20 .... 108 C2
Christies Av *RSEV* TN14 .... 77 H5
Christmas La *HOO/HM* ME3................ 33 F3
Christmas St *GILL* ME7 .... 5 E1
Christy Rd *BH/WHM* TN16 .... 97 G2
Chulkhurst *HDCN* TN27 .... 217 H4
Church Av *SCUP* DA14 .... 38 B3
Church CI *HOO/HM* ME3 .... 15 G8
  WBY/YAL ME18 .... 194 A6
Church Crs *RMAID* ME17 .... 137 K8
Church Farm CI *HOO/HM* ME3 ...... 51 F2
Church Farm Rd *RSIT* ME9............... 71 H3
Church Fld *DART* DA1 .... 23 G8
  EDEN TN8 .... 164 D5
  SEV TN13 .... 8 B1
  SNOD ME6 .... 86 A5
Church Flds *E/WMAL* ME19 .... 107 K6
Churchfields Ter *ROCH* ME1 .... 2 B4
Church Gn *STPH/PW* TN12 .... 176 C8
  STPH/PW TN12 .... 198 A4
  STRD ME2 .... 49 H6
Church HI *BGR/WK* TN15 .... 126 E6
  BH/WHM TN16 .... 119 H1
  DART DA1 .... 22 B3
  DART DA1 .... 41 G1
  GRH DA9 .... 24 D4
  HDCN TN27 .... 161 J6
  ORP BR6 .... 56 B4
  RASHW TN26 .... 219 K7
  RMAID ME17 .... 155 H7
  RMAID ME17 .... 155 H4
  RSEV TN14 .... 98 C2
  RSIT ME9 .... 91 J7
  WALD ME5 .... 4 C6
Church Hill Wd *STMC/STPC* BR5 ...... 56 A2
Church Hollow *PUR* RM19 .... 12 E5
Churchill Av *WALD* ME5 .... 68 A8
Churchill CI *DART* DA1 .... 24 A7
Churchill Rd *EYN* DA4 .... 60 B1
  GVW DA11 .... 27 G7
Churchill Sq *E/WMAL* ME19 .... 129 J3
Church La *BGR/WK* TN15 .... 103 F4
  CHAT ME4 .... 3 F2
  E/WMAL ME19 .... 106 C1
  GVE DA12 .... 29 F8
  MAID/SHEP ME15 .... 131 H7
  OXTED RH8 .... 118 C8
  PUR RM19 .... 12 E5
  RMAID ME17 .... 137 J8
  RMAID ME17 .... 157 K6
  RSIT ME9 .... 72 A8
  RSIT ME9 .... 91 H6
  RTON TN11 .... 172 D8
  RYE TN31 .... 245 F8
  STPH/PW TN12 .... 151 H7
  TON TN9 .... 170 C4
  WARL CR6 .... 96 A3
Church Ms *RHAM* ME8 .... 70 C6
Church Pth *GILL* ME7 .... 5 E2
  GRH DA9 .... 24 E5
  GVW DA11 .... 26 D5
Church Rd *BGR/WK* TN15 .... 80 D3
  BGR/WK TN15 .... 102 D8
  BGR/WK TN15 .... 125 J2
  BH/WHM TN16 .... 97 H4
  BH/WHM TN16 .... 121 H3
  CRBK TN17 .... 212 D6
  CRBK TN17 .... 222 D4
  E/WMAL ME19 .... 107 G5
  E/WMAL ME19 .... 107 H3
  EYN DA4 .... 41 K4
  GRH DA9 .... 24 D4
  GVE DA12 .... 45 K4
  HART DA3 .... 43 G2
  HAWK TN18 .... 243 G2
  HAYES BR2 .... 74 C3
  MAID/BEAR ME14 .... 114 B5
  MAID/SHEP ME15 .... 6 B5
  MAID/SHEP ME15 .... 134 B6
  MEO DA13 .... 45 K6
  ORP BR6 .... 75 H1
  ORP BR6 .... 76 E2

RMAID ME17 .... 156 E6
RMAID ME17 .... 159 K7
RMAID ME17 .... 159 J1
RRTW TN3 .... 210 E8
RSEV TN14 .... 122 A5
RSEV TN14 .... 145 K3
RSIT ME9 .... 95 F2
RTON TN11 .... 147 H8
SCUP DA14 .... 38 B2
SIT ME10 .... 94 C1
STH/RUST TN4 .... 10 B4
STH/RUST TN4 .... 189 H4
STPH/PW TN12 .... 173 K8
SWCM DA10 .... 26 A5
SWLY BR8 .... 41 G6
SWLY BR8 .... 39 H8
TENT TN30 .... 230 A7
WBY/YAL ME18 .... 128 C3
Church Ter *RMAID* ME17 .... 4 C6
Churchside CI *BH/WHM* TN16 ...... 97 G5
Church Sq *RMAID* ME17 .... 160 D1
Church St *BGR/WK* TN15 .... 102 E7
  CHAT ME4 .... 4 A4
  EDEN TN8 .... 164 D5
  GILL ME7 .... 5 E2
  GVW DA11 .... 27 J5
  HOO/HM ME3 .... 30 B7
  HOO/HM ME3 .... 31 G1
  HOO/HM ME3 .... 51 F1
  MAID/BEAR ME14 .... 7 D3
  MAID/SHEP ME15 .... 6 B5
  MAID/SHEP ME15 .... 155 F1
  MEO DA13 .... 44 B3
  RMAID ME17 .... 155 H3
  ROCH ME1 .... 3 D4
  RSEV TN14 .... 78 C6
  RSIT ME9 .... 94 D7
  RTON TN11 .... 150 A6
  SIT ME10 .... 93 K2
  TON TN9 .... 170 C4
  WBY/YAL ME18 .... 130 E7
Church Vw *HDCN* TN27 .... 217 J4
  SOCK/AV RM15 .... 13 C2
Church Wk *DART* DA1 .... 41 G1
  E/WMAL ME19 .... 108 E7
  GVE DA12 .... 28 A6
  HDCN TN27 .... 200 A1
Church Wy *OXTED* RH8 .... 140 D3
Churn La *STPH/PW* TN12 .... 194 D3
Chute CI *RHAM* ME8 .... 90 A2
Chyngton CI *BFN/LL* DA15 .... 38 A1
Cimba Wd *GVE* DA12 .... 46 B2
Cinder Hill La *RTON* TN11 .... 168 A5
Cinnabar CI *WALD* ME5 .... 88 B5
Cirrus Crs *GVE* DA12 .... 46 B3
City Wy *ROCH* ME1 .... 3 D4
Civic Sq *TIL* RM18............................ 27 H1
Clacket La *BH/WHM* TN16 .... 119 J3
Clandon Rd *WALD* ME5..................... 88 C5
Clanricarde Gdns *RTW* TN1 .... 10 C4
Clanricarde Rd *STH/RUST* TN4 ...... 10 B4
Clapper La *STPH/PW* TN12............. 197 K2
Clare Av *TON* TN9 .... 169 K5
Clare La *E/WMAL* ME19 .... 108 C6
Claremont Crs *DART* DA1 .... 22 B3
Claremont Gdns *RTW* TN1 .... 11 D5
Claremont Rd *MAID/BEAR* ME14 .... 7 E2
  RTW TN1 .... 11 D5
  SWLY BR8 .... 40 B5
Claremont Wy *CHAT* ME4 .... 3 F5
Clarence Ct *MAID/BEAR* ME14...... 134 A2
Clarence Crs *SCUP* DA14 .... 38 C1
Clarence PI *GVE* DA12 .... 27 J6
Clarence Rd *BH/WHM* TN16 .... 97 K5
  CHAT ME4 .... 4 B6
  RTW TN1 .... 10 C4
  SCUP DA14 .... 38 C1
Clarence Rw *GVE* DA12 .... 27 J5
  RTW TN1 .... 10 C3
Clarendon CI *MAID/BEAR* ME14 .... 134 C2
  SIT ME10 .... 94 A5
  STMC/STPC BR5 .... 38 B8
Clarendon Gdns *RDART* DA2 .... 24 C7
  RTWE/PEM TN2 .... 10 C6
  STRD ME2 .... 49 F5
Clarendon Gn *STMC/STPC* BR5 .... 38 B8
Clarendon Gv *STMC/STPC* BR5 ...... 56 B1
Clarendon Pth *STMC/STPC* BR5 ...... 56 B1
Clarendon PI *RDART* DA2 .... 40 A3
Clarendon Rd *GVE* DA12................. 27 J5
  SEV TN13 .... 8 C3
Clarendon Wy *CHST* BR7 .... 38 A8
  RTWE/PEM TN2 .... 10 B6
Clare Wy *SEV* TN13 .... 124 A7
Clarewood Dr *E/WMAL* ME19 .... 108 C6
Claridge CI *GILL* ME7 .... 89 G2
Clarkes Green Rd *BGR/WK* TN15.. 102 E1
Clark Ms *DIT/AY* ME20.................. 109 K5
Clarks La *RSEV* TN14 .... 77 G7
  WARL CR6 .... 119 F2
Claston CI *DART* DA1 .... 22 B3
Clavadal Rd *STPH/PW* TN12 .... 173 J7
Clavell CI *RHAM* ME8....................... 90 A3

Claxfield Rd *RSIT* ME9....................... 95 H7
Claygate *MAID/SHEP* ME15 .... 133 K5
Claygate Cross *BGR/WK* TN15 ...... 127 G3
Claygate La *RTON* TN11 .... 149 F1
Claygate Rd *STPH/PW* TN12 .... 175 F4
  WBY/YAL ME18 .... 174 C2
Clayhill *CRBK* TN17 .... 212 C7
Clay Hill Rd *RRTW* TN3 .... 210 A6
Clayton Croft Rd *RDART* DA2 .... 22 D8
Clayton's La *RRTW* TN3 .... 204 B4
Claywood La *RDART* DA2 .... 43 J1
Clearway *BGR/WK* TN15 .... 106 C5
Cleave Av *ORP* BR6 .... 75 K2
Cleave Rd *GILL* ME7............................ 5 E6
Cleavers *CRBK* TN17 .... 215 H6
Cleavesland *WBY/YAL* ME18 .... 174 C1
Cleeve Av *RTWE/PEM* TN2 .... 11 F5
Clematis Av *RHAM* ME8 .... 89 J1
Clement Ct *MAIDW* ME16................. 6 A2
Clement St *SWLY* BR8 .... 41 G4
Clenches Farm Rd *SEV* TN13 .... 8 C5
Clerks Fld *HDCN* TN27 .... 200 A1
Clermont CI *GILL* ME7 .... 89 H2
Cleveland *RTWE/PEM* TN2.............. 11 F2
Cleveland Rd *GILL* ME7 .... 5 D2
Cleve Rd *SCUP* DA14 .... 38 E1
Cleves Rd *RSEV* TN14 .... 102 C4
Clewson Ri *MAID/BEAR* ME14 .... 111 H6
Cliffe Rd *STRD* ME2 .... 49 G6
Cliff HI *RMAID* ME17 .... 155 J2
Cliff Hill Rd *RMAID* ME17 .... 155 J2
Cliff Reach *GRH* DA9 .... 24 D5
Clifton CI *MAID/BEAR* ME14........... 7 E1
  ORP BR6 .... 75 H1
  STRD ME2 .... 48 C7
Clifton Gv *GVW* DA11 .... 27 J6
Clifton Marine Pde *GVW* DA11 ...... 27 H5
Clifton PI *RTW* TN1 .... 11 D5
Clifton Rd *GILL* ME7 .... 5 E4
  GVW DA11 .... 27 H5
  RTWE/PEM TN2 .... 190 C7
Clinch St *HOO/HM* ME3 .... 33 G1
Clinton Av *STRD* ME2 .... 48 C6
Clinton CI *RMAID* ME17.................. 154 B3
Clinton La *EDEN* TN8 .... 165 K3
Clipper Bvd *GRH* DA9 .... 24 D3
Clipper Bvd West *GRH* DA9 .... 24 C2
Clipper CI *STRD* ME2......................... 3 E1
Clipper Crs *GVE* DA12 .... 46 C2
Clive Av *DART* DA1.......................... 22 C5
Clive Rd *DART* DA1 .... 27 J5
  ROCH ME1 .... 2 C5
  SIT ME10 .... 93 G1
Clockhouse La *RTWE/PEM* TN2 ..... 191 F8
Cloisterham Rd *ROCH* ME1 .... 67 J7
Cloonmore Av *ORP* BR6 .... 76 A1
The Close *BGR/WK* TN15 .... 104 D8
  BGR/WK TN15 .... 107 K1
  E/WMAL ME19 .... 166 C4
  EDEN TN8 .... 166 C4
  HART DA3 .... 44 C7
  RDART DA2 .... 41 F1
  ROCH ME1 .... 2 C4
  RRTW TN3 .... 205 F8
  SCUP DA14 .... 38 C3
  SEV TN13 .... 8 C3
Cloth Hall Gdns *HDCN* TN27 .... 217 K4
Cloudesley CI *ROCH* ME1 .... 67 G5
Clovelly Wy *ORP* BR6 .... 56 A4
Clover Bank Vw *WALD* ME5............ 68 C8
Clover Lay *RHAM* ME8 .... 70 E4
Clover Rd *HOO/HM* ME3 .... 51 F3
The Clovers *GVW* DA11 .... 45 F2
Clover St *CHAT* ME4 .... 3 F4
Clover Wy *STPH/PW* TN12 .... 193 J1
Clyde Rd *TONN* TN10 .... 170 C1
The Coach Dr *MEO* DA13 .... 83 F2
Coach Rd *BGR/WK* TN15................. 126 A3
  HDCN TN27 .... 160 E8
Coalpit La *RSIT* ME9 .... 117 G8
Cobb CI *STRD* ME2............................ 48 C6
Cobbets Wy *EDEN* TN8.................. 164 C6
Cobbett CI *E/WMAL* ME19 .... 108 D6
Cobbett's Ride *RTWE/PEM* TN2 ..... 10 B6
Cobblestones *GILL* ME7 .... 89 C1
Cobbs CI *STPH/PW* TN12 .... 173 H8
  WBY/YAL ME18 .... 130 C7
Cob CI *BGR/WK* TN15 .... 104 C8
Cobden Rd *SEV* TN13 .... 9 E2
Cobdown CI *DIT/AY* ME20 .... 109 F4
Cobdown Gv *RHAM* ME8 .... 70 D4
Cob Dr *GVE* DA12 .... 47 H3
Cobfield *RMAID* ME17 .... 156 C5
Cobham Av *SIT* ME10 .... 93 K2
Cobhambury Rd *GVE* DA12 .... 64 D1
Cobham CI *MAIDW* ME16 .... 6 A2
  STRD ME2 .... 48 D7
Cobhams *RRTW* TN3 .... 188 C6
Cobham St *GVW* DA11 .... 27 H6
Cobtree CI *WALD* ME5 .... 68 D6
Cobtree Rd *RMAID* ME17 .... 154 C3
Cockerhurst Rd *RSEV* TN14 .... 78 B4
Cockmannings La *STMC/STPC* BR5 .. 56 E5
Cockmannings Rd *STMC/STPC* BR5 .. 56 E4
Cockmount La *WADH* TN5 .... 220 A8

Cocksett Av *ORP* BR6 .... 75 K2
Cocksure La *SCUP* DA14 .... 39 H2
Codrington Crs *GVE* DA12 .... 45 K3
Codrington Gdns *GVE* DA12 .... 46 A3 🖸
Cogate Rd *STPH/PW* TN12 .... 173 G8
Colchester Cl *WALD* ME5 .... 68 A7
Cold Arbor Rd *SEV* TN13 .... 123 F3
Cold Blow Crs *BXLY* DA5 .... 22 A7
Coldblow La *MAID/BEAR* ME14 ...... 113 J5
Coldbridge La *RMAID* ME17 .... 181 K1
Coldharbour La *DIT/AY* ME20 ...... 110 A5
MAID/BEAR ME14 .... 113 K5
Cold Harbour La *RSIT* ME9 .... 72 E8
Coldharbour La *RTON* TN11 .... 147 J8
Coldharbour Rd *CRBK* TN17 .... 236 C1
GVW DA11 .... 27 F8
RTON TN11 .... 187 F6
Coldred Rd *MAID/SHEP* ME15 .... 156 B2 🖸
Coldrum La *E/WMAL* ME19 .... 106 F1
Coldshott *OXTED* RH8 .... 140 D4
Colebrook Rd *STH/RUST* TN4 ...... 190 C7
Colegate Dr *MAID/BEAR* ME14 .... 134 E2
Coleridge Av *GILL* ME7 .... 4 B4
Coleridge Cl *DART* DA1 .... 23 K3
TIL RM18 .... 27 K1
Coleridge Wy *ORP* BR6 .... 56 B3 🖸
Coleshall Cl *MAID/SHEP* ME15 .... 134 B8
Coles La *BH/WHM* TN16 .... 121 J2
Colets Orch *RSEV* TN14 .... 101 K3 🖸
Colewood Dr *STRD* ME2 .... 48 A6
Colin Blythe Rd *TONN* TN10 .... 171 F1
Colin Chapman Wy *HART* DA3 ..... 60 E7
Colin Cl *RDART* DA2 .... 24 A5
College Av *GILL* ME7 .... 4 B4
MAID/SHEP ME15 .... 6 C4
TON TN9 .... 170 A7
College Dr *RTWE/PEM* TN2 .... 11 F3
College Rd *CHAT* ME4 .... 4 A1
DIT/AY ME20 .... 109 F3
GVW DA11 .... 26 C4
MAID/SHEP ME15 .... 6 C4
SIT ME10 .... 93 J3
SWLY BR8 .... 40 B5
College Yd *ROCH* ME1 .... 2 C2
Coller Crs *RDART* DA2 .... 42 D3
Collet Rd *RSEV* TN14 .... 102 C4
Collet Wk *RHAM* ME8 .... 90 A2
Colliers Wd *HAYES* BR2 .... 74 E1 🖸
Collington Cl *GVW* DA11 .... 27 F6 🖸
Collington Ter
MAID/SHEP ME15 .... 156 B2 🖸
Collingwood Rd *DIT/AY* ME20 ...... 87 H7
Collison Pl *TONN* TN10 .... 230 D7
Collis St *STRD* ME2 .... 49 F6
Colne Rd *TONN* TN10 .... 170 B1
Colney Rd *DART* DA1 .... 23 J5
Colonel's Wy *STH/RUST* TN4 ...... 190 A4
Coltsfoot Dr *MAID/BEAR* ME14 .. 134 B2 🖸
Coltsfoot La *OXTED* RH8 .... 140 D4
Coltstead *HART* DA3 .... 61 K6 🖸
Columbine Cl *E/WMAL* ME19 .... 108 D5 🖸
STRD ME2 .... 48 D7
Columbine Rd *E/WMAL* ME19 .... 108 D5
STRD ME2 .... 48 D7
Colyer Rd *GVW* DA11 .... 26 E8
Combe Bank Dr *RSEV* TN14 ...... 122 A2
Comet Cl *PUR* RM19 .... 12 E4
Comforts Farm Av *OXTED* RH8 .. 140 D4
Command Rd *MAID/BEAR* ME14 .. 111 F6
Commercial Pl *GVE* DA12 .... 27 K5
Commercial Rd *RTW* TN1 .... 11 D2
STPH/PW TN12 .... 173 H8
STRD ME2 .... 2 B1
TON TN9 .... 170 C6
Commissioner's Rd *STRD* ME2 ..... 49 H6
Commodore Rd *MAID/BEAR* ME14 .. 7 F2
Common La *HOO/HM* ME3 .... 15 H8
RDART DA2 .... 22 D8
Common Rd *BGR/WK* TN15 ...... 126 B2
CRBK TN17 .... 215 G5
HOO/HM ME3 .... 15 J6
ROCH ME1 .... 87 G4
RTON TN11 .... 150 A4
Common Vw *STH/RUST* TN4 ...... 206 B3
Common Wall *HOO/HM* ME3 .... 15 J8
Commonwealth Cl *SIT* ME10 .... 94 C3
Commority Rd *MEO* DA13 .... 83 J6
Compass Cl *ROCH* ME1 .... 67 H5
Compasses Rd *RTON* TN11 .... 167 K4
Comp La *BGR/WK* TN15 .... 105 J8
E/WMAL ME19 .... 106 C7
Compton Cl *WALD* ME5 .... 88 E4 🖸
Concord Av *WALD* ME5 .... 88 E3
Concord Cl *RTWE/PEM* TN2 ...... 11 E3 🖸
STPH/PW TN12 .... 173 G8
Coneyburrow Rd *RTWE/PEM* TN2 .. 207 K1
Conghurst La *HAWK* TN18 .... 242 B1
Conifer Av *HART* DA3 .... 61 K3
Conifer Dr *MEO* DA13 .... 83 G4
WALD ME5 .... 88 E5
Conifer Wy *SWLY* BR8 .... 39 K6
Coniston Av *STH/RUST* TN4 ...... 10 A3
Coniston Cl *DART* DA1 .... 22 E7
GILL ME7 .... 51 H8
Connaught Cl *MAID/SHEP* ME15 .. 156 B1 🖸

Connaught Rd *CHAT* ME4 .... 4 B6
GILL ME7 .... 5 D3 🖸
SIT ME10 .... 93 K3
Connaught Wy *STH/RUST* TN4 ..... 10 B2
Conrad Cl *RHAM* ME8 .... 90 A2 🖸
Consort Rd *MAID/BEAR* ME14 .... 7 E2
Constable Rd *GVW* DA11 .... 45 K1
TONN TN10 .... 170 E1 🖸
Constitutional Hill Rd
STH/RUST TN4 .... 189 J5
Constitution Hl *GVE* DA12 .... 27 K7
SNOD ME6 .... 85 J6
WALD ME5 .... 4 B5 🖸
Constitution Rd *WALD* ME5 .... 4 B5
Contessa Cl *ORP* BR6 .... 75 K1
Convalescent La *CRBK* TN17 .... 215 F4 🖸
Conway Cl *STRD* ME2 .... 48 D5 🖸
Conway Ms *GILL* ME7 .... 4 A2
Conway Rd *MAIDW* ME16 .... 110 C8
Conyerd Rd *BGR/WK* TN15 .... 105 F7
Cooden Cl *RHAM* ME8 .... 70 D4
Cook Cl *WALD* ME5 .... 68 D8
Cookham Hl *ROCH* ME1 .... 2 A6
Cookham Rd *SWLY* BR8 .... 39 H6
Cookham Wood Rd *ROCH* ME1 ..... 67 G6
Cooks La *SIT* ME10 .... 73 K8
Cooling Cl *MAID/BEAR* ME14 .... 7 F1
Cooling Common *HOO/HM* ME3 ... 31 H6
Cooling Rd *HOO/HM* ME3 .... 31 J2
STRD ME2 .... 49 G4
Cooling St *HOO/HM* ME3 .... 31 J4
Coombe Av *RSEV* TN14 .... 101 K7
Coombe Dr *SNOD* ME6 .... 85 K7
WALD ME5 .... 88 C3
Coombe Dr *SIT* ME10 .... 94 D2
Coombe Farm La *HOO/HM* ME3 ... 18 B8
Coombe Lands *TENT* TN30 .... 247 J2
Coombe La *TENT* TN30 .... 230 A7
Coombe Rd *GVE* DA12 .... 27 K8
HOO/HM ME3 .... 51 F1
MAID/SHEP ME15 .... 6 C5
RSEV TN14 .... 102 A2
Coomb Fld *EDEN* TN8 .... 164 C6
Coombfield Dr *RDART* DA2 .... 42 C2
Cooper Cl *GRH* DA9 .... 24 D4
Cooper Rd *SNOD* ME6 .... 85 J8
WALD ME5 .... 88 B3
Coopers Cl *EYN* DA4 .... 42 B6
Coopers La *RRTW* TN3 .... 188 A3
Cooper's Rd *GVW* DA11 .... 27 F7
Copenhagen Rd *GILL* ME7 .... 4 C4
Coplands Ri *RYE* TN31 .... 244 E7
Coppards La *RYE* TN31 .... 245 F6
Copper Beech Cl *GVE* DA12 ..... 28 A6 🖸
STMC/STPC BR5 .... 56 D2 🖸
Copperfield Cl *GVE* DA12 .... 28 D7
Copperfield Crs *STRD* ME2 .... 48 B4
Copperfield Rd *ROCH* ME1 .... 2 A6
Copperfields *BGR/WK* TN15 ...... 102 D4
Copperfields Wk *BGR/WK* TN15 .. 102 D4
Coppergate *GILL* ME7 .... 89 C1
Copperhouse La *GILL* ME7 .... 51 J8 🖸
Copperhouse Rd *STRD* ME2 .... 48 B7
Copper La *STPH/PW* TN12 .... 196 D5
Copperpenny Dr *GILL* ME7 .... 89 J3
Copper Tree Ct *MAID/SHEP* ME15 .. 155 C1
Coppice Ct *GILL* ME7 .... 89 J2 🖸
Coppice Rd *WALD* ME5 .... 88 D4
The Coppice *BGR/WK* TN15 ...... 125 H5
DIT/AY ME20 .... 109 J3
MEO DA13 .... 83 J6
RTWE/PEM TN2 .... 191 K7
Coppice Vw *MAID/BEAR* ME14 .. 112 A8
Copping's Rd *RTON* TN11 .... 167 K3
Coppins La *RSIT* ME9 .... 93 G4
Copse Bank *BGR/WK* TN15 .... 102 D7
Copse Cl *CHAT* ME4 .... 67 K5
Copsehill *DIT/AY* ME20 .... 108 C4
Copse Rd *RTON* TN11 .... 169 J2
Copse Side *HART* DA3 .... 43 K8
The Copse *HOO/HM* ME3 .... 51 F3
Copsewood Wy *MAID/SHEP* ME15 .. 134 C3
Copthall Av *HAWK* TN18 .... 235 F5
Copt Hall Rd *BGR/WK* TN15 ...... 126 A2
MEO DA13 .... 63 J1
Cordelia Crs *ROCH* ME1 .... 66 E4
Cork La *STPH/PW* TN12 .... 197 K6
Cork St *DIT/AY* ME20 .... 86 E8
Corkwell St *CHAT* ME4 .... 3 E5
Cormorant Cl *STRD* ME2 .... 48 B7 🖸
Cornell Cl *SCUP* DA14 .... 39 F4
Corner Farm Rd *STPH/PW* TN12 .. 198 A2 🖸
Cornflower Wy *TONN* TN10 .... 148 D8
Cornflower Cl *MAID/BEAR* ME14 .. 134 A2
Cornford Cl *RTWE/PEM* TN2 ... 191 H8 🖸
Cornford La *RTWE/PEM* TN2 .... 207 K2
RTWE/PEM TN2 .... 208 A3
Cornford Pk *RTWE/PEM* TN2 .... 191 J8
MEO DA13 .... 63 J1
Corn Mill Dr *ORP* BR6 .... 56 A4
Cornott La *MAID/SHEP* ME15 .... 134 A7
Cornwall Crs *ROCH* ME1 .... 86 B2
Cornwall Dr *STMC/STPC* BR5 ..... 38 C5
Cornwallis Av *CHAT* ME4 .... 67 K5

GILL ME7 .... 5 F4
RMAID ME17 .... 154 E6
TONN TN10 .... 170 E2
Cornwallis Rd *MAIDW* ME16 .... 6 A3
Cornwall Rd *DART* DA1 .... 23 F2 🖸
GILL ME7 .... 4 C2 🖸
ROCH ME1 .... 2 C5
Cornwell Av *GVE* DA12 .... 45 K1
Corona Ter *SNOD* ME6 .... 85 J8 🖸
Coronation Rd *HOO/HM* ME3 ...... 37 C1
WALD ME5 .... 4 C6 🖸
Corporation Rd *GILL* ME7 .... 5 D2
Corporation St *ROCH* ME1 .... 2 C2
Corral Cl *WALD* ME5 .... 5 D6
Corrance Gn *MAID/SHEP* ME15 .. 133 G6 🖸
Correnden Rd *RTON* TN11 .... 170 A3
Cortland Cl *SIT* ME10 .... 73 K8 🖸
Cortland Ms *SIT* ME10 .... 73 K8 🖸
Cossack St *ROCH* ME1 .... 2 C5
Cossington Rd *WALD* ME5 .... 88 C5
Costells Meadow *BH/WHM* TN16 .. 120 D5
Cot La *HDCN* TN27 .... 218 A3
Cotmandene Crs *STMC/STPC* BR5 .. 38 C3
Cotman's Ash La *BGR/WK* TN15 .. 103 H2
Cotman Wy *STPH/PW* TN12 ..... 151 G8
Cotswold Gdns *MAID/SHEP* ME15 .. 134 C5
Cotswold Ri *ORP* BR6 .... 56 A3 🖸
Cotswold Rd *GVW* DA11 .... 45 F1
Cottage Rd *CHAT* ME4 .... 3 F2
Cottages Crs *SEV* TN13 .... 101 G2
Cottall Av *CHAT* ME4 .... 3 F6
Cottenham Cl *E/WMAL* ME19 .... 108 D7
Cotton La *GRH* DA9 .... 24 B4
Couchman Green La
STPH/PW TN12 .... 178 B7
Coulman St *GILL* ME7 .... 5 D3
Coulters Cl *MAID/BEAR* ME14 .. 133 K2
Coulton Av *GVW* DA11 .... 27 F6
Council Av *GVW* DA11 .... 26 D5
County Gv *E/WMAL* ME19 .... 107 K5
County Rd *MAID/BEAR* ME14 .... 7 D2
Court Crs *SWLY* BR8 .... 58 B1
Court Dr *MAIDW* ME16 .... 6 A5
Courtenay Rd *MAID/SHEP* ME15 ... 6 C5
Courtenay Rd *RHAM* ME8 .... 69 J6
Courtfield Av *WALD* ME5 .... 88 D3
Courthope *STPH/PW* TN12 .... 173 J8
Courtlands *RTON* TN11 .... 170 A3
WBY/YAL ME18 .... 130 E6
Court La *MAID/BEAR* ME14 .... 112 E1
RTON TN11 .... 150 C6
Court Lodge Rd *GILL* ME7 .... 5 F2
Court Rd *RDART* DA2 .... 42 D3
ROCH ME1 .... 86 C5
SIT ME10 .... 73 K7
STH/RUST TN4 .... 10 A3
Court Road (Orpington By-pass)
ORP BR6 .... 56 C7
Cousley Wood Rd *WADH* TN5 .... 220 C8
Coutts Av *GVE* DA12 .... 47 H2
Coventry Cl *STRD* ME2 .... 48 C3 🖸
Coventry Rd *TONN* TN10 .... 170 D1
Coverdale Av *MAID/SHEP* ME15 .. 133 G6
Coverdale Cl *WALD* ME5 .... 68 C7
The Covert *MEO* DA13 .... 83 F7
WALD ME5 .... 88 C5 🖸
Covet Wood Cl *STMC/STPC* BR5 .. 56 A3
Covey Hall Rd *SNOD* ME6 .... 85 K6
Cowbeck Cl *RHAM* ME8 .... 70 A8 🖸
Cowden Cl *HAWK* TN18 .... 234 E6
Cowden La *HAWK* TN18 .... 234 E7
Cowden Rd *MAID/BEAR* ME14 ... 7 F2 🖸
ORP BR6 .... 56 A4
Cowdrey Cl *MAIDW* ME16 .... 132 B5
ROCH ME1 .... 2 B6
Cowdrey Ct *DART* DA1 .... 22 E6
Cow La *EDEN* TN8 .... 185 K4
Cowley Av *GRH* DA9 .... 24 E4
Cowper Rd *GILL* ME7 .... 5 D5
SIT ME10 .... 94 C2
Cowstead Rd *RSIT* ME9 .... 91 J2
Cox's Cl *SNOD* ME6 .... 85 J6
Cox St *MAID/BEAR* ME14 .... 112 E2
Cozenton Cl *RHAM* ME8 .... 70 B5
Crabbs Croft Cl *ORP* BR6 .... 75 H1 🖸
Crabtree Cl *E/WMAL* ME19 ...... 129 J4
Crabtree La *RMAID* ME17 .... 161 H6
Crabtree Rd *RHAM* ME8 .... 70 A6
Craddock Wy *RHAM* ME8 .... 90 A1 🖸
Cradducks La *STPH/PW* TN12 .. 198 D5
Cradles Rd *RSIT* ME9 .... 91 F5
Cramptons Rd *CRBK* TN17 .... 215 G6
Crampton's Rd *RSEV* TN14 ...... 101 K7
Cranborne *MAID/SHEP* ME15 .... 133 J5
Cranbourne Av *MAID/SHEP* ME15 .. 133 H6
Cranbrook Cl *MAID/SHEP* ME15 .. 134 B7
RHAM ME8 .... 69 J3 🖸
Cranbrook Dr *SIT* ME10 .... 93 J5
Cranbrook Rd *CRBK* TN17 .... 213 F6
CRBK TN17 .... 226 A5
HAWK TN18 .... 235 F2
HDCN TN27 .... 216 C2
STPH/PW TN12 .... 198 B2
TENT TN30 .... 229 J6
Crandalls *RTON* TN11 .... 168 D5

Crane La CRBK TN17 .... 225 K1
Cranford Cl RHAM ME8 .... 70 A5
Cranford Rd DART DA1 .... 23 H7
  TONN TN10 .... 171 G1
Cranleigh Cl ORP BR6 .... 56 B7
Cranleigh Dr SWLY BR8 .... 58 B1
Cranleigh Gdns MAIDW ME16 .... 110 C7 🔲
  ROCH ME1 .... 3 D5
Cranmer Cl MAID/SHEP ME15..... 133 H6
Cranmere Ct STRD ME2 .... 49 H6
Cranmer Rd SEV TN13 .... 8 A2
Cranwell Rd STH/RUST TN4 .... 206 B2
Craven Rd ORP BR6 .... 56 E7
Crawfords SWLY BR8 .... 40 B5
Crawshay Cl SEV TN13 .... 8 C2
Cray Av STMC/STPC BR5 .... 56 C2
Craybrooke Rd SCUP DA14 .... 38 C2
Crayburne MEO DA13 .... 44 A3
Cray Cl DART DA1 .... 22 D4
Crayford Cl MAID/BEAR ME14 ...... 7 F1 🔲
Crayford High St DART DA1 .... 22 B3
Crayford Rd DART DA1 .... 22 C4
Crayford Wy DART DA1 .... 22 D3
Craylands STMC/STPC BR5 .... 38 D8
Craylands La SWCM DA10 .... 25 J4
Craylands Sq SWCM DA10 .... 25 J4 🔲
Cray Rd SCUP DA14 .... 38 D4
  SWLY BR8 .... 57 K3
Craythorne TENT TN30 .... 230 B3
Cray Valley Rd STMC/STPC BR5... 56 B2
Crayne Ct CHAT ME4 .... 26 C4
Cremers Rd SIT ME10 .... 94 C1
Cremorne Rd GVW DA11 .... 27 G6 🔲
Crendon Pk STH/RUST TN4 .... 190 A5
Crescent Gdns BFN/LL DA15 .... 38 A1
  SOCK/AV RM15 .... 13 G2 🔲
The Crescent BGR/WK TN15 .... 105 C6
  CHAT ME4 .... 50 C5
  GRH DA9 .... 25 H5
  GVW DA11 .... 27 G8
  HART DA3 .... 43 K8
  MAID/BEAR ME14 .... 111 F6
  SCUP DA14 .... 38 A2
  SEV TN13 .... 9 F1
  STH/RUST TN4 .... 189 J2
  TON TN9 .... 170 B4
Crescent Wk SOCK/AV RM15 .... 13 G2
Crescent Wy ORP BR6 .... 75 K1
  SOCK/AV RM15 .... 13 H1
  WALD ME5 .... 87 J1
Cressey Ct CHAT ME4 .... 3 E4
Crest Cl RSEV TN14 .... 77 J6 🔲
Crest Rd ROCH ME1 .... 67 H5
Crest Vw GRH DA9 .... 25 F5 🔲
Crestway WALD ME5 .... 68 C6
Crete Hall Rd GVW DA11 .... 26 E5
Creve Coeur Cl
  MAID/BEAR ME14 .... 134 C1 🔲
Cricketers Cl MAID/BEAR ME17 .. 137 H8
Cricketers Dr MEO DA13 .... 63 H7
Cripple Hl RASHW TN26 .... 219 J5
Cripple St MAID/SHEP ME15 ...... 133 G7
Crismill La MAID/BEAR ME14 ..... 135 H2
Crismill Rd MAID/BEAR ME14 .... 135 G2
Crispe Cl RHAM ME8 .... 90 A2
Crispin Ct RMAID ME17 .... 154 C3 🔲
Crispin Rd STRD ME2 .... 48 D6
Crispin Wy E/WMAL ME19 .... 129 J3
Crittenden Rd STPH/PW TN12 .. 192 E2
Crockenhall Wy MEO DA13 .... 45 F6
Crockenhill Rd STMC/STPC BR5.. 56 E2
Crockenhill La SWLY BR8 .... 58 D4
Crocken Hill Rd HDCN TN27 .... 182 C4
Crockers La RYE TN31 .... 244 E6
Croft Cl RMAID ME17 .... 158 B4
  TONN TN10 .... 171 F1
  WALD ME5 .... 88 D5
Croft Ct EDEN TN8 .... 164 C5
The Crofters RHAM ME8 .... 70 C7
Croft Gdns RMAID ME17 .... 160 D1
Croft La EDEN TN8 .... 164 C5
Croft Rd BH/WHM TN16 .... 120 B5
Croftside MEO DA13 .... 83 H6 🔲
The Croft E/WMAL ME19 .... 108 C4
  SWLY BR8 .... 39 K8
Croft Wy SEV TN13 .... 8 B4
Cromer La SIT ME10 .... 93 K6
Cromer Rd SIT ME10 .... 93 K6
  STRD ME2 .... 49 G6
Cromer St TON TN9 .... 170 A5
Crompton Gdns MAID/SHEP ME15.. 7 E4
Cromwell Rd MAID/BEAR ME14 .. 7 D2 🔲
  RTWE/PEM TN2 .... 11 E4
Cromwell Ter CHAT ME4 .... 4 A5
Cronin Cl DIT/AY ME20 .... 108 D2
Crooked La GVE DA12 .... 27 J5
Crook Rd STPH/PW TN12 .... 194 A5
Crosier Cl RSIT ME9 .... 71 H3
Crosley Rd GILL ME7 .... 5 D6
Cross Dr RMAID ME17 .... 157 G5
Cross Keys MAID/BEAR ME14 .... 134 C2
Cross La SIT ME10 .... 73 K8 🔲
Cross La East GVE DA12 .... 27 J8
Cross Lane Gdns WADH TN5 .... 232 B5

Cross La West GVW DA11 .... 27 J8
Crossley Cl BH/WHM TN16 .... 97 H2
Cross Rd DART DA1 .... 23 F5
  GVW DA11 .... 27 G5
  RDART DA2 .... 41 J2
  SCUP DA14 .... 38 C2 🔲
  STMC/STPC BR5 .... 56 C2 🔲
Cross St CHAT ME4 .... 4 A4
  GILL ME7 .... 4 C2
  MAID/BEAR ME14 .... 7 D1
  STRD ME2 .... 49 G6
Cross Wy ROCH ME1 .... 2 B5
Crossway WALD ME5 .... 67 K8
Crossways BH/WHM TN16 .... 97 G2
  SIT ME10 .... 93 K5
Crossways Bvd GVW DA11 .... 24 D4
The Crossway STH/RUST TN4 ..... 206 C4
Crouch Hill Ct RSIT ME9 .... 72 B3 🔲
Crouch House Rd EDEN TN8 .... 164 A3
Crouch La BGR/WK TN15 .... 105 G8
  HAWK TN18 .... 237 H6
Crow Dr RSEV TN14 .... 100 E2
Crow Hill Rd BGR/WK TN15 .... 105 G7
Crowhurst La BGR/WK TN15 .... 81 C1
  BGR/WK TN15 .... 126 E1
  LING RH7 .... 162 B1
Crowhurst Rd BGR/WK TN15 .... 105 F8
  LING RH7 .... 162 B8
Crowhurst Village Rd LING RH7 .. 162 C4
Crowhurst Wy STMC/STPC BR5.. 56 D2
Crow La ROCH ME1 .... 2 C3
Crown Acres STPH/PW TN12 ..... 151 J8
Crown Cl ORP BR6 .... 56 B8
Crownfields MAID/BEAR ME14 .. 134 A2 🔲
  SEV TN13 .... 9 D4
Crown Gn GVE DA12 .... 47 H3 🔲
Crown La GVE DA12 .... 47 H2
Crown Quay La SIT ME10 .... 94 A2 🔲
Crown Rd EDEN TN8 .... 164 D3
  ORP BR6 .... 76 B1
  RSEV TN14 .... 78 C5
  SIT ME10 .... 93 K1
Crown St GILL ME7 .... 5 D2
Crowther Cl STPH/PW TN12 ..... 198 A6
Croxley Cl STMC/STPC BR5 .... 38 C7
Croxley Gn STMC/STPC BR5........ 38 C6
Croydon Cl WALD ME5 .... 88 C2
Croydon Rd BH/WHM TN16 ...... 120 B5
  WARL CR6 .... 118 B1
Cruden Rd GVE DA12 .... 46 C1
Crump's La RMAID ME17 .... 180 C3
Crundale Rd RHAM ME8 .... 69 K3
Crundwell Rd STH/RUST TN4 ..... 189 K5
Crusader Cl GILL ME7 .... 69 H6
  PUR RM19 .... 12 E4
Crutches La STRD ME2 .... 48 A6
Cryalls La RSIT ME9 .... 93 G4
  SIT ME10 .... 93 H2
Cryals Rd STPH/PW TN12 .... 209 K2
Cuckolds Green Rd HOO/HM ME3.. 34 D1
Cuckoo La RTON TN11 .... 149 G1
  STPH/PW TN12 .... 210 B2
Cuckoowood Av
  MAID/BEAR ME14 .... 111 F5
Cudham Cl MAID/BEAR ME14 ...... 7 F1
Cudham La North RSEV TN14 ...... 98 C1
Cudham La South RSEV TN14 ...... 98 C1
Cudham Park Rd RSEV TN14 .... 75 K5
Cudham Rd BH/WHM TN16 .... 97 J6
  ORP BR6 .... 75 F6
Cugley Rd RDART DA2 .... 24 A6
Culcroft HART DA3 .... 62 A1
Culpeper Cl RMAID ME17 .... 136 B4
  STRD ME2 .... 3 D1
Culpepers CRBK TN17 .... 212 D7
Culpepper Rd RHAM ME8 .... 90 A2
  RMAID ME17 .... 154 B3
Culverden Av STH/RUST TN4 ...... 10 B1
Culverden Down STH/RUST TN4.. 10 B2
Culverden Pk STH/RUST TN4 .... 10 B1
Culverden Park Rd STH/RUST TN4.. 10 B1
Culverden Sq STH/RUST TN4 ...... 10 C2
Culverden St RTW TN1 .... 10 C3 🔲
Culver Dr OXTED RH8 .... 140 A4
Culvey Cl HART DA3 .... 61 K2
Cumberland Av GVE DA12 .... 27 K6 🔲
  MAID/SHEP ME15 .... 133 K6
Cumberland Dr DART DA1 .... 23 J6
  RSIT ME9 .... 72 A3
Cumberland Rd GILL ME7 .... 4 C1
Cumberland Yd RTW TN1 .... 10 C5 🔲
Cumbrian Av BXLYHN DA7 .... 22 B1
Cunningham Ct STH/RUST TN4 . 190 B7 🔲
Cunningham Crs WALD ME5 .... 88 B6
Cunningham Rd STH/RUST TN4 . 190 B7
Curlew Av RSIT ME9 .... 72 A3
Curlew Crs STRD ME2 .... 48 B8
The Curlews GVE DA12 .... 28 A8
Currie Rd STH/RUST TN4 .... 10 C1
Curteis Rd TENT TN30 .... 230 B6
Curtismill Cl STMC/STPC BR5...... 38 C8
Curtismill Wy STMC/STPC BR5 ... 38 C8
Curzon Rd CHAT ME4 .... 3 F5
  MAID/BEAR ME14 .... 7 D1
Cutmore St GVW DA11 .... 27 J6

Cutter Ridge Rd MEO DA13........... 64 D5
The Cut HDCN TN27 .... 201 H7
Cutty Sark Ct GRH DA9 .... 25 F4 🔲
Cuxton Rd MAID/SHEP ME15 ..... 156 B1
  STRD ME2 .... 2 A2
Cyclamen Rd SWLY BR8 .... 58 A1
Cygnet Cl DIT/AY ME20 .... 108 E4
Cygnet Rd WALD ME5 .... 88 D4
Cygnet Vw WTHK RM20 .... 13 K3
Cypress Av HOO/HM ME3 .... 51 F3 🔲
Cypress Cl GILL ME7 .... 5 F2
Cypress Gv RTWE/PEM TN2 ...... 207 H6 🔲
Cypress Rd STRD ME2 .... 49 H5
Cyril Rd ORP BR6 .... 56 B4

D

Dacre Av SOCK/AV RM15 .... 13 H1
Dacre Crs SOCK/AV RM15 .... 13 H1
Daffodil Rd STRD ME2 .... 48 D7
Dagmar Rd CHAT ME4 .... 4 B6
Dahlia Dr SWLY BR8 .... 40 C7
Dairy Cl EYN DA4 .... 42 A5
Dairy La EDEN TN8 .... 142 B5
  STPH/PW TN12 .... 175 K2
Dale Cl DART DA1 .... 22 C5
Dale Rd DART DA1 .... 22 C5
  MEO DA13 .... 44 B2
  ROCH ME1 .... 2 C5
  SWLY BR8 .... 39 K8
Daleside ORP BR6 .... 76 B1
Daleside Cl ORP BR6 .... 76 B2
Dale St CHAT ME4 .... 3 E6
  RTW TN1 .... 11 D3
Dale Vw ERITH DA8 .... 22 D1
Dalewood SIT ME10 .... 94 B4
Dalison Ct STRD ME2 .... 86 A2
Daltons Rd SWLY BR8 .... 57 K6
Dalton St GILL ME7 .... 4 C2 🔲
Damiem Cl CHAT ME4 .... 4 A6
Damigos Rd GVE DA12 .... 28 C7
Damon Cl SCUP DA14 .... 38 C1
Damson Dr HOO/HM ME3 .... 51 F3 🔲
Dane Cl ORP BR6 .... 75 J1
  RSIT ME9 .... 91 C1
  WALD ME5 .... 88 D4
Dane Ct RMAID ME17 .... 154 C4
Dane La RSIT ME9 .... 91 C1
Danemore TENT TN30 .... 230 B6
Dane Rd SEV TN13 .... 101 G4
Danes Cl GVE DA12 .... 44 D1
Danes Hl GILL ME7 .... 51 H8
Danes Md SIT ME10 .... 73 K4
Danns La WBY/YAL ME18 .... 129 J6
Danson Wy RHAM ME8 .... 70 A5
Danvers Rd TON TN9 .... 170 B5
Darby Gdns HOO/HM ME3 .... 48 A3
Darent Cl SEV TN13 .... 122 E1
Darenth Av TONN TN10 .... 170 B1
Darenth Dr GVE DA12 .... 28 D7
Darenth Gdns BH/WHM TN16 .. 120 D5 🔲
Darenth Hl RDART DA2 .... 42 A3
Darenth La SEV TN13 .... 101 C8
Darenth Park Av RDART DA2 .... 24 C8
Darenth Ri WALD ME5 .... 88 C3
Darenth Rd DART DA1 .... 23 J7
Darenth Rd South RDART DA2 ..... 42 A2
Darenth Wy RSEV TN14 .... 78 D6
Darenth Wood Rd RDART DA2 .... 24 D7
Darent Md EYN DA4 .... 42 A6
Darent Valley Pth DART DA1 .... 12 B8
  EYN DA4 .... 60 A2
  RSEV TN14 .... 101 J2
  SEV TN13 .... 100 D8
Dargate Cl MAIDW ME16 .... 110 C7
Dargets Rd WALD ME5 .... 88 B3
Darland Av GILL ME7 .... 5 E6
Dariton Cl DART DA1 .... 22 C1
Darman La STPH/PW TN12 .... 174 B3
Darnets Fld RSEV TN14 .... 101 H4
Darnley Cl MEO DA13 .... 48 C8
Darnley Dr STH/RUST TN4 .... 189 J2
Darnley Rd GVW DA11 .... 27 H5 🔲
  STRD ME2 .... 48 D8
Darnley St GVW DA11 .... 27 H6
Darns Hl SWLY BR8 .... 57 K4
Dart Cl STRD ME2 .... 48 E7
Dartford Rd DART DA1 .... 22 D5
  EYN DA4 .... 59 J3
  SEV TN13 .... 9 E3
Darwin Cl ORP BR6 .... 75 J1
Darwin Dr TONN TN10 .... 148 D3
Dashmonden Cl STRD ME2 .... 49 H4
Dashwood Rd GVW DA11 .... 27 H7
Davenport Av GILL ME7 .... 5 E2
Davis Cl STRD ME2 .... 77 F7
Davis Cl SEV TN13 .... 9 E1
Davis Rd SOCK/AV RM15 .... 13 H1
Davy's Pl GVE DA12 .... 46 B4
Dawell Dr BH/WHM TN16 .... 97 G4
Dawes Cl GRH DA9 .... 24 E4
Dawes St GILL ME7 .... 4 C3
Dawson Av STMC/STPC BR5 .... 38 C7

Dawson Dr *SWLY* BR8 .... 40 B5
Dayton Dr *ERITH* DA8 .... 12 B5
Deacon Cl *STRD* ME2 .... 48 D6 🅳
Deakin Leas *TON* TN9 .... 170 B7
Deakins Ter *ORP* BR6 .... 56 B4 🅳
Deanery La *EDEN* TN8 .... 142 C5
Dean La *MEO* DA13 .... 64 A7
Dean Rd *SIT* ME10 .... 73 K8
   STRD ME2 .... 48 D6
Deans Hill Rd *RSIT* ME9 .... 115 J1
Dean St *MAID/SHEP* ME15 .... 132 D6
Deanwood Dr *RHAM* ME8 .... 70 A8
Decoy Hill Rd *HOO/HM* ME3 .... 17 C8
Deepdene *WADH* TN5 .... 220 B8
Deerhurst Cl *HART* DA3 .... 44 D8 🅳
Deerhurst Gdns *MAIDW* ME16 .... 6 A3 🅳
Deerleap La *RSEV* TN14 .... 76 E8
Defiant Cl *WALD* ME5 .... 68 C8
Defoe Cl *WALD* ME5 .... 68 C8 🅳
Delagarde Rd *BH/WHM* TN16 .... 120 C5
Delarue Cl *RTON* TN11 .... 148 D6
Delce Rd *ROCH* ME1 .... 3 D4
Del Gdns *SNOD* ME6 .... 85 K6 🅳
Delius Dr *TONN* TN10 .... 149 F8
Dell Dr *RTWE/PEM* TN2 .... 11 F3
The Dell *BXLY* DA5 .... 22 B7
Delmonden Rd *HAWK* TN18 .... 234 C6
Delves Av *RTWE/PEM* TN2 .... 11 F5
De Mere Cl *RHAM* ME8 .... 70 A8
Denbeigh Dr *TONN* TN10 .... 148 D8
Denberry Dr *SCUP* DA14 .... 38 C1
Denbigh Av *RHAM* ME8 .... 70 A5
Denbigh Cl *SIT* ME10 .... 73 K7
Denbigh Rd *STH/RUST* TN4 .... 190 C7 🅳
Dene Cl *RDART* DA2 .... 40 B2
Dene Dr *HART* DA3 .... 44 C7
   ORP BR6 .... 56 C7
Dene Holm Rd *GVW* DA11 .... 44 E1
Dene Lodge Cl *BGR/WK* TN15 .... 105 F7
Dene Rd *DART* DA1 .... 23 J6
Denesway *MEO* DA13 .... 63 H3
The Dene *SEV* TN13 .... 9 D5
Dene Wk *HART* DA3 .... 43 K8
Dene Wy *RRTW* TN3 .... 188 E7
Denham Rd *RSIT* ME9 .... 72 A7
Denison Ms *HOO/HM* ME3 .... 35 F2 🅳
Den La *STPH/PW* TN12 .... 175 G3
Dennettsland Rd *EDEN* TN8 .... 142 C5
Dennis Rd *GVW* DA11 .... 45 H1
Denton Cl *MAID/SHEP* ME15 .... 134 A6
Denton Court Rd *GVE* DA12 .... 28 B7
Denton Rd *BXLY* DA5 .... 22 B7
   DART DA1 .... 22 B6
Denton St *GVE* DA12 .... 28 B6
Denver Rd *DART* DA1 .... 22 C6
Derby Cl *RTON* TN11 .... 147 J8
   SIT ME10 .... 73 J8
Derby Rd *MAID/SHEP* ME15 .... 133 J6
   WALD ME5 .... 5 E6
Dering Cl *HDCN* TN27 .... 203 J2
Dering Wy *GVE* DA12 .... 28 E7
Deringwood Dr *MAID/SHEP* ME15 .. 134 B3
Dernier Rd *TON* TN9 .... 170 C2
Derry Downs *STMC/STPC* BR5 .... 56 D5
Derwent Cl *DART* DA1 .... 22 E7
Derwent Dr *STH/RUST* TN4 .... 10 A2
Derwent Rd *TONN* TN10 .... 170 C1
Derwent Wy *RHAM* ME8 .... 70 A6
Detillens La *OXTED* RH8 .... 118 E8
Detling Cl *RHAM* ME8 .... 69 K4
Detling Hl *MAID/BEAR* ME14 .... 112 C5
Detling Rd *GVW* DA11 .... 26 E7
Devon Cl *RHAM* ME8 .... 70 C5
   WALD ME5 .... 68 D7
Devon Rd *EYN* DA4 .... 42 A6
   MAID/SHEP ME15 .... 7 F6
Devonshire Av *DART* DA1 .... 22 E5
Devonshire Cl *RTWE/PEM* TN2 .. 206 E6 🅳
Devonshire Rd *GILL* ME7 .... 5 D1 🅳
   GVW DA11 .... 45 H1
   ORP BR6 .... 56 B4 🅳
Dewlands Av *RDART* DA2 .... 24 A6
Dhekelia Cl *MAID/BEAR* ME14 .. 111 G7
Dial Cl *GILL* ME7 .... 5 F2
   GRH DA9 .... 25 H4
Dial Rd *GILL* ME7 .... 5 F2
Dibden La *RSEV* TN14 .... 8 A6
Dickens Av *DART* DA1 .... 23 K3
Dickens Cl *HART* DA3 .... 61 K2
   RMAID ME17 .... 157 G2
Dickens Dr *E/WMAL* ME19 .... 108 C5
Dickensian Cl *HOO/HM* ME3 .... 34 D3
Dickens Rd *GVW* DA11 .... 28 B7
   MAID/BEAR ME14 .... 110 E7
   ROCH ME1 .... 2 C6
Dickens Wy *HAWK* TN18 .... 235 C5
Dickley La *RMAID* ME17 .... 138 A8
Digdog La *CRBK* TN17 .... 216 B3
Dignals Cl *RHAM* ME8 .... 70 C4
Dillon Wy *RTWE/PEM* TN2 .... 11 F1
Dillywood La *HOO/HM* ME3 .... 48 D4
Dimmock Cl *STPH/PW* TN12 .... 173 K8
Dingleden La *CRBK* TN17 .... 237 H4
Dippers Cl *BGR/WK* TN15 .... 102 D4

Discovery Dr *E/WMAL* ME19 .... 129 J3
Dislingbury Rd *RTON* TN11 .... 191 H3
Disraeli Cl *MAID/SHEP* ME15 .... 156 A1 🅳
Ditton Court Cl *DIT/AY* ME20 .... 109 F5 🅳
Ditton Pl *DIT/AY* ME20 .... 109 F5
Dixon Cl *MAID/SHEP* ME15............ 6 C5
Dixter La *RYE* TN31 .... 244 D7
Dixter Rd *RYE* TN31 .... 244 D6
Dixwell Rd *RHAM* ME8 .... 90 A1
Dobbie Cl *SIT* ME10 .... 73 K8
Dobson Rd *GVE* DA12 .... 46 B3
Dock Rd *CHAT* ME4 .... 3 F3
Doctor Hope's Rd *CRBK* TN17 .... 225 K2
Doddington Ct *MAIDW* ME16 .... 6 B2 🅳
Doddington Rd *RHAM* ME8 .... 69 K4
Dodd Rd *TONN* TN10 .... 170 C1
Doggets *EDEN* TN8 .... 164 C6 🅳
Doggetts Rw *HOO/HM* ME3 .... 21 G8 🅳
Doggett's Sq *STRD* ME2 .... 2 B1 🅳
Dogwood Cl *GVW* DA11 .... 45 F1 🅳
   WALD ME5 .... 88 E5 🅳
Dolphin Dr *RHAM* ME8 .... 90 B1
Dolphin Rd *SIT* ME10 .... 94 C1
Dombey Cl *HOO/HM* ME3 .... 48 B3
   ROCH ME1 .... 2 C5 🅳
Donald Moor Av *RSIT* ME9 .... 95 K4
Doncaster Cl *MAID/SHEP* ME15 .. 134 B8 🅳
Donet Cl *RHAM* ME8 .... 89 K1
Dongola Rd *STRD* ME2 .... 49 F5
Donkey Fld *RTON* TN11 .... 168 C5
Donkey La *EYN* DA4 .... 60 A6
Doon Brae *STH/RUST* TN4 .... 190 A4
Dorado Gdns *ORP* BR6 .... 56 E7
Dorchester Cl *DART* DA1 .... 23 J6
   HOO/HM ME3 .... 31 G7 🅳
   STMC/STPC BR5 .... 56 C5 🅳
Dorchester Rd *GVE* DA12 .... 46 A1
Doric Av *STH/RUST* TN4 .... 189 K5
Doric Cl *STH/RUST* TN4 .... 189 K5
Dorking Rd *RTW* TN1 .... 11 E1
Dormers Dr *MEO* DA13 .... 63 J4 🅳
Dornden Dr *RRTW* TN3 .... 205 K2
Dornden Gdns *WALD* ME5 .... 88 C4
Dorney Ri *STMC/STPC* BR5 .... 56 A1
Dorothy Av *CRBK* TN17 .... 225 K2
Dorrit Wy *ROCH* ME1 .... 3 D6
Dorset Crs *GVE* DA12 .... 46 B2
Dorset Rd *RTWE/PEM* TN2 .... 11 F5
Dorset Sq *RHAM* ME8 .... 70 A5
Dorset Wy *MAID/SHEP* ME15 .... 133 J6
Dotterel Cl *WALD* ME5 .... 88 E5
Doubleday Dr *RSIT* ME9 .... 94 E4
Doubleton La *RTON* TN11 .... 187 J1
Douglas Rd *MAIDW* ME16 .... 6 B4
   RMAID ME17 .... 160 D1 🅳
   TON TN9 .... 170 A6
Doust Wy *ROCH* ME1 .... 3 D4
Dove Cl *WALD* ME5 .... 68 C8
Dovedale Rd *RDART* DA2 .... 24 B7 🅳
Doveney Cl *STMC/STPC* BR5 .... 56 E1
Dove Rd *TONN* TN10 .... 148 C8
Dover Rd *GVW* DA11 .... 26 E6
Dover Rd East *GVW* DA11 .... 27 F6
Dover St *MAIDW* ME16 .... 132 C4
   SIT ME10 .... 93 K2 🅳
Doves Cft *RSIT* ME9 .... 93 H7
Dowding Rd *BH/WHM* TN16 .... 97 H2
Dowding Wy *RTWE/PEM* TN2 .... 190 E5
Dower House Crs *STH/RUST* TN4 .. 189 J3
Dowgate Cl *TON* TN9 .... 170 D7
Dowlerville Rd *ORP* BR6 .... 76 A2
Dowling Cl *SNOD* ME6 .... 85 H7 🅳
The Downage *GVW* DA11 .... 27 H8
Down Av *RRTW* TN3 .... 221 J3
Downderry Wy *DIT/AY* ME20 .... 109 F5
Downe Av *RSEV* TN14 .... 75 H7
Downe Ct *ROCH* ME1 .... 67 K6
Downe Rd *HAYES* BR2 .... 98 C4
   RSEV TN14 .... 98 C1
Downlands *RMAID* ME17 .... 137 K8
Downs Av *DART* DA1 .... 23 K6
Downs Cl *HDCN* TN27 .... 200 C1
   MAID/BEAR ME14 .... 111 G6 🅳
   SIT ME10 .... 93 J4
Downside *STRD* ME2 .... 2 A1
Downs Rd *MAID/BEAR* ME14.......... 111 H6
   MEO DA13 .... 44 E3
   WBY/YAL ME18 .... 152 E5
The Downs *WALD* ME5 .... 87 J5
Downs Vw *HART* DA3 .... 61 K1
Downs Vw *ROCH* ME1 .... 86 E5
Downsview *E/WMAL* ME19 .... 83 H8
   WALD ME5 .... 68 D6
Downs View Cl *ORP* BR6 .... 76 D5
Downsview Cl *SWLY* BR8 .... 40 C8 🅳
Downs View Rd *MAID/BEAR* ME14.. 111 G6
Downsview Rd *SEV* TN13............... 8 B4
Downsway *ORP* BR6 .... 75 K1 🅳
Downs Wy *OXTED* RH8 .... 118 C6
Downs Wd *MEO* DA13 .... 83 G6
Drage Rd *STPH/PW* TN12 .... 151 G8
Drake's Av *STRD* ME2 .... 48 E6
Drakes Cl *RSIT* ME9 .... 71 H4
Draper St *STH/RUST* TN4 .... 189 K4
Dray Corner Rd *HDCN* TN27 .... 179 H7

Dray Ct *RTON* TN11 .... 150 A6 🅳
Dray's Fld *RSIT* ME9 .... 116 A7
Drayton Cl *HOO/HM* ME3 .... 33 F3
Drayton Rd *TON* TN9 .... 170 C6
Drewery Dr *RHAM* ME8 .... 89 K1
Driffield Gdns *STH/RUST* TN4 .... 169 J7
The Drive *CHST* BR7 .... 38 A6
   GVE DA12 .... 46 A2
   HART DA3 .... 44 C8
   ORP BR6 .... 56 A6
   RTWE/PEM TN2 .... 10 C6
   SCUP DA14 .... 38 C1
   SEV TN13 .... 8 B7
   TON TN9 .... 170 B7
The Drove Wy *MEO* DA13 .... 45 F5
Drudgeon Wy *RDART* DA2 .... 38 B5
Drury Rd *TENT* TN30 .... 230 A6
Dry Bank Ct *TONN* TN10.................... 170 B2
Dryden Wy *ORP* BR6 .... 56 B5
Dryhill La *SEV* TN14 .... 122 D2
Dry Hill Park Crs *TONN* TN10 .... 170 C3
Dry Hill Park Rd *TONN* TN10 .... 170 B3
Dry Hill Rd *TONN* TN10 .... 170 B3
Dryland Av *ORP* BR6 .... 56 A8
Dryland Rd *BGR/WK* TN15 .... 105 F8
   SNOD ME6 .... 85 J6
Duchess Cl *STRD* ME2 .... 48 D6
Duchess of Kent Dr *WALD* ME5 .... 88 C3
Duchess' Wk *BGR/WK* TN15.......... 124 C4
Ducketts Rd *DART* DA1 .... 22 C4
Dudely Rd *GVW* DA11 .... 27 F6
Dudley Rd *RTW* TN1 .... 10 C3 🅳
Dudsbury Rd *DART* DA1 .... 22 E5
Dukes Meadow *RTON* TN11.......... 167 H4
Dukes Meadow Dr *GILL* ME7 .... 69 G8
Dukes Rd *RTW* TN1 .... 11 E2
Dully Rd *HART* DA3 .... 117 K2
Dumbourne La *TENT* TN30 .... 240 C4
Duncan Rd *GILL* ME7 .... 5 D3
Dundale Rd *RRTW* TN3 .... 209 F5
Dunedin Cl *SIT* ME10 .... 93 H3
Dunera Dr *MAID/BEAR* ME14 .... 111 F7
Dunkin Rd *DART* DA1 .... 23 K3
Dunkirk Cl *GVE* DA12 .... 45 K3
Dunkirk Dr *WALD* ME5 .... 68 A8
Dunk's Green Rd *RTON* TN11 .... 149 G1
Dunning's La *ROCH* ME1 .... 2 C4 🅳
The Dunnings *MAIDW* ME16 .... 132 A4
Dunn Street Rd *GILL* ME7 .... 89 H6
Dunstan Gv *STH/RUST* TN4 .... 11 D2
Dunstan Rd *STH/RUST* TN4 .... 11 D1
Durant Rd *SWLY* BR8 .... 40 D4
Durham Cl *MAID/SHEP* ME15 .... 133 K5
Durham Rd *RHAM* ME8 .... 69 K7
   SCUP DA14 .... 38 C1
Durley Gdns *ORP* BR6.................... 56 C8
Durndale La *GVW* DA11 .... 45 F2
Durrant Wy *ORP* BR6 .... 75 J1
   SWCM DA10 .... 25 K6
Durrell Gdns *WALD* ME5 .... 68 C5 🅳
Duval Dr *ROCH* ME1 .... 67 K6
Dux Court Rd *HOO/HM* ME3 .... 32 D6
Dux Hl *BGR/WK* TN15 .... 127 F6
Dux La *BGR/WK* TN15 .... 127 F5
Dwelly La *LING* RH7 .... 163 G2
Dyke Dr *STMC/STPC* BR5 .... 56 D4
Dykewood Cl *BXLY* DA5 .... 40 A1
Dynes Rd *RSEV* TN14 .... 102 C4
Dynevor Rd *STH/RUST* TN4 .... 190 C7
Dyngley Cl *SIT* ME10 .... 73 K8 🅳

E

Eagle Cl *DIT/AY* ME20 .... 108 E4
Eagles Cl *SIT* ME10 .... 94 D2
Eagles Dr *BH/WHM* TN16 .... 97 H5
Eagles Rd *GRH* DA9 .... 25 G3
Eaglestone Cl *BGR/WK* TN15 .... 105 G6 🅳
Eagle Wy *GVW* DA11 .... 26 B4
Ealing Cl *WALD* ME5 .... 88 C2
Eardemont Cl *DART* DA1 .... 22 C3
Eardley Rd *SEV* TN13 .... 9 D3
Earl Cl *WALD* ME5 .... 88 C2
Earl Rd *GVW* DA11 .... 27 F8
Earl's Rd *STH/RUST* TN4 .... 10 B3
Earl St *MAID/BEAR* ME14 .... 6 C3
   MAIDW ME16 .... 6 C3
East Cliff Rd *STH/RUST* TN4.......... 10 C1
Eastcote *ORP* BR6 .... 56 A5
Eastcourt Gn *RHAM* ME8 .... 69 J3
Eastcourt La *GILL* ME7 .... 69 K1
   RHAM ME8 .... 69 J4
East Cross *TENT* TN30 .... 230 A7
East Dr *STMC/STPC* BR5 .... 56 C3
Easterfields *E/WMAL* ME19 .... 131 C1
Eastern Av *SOCK/AV* RM15.......... 13 G2
   WTHK RM20 .... 13 K5
Eastern Rd *GILL* ME7 .... 5 F2
Eastern Vw *BH/WHM* TN16 .... 97 G4
Eastfield Gdns *TONN* TN10 .... 170 E1 🅳
Eastgate *ROCH* ME1 .... 2 C3
Eastgate Rd *TENT* TN30 .... 230 B5
Eastgate Ter *ROCH* ME1 .... 2 C3 🅳

East Hall HI *RMAID* ME17 .... 156 A8
East Hall La *SIT* ME10 .... 94 D1
East Hall Rd *STH/STPC* BR5 ..... 57 F4
East HI *BH/WHM* TN16 .... 97 F5
  DART DA1 .... 23 J6
  EYN DA4 .... 42 C6
  OXTED RH8 .... 118 D8
  TENT TN30 .... 230 B6
East Hill Dr *DART* DA1 .... 23 J6 🔟
East Hill Rd *BGR/WK* TN15 .... 80 A7
  OXTED RH8 .... 118 C8
East Kent Av *GVW* DA11 .... 26 D5
Eastlands CI *OXTED* RH8 .... 118 B6
  STH/RUST TN4 .... 206 D6
Eastlands Wy *OXTED* RH8 .... 118 B6
Eastling CI *RHAM* ME8 .... 70 A3
East Milton Rd *GVE* DA12 .... 28 A6
East Park Rd *DIT/AY* ME20 .... 110 A5
East Rochester Wy *DART* DA1 ... 22 A6
East Rw *ROCH* ME1 .... 2 C5
Eastry CI *MAIDW* ME16 .... 110 C7
East St *CHAT* ME4 .... 4 A5
  E/WMAL ME19 .... 107 F4
  GILL ME7 .... 5 D2
  MAID/SHEP ME15 .... 153 K6
  RMAID ME17 .... 159 J1
  SIT ME10 .... 94 B2
  SNOD ME6 .... 86 A6
  TON TN9 .... 170 C4
East St (North) *E/WMAL* ME19 . 107 F3
East Sutton Rd *HDCN* TN27 ..... 179 J5
  RMAID ME17 .... 157 H7
East Ter *GVE* DA12 .... 27 K5
East Weald Dr *TENT* TN30 .... 230 B5
Eastwell Barn Ms *TENT* TN30 . 230 A6 🔟
Eastwell CI *MAID/BEAR* ME14 ..... 7 F2
  STPH/PW TN12 .... 173 G7
Eastwell Mdw *TENT* TN30 .... 230 A6
Eastwood Rd *SIT* ME10 .... 93 J1
Eccles Rw *DIT/AY* ME20 .... 86 E8
Eccleston Rd *MAID/SHEP* ME15 .. 6 C5
Echo CI *MAID/SHEP* ME15 .... 134 B8
Echo Ct *GVE* DA12 .... 27 K8
Eclipse Dr *SIT* ME10 .... 73 K6
Eddington CI *MAID/SHEP* ME15 .133 J6
Eden Av *WALD* ME5 .... 68 A7
Edenbridge CI *STMC/STPC* BR5 .. 56 E2
Eden CI *BXLY* DA5 .... 40 A2
Eden PI *GVE* DA12 .... 27 J6
Eden Rd *BXLY* DA5 .... 39 K2
  HOO/HM ME3 .... 33 F7
  RTW TN1 .... 10 C5
Eden Valley Wk *EDEN* TN8 ...... 163 K8
  RTON TN11 .... 168 C7
Edgar CI *SWLY* BR8 .... 40 C8
Edgar Rd *BH/WHM* TN16 .... 97 H8
  RSEV TN14 .... 102 C4
Edgefield CI *DART* DA1 .... 24 A7 🔟
Edgehill Gdns *MAID* DA13 .... 45 G6
Edgeler Ct *SNOD* ME6 .... 85 J7
Edgewood Dr *ORP* BR6 .... 76 A1
Edgington Wy *SCUP* DA14 .... 38 D5
Edinburgh Ms *TIL* RM18 .... 27 J1 🔟
Edinburgh Rd *CHAT* ME4 .... 4 C6
  GILL ME7 .... 5 D3 🔟
  HOO/HM ME3 .... 37 F1
Edinburgh Sq *MAID/SHEP* ME15 .133 J8
Edith Rd *ORP* BR6 .... 76 B1
Ediva Rd *MEO* DA13 .... 63 H2
Edmund CI *MAIDW* ME16 .... 132 A3
  MEO DA13 .... 63 H2
Edmund Rd *STMC/STPC* BR5 ..... 56 D3
Edmunds Av *STMC/STPC* BR5 .. 38 E8
Edna Rd *MAID/BEAR* ME14 ..... 111 F7
Edward Rd *BH/WHM* TN16 .... 97 J5
Edwards CI *RHAM* ME8 .... 89 K1
Edwards Gdns *SWLY* BR8 ..... 58 A1 🔟
Edward St *CHAT* ME4 .... 4 A6
  STH/RUST TN4 .... 189 K5
  STRD ME2 .... 2 B1
Edward Wk *E/WMAL* ME19 ..... 108 D6
Edwin Petty PI *RDART* DA2 .. 24 B6 🔟
Edwin Rd *RDART* DA2 .... 40 E1
  RHAM ME8 .... 69 K5
Edwin St *GVE* DA12 .... 27 K8
Egerton Av *SWLY* BR8 .... 40 C6
Egerton CI *DART* DA1 .... 22 E7
Egerton House Rd *HDCN* TN27 .. 182 E2
Egerton Rd *HDCN* TN27 .... 161 J8
  MAID/BEAR ME14 .... 110 E7
Eggpie La *RTON* TN11 .... 146 B6
Eglantine La *EYN* DA4 .... 60 A3
Eglinton Rd *SWCM* DA10 .... 26 A5
Egremont Rd *MAID/SHEP* ME15 .134 B4
Egret CI *CHAT* ME4 .... 50 C6
Elaine Av *STRD* ME2 .... 4 A4
Elder CI *HOO/HM* ME3 .... 51 F3 🔟
  RMAID ME17 .... 158 B4
Elder Ct *RHAM* ME8 .... 69 J8 🔟
Eldon St *CHAT* ME4 .... 4 A4
Eldon Wy *STPH/PW* TN12 ...... 173 H7
Eldred Dr *STMC/STPC* BR5 .... 56 E6
Elford Rd *HOO/HM* ME3 .... 51 G1
Elgal CI *ORP* BR6 .... 75 G1

Elgar CI *TONN* TN10 .... 148 E8
Elham Rd *RHAM* ME8 .... 69 J4
Eliot Rd *DART* DA1 .... 24 A4
Elizabeth CI *TIL* RM18 .... 27 J1 🔟
Elizabeth Ct *RHAM* ME8 .... 69 K5 🔟
Elizabeth St *GRH* DA9 .... 24 D4
Elizabeth Wy *STMC/STPC* BR5 ... 56 D2
Ellenborough Rd *SCUP* DA14 ... 38 E4
Ellenswood CI
  MAID/SHEP ME15 .... 134 C5 🔟
Ellerman Rd *TIL* RM18 .... 27 G1 🔟
Ellice Rd *OXTED* RH8 .... 118 D8
Ellingham Leas *MAID/SHEP* ME15 .. 133 J6
Elliotts La *BH/WHM* TN16 ...... 121 J3
Elliott St *GVE* DA12 .... 28 A6
Ellison Wy *RHAM* ME8 .... 70 D4
Ellis Waterton CI *SWLY* BR8 .. 58 A1 🔟
Ellis Wy *DART* DA1 .... 23 J8 🔟
Elm Av *CHAT* ME4 .... 67 K5
  HOO/HM ME3 .... 50 B2
Elm CI *DART* DA1 .... 23 F7
  HDCN TN27 .... 183 F3
  HOO/HM ME3 .... 48 B3
Elm Crs *E/WMAL* ME19 .... 108 D6
Elmcroft Rd *ORP* BR6 .... 56 B4
Elm Dr *SWLY* BR8 .... 40 A7
Elmfield *RHAM* ME8 .... 69 H3
  TENT TN30 .... 230 B6
Elmfield CI *GVW* DA11 .... 27 J7
  RSEV TN14 .... 145 K4
Elm Gv *MAID/SHEP* ME15 .... 7 E8
  ORP BR6 .... 56 A5
  RTON TN11 .... 169 K2
  SIT ME10 .... 94 C2
Elmhurst Av *RTWE/PEM* TN2 .. 191 K6
Elmhurst Gdns *ROCH* ME1 .... 3 D5
Elm La *TON* TN9 .... 170 C3
Elm Rd *BH/WHM* TN16 .... 120 E4
  DART DA1 .... 23 G7
  GILL ME7 .... 5 E2
  GRH DA9 .... 25 G3
  GVE DA12 .... 45 K1
  HOO/HM ME3 .... 51 F3 🔟
  ORP BR6 .... 76 B3
  SCUP DA14 .... 38 B2
  SOCK/AV RM15 .... 13 H1
  STH/RUST TN4 .... 189 K5
Elmshurst Gdns *TONN* TN10 .. 148 C3
Elmstone CI *MAIDW* ME16 ..... 132 B4
Elmstone Hole Rd *RMAID* ME17 .159 H6
Elmstone La *MAIDW* ME16 ..... 132 A4
Elmstone Rd *RHAM* ME8 .... 70 A7
Elm Tree Dr *ROCH* ME1 .... 2 A6
Elmwood Rd *HOO/HM* ME3 ...... 32 A4
Elphick's PI *RTWE/PEM* TN2 .. 207 G6 🔟
Elvington CI *MAIDW* ME16 ...... 6 A2 🔟
Elwill Wy *MEO* DA13 .... 45 G6
Ely CI *ERITH* DA8 .... 22 C1
  RHAM ME8 .... 70 D4
Ely Gdns *TON* TN9 .... 170 D2
Embassey Ct *SCUP* DA14 .... 38 C1
Embassy Rd *GILL* ME7 .... 69 G5 🔟
Emerald CI *ROCH* ME1 .... 67 J7
Emersons Av *SWLY* BR8 .... 40 C5
Emily Rd *WALD* ME5 .... 68 C8
Emmett Hill La *WBY/YAL* ME18 .174 D2
Emmetts Rd *BH/WHM* TN16 ... 143 J1
Empress Rd *GVE* DA12 .... 28 B6
Emsworth Gv *MAID/BEAR* ME14 .111 K8
Englefield CI *STMC/STPC* BR5 .. 56 A1 🔟
Englefield Crs *HOO/HM* ME3 .... 31 G7
  STMC/STPC BR5 .... 56 B2
Englefield Pth *STMC/STPC* BR5 . 56 B1 🔟
Ensfield Rd *RTON* TN11 .... 168 D7
Enterprise CI *STRD* ME2 .... 49 J6
Enterprise Rd *MAID/SHEP* ME15 .... 7 D6
Epaul La *ROCH* ME1 .... 2 C2 🔟
Epps Rd *SIT* ME10 .... 93 K3
Epsom CI *E/WMAL* ME19 .... 107 K6
  MAID/SHEP ME15 .... 134 B8 🔟
Eridge Green CI *STMC/STPC* BR5 .. 56 D5
Eridge Rd *RRTW* TN3 .... 205 G8
  STH/RUST TN4 .... 10 B5
Erith CI *MAID/BEAR* ME14 ..... 111 G6
Erith Ct *PUR* RM19 .... 12 E4
Ernest Dr *MAIDW* ME16 .... 132 B1
Ernest Rd *CHAT* ME4 .... 4 A5
Erskine Park Rd *STH/RUST* TN4 . 206 A2
Erskine Rd *MEO* DA13 .... 83 J6
Eshcol Rd *HOO/HM* ME3 .... 33 K8
Eskdale CI *RDART* DA2 .... 24 B8
Esplanade *ROCH* ME1 .... 2 B2
Essex Dr *DART* DA1 .... 23 G5 🔟
  GVW DA11 .... 27 H7
  HART DA3 .... 43 J7
  MAID/SHEP ME15 .... 134 A8
  STRD ME2 .... 85 K1
Estelle CI *ROCH* ME1 .... 67 J7
Estridge Wy *TONN* TN10 .... 171 F1
Etfield Gv *SCUP* DA14 .... 38 C3
Ethelbert Rd *ROCH* ME1 .... 2 C4
  STMC/STPC BR5 .... 38 E2

Ethelberry Rd *RDART* DA2 .... 41 H2
Etherington HI *RRTW* TN3 ...... 189 G6
Ethnam La *HAWK* TN18 .... 244 B3
Eton CI *WALD* ME5 .... 88 C2
Eton Rd *ORP* BR6 .... 56 C8
Eton Wy *DART* DA1 .... 23 F3
Euclid Wy *WTHK* RM20 .... 13 K4
Eurolink Wy *SIT* ME10 .... 94 B2
Evans CI *GRH* DA9 .... 25 F4
Eva Rd *GILL* ME7 .... 5 D5
Evelyn CI *STRD* ME2 .... 49 H6
Evelyn Rd *MAIDW* ME16 .... 6 B4
  RSEV TN14 .... 102 A3
Evenden Rd *MEO* DA13 .... 63 H4
Everest CI *GVW* DA11 .... 45 F1 🔟
Everest Dr *HOO/HM* ME3 .... 51 F2
Everest La *STRD* ME2 .... 49 G5
Everest Ms *HOO/HM* ME3 .... 51 F2
Everest PI *SWLY* BR8 .... 58 A1 🔟
Everglade *BH/WHM* TN16 .... 97 H5
Everglade CI *HART* DA3 .... 62 A1 🔟
The Everglades *GILL* ME7 .... 69 G8
Evergreen CI *E/WMAL* ME19 .. 108 C4 🔟
  GILL ME7 .... 89 H1
  HOO/HM ME3 .... 47 K3
  RSIT ME9 .... 73 J2
Eversley Av *BXLYHN* DA7 .... 22 B1
Eversley CI *MAIDW* ME16 ...... 110 C8 🔟
Eversley Cross *BXLYHN* DA7 .... 22 B1
Evesham Rd *GVE* DA12 .... 28 A8 🔟
Evry Rd *SCUP* DA14 .... 38 D4
Ewart Rd *CHAT* ME4 .... 67 K5
Ewehurst La *RRTW* TN3 .... 188 D3
Ewell Av *E/WMAL* ME19 .... 107 J6
Ewell La *MAID/SHEP* ME15 ..... 153 H1
Ewins CI *STPH/PW* TN12 .... 173 J8
Exedown Rd *BGR/WK* TN15 .... 104 C2
Exeter CI *TON* TN9 .... 170 D2
Exeter Rd *GVE* DA12 .... 46 A1
Exmouth Rd *GILL* ME7 .... 4 C1 🔟
Exton CI *WALD* ME5 .... 88 C2
Exton Gdns *MAID/BEAR* ME14 .134 B1
Eyhorne St *RMAID* ME17 .... 136 A5
Eynsford Ri *EYN* DA4 .... 59 G8
Eynsford Rd *EYN* DA4 .... 59 J5
  GRH DA9 .... 25 H4
  MAIDW ME16 .... 110 D7
  SWLY BR8 .... 58 B3
Eynswood Dr *SCUP* DA14 .... 38 C3

F

Fackenden La *BGR/WK* TN15 ..... 79 K8
Factory Rd *GVW* DA11 .... 26 D5
Faesten Wy *BXLY* DA5 .... 40 B1
Fagus CI *WALD* ME5 .... 88 C5
Fairbourne La *RMAID* ME17 ... 159 G3
Fairby La *HART* DA3 .... 61 K3
Fairchildes Rd *WARL* CR6 .... 96 B2
Fairfax CI *RHAM* ME8 .... 90 A1
Fairfax Rd *CHAT* ME4 .... 46 B3
Fairfield Av *RTWE/PEM* TN2 .. 11 E2 🔟
Fairfield CI *BGR/WK* TN15 ...... 102 E5
Fairfield Crs *TON* TN9 .... 170 C6 🔟
Fairfield Rd *BGR/WK* TN15 ...... 105 F6
Fairfield Wy *RTON* TN11 .... 169 J1
Fairhurst Dr *MAID/SHEP* ME15 .154 B2
Fairlawn CI *WBY/YAL* ME18 .... 130 E6
Fairlead Rd *ROCH* ME1 .... 67 J5
Faireas *SIT* ME10 .... 94 C4
Fairlight CI *STH/RUST* TN4 ..... 190 A4
Fairlight Cross *HART* DA3 .... 44 C8
Fairman's La *STPH/PW* TN12 .. 193 K8
Fairmeadow *MAID/BEAR* ME14 ... 6 C2
  MAIDW ME16 .... 6 C3
Fairmead Rd *EDEN* TN8 .... 164 B1
Fairmile Rd *RTWE/PEM* TN2 .. 207 K1
Fairseat La *BGR/WK* TN15 .... 82 B5
  BGR/WK TN15 .... 105 H2
Fairtrough Rd *ORP* BR6 .... 76 C8
Fairview *HAWK* TN18 .... 235 F4
Fairview Av *RHAM* ME8 .... 89 J1
Fairview Dr *HOO/HM* ME3 .... 48 A2
Fairview Gdns *MEO* DA13 .... 63 J2
Fairview Rd *MEO* DA13 .... 44 E5
  SIT ME10 .... 94 B3
Fairway CI *ROCH* ME1 .... 67 H5
Fairway Dr *RDART* DA2 .... 24 A4
The Fairways *STH/RUST* TN4 .. 190 A7 🔟
The Fairway *GVW* DA11 .... 27 H5
  ROCH ME1 .... 67 H5
  SIT ME10 .... 93 K5
Falcon CI *DART* DA1 .... 23 J4
Falcon Ms *GVW* DA11 .... 27 F7 🔟
Falcons CI *BH/WHM* TN16 .... 97 H4
Falkland PI *WALD* ME5 .... 87 K5
Fallowfield *RDART* DA2 .... 43 G1
  SIT ME10 .... 94 B4
  WALD ME5 .... 68 C6
Fallowfield CI *MAID/BEAR* ME14 ..134 A2 🔟
Falmouth PI *STPH/PW* TN12 .. 172 E7
Fanconi Rd *WALD* ME5 .... 88 C3

Fane Wy *RHAM* ME8 .... 90 A2
Fanns Ri *PUR* RM19 .... 12 E4
Fant La *SIT* ME9 .... 73 J2
Fant La *MAIDW* ME16 .... 132 B4
Faraday Ride *TONN* TN10 .... 148 D7
Faraday Rd *MAID/BEAR* ME14 .... 111 J7
Faraday Wy *STMC/STPC* BR5 .... 56 C1
Farleigh Court Rd *WARL* CR6 .... 96 A2
Farleigh Hl *MAID/SHEP* ME15 .... 6 B6
Farleigh La *MAIDW* ME16 .... 132 A3
Farley Cl *WALD* ME5 .... 88 E4
Farleycroft *BH/WHM* TN16 .... 120 B5
Farley La *BH/WHM* TN16 .... 120 B6
Farley Nursery *BH/WHM* TN16 .... 120 C6
Farley Pk *OXTED* RH8 .... 140 B1
Farley Rd *GVE* DA12 .... 28 C6
Farlow Cl *GVW* DA11 .... 45 G1
Farm Av *SWLY* BR8 .... 39 K8
Farmcombe Cl *RTW* TN1 .... 11 D5 **3**
Farmcombe La *RTW* TN1 .... 11 D5
Farmcombe Rd *RTW* TN1 .... 11 D5
Farm Crs *SIT* ME10 .... 94 B4
Farmcroft *GVW* DA11 .... 27 H8
Farmdale Rd *ROCH* ME1 .... 66 E3 **3**
Farmdale Av *ROCH* ME1 .... 66 E4
Farmer Cl *RMAID* ME17 .... 155 J8
Farm Ground Cl *TON* TN9 .... 170 E6
Farm Holt *HART* DA3 .... 62 A5
Farm La *RTON* TN11 .... 170 A2
Farm Pl *DART* DA1 .... 22 D3
Farm Rd *RSEV* TN14 .... 102 A7
Farm Rd *WALD* ME5 .... 87 K3
Farmstead Dr *EDEN* TN8 .... 164 D3
Farnaby Dr *SEV* TN13 .... 8 B5
Farnborough Cl *MAIDW* ME16 .... 132 C4 **3**
Farnborough Hl *ORP* BR6 .... 75 J1
Farnborough Wy *ORP* BR6 .... 75 K2
Farne Cl *MAID/SHEP* ME15 .... 133 G8
Farnham Beeches *RRTW* TN3 .... 205 K2
Farnham Cl *RHAM* ME8 .... 70 C8
Farnham La *RRTW* TN3 .... 205 K3
Farningham Cl *MAID/BEAR* ME14 .... 7 F1
Farningham Hill Rd *SWLY* BR8 .... 59 F2
Farnol Rd *DART* DA1 .... 23 K4 **3**
Farraday Cl *ROCH* ME1 .... 67 J6
Farrant Cl *ORP* BR6 .... 76 B3 **3**
Farrier Cl *MAID/BEAR* ME14 .... 133 K1
Farriers Cl *GVE* DA12 .... 28 C7 **3**
Farriers Ct *RHAM* ME8 .... 71 F6
Farrington Av *STMC/STPC* BR5 .... 38 C3
Fartherwell Av *E/WMAL* ME19 .... 107 J6
Fartherwell Rd *E/WMAL* ME19 .... 107 H7
Farthingfield *BGR/WK* TN15 .... 105 G3 **3**
Farthing St *ORP* BR6 .... 74 E3
Farwell Rd *SCUP* DA14 .... 38 C2
Fauchon's Cl *MAID/BEAR* ME14 .... 134 B3
Fauchon's La *MAID/BEAR* ME14 .... 134 B3
Faversham Rd *RMAID* ME17 .... 138 E7
Fawkes Av *DART* DA1 .... 23 J8
Fawkham Av *HART* DA3 .... 44 D8 **3**
Fawkham Green Rd *HART* DA3 .... 61 G7
Fawkham Rd *BGR/WK* TN15 .... 60 E8
Fawkham Rd *HART* DA3 .... 61 J1
Fawley Cl *MAID/BEAR* ME14 .... 110 E7 **3**
Featherbed La *RSIT* ME9 .... 73 K4
Featherby Rd *GILL* ME7 .... 69 H1
Featherby Rd *RHAM* ME8 .... 69 H3
Felderland Cl *RMAID* ME17 .... 156 A1 **3**
Felderland Dr *RMAID* ME17 .... 156 A1 **3**
Felderland Rd *RMAID* ME17 .... 156 A1 **3**
Feldspar Cl *WALD* ME5 .... 88 A5 **3**
Fell Md *STPH/PW* TN12 .... 151 H8
Fellowes Wy *RTON* TN11 .... 169 J1
Felstead Rd *ORP* BR6 .... 56 B6
Felton Lea *SCUP* DA14 .... 38 A3
Fen Meadow *BGR/WK* TN15 .... 104 C6
Fennel Cl *MAIDW* ME16 .... 132 B3
Fennel Cl *ROCH* ME1 .... 2 B5
Fen Pond Rd *BGR/WK* TN15 .... 104 D7
Fens Wy *SWLY* BR8 .... 40 D4
Ferbies *RRTW* TN3 .... 188 E7 **3**
Ferguson Av *GVE* DA12 .... 45 K2
Fernbank Cl *WALD* ME5 .... 87 K5
Ferndale *RTWE/PEM* TN2 .... 11 F2
Ferndale Cl *RTWE/PEM* TN2 .... 11 E3 **3**
Ferndale *RTWE/PEM* TN2 .... 11 E5 **3**
Ferndale *GILL* ME7 .... 5 E3
Ferndale *GVE* DA12 .... 27 J8
Ferndale Wy *ORP* BR6 .... 75 J1
Ferndell Av *BXLY* DA5 .... 40 A1
Ferndene *HART* DA3 .... 44 E8
Fern Down *MEO* DA13 .... 83 J6
Ferndown Cl *GILL* ME7 .... 89 H1
Fernheath Wy *RDART* DA2 .... 40 A3
Fernhill *MAIDW* ME16 .... 132 A4
Fernholt *TONN* TN10 .... 148 C7
Fernhurst Crs *STH/RUST* TN4 .... 190 A4
Fernleigh Ri *DIT/AY* ME20 .... 109 F4
Fernside La *SEV* TN13 .... 124 A8
The Ferns *BGR/WK* TN15 .... 105 J7
The Ferns *DIT/AY* ME20 .... 109 F3
The Ferns *RTW* TN1 .... 11 D3 **2**

Ferrier Cl *RHAM* ME8 .... 90 B2
Ferry La *ROCH* ME1 .... 86 B2
Ferry Rd *RSIT* ME9 .... 73 K2
Ferry Rd *STRD* ME2 .... 86 A2 **3**
Ferry Rd *TIL* RM18 .... 27 H1
Festival Av *HART* DA3 .... 44 E8
Ffinch Cl *DIT/AY* ME20 .... 109 H6
Fiddlers Cl *GRH* DA9 .... 25 G3
Field Cl *MAID* ME5 .... 67 K8
Field Ct *OXTED* RH8 .... 118 C7
Field Dr *EDEN* TN8 .... 164 D3
Fielding Dr *DIT/AY* ME20 .... 108 E3
The Fieldings *SIT* ME10 .... 93 K4
Field Mill Rd *HDCN* ME27 .... 183 C5
Field Rd *BGR/WK* TN15 .... 83 F1
Field Rd *MEO* DA13 .... 63 G8
Field Rd *SOCK/AV* RM15 .... 13 G1
Fields La *WBY/YAL* ME18 .... 130 C7
Fieldways *HAWK* TN18 .... 235 G5
Fieldworks Rd *CHAT* ME4 .... 4 A1
Fiennes Wy *SEV* TN13 .... 9 E6
Filborough Wy *GVE* DA12 .... 28 E7
Filey Cl *BH/WHM* TN16 .... 97 F6
Filmer La *RSEV* TN14 .... 102 C8
Filston La *RSEV* TN14 .... 78 B8
The Finches *SIT* ME10 .... 93 H6
Finchley Cl *DART* DA1 .... 23 K5
Findlay Cl *RHAM* ME8 .... 90 A1
Finglesham Cl *STMC/STPC* BR5 .... 56 E5 **3**
Finglesham Ct *MAID/SHEP* ME15 .... 133 J6
Fintonagh Dr *MAID/BEAR* ME14 .... 111 H7
Finucane Dr *STMC/STPC* BR5 .... 56 D4
Finwell Rd *RHAM* ME8 .... 70 D4
Fircroft Wy *EDEN* TN8 .... 164 C3
Firecrest Hl *HART* DA3 .... 44 C8 **3**
Firethorn Cl *GILL* ME7 .... 5 E2 **3**
Firmingers Rd *ORP* BR6 .... 77 J1
Firmin Rd *DART* DA1 .... 23 F4
Firs Cl *DIT/AY* ME20 .... 109 H3
First Av *CHAT* ME4 .... 4 C6
First Av *GILL* ME7 .... 5 E6
First Av *GVW* DA11 .... 27 F7
First La *MAID/SHEP* ME15 .... 135 G4
First St *RRTW* TN3 .... 205 J3
Fir Tree Cl *ORP* BR6 .... 76 A1
Fir Tree Cl *RTON* TN11 .... 169 J1 **3**
Fir Tree Cl *STPH/PW* TN12 .... 198 B3
Fir Tree Gv *GILL* ME7 .... 89 J3
Fir Tree Gv *WALD* ME5 .... 88 E5
Fir Tree Rd *STH/RUST* TN4 .... 10 B5
Fishermen's Hl *GVW* DA11 .... 26 C3 **3**
Fisher Rd *WALD* ME5 .... 68 C7
Fishers Cl *STPH/PW* TN12 .... 198 B1
Fishers Rd *STPH/PW* TN12 .... 198 B1
Fisher St *MAID/BEAR* ME14 .... 7 D1
Fishponds Rd *HAYES* BR2 .... 74 C1
Fitzwilliam Rd *MAID/BEAR* ME14 .... 134 B1
Fiveash Rd *GVW* DA11 .... 27 G6
Five Bells La *ROCH* ME1 .... 3 D4 **3**
Five Fields La *EDEN* TN8 .... 165 J2
Five Oak Green Rd *RTON* TN11 .... 171 J8
Five Oak La *STPH/PW* TN12 .... 197 G5
Five Wents *SWLY* BR8 .... 40 D7
Flack Gdns *HOO/HM* ME3 .... 17 J2
Flamborough Cl *BH/WHM* TN16 .... 97 F6
Flamingo Cl *MAID/SHEP* ME5 .... 68 B7 **3**
Flaxman Dr *MAIDW* ME16 .... 110 C8
Flaxmans Ct *SIT* ME10 .... 4 A2 **3**
Flaxmore Pl *STH/RUST* TN4 .... 190 A4 **3**
Fleet Av *RDART* DA2 .... 24 B7
Fleet Rd *GVW* DA11 .... 44 D1
Fleet Rd *RDART* DA2 .... 24 B7
Fleet Rd *ROCH* ME1 .... 67 J5
Fleming Wy *TONN* TN10 .... 148 E7
Fletcher Rd *STPH/PW* TN12 .... 198 A3
Flimwell Cl *WADH* TN5 .... 233 H2
Flint Cl *ORP* BR6 .... 76 A2 **3**
Flint Down Cl *STMC/STPC* BR5 .... 38 B6 **3**
Flint Gn *WALD* ME5 .... 88 D4
Flint La *RMAID* ME17 .... 138 D6
The Floats *SEV* TN13 .... 101 G8
Flood Hatch *MAID/SHEP* ME15 .... 6 A5 **3**
Florance La *RRTW* TN3 .... 204 E8
Florence Rd *MAIDW* ME16 .... 6 B4
Florence St *STRD* ME2 .... 49 G6 **3**
Florin Dr *ROCH* ME1 .... 2 B4
Flowerhill Wy *MEO* DA13 .... 45 F5
Flowerhill Wy *MEO* DA13 .... 45 F5
Flume End *MAIDW* ME16 .... 6 A5 **3**
The Flyers Wy *BH/WHM* TN16 .... 120 B5
Foalhurst Cl *TONN* TN10 .... 170 E2
Foley Rd *BH/WHM* TN16 .... 97 H5
Foley St *MAID/BEAR* ME14 .... 7 D2
Fontwell Cl *MAID/SHEP* ME15 .... 134 B8 **3**
Foord Cl *RDART* DA2 .... 24 D8
Foord Rd *RMAID* ME17 .... 160 D1
Foord St *ROCH* ME1 .... 2 C4
Footbury Hill Rd *ORP* BR6 .... 56 B5
Foots Cray High St *SCUP* DA14 .... 38 D4
Force Green La *BH/WHM* TN16 .... 120 D3
Fordcombe Cl *MAID/SHEP* ME15 .... 134 B7 **3**
Fordcombe Rd *RRTW* TN3 .... 204 E1

Rton TN11 .... 187 J3
Fordcroft Rd *STMC/STPC* BR5 .... 56 C2
Fordingbridge Cl *MAIDW* ME16 .... 132 B1 **3**
Ford La *BGR/WK* TN15 .... 106 B4
Ford Rd *GVW* DA11 .... 26 C4 **3**
Fordwich Cl *MAIDW* ME16 .... 110 B7
Fordwich Rd 56 A4
Foremans Barn Rd
   MAID/SHEP ME15 .... 153 K3
Forestdale Rd *WALD* ME5 .... 88 B6
Forest Dr *WALD* ME5 .... 88 A4
Foresters Cl *WALD* ME5 .... 88 A4
Forest Gv *TONN* TN10 .... 170 C1
Forest Hl *MAID/SHEP* ME15 .... 6 C6
Forest Rd *RTWE/PEM* TN2 .... 11 E6
Forest Rd *STPH/PW* TN12 .... 173 H8
Forest Wy *E/WMAL* ME19 .... 129 J3
Forest Wy *RTWE/PEM* TN2 .... 11 E6
Forest Wy *RTWE/PEM* TN2 .... 191 K6
Forest Wy *STMC/STPC* BR5 .... 56 B2
Forge Cft *EDEN* TN8 .... 164 C5
Forgefield *BH/WHM* TN16 .... 97 H3
Forge La *BGR/WK* TN15 .... 60 B1
Forge La *EYN* DA4 .... 60 B1
Forge La *GILL* ME7 .... 5 E2
Forge La *GILL* ME7 .... 89 H5
Forge La *GVE* DA12 .... 28 C8
Forge La *GVE* DA12 .... 47 H3
Forge La *HDCN* ME27 .... 182 C5
Forge La *HDCN* TN27 .... 200 B1
Forge La *HOO/HM* ME3 .... 32 E3
Forge La *HOO/HM* ME3 .... 48 B3
Forge La *MAID/BEAR* ME14 .... 111 J3
Forge La *MAID/SHEP* ME15 .... 132 B7
Forge La *RMAID* ME17 .... 135 H7
Forge La *RMAID* ME17 .... 178 B1
Forge La *RSIT* ME9 .... 71 J3
Forge La *WBY/YAL* ME18 .... 128 C8
Forge La *WBY/YAL* ME18 .... 174 E2
Forge Meadow *RMAID* ME17 .... 137 H8
Forge Mdw *HDCN* TN27 .... 200 B1
Forge Meads *TENT* TN30 .... 247 K3
Forge Rd *SIT* ME10 .... 73 K8
Forge Wy *STH/RUST* TN4 .... 189 K5
Forge Wy *RSEV* TN14 .... 78 C6
Formby Rd *STRD* ME2 .... 65 K8
Forsham La *RMAID* ME17 .... 178 E1
Forson Cl *TENT* TN30 .... 230 B6
Forstall *RTON* TN11 .... 205 K2 **3**
Forstal La *RMAID* ME17 .... 154 D2
The Forstall *RTON* TN11 .... 168 E4
Forstal Rd *DIT/AY* ME20 .... 110 A4
Forstal Rd *HDCN* TN27 .... 182 C5
The Forstal *RTON* TN11 .... 150 A6
   RTWE/PEM TN2 .... 192 A6 **3**
Forsters *RMAID* ME17 .... 157 C2
Forsyth Cl *DIT/AY* ME20 .... 108 E5 **3**
Fort Pitt Hl *ROCH* ME1 .... 3 E4
Fort Pitt St *CHAT* ME4 .... 3 E5
Fort Rd *RSEV* TN14 .... 100 E2
Fort Rd *TIL* RM18 .... 27 J3
Fortrye Cl *GVW* DA11 .... 27 F8
Fort St *ROCH* ME1 .... 3 D4
Forward Wy *ROCH* ME1 .... 67 H8
Fosse Bank *TON* TN9 .... 170 A7
Fosse Bank Cl *TON* TN9 .... 170 A7
Fosse Rd *TON* TN9 .... 170 B4
Fosten La *HDCN* TN27 .... 217 H6
Foster St *MAID/SHEP* ME15 .... 7 D4
Fostington Wy *WALD* ME5 .... 88 A5
Foulds Cl *RHAM* ME8 .... 89 J2
Fountain La *MAIDW* ME16 .... 132 A4
Fountain Rd *STRD* ME2 .... 48 D5
Fountain Wk *SIT* ME10 .... 93 K2 **3**
Fountain Wk *GVW* DA11 .... 27 F5
Four Elms Hl *HOO/HM* ME3 .... 49 K3
Four Elms Rd *EDEN* TN8 .... 165 F2
Four Oaks Rd *STPH/PW* TN12 .... 179 C7
Fourth Av *GILL* ME7 .... 5 E4
Fourwents Rd *HOO/HM* ME3 .... 32 E8
Fowey Cl *MAID* ME5 .... 88 D1
Fowler Cl *RHAM* ME8 .... 89 K3
Fowler Cl *SCUP* DA14 .... 38 C4
Foxburrow Cl *RHAM* ME8 .... 90 A1
Foxbury Cl *ORP* BR6 .... 76 B1 **3**
Foxbury Dr *ORP* BR6 .... 76 B2
Foxbush *RTON* TN11 .... 147 G8
Fox Cl *ORP* BR6 .... 76 B1
Foxden Dr *MAID/SHEP* ME15 .... 134 B5
Foxearth Cl *BH/WHM* TN16 .... 97 J5
Foxendown La *MEO* DA13 .... 63 J3
Foxglove Crs *WALD* ME5 .... 87 K2
Foxglove Ri *MAID/BEAR* ME14 .... 110 E7
Foxgrove *SIT* ME10 .... 73 K7
Fox Hl *SIT* ME10 .... 94 E3
Foxhole La *HAWK* TN18 .... 235 K6
Foxhole La *STPH/PW* TN12 .... 192 E6
Fox La *HAYES* BR2 .... 74 A1
Fox St *GILL* ME7 .... 4 C2
Foxwood Gv *GVW* DA11 .... 27 F7
Foxwood Rd *RDART* DA2 .... 43 C1
Foxwood Wy *HART* DA3 .... 44 D7
Framley Rd *TONN* TN10 .... 171 F1

Francis Dr *WALD* ME5 .... 88 B4
Francis La *MAID/SHEP* ME15 ... 156 B1
Francis Rd *DART* DA1 .... 23 G4
RTON TN11 .... 147 H8
STMC/STPC BR5 .... 38 E8
Frankapps Cl *RSIT* ME9 .... 72 A8 🔢
Frankfield Ri *RTWE/PEM* TN2 .... 10 B6
Franklin Dr *MAID/BEAR* ME14 .. 133 K2
Franklin Rd *GILL* ME7 .... 5 D3
GVE DA12 .... 46 A3
Franks Ct *RHAM* ME8 .... 69 J5
Frank's Hollow Rd *RRTW* TN3 .. 189 C5
Franks La *EYN* DA4 .... 60 A2
Frank Woolley Rd *TONN* TN10 .. 171 F1
Frant Fld *EDEN* TN8 .... 164 D5
Frant Rd *RTWE/PEM* TN2 .... 207 F7
Frederick Rd *GILL* ME7 .... 4 C1
Frederick St *GILL* ME10 .... 93 K2
Free Heath Rd *RRTW* TN3 .... 220 E3
The Freehold *RTON* TN11 .... 149 K5
Freelands Rd *SNOD* ME6 .... 85 H6
Freeman Gdns *CHAT* ME4 .... 3 F6 🔢
Freeman Rd *GVE* DA12 .... 46 B1
Freeman Wy *MAID/SHEP* ME15 .. 134 A7
Freesia Cl *GILL* ME7 .... 5 F2
ORP BR6 .... 76 A1 🔢
Freight La *CRBK* TN17 .... 225 J3
Fremlin Cl *STH/RUST* TN4 ...... 206 A2
Fremlins Rd *MAID/BEAR* ME14 .. 134 E2
Frensham Cl *SIT* ME10 .... 94 C2
Frensham Rd *CRBK* TN17 .... 238 C5
Frensham Wk *WALD* ME5 .... 88 A5 🔢
Freshland Rd *RHAM* ME16 .... 132 B2
Freshwater Rd *WALD* ME5 .... 68 C7
Frewen Cl *RYE* TN31 .... 244 E7
Friar Rd *STMC/STPC* BR5 .... 56 B2
Friars Av *WALD* ME5 .... 88 A4
Friars Wy *RTWE/PEM* TN2 .... 11 F1
Friary Pl *STRD* ME2 .... 2 B1
Friday St *RHAM* ME17 .... 157 H2
Friezland Rd *STH/RUST* TN4 .... 206 C5
Friezley La *CRBK* TN17 .... 214 D4
Frimley Ct *SCUP* DA14 .... 38 D3
Frindsbury Hl *STRD* ME2 .... 49 H5
Frindsbury Rd *STRD* ME2 .... 49 G6
Frinstead Cl *STMC/STPC* BR5 ... 56 E1
Frinstead Rd *RHAM* ME8 .... 69 K3 🔢
Frinstead Rd *RSIT* ME9 .... 116 E5
Friston Wy *ROCH* ME1 .... 67 J6
Frithwood Cl *MAID/SHEP* ME15 .. 134 A5
Frittenden Rd *STPH/PW* TN12 .. 198 B4
STRD ME2 .... 49 J5
Frobisher Cl *SIT* ME10 .... 73 K8 🔢
Frobisher Gdns *ROCH* ME1 .... 2 C6 🔢
Frobisher Wy *GRH* DA9 .... 25 G3
GVE DA12 .... 46 B3
Froghole La *EDEN* TN8 .... 142 E3
Frog La *E/WMAL* ME19 .... 108 A6
RTW TN1 .... 10 C5
Frognal Av *SCUP* DA14 .... 38 B4
Frognal Cl *RSIT* ME9 .... 95 J4
Frognal Gdns *RSIT* ME9 .... 95 J4
Frognal La *SCUP* DA14 .... 38 B3
Frognal Pl *SCUP* DA14 .... 38 B3
Frogs Hole La *CRBK* TN17 ...... 228 B4
Frog's La *CRBK* TN17 .... 238 D5
Frost Crs *WALD* ME5 .... 68 B7
Froyle Cl *MAIDW* ME16 .... 110 C8
Fruiterer's Cl *RSIT* ME9 .... 94 B7
Fry Cl *HOO/HM* ME3 .... 21 F8 🔢
Frythe Cl *CRBK* TN17 .... 225 K2
Frythe Crs *CRBK* TN17 .... 225 K2
Frythe Wk *CRBK* TN17 .... 225 K2
Frythe Wy *CRBK* TN17 .... 225 K2
Fuggles Cl *STPH/PW* TN12 ...... 173 G8
Fuggles Ct *CRBK* TN17 .... 227 F8
Fulbert Dr *MAID/BEAR* ME14... 134 B1
Fuller Cl *ORP* BR6 .... 76 A1
Fullers Cl *MAID/BEAR* ME14 .... 134 C2
Fullers Hl *BH/WHM* TN16 .... 120 D5
Fullers La *RYE* TN31 .... 244 E8
Fulmar Rd *STRD* ME2 .... 66 C1
Fulston Pl *SIT* ME10 .... 94 A5
Fulwich Rd *DART* DA1 .... 23 H4
Furfield Cl *MAID/SHEP* ME15 ... 156 A1
Furnace Av *RRTW* TN3 .... 221 H3
Furnace La *RRTW* TN3 .... 221 F2
STPH/PW TN12 .... 194 C5
Furner Cl *DART* DA1 .... 22 C2
Furrell's Rd *ROCH* ME1 .... 3 D3 🔢
Furzefield Av *RRTW* TN3 .... 188 E6
Furzehill Sq *STMC/STPC* BR5 ... 56 C1 🔢

G

Gabion Av *PUR* RM19 .... 13 H4
Gable Cl *DART* DA1 .... 22 D4
The Gables *HART* DA3 .... 44 D7
Gabriel Gdns *GVE* DA12 .... 46 B3
Gabriel's Hl *MAID/SHEP* ME15 .. 7 D3 🔢
Gabriel Spring Rd *EYN* DA4 ...... 60 C6

Gabriel Spring Rd (East) *EYN* DA4 .... 60 D6
Gadby Rd *SIT* ME10 .... 93 H1
Gadsby La *RASHW* TN26 .... 219 K4
Gainsborough Av *DART* DA1 ..... 23 F4
Gainsborough Cl *RHAM* ME8 ..... 70 A8
SIT ME10 .... 93 G1 🔢
Gainsborough Dr *GVW* DA11 .... 44 E1
MAIDW ME16 .... 132 B2 🔢
Gainsborough Gdns *TONN* TN10 .. 170 E1 🔢
Galahad Av *STRD* ME2 .... 48 D8
Galena Cl *WALD* ME5 .... 88 B5 🔢
Gallants La *MAID/SHEP* ME15 .. 131 K8
Galleon Bvd *GRH* DA9 .... 24 C3
Galleon Cl *ROCH* ME1 .... 67 H6
Galley Hill Rd *SWCM* DA10 ...... 26 A4
The Gallops *MEO* DA13 .... 83 G6
Gamma Rd *HOO/HM* ME3 .... 34 A7
Gandy's La *RMAID* ME17 .... 155 J4
Garden Cl *MAID/SHEP* ME15 ... 134 A7
Gardenia Cl *STRD* ME2 .... 49 G2
Garden Pl *RDART* DA2 .... 41 G1
Garden Rd *RTW* TN1 .... 11 D3 🔢
SEV TN13 .... 9 F1
TON TN9 .... 170 D4
Garden Rw *GVW* DA11 .... 45 G1 🔢
Garden St *GILL* ME7 .... 4 A2
RTW TN1 .... 11 D3 🔢
Garden Wy *WBY/YAL* ME18 ... 129 H4
Gardiner Cl *STMC/STPC* BR5 .... 38 D7
Gardiner St *GILL* ME7 .... 4 C2
Gardyne Ms *TON* TN9 .... 170 B6 🔢
Garfield Rd *GILL* ME7 .... 5 D2
Garlands *RTON* TN11 .... 147 H6
Garlinge Rd *STH/RUST* TN4 .... 190 A5
Garner Dr *E/WMAL* ME19 .... 108 E5
Garrick St *GVW* DA11 .... 27 J5 🔢
Garrington Cl *MAID/BEAR* ME14 .. 7 F1
Garrolds Cl *SWLY* BR8 .... 40 A7
Garrow *HART* DA3 .... 44 C8
Garth Rd *SEV* TN13 .... 124 A7
Garwock Dr *SEV* TN13 .... 9 F3
Gascoyne Dr *DART* DA1 .... 22 C2
Gasson Rd *SWCM* DA10 .... 25 K5
Gassons Rd *SNOD* ME6 .... 85 H6 🔢
Gatcombe Cl *MAIDW* ME16 .... 132 B1
WALD ME5 .... 88 B1
Gate Farm Rd *RRTW* TN3 ...... 189 G2
Gatefield Cottages *CRBK* TN17 .. 238 D2
Gatland La *MAIDW* ME16 .... 132 B4
Gattons Wy *SCUP* DA14 .... 39 G2
Gatwick Rd *GVE* DA12 .... 27 J8
Gault Cl *MAID/SHEP* ME15 ..... 134 C4
Gayhurst Cl *RHAM* ME8 .... 70 A8
Gayhurst Dr *SIT* ME10 .... 93 H1
Gaze Hill Av *SIT* ME10 .... 94 B3
Gazelle Gld *GVE* DA12 .... 46 C3
Gean Cl *WALD* ME5 .... 88 B5
Gedge's Hl *STPH/PW* TN12 .... 193 H4
Genesta Cl *SIT* ME10 .... 73 K7
Genesta Gld *GVE* DA12 .... 46 D3
Geneva Av *RHAM* ME8 .... 69 H4
Gentian Cl *MAID/BEAR* ME14 .. 134 A1
George La *RMAID* ME17 .... 135 J7
ROCH ME1 .... 2 C2 🔢
Georges Cl *STMC/STPC* BR5 .... 38 D7
George's Rd *BH/WHM* TN16 ..... 97 H7
George St *MAID/SHEP* ME15 ..... 7 D4
MAID/SHEP ME15 .... 154 A8
SIT ME10 .... 94 C3 🔢
STPH/PW ME7 .... 178 A8
TON TN9 .... 170 B6
George Summers Cl *STRD* ME2 .. 49 K6
Georgian Dr *RMAID* ME17 ...... 154 D3
Georgian Wy *RHAM* ME8 .... 89 K2
Gerald Av *CHAT* ME4 .... 3 F6
Gerald Rd *GVE* DA12 .... 28 B6
Gerdview Dr *RDART* DA2 .... 41 F2
Gerrard Av *ROCH* ME1 .... 67 J6
Gerrards Dr *SIT* ME10 .... 94 A4
Ghyll Side Rd *RYE* TN31 .... 244 E7
Gibbet La *STPH/PW* TN12........ 194 D8
Gibbetts *RRTW* TN3 .... 205 J3
Gibbons Rd *SIT* ME10 .... 93 C1
Gibbs Brook La *OXTED* RH8 .... 140 B7
Gibbs Hl *HDCN* TN27 .... 200 C1 🔢
WBY/YAL ME18 .... 151 K1
Gibraltar Av *GILL* ME7 .... 4 A1
Gibraltar Hl *CHAT* ME4 .... 3 F4
Gibraltar La *MAID/BEAR* ME14 .. 110 K6
Gibson Cl *GVW* DA11 .... 45 G1
Gibson Dr *E/WMAL* ME19 .... 129 H2
Gibson St *SIT* ME10 .... 93 K2
Giddyhorn La *MAIDW* ME16 .... 132 C2
Gifford Cl *GILL* ME7 .... 69 K2
Giggs Hl *STMC/STPC* BR5 .... 38 D7
Gighill Rd *DIT/AY* ME20 .... 108 D3
Gilbert Cl *GILL* ME7 .... 89 H1
SWCM DA10 .... 25 J5
Gildenhill Rd *SWLY* BR8 .... 41 F5
Gill Av *STRD* ME2 .... 49 J3
Gill Crs *GVW* DA11 .... 45 G1
Gilletts La *E/WMAL* ME19 ...... 108 E8
Gillies Rd *BGR/WK* TN15 .... 80 D1
Gillingham Gn *GILL* ME7 .... 5 E2
Gillingham Rd *GILL* ME7 .... 5 D3

Gillmans Rd *STMC/STPC* BR5 ... 56 C5
Gill's Rd *EYN* DA4 .... 42 D6
The Gill *RTWE/PEM* TN2 .... 192 A6
Gilroy Wy *STMC/STPC* BR5 ...... 56 C4
Gimble Wy *RTWE/PEM* TN2 ... 191 K6
Gingerbread La *HAWK* TN18 ... 233 K3
Ginsbury Cl *STRD* ME2 .... 3 D2
Gipps Cross La *RRTW* TN3 ...... 205 J3 🔢
The Glades *GVE* DA12 .... 46 A4
The Glade *SEV* TN13 .... 9 D2
WALD ME5 .... 88 B4
Gladstone Dr *SIT* ME10 .... 94 D3
Gladstone Rd *CHAT* ME4 .... 3 E6
DART DA1 .... 23 J7
MAID/BEAR ME14 .... 7 D1
ORP BR6 .... 75 H1
STH/RUST TN4 .... 206 A2 🔢
TON TN9 .... 170 B5
Gladwyn Cl *RHAM* ME8 .... 90 A2 🔢
Glamford Rd *STRD* ME2 .... 66 C1
Glanvis Cl *WALD* ME5 .... 88 B1
Glanville Rd *GILL* ME7 .... 5 D3 🔢
STRD ME2 .... 2 A1
Glassenbury Rd *CRBK* TN17 ... 224 E2
Glastonbury Rd *STMC/STPC* BR5 .. 56 D5
Gleaming Wood Dr
MAID/BEAR ME14 .... 88 E6
Gleaners Cl *MAID/BEAR* ME14 .. 134 A2
Glebe Cl *HDCN* TN27 .... 202 B3
The Glebefield *SEV* TN13 .... 8 B2
Glebe Gdns *RMAID* ME17 .... 160 E1
Glebeland *HDCN* TN27 .... 183 F2
Glebelands *DART* DA1 .... 22 C3
HDCN TN27 .... 217 J5
RRTW TN3 .... 189 G3
RTON TN11 .... 187 J3
Glebe La *MAIDW* ME16 .... 131 K5
SEV TN13 .... 9 D5
SIT ME10 .... 94 C4
Glebe Meadow *WBY/YAL* ME18... 130 B7
Glebe Pl *EYN* DA4 .... 60 B3
Glebe Rd *GILL* ME7 .... 5 E5
GVW DA11 .... 27 G7
RSEV TN14 .... 145 K3
The Glebe *RTWE/PEM* TN2 .... 191 K6
STH/RUST TN4 .... 189 H3
STRD ME2 .... 66 B4
Gleeson Dr *ORP* BR6 .... 76 A1
Glenbrook Gv *SIT* ME10 .... 73 K7
Glencoe Rd *CHAT* ME4 .... 4 A1
Glendale *SWLY* BR8 .... 58 C2
Glendale Rd *GVW* DA11 .... 45 F2
Glendon Crs *ORP* BR6 .... 56 B3
Gleneagles Dr *MAID/SHEP* ME15 .. 6 C1
Glenmore Pk *RTWE/PEM* TN2 .. 206 E6
Glenrosa Gdns *GVE* DA12 .... 46 C3
Glentrammon Av *ORP* BR6 .... 76 A2
Glentrammon Cl *ORP* BR6 .... 76 A2
Glentrammon Gdns *ORP* BR6 .... 76 A2
Glentrammon Rd *ORP* BR6 .... 76 A2
Glen Vw *GVE* DA12 .... 27 K7
Glenwood Cl *GILL* ME7 .... 69 G7
MAIDW ME16 .... 132 C1
TENT TN30 .... 230 B3 🔢
WALD ME5 .... 68 D5
Glistening Gld *RHAM* ME8 .... 70 B8
Gload Crs *STMC/STPC* BR5 ...... 56 E6
Globe La *CHAT* ME4 .... 3 F3
Gloucester Cl *RHAM* ME8 .... 70 D6 🔢
Gloucester Rd *DART* DA1 .... 22 E5
GVE DA12 .... 45 K2
MAID/SHEP ME15 .... 133 K6
WADH TN5 .... 220 B8
Gloxinia Rd *MEO* DA13 .... 44 C4
Glyn Davies Cl *SEV* TN13 ...... 101 G7
Glyn Dr *SCUP* DA14 .... 38 C2
Goad Av *WALD* ME5 .... 88 C3
Goatsfield Rd *BH/WHM* TN16 ... 97 G7
Goddards Cl *CRBK* TN17 .... 225 H2
Godden Cl *RYE* TN31 .... 244 E6
Godden Rd *SNOD* ME6 .... 85 J6
Goddings Dr *ROCH* ME1 .... 2 A5
Goddington Cha *ORP* BR6 .... 56 C8
Goddington La *ORP* BR6 .... 56 D7
RMAID ME17 .... 137 F8
Goddington Rd *STRD* ME2 .... 49 G6
Godfrey Evans Cl *TONN* TN10 .. 171 F1
Godstone Rd *OXTED* RH8 .... 140 A1
Golden Sq *TENT* TN30 .... 230 B6
Golden Wood Cl *WALD* ME5 ..... 88 E6
Goldfinch Cl *DIT/AY* ME20 ...... 108 E4
ORP BR6 .... 76 B1
STPH/PW TN12 .... 193 J1 🔢
Golding Cl *DIT/AY* ME20 .... 109 C5
Golding Gdns *STPH/PW* TN12 .. 151 J8
Golding Rd *SEV* TN13 .... 9 E1
Goldings *STPH/PW* TN12 .... 193 G1 🔢
Goldings Cl *E/WMAL* ME19....... 129 J4
The Goldings *RHAM* ME8 .... 69 K6
Goldsel Rd *SWLY* BR8 .... 58 B1
Goldsmid Rd *TON* TN9 .... 170 C7
Goldsmith Ct *TENT* TN30 .... 230 B5 🔢
Goldsmith Rd *RHAM* ME8 .... 90 D1
Goldstone Wk *WALD* ME5 .... 88 B5 🔢
Gold St *GVE* DA12 .... 64 B2

Goldsworth Dr *STRD* ME2 .... 49 F5 🔲
Goldthorne Cl *MAID/BEAR* ME14 ...... 7 F3 🔲
Golf Links Av *GVW* DA11.................... 45 J3
Colford Rd *CRBK* TN17.................... 226 B1
Gooch Cl *MAIDW* ME16.................... 110 D6
Goodall Rd *RHAM* ME8.................... 90 B1
Goodbury Rd *RORP* BR6.................... 80 A8
Goodley Stock Rd *EDEN* TN8............ 120 B8
Goodmead Rd *ORP* BR6.................... 56 B4
Goodnestone Rd *SIT* ME10.................... 94 C3
Goods Hl *TENT* TN30.................... 229 H6
Goods Station Rd *RTW* TN1.................... 11 D3
Goodwin Dr *MAID/BEAR* ME14 ...... 111 H6
Goodwin Rd *HOO/HM* ME3.................... 31 G7
The Goodwins *RTWE/PEM* TN2 .... 10 B6 🔲
Goodwood Cl *HOO/HM* ME3.................... 33 F3
  MAID/SHEP ME15.................... 134 B8 🔲
Goodwood Crs *GVE* DA12.................... 45 K4
Goodworth Rd *BGR/WK* TN15.................... 105 F3
Goose Cl *WALD* ME5.................... 68 B7 🔲
Goose Green Cl *STMC/STPC* BR5...... 38 B7
Gooseneck La *HDCN* TN27.................... 200 A1
Gordon Cl *SIT* ME10.................... 94 D2 🔲
Gordon Pl *CVE* DA12.................... 27 K5 🔲
Gordon Rd *CHAT* ME4.................... 4 A6
  DART DA1.................... 23 G6
  GILL ME7.................... 4 A1 🔲
  GVW DA11.................... 27 F6
  HOO/HM ME3.................... 50 E1
  SEV TN13.................... 9 D4
  STH/RUST TN4.................... 190 C1
  STRD ME2.................... 49 F6
Gordons Wy *OXTED* RH8.................... 118 B7
Gordon Ter *ROCH* ME1.................... 2 C4
Gore Court Rd *MAID/SHEP* ME15 .... 156 F5
  SIT ME10.................... 93 K4
Gore Green Rd *HOO/HM* ME3.................... 30 C7
Gore La *CRBK* TN17.................... 212 D3
Gore Rd *RDART* DA2.................... 24 C8
  RSIT ME9.................... 115 K1
Gorham Cl *SNOD* ME6.................... 85 J7
Gorham Dr *MAID/SHEP* ME15 .... 134 C5
  TON TN9.................... 170 D6
Gorringe Av *EYN* DA4.................... 42 C7
Gorse Av *WALD* ME5.................... 67 J8
Gorse Crs *DIT/AY* ME20.................... 109 H6
Gorse Rd *RTWE/PEM* TN2.................... 207 K1
  SIT ME10.................... 94 D1
  STMC/STPC BR5.................... 57 H6
  STRD ME2.................... 48 E6
Gorse Wy *HART* DA3.................... 62 A2
Gorse Wood Rd *HART* DA3.................... 62 A1
Goss Hl *SWLY* BR8.................... 41 F4
Gothic Cl *DART* DA1.................... 41 G1
Goudhurst Cl *MAIDW* ME16.................... 6 B3 🔲
Goudhurst Rd *CRBK* TN17.................... 214 E6
  RHAM ME8.................... 69 J3
  STPH/PW TN12.................... 196 B3
  STPH/PW TN12.................... 212 A1
Gouge Av *GVW* DA11.................... 27 F7
Gould Rd *WALD* ME5.................... 88 C3
Gover Hl *WBY/YAL* ME18.................... 128 A8
Gover Vw *WBY/YAL* ME18.................... 128 A7
Grace Av *MAIDW* ME16.................... 6 A1
Gracious La *SEV* TN13.................... 145 J1
Gracious Lane End *RSEV* TN14 ...... 145 H1
Grafton Av *ROCH* ME1.................... 67 K6
Grafton Rd *SIT* ME10.................... 94 A2
Grainey Fld *RSIT* ME9.................... 91 H2
Grain Rd *HOO/HM* ME3.................... 34 E3
  RHAM ME8.................... 89 K3
Grampian Cl *ORP* BR6.................... 56 A3
  RTWE/PEM TN2.................... 11 F2
Grampian Wy *MAID/SHEP* ME15.... 134 C5
Granada St *MAID/SHEP* ME15 ...... 7 D3 🔲
Granary *STPH/PW* TN12.................... 173 K8
Granary Cl *MAID/BEAR* ME14......... 134 A1
  RHAM ME8.................... 70 C5
Granby Rd *GVW* DA11.................... 26 E5
Grandshore La *CRBK* TN17.................... 215 H1
Grandsire Gdns *HOO/HM* ME3.................... 33 F8
Grand View Av *BH/WHM* TN16 ...... 97 G4
Grange Cl *BFN/LL* DA15.................... 38 B1
  RTWE/PEM TN16.................... 120 D5 🔲
  E/WMAL ME19.................... 108 A4
  EDEN TN8.................... 164 C5 🔲
Grange Crs *RDART* DA2.................... 24 A5
  TENT TN30.................... 230 A3
Grange Dr *ORP* BR6.................... 76 D4
Grange Gdns *STH/RUST* TN4.................... 206 C2
Grange Hl *BGR/WK* TN15.................... 126 E6
  WALD ME5.................... 4 B5
Grange La *HART* DA3.................... 62 C4
  MAID/BEAR ME14.................... 111 H5
Grange Rd *BGR/WK* TN15.................... 105 J7
  GILL ME7.................... 5 E2
  GVW DA11.................... 27 H6
  SEV TN13.................... 8 C6
  SOCK/AV RM15.................... 13 G1
  STH/RUST TN4.................... 206 C2
  STRD ME2.................... 2 B1
  TENT TN30.................... 229 K3
The Grange *BGR/WK* TN15.................... 80 E4
  E/WMAL ME19.................... 108 E2
  EYN DA4.................... 42 C6

Grange Wy *HART* DA3.................... 62 A3
  ROCH ME1.................... 2 C5
Grangeways Cl *GVW* DA11.................... 45 G2 🔲
Grant Cl *GILL* ME7.................... 69 J5
Granton Rd *SCUP* DA14.................... 38 C4
Grant Rd *HOO/HM* ME3.................... 49 H3
Grants La *OXTED* RH8.................... 141 H8
Granville Ms *SCUP* DA14.................... 38 B2
Granville Rd *BH/WHM* TN16.................... 120 C5
  GILL ME7.................... 5 E3
  GVW DA11.................... 27 G6
  MAID/BEAR ME14.................... 7 D1
  OXTED RH8.................... 118 D8
  RTW TN1.................... 11 D2
  SCUP DA14.................... 38 B2
  SEV TN13.................... 8 C3
Grapple Rd *MAID/BEAR* ME14 ...... 111 G7
Grasmere Gv *STRD* ME2.................... 49 H4
Grassington Rd *SCUP* DA14.................... 38 B2
Grasslands *RMAID* ME17.................... 157 G2
Grasmere *DIT/AY* ME20.................... 108 C5
Grassy Gld *GILL* ME7.................... 69 J8
Grassy La *SEV* TN13.................... 9 D6
Gravelly Bottom Rd *RMAID* ME17 .. 157 K4
Gravelly Ways *STPH/PW* TN12 ...... 174 A2
Gravel Pit Wy *ORP* BR6.................... 56 B6
Gravel Rd *EYN* DA4.................... 42 A5
Gravel Wk *ROCH* ME1.................... 3 D3
Graveney Cl *HOO/HM* ME3.................... 31 H7
Graveney Rd *MAID/SHEP* ME15 .... 134 B7
Gravesend Rd *BGR/WK* TN15.................... 83 F6
  CVE DA12.................... 47 J2
  HOO/HM ME3.................... 48 B4
  STRD ME2.................... 48 E6
Graylings Ct *SIT* ME10.................... 93 H4
Grayne Av *HOO/HM* ME3.................... 37 G1
Grays Farm Rd *STMC/STPC* BR5.... 38 C4
Grayshott St *SIT* ME10.................... 94 A3
Gray Rd *BH/WHM* TN16.................... 98 B8
Great Bounds Dr *STH/RUST* TN4.... 189 J3
Great Brooms Rd *STH/RUST* TN4 .. 190 B6
Great Courtlands *RRTW* TN3.................... 205 K3
Great Elms *RTON* TN11.................... 150 A5
Great Footway *RRTW* TN3.................... 205 J2
Great Lines *GILL* ME7.................... 4 B3
Greatness La *RSEV* TN14.................... 102 A3
Greatness Rd *RSEV* TN14.................... 102 A8
Great Queen St *DART* DA1.................... 23 J5
Great South Av *CHAT* ME4.................... 68 B5
Great Till Cl *RSEV* TN14.................... 101 G3
Grebe Cl *HOO/HM* ME3.................... 35 F2 🔲
Grecian Cl *RTW* TN1.................... 11 D5 🔲
Grecian St *MAID/BEAR* ME14.................... 7 F2
Greenacre Cl *SWLY* BR8.................... 58 B1 🔲
  WALD ME5.................... 88 B1 🔲
Greenacres *OXTED* RH8.................... 118 C6
Greenbank *WALD* ME5.................... 68 C6 🔲
Green Bank Cl *GILL* ME7.................... 89 H1 🔲
Greenbanks *DART* DA1.................... 23 H8
Greenborough Cl
  MAID/SHEP ME15.................... 134 A8
Green Cl *ROCH* ME1.................... 3 D6
Green Court Rd *SWLY* BR8.................... 58 A2
Green Farm Cl *ORP* BR6.................... 76 A1
Green Farm La *GVE* DA12.................... 47 H1
Greenfield *EDEN* TN8.................... 164 D5
Greenfield Cl *DIT/AY* ME20.................... 87 F3
  STH/RUST TN4.................... 206 D3 🔲
Greenfield Rd *GILL* ME7.................... 5 D2
  RDART DA2.................... 40 A3
Greenfields *MAID/SHEP* ME15...... 134 A6
Greenfields *HOO/HM* ME3.................... 49 J3 🔲
Greenfinches *GILL* ME7.................... 69 G8
  HART DA3.................... 44 C8
Greenfrith Dr *TONN* TN10.................... 148 B7
Green Gdns *ORP* BR6.................... 75 H1
Green Hedges *TENT* TN30.................... 230 B6 🔲
Green Hl *MAID/SHEP* ME15.................... 134 C5
  ORP BR6.................... 74 D7
Greenhill La *HDCN* TN27.................... 182 E7
Green Hill La *RMAID* ME17.................... 159 H6
Greenhill Rd *GVW* DA11.................... 27 G8 🔲
  RSEV TN14.................... 102 A2
Greenhithe Head *MAID/SHEP* ME15 .. 7 D4 🔲
Greenhurst La *OXTED* RH8.................... 105 H7
Greenlands *BGR/WK* TN15.................... 105 H7
Green Lands *GVE* DA12.................... 64 A2
Green La *CRBK* TN17.................... 228 A3
  E/WMAL ME19.................... 106 C1
  EDEN TN8.................... 143 H1
  HDCN TN27.................... 202 A5
  HOO/HM ME3.................... 15 G8
  HOO/HM ME3.................... 21 G8
  MEO DA13.................... 63 J4
  RMAID ME17.................... 155 J3
  RMAID ME17.................... 157 G3
  RMAID ME17.................... 159 K5
  RMAID ME17.................... 178 B1
  RSIT ME9.................... 91 J5
  RSIT ME9.................... 94 C1
  STPH/PW TN12.................... 175 J5
  STPH/PW TN12.................... 193 J1
The Green La *RTON* TN11.................... 168 D5 🔲
Greenleas *RTWE/PEM* TN2.................... 191 J8
Greenleigh Av *STMC/STPC* BR5...... 56 C1

Greenoak Ri *BH/WHM* TN16.................... 97 G5
Green Rd *STPH/PW* TN12.................... 211 K1
Green Sands *MAID/BEAR* ME14...... 134 C4
Greensand Wy *EDEN* TN8.................... 142 C2
  HDCN TN27.................... 183 F4
  MAID/SHEP ME15.................... 153 J4
  OXTED RH8.................... 118 C5
  OXTED RH8.................... 140 C2
  RMAID ME17.................... 155 J5
  RSEV TN14.................... 145 F3
  RTON TN11.................... 149 F1
  WBY/YAL ME18.................... 151 J3
Greenside *MAID/SHEP* ME15.................... 7 E4
  RASHW TN26.................... 219 K7
  SWLY BR8.................... 40 A7 🔲
Green St *GILL* ME7.................... 4 C3
Green Street Green Rd *DART* DA1 .. 23 K7
  RDART DA2.................... 42 B1
The Green *BH/WHM* TN16.................... 110 D5
  RDART DA2.................... 24 C8
  RRTW TN3.................... 205 H3
  RSIT ME9.................... 72 A3 🔲
  RTON TN11.................... 168 D5
  SCUP DA14.................... 38 B3
  SEV TN13.................... 9 F1
  STMC/STPC BR5.................... 38 C5
Greentrees Av *TONN* TN10.................... 171 F1
Greenvale Gdns *RHAM* ME8.................... 69 J4
Green View Av *RTON* TN11.................... 168 E5
Greenview Crs *RTON* TN11.................... 169 J2
Green Wk *DART* DA1.................... 22 C5
Green Wy *HART* DA3.................... 61 K2
  MAIDW ME16.................... 132 B3
  RTWE/PEM TN2.................... 190 E6
Greenway *BH/WHM* TN16.................... 97 G7
  CRBK TN17.................... 225 H2
  WALD ME5.................... 67 J8
Greenway Court Rd *RMAID* ME17 .. 136 D7
Greenway La *RMAID* ME17.................... 136 E7
Greenways *HART* DA3.................... 44 E8
  MAID/BEAR ME14.................... 134 B1
  WALD ME5.................... 94 C3
The Greenways *STPH/PW* TN12 .... 193 H1 🔲
The Greenway *OXTED* RH8.................... 140 E4
Greenwich Cl *MAIDW* ME16.................... 6 A3
  WALD ME5.................... 88 C2 🔲
Greenwood Rd *BXLY* DA5.................... 40 A2
Greenwood Wy *SEV* TN13.................... 8 B4
Greggs Wood Rd *RTWE/PEM* TN2 .. 190 E7
Gregory Cl *RHAM* ME8.................... 90 B2
Grenadier Cl *RHAM* ME8.................... 70 E4
Grenville Cl *MEO* DA13.................... 63 H7
Gresham Av *HART* DA3.................... 62 A2
Gresham Cl *OXTED* RH8.................... 118 D8
  RHAM ME8.................... 70 C5 🔲
Gresham Rd *OXTED* RH8.................... 118 D8
  RMAID ME17.................... 154 D3
Cresswell Cl *SCUP* DA14.................... 38 B1
Greybury La *EDEN* TN8.................... 184 B8
Greyfriars Cl *MAIDW* ME16.................... 6 A2
Greyhound Wy *DART* DA1.................... 22 B4
Greys Park Cl *HAYES* BR2.................... 74 B1
Greystone Pk *RSEV* TN14.................... 122 A4
Greystones *RSEV* TN14.................... 102 C4
Greystones Rd *MAID/SHEP* ME15 .. 134 C4
Grey Wethers *MAID/BEAR* ME14.... 110 C3
Gribble Bridge La *HDCN* TN27.................... 229 F1
Grice Av *BH/WHM* TN16.................... 74 A8
Grieves Rd *GVW* DA11.................... 45 C1
Griffin Wk *GRH* DA9.................... 24 E4
Grigg La *HDCN* TN27.................... 181 H7
Griggs Wy *BGR/WK* TN15.................... 105 C7
Grizedale Cl *ROCH* ME1.................... 67 J6
Gromenfield *RRTW* TN3.................... 205 F7 🔲
Groombridge Hl *RRTW* TN3.................... 205 F6
Groombridge Rd *RRTW* TN3.................... 204 D6
Groombridge Sq
  MAID/SHEP ME15.................... 134 B8 🔲
Grosvenor Av *ROCH* ME1.................... 3 E5
  STH/RUST TN4.................... 11 D2
Grosvenor Crs *DART* DA1.................... 23 C4
Grosvenor Pk *RTW* TN1.................... 11 D5
Grosvenor Rd *GILL* ME7.................... 69 G5
Grosvenor Wk *RTW* TN1.................... 10 C5 🔲
Grove Av *RTW* TN1.................... 10 C5 🔲
Grove Green La *MAID/BEAR* ME14 .. 134 A1
Grove Green Rd *MAID/BEAR* ME14 .. 134 B1
Groveherst Rd *DART* DA1.................... 23 J2
Grove Hill Gdns *RTW* TN1.................... 11 D5
Grove Hill Rd *RTW* TN1.................... 10 C4
Grovehurst La *STPH/PW* TN12 .... 212 B1
Grovehurst Rd *RSIT* ME9.................... 73 K3
  SIT ME10.................... 73 K5
Grovelands *RMAID* ME17.................... 160 E1
Grovelands Rd *STMC/STPC* BR5...... 38 B5
Grove Park Av *SIT* ME10.................... 93 F1
Grove Rd *BGR/WK* TN15.................... 124 E1
  BH/WHM TN16.................... 97 G7
  CHAT ME4.................... 4 B6
  EDEN TN8.................... 187 F5
  GILL ME7.................... 5 J5
  GVW DA11.................... 26 C4
  MAID/SHEP ME15.................... 135 J8
  RSEV TN14.................... 102 A8

STRD ME2 .... 49 G6
The Groves *SNOD* ME6 .... 85 J7
The Grove *BGR/WK* TN15 .... 80 E5
  BH/WHM TN16 .... 97 H5
  GVE DA12 .... 27 J6
  MAID/BEAR ME14 .... 134 C3
  RTWE/PEM TN2 .... 191 K6
  SCUP DA14 .... 39 F3
  SWCM DA10 .... 25 K4
  SWLY BR8 .... 40 C8 ▣
Grovewood Dr
  MAID/BEAR ME14 .... 133 K2 ▣
  MAID/BEAR ME14 .... 134 B2 ▣
Grub St *OXTED* RH8 .... 119 C8
Guardian Ct *RHAM* ME8 .... 69 K5
Guestwick *TONN* TN10 .... 171 F1
Guildables La *EDEN* TN8 .... 141 J7
  OXTED RH8 .... 141 J5
Guildford Gdns *STRD* ME2 .... 48 B8 ▣
Guildford Rd *RTW* TN1 .... 11 D4 ▣
Gullands *RMAID* ME17 .... 157 G2
Gun Back La *STPH/PW* TN12 .... 211 K1 ▣
Gundulph Rd *CHAT* ME4 .... 3 E4
Gundulph Sq *MEO1* .... 2 C2 ▣
Gunfleet Cl *GVE* DA12 .... 28 B6
Gunlands *STPH/PW* TN12 .... 194 E8
Gun La *STRD* ME2 .... 2 B1
Gunnis Cl *RHAM* ME8 .... 89 K2
Gunn Rd *SWCM* DA10 .... 25 K4
Guston Rd *MAID/BEAR* ME14 .... 7 F2
Gwynn Rd *GVW* DA11 .... 26 D8
Gybbon Ri *STPH/PW* TN12 .... 198 A3
Gybbons Rd *CRBK* TN17 .... 238 D5

H

Hackney Rd *MAIDW* ME16 .... 132 C4
Haddon Cl *STMC/STPC* BR5 .... 56 D2
Hadleigh Ct *GILL* ME7 .... 89 H3
Hadley Cl *MEO* DA13 .... 63 J6
Hadlow Pk *RTON* TN11 .... 147 H6
Hadlow Rd *MAID/BEAR* ME14 .... 7 F2
  SCUP DA14 .... 38 B2
  TON TN9 .... 170 C4
  TONN TN10 .... 170 E2
Hadlow Stair Rd *TONN* TN10 .... 171 F2
Hadlow Wy *MEO* DA13 .... 45 F5 ▣
Haffenden Cl *STPH/PW* TN12 .... 176 D8
Haffenden Rd *TENT* TN30 .... 230 A5
Haig Av *CHAT* ME4 .... 4 A1
  CHAT ME4 .... 67 J5
  GILL ME7 .... 5 E4
Haig Gdns *GVE* DA12 .... 27 K6
Haig Rd *BH/WHM* TN16 .... 97 J4
Haileybury Rd *ORP* BR6 .... 56 B8
Hailstone Cl *RTON* TN11 .... 150 A6 ▣
Haldane Gdns *GVW* DA11 .... 26 D7
Halden Cl *MAID/SHEP* ME15 .... 134 B8
Halden La *CRBK* TN17 .... 228 C5
Hale Ct *STPH/PW* TN12 .... 151 J7
Hale La *RSEV* TN14 .... 101 H4
Hale Oak Rd *EDEN* TN8 .... 167 G2
  RSEV TN14 .... 145 J5
Hale Rd *HOO/HM* ME3 .... 49 H1
Hales Cl *TENT* TN30 .... 230 B6
Hales Rd *SIT* ME10 .... 93 J5
Hale St *STPH/PW* TN12 .... 151 J5
Haleys Pl *ROCH* ME1 .... 87 F6 ▣
Half Moon La *RTON* TN11 .... 147 H8
Halfpence La *GVE* DA12 .... 46 E7
Halfpenny Cl *MAIDW* ME16 .... 132 A4
Halfway Ct *PUR* RM19 .... 12 E4
Halifax Cl *WALD* ME5 .... 68 C8
Hall Av *SOCK/AV* RM15 .... 13 C1
Hall Cl *SIT* ME10 .... 73 K8
Hall Crs *SOCK/AV* RM15 .... 13 C2
Hallford Wy *DART* DA1 .... 23 F5
Hall Hl *BGR/WK* TN15 .... 125 F2
  OXTED RH8 .... 140 B3
Hall Rd *DART* DA1 .... 23 J3
  DIT/AY ME20 .... 109 K5
  GVW DA11 .... 26 E8
  HOO/HM ME3 .... 34 C8
  ROCH ME1 .... 86 B5
  SOCK/AV RM15 .... 13 C2
  WALD ME5 .... 88 D3
Hallsfield Rd *WALD* ME5 .... 87 J3
Hall's Hole Rd *RTWE/PEM* TN2 .... 207 K3
Hallsland Wy *OXTED* RH8 .... 140 D4
Hall Ter *SOCK/AV* RM15 .... 13 H1
Hallwards *STPH/PW* TN12 .... 198 A4
Hallwood Cl *RHAM* ME8 .... 90 A1
Halstead La *RSEV* TN14 .... 100 A2
Halstow Cl *MAID/SHEP* ME15 .... 155 H1
Hambledon Ct *MAIDW* ME16 .... 132 B3 ▣
Hamble Rd *TONN* TN10 .... 170 B1
Hamelin Rd *GILL* ME7 .... 69 G6
Hamerton Rd *GVW* DA11 .... 26 C4 ▣
Hamfield Cl *OXTED* RH8 .... 118 A6
Hamilton Crs *SIT* ME10 .... 93 H3
Hamilton Rd *BFN/LL* DA15 .... 38 B2
  GILL ME7 .... 5 D1
Ham La *GILL* ME7 .... 89 F3

RMAID ME17 .... 160 B1
Hamlin Rd *SEV* TN13 .... 101 G8
Hammonds *HAWK* TN18 .... 235 C4 ▣
Hammonds Sq *SNOD* ME6 .... 85 K6
Hamond Hl *CHAT* ME4 .... 3 E4 ▣
Hampshire Cl *WALD* ME5 .... 68 D7 ▣
Hampshire Drive Rd
  MAID/SHEP ME15 .... 133 J6
Hampson Wy *MAID/BEAR* ME14 .... 134 C2
Hampstead La *WBY/YAL* ME18 .... 152 A5
Hampton Cl *MAID* ME5 .... 88 D1
Hampton Crs *GVE* DA12 .... 28 B8
Hampton Rd *MAID/BEAR* ME14 .... 7 F1
Hamptons Rd *RTON* TN11 .... 149 F1
Ham River Hl *HOO/HM* ME3 .... 31 F8
Ham Shades Cl *BFN/LL* DA15 .... 38 A1
Hamwick Gn *WALD* ME5 .... 88 C8
Hanbury Cl *WBY/YAL* ME18 .... 130 C7
Hanbury Dr *BH/WHM* TN16 .... 74 A8
Hancock Cl *DART* DA2 .... 49 G5
Handel Wk *TONN* TN10 .... 149 G8
Hanford Rd *SOCK/AV* RM15 .... 13 C1 ▣
Hang Grove Hl *ORP* BR6 .... 75 G8
Hanmer Wy *STPH/PW* TN12 .... 198 A4
Hanover Cl *SIT* ME10 .... 93 K4
Hanover Dr *RHAM* ME8 .... 89 K2
Hanover Rd *RMAID* ME17 .... 154 C3
  RTW TN1 .... 10 C3 ▣
Hanway *RHAM* ME8 .... 69 H4
Harbledown Pl *STMC/STPC* BR5 .... 56 D1 ▣
Harbourland Cl
  MAID/BEAR ME14 .... 111 H6 ▣
Harbourne La *RASHW* TN26 .... 230 E2
  TENT TN30 .... 230 D2
The Harbour *RMAID* ME17 .... 179 C1 ▣
Harcourt Gdns *RHAM* ME8 .... 90 B2
Harden Rd *GVW* DA11 .... 27 G8
Hardie Cl *E/WMAL* ME19 .... 108 D5 ▣
Hardinge Av *STH/RUST* TN4 .... 189 J3
Hardinge Cl *RHAM* ME8 .... 89 K2
Hards Town *CHAT* ME4 .... 4 A4
Hardwick Crs *DART* DA1 .... 24 A5 ▣
Hardwick Rd *RTON* TN11 .... 147 J8
Hardy Av *GVW* DA11 .... 27 F8
Hardy Cl *WALD* ME5 .... 68 C8
Hardy Gv *DART* DA1 .... 23 K3
Hardy St *MAID/BEAR* ME14 .... 7 D3
Harebell Cl *MAID/BEAR* ME14 .... 134 A1 ▣
Haredale Cl *ROCH* ME1 .... 67 J7
Harescroft *RTWE/PEM* TN2 .... 206 E7 ▣
Harfst Wy *SWLY* BR8 .... 39 K6
Hargate Cl *RTWE/PEM* TN2 .... 206 E7
Harland Wy *STH/RUST* TN4 .... 189 K3
Harlech Cl *STRD* ME2 .... 48 E5
Harman Av *GVW* DA11 .... 45 J3
Harmer Rd *SWCM* DA10 .... 26 A5
Harmer St *GVE* DA12 .... 27 J6
Harmers Wy *HDCN* TN27 .... 183 F3
Harmony St *STH/RUST* TN4 .... 206 C2
Harold Av *GILL* ME7 .... 5 E4
Harold Rd *RDART* DA2 .... 41 J2
  SIT ME10 .... 94 C2
  STRD ME2 .... 66 A3
Harp Farm Rd *MAID/BEAR* ME14 .... 88 D7
Harple La *MAID/BEAR* ME14 .... 112 B5
Harptree Dr *WALD* ME5 .... 88 A1
Harrier Dr *SIT* ME10 .... 94 B4
Harries Rd *RTWE/PEM* TN2 .... 190 D7
Harris Cl *GVW* DA11 .... 45 F1
Harrison Dr *HOO/HM* ME3 .... 33 F2
  RMAID ME17 .... 137 J8
Harrison Rd *BGR/WK* TN15 .... 105 F7
Harrisons Whf *PUR* RM19 .... 12 E5
Harrison Wy *SEV* TN13 .... 8 C1
Harrowby Gdns *GVW* DA11 .... 27 F8
Harrow Ct *RSIT* ME9 .... 91 G6
Harrow Gdns *ORP* BR6 .... 77 G1
Harrow Rd *GILL* ME7 .... 69 G8
  RSEV TN14 .... 100 A2
Harrow Wy *MAID/BEAR* ME14 .... 134 A1
Harrys Rd *RSIT* ME9 .... 95 K3
Hart Dyke Rd *STMC/STPC* BR5 .... 56 D5 ▣
  SWLY BR8 .... 40 A8
Hartfield Cl *TONN* TN10 .... 170 E1
Hartfield Pl *GVW* DA11 .... 26 E6 ▣
Hartfield Rd *EDEN* TN8 .... 185 D2
Hartington Cl *ORP* BR6 .... 75 H1
Hartington St *CHAT* ME4 .... 4 A5
Hartlake Rd *RTON* TN11 .... 171 J6
Hartley Bottom Rd *HART* DA3 .... 62 C5
Hartley Cl *MAID/SHEP* ME15 .... 134 B8
Hartley Court Gdns *CRBK* TN17 .... 225 G3 ▣
Hartley Hl *HART* DA3 .... 62 B5
Hartley Rd *BH/WHM* TN16 .... 120 D5
  CRBK TN17 .... 225 G4
  HART DA3 .... 43 K7
Hartlip Hl *RSIT* ME9 .... 71 H7
Hartnokes *HAWK* TN18 .... 235 G4
Hartnup St *MAIDW* ME16 .... 132 C4
Hartpiece Cl *RHAM* ME8 .... 70 C4 ▣
Hart Shaw *HART* DA3 .... 44 C7
Hartshill Rd *GVW* DA11 .... 27 G8
Hartsland Rd *SEV* TN13 .... 9 E2
Hart St *MAIDW* ME16 .... 6 C4
Harty Av *RHAM* ME8 .... 89 J3

Harvel Av *STRD* ME2 .... 48 D7
Harvel Cl *CHST* BR7 .... 38 B8
Harvel Rd *MEO* DA13 .... 83 J3
Harvel Rd *MEO* DA13 .... 83 F7
Harvel St *MEO* DA13 .... 83 K3
Harvesters Cl *RHAM* ME8 .... 70 B8
Harvesters Wy
  MAID/BEAR ME14 .... 133 K2 ▣
Harvest Rdg *E/WMAL* ME19 .... 108 B4
Harvest Wy *TONN* TN10 .... 148 D8
Harvest Wy *SWLY* BR8 .... 57 K4
Harvey Dr *SIT* ME10 .... 94 B4
Harvey Rd *RHAM* ME8 .... 70 B6
Harvill Rd *SCUP* DA14 .... 38 E5
Harwood Rd *RHAM* ME8 .... 70 E5 ▣
Hasletts Cl *STH/RUST* TN4 .... 11 D1
Haslewood Cl *HDCN* TN27 .... 202 B4 ▣
Hasted Cl *GRH* DA9 .... 25 H5
Hasted Rd *RSIT* ME9 .... 72 A7
Hasteds *RMAID* ME17 .... 136 A4
Haste Hill Cl *MAID/SHEP* ME15 .... 155 G3
Haste Hill Rd *MAID/SHEP* ME15 .... 155 G3
Hastings Rd *CRBK* TN17 .... 238 B5
  HAWK TN18 .... 235 F7
  MAID/SHEP ME15 .... 7 E4
  RTWE/PEM TN2 .... 191 K8
  STPH/PW TN12 .... 209 G5
Hatches La *RTON* TN11 .... 151 F8
Hatch Rd *RMAID* ME17 .... 160 C1
Hatfield Rd *STRD* ME2 .... 49 F6
Hatham Green La *BGR/WK* TN15 .... 81 J5
Hathaway Ct *ROCH* ME1 .... 2 B3
Hatherall Rd *MAID/BEAR* ME14 .... 7 E1
Hatherley Rd *SCUP* DA14 .... 38 B1
Hatmill La *STPH/PW* TN12 .... 193 J7
Hatton Cl *GVW* DA11 .... 45 F1
Hatton Rd *WALD* ME5 .... 88 D3
Havelock Rd *DART* DA1 .... 22 E6
  GVW DA11 .... 27 G7
  TON TN9 .... 170 B3
Haven Cl *MEO* DA13 .... 45 G6
  ROCH ME1 .... 2 C6
  SCUP DA14 .... 38 D4
  SWLY BR8 .... 40 C7
Havengore Av *GVE* DA12 .... 28 B6
Haven Hl *BGR/WK* TN15 .... 82 B2
Haven St *HOO/HM* ME3 .... 49 H1
Haven Wy *CHAT* ME4 .... 50 C5
Havering Cl *RTWE/PEM* TN2 .... 191 F8
Havisham Cl *ROCH* ME1 .... 3 D6 ▣
Havisham Rd *GVW* DA12 .... 28 D7
Havock Cl *MAID/BEAR* ME14 .... 6 C3 ▣
Hawbeck Rd *RHAM* ME8 .... 89 K3
Hawden Cl *RTON* TN11 .... 169 K2
Hawden La *RTON* TN11 .... 169 K3
Hawden Rd *TONN* TN10 .... 170 B4
Hawfield Bank *ORP* BR6 .... 56 E7 ▣
Hawkenbury Cl *RTWE/PEM* TN2 .... 11 F5 ▣
Hawkenbury Md
  RTWE/PEM TN2 .... 11 F6 ▣
Hawkenbury Rd *RTWE/PEM* TN2 .... 207 K5
  STPH/PW TN12 .... 178 E8
Hawkes Pl *SEV* TN13 .... 8 C6
Hawkes Rd *DIT/AY* ME20 .... 109 K1
Hawkhurst Rd *BUR/ETCH* TN19 .... 233 J4
  HAWK TN18 .... 225 F7
  RHAM ME8 .... 69 H3
Hawkins Av *GVE* DA12 .... 45 K2
Hawkins Cl *CHAT* ME4 .... 4 A2
  SIT ME10 .... 73 K8
Hawkwood *MAIDW* ME16 .... 132 B1 ▣
Hawkwood Cl *ROCH* ME1 .... 3 D4 ▣
Hawley Cl *DART* DA1 .... 23 H8
Hawser Rd *ROCH* ME1 .... 67 H5
Hawstead La *ORP* BR6 .... 77 G1
Hawthorn Cl *EDEN* TN8 .... 164 C4 ▣
  GVE DA12 .... 45 J2
Hawthorne Av *BH/WHM* TN16 .... 97 H2
  RHAM ME8 .... 69 K4
Hawthorn Rd *DART* DA1 .... 23 G8
  SIT ME10 .... 93 K2
  STRD ME2 .... 48 E8
Hawthorns *HART* DA3 .... 62 A1
  WALD ME5 .... 88 A5 ▣
The Hawthorns *DIT/AY* ME20 .... 109 J5
  OXTED RH8 .... 140 E4 ▣
Hawthorn Wk *RTWE/PEM* TN2 .... 190 E6 ▣
  TONN TN10 .... 148 C7
Haxted Rd *LING* RH7 .... 162 C7
Haydens Cl *STMC/STPC* BR5 .... 56 D4
Haydens Ms *TON* TN9 .... 170 C3
The Haydens *TON* TN9 .... 170 C3
Hayes Cl *HOO/HM* ME3 .... 48 B3
Hayesden La *RRTW* TN3 .... 188 E2
Hayes La *RSIT* ME9 .... 91 J8
Hayes Rd *RDART* DA2 .... 24 D6
Hayfield *E/WMAL* ME19 .... 108 B4
Hayfield Rd *STMC/STPC* BR5 .... 56 B2
Hayfields *WALD* ME5 .... 88 E4
Hayle Mill Rd *MAID/SHEP* ME15 .... 133 F6
Hayle Rd *MAID/SHEP* ME15 .... 7 F4
Hayley Cl *STRD* ME2 .... 66 B4
Haymans Hl *STPH/PW* TN12 .... 195 F7
Hayman Wk *DIT/AY* ME20 .... 86 E8 ▣
Haymen St *CHAT* ME4 .... 3 E5

Haynes Rd *GVW* DA11 ..... 45 G1
Hayrick Cl *MAID/BEAR* ME14 ..... 134 A1
Haysel *SIT* ME10 ..... 94 B4
Haywain Cl *MAID/BEAR* ME14 ..... 134 B2
  STPH/PW TN12 ..... 193 J1
The Haywain *OXTED* RH8 ..... 140 B1
Hayward Av *STRD* ME2 ..... 49 G6
Hayward Ci *DART* DA1 ..... 22 A4
Haywood Ri *ORP* BR6 ..... 75 K1
Hazel Av *HOO/HM* ME3 ..... 50 E3
  MAIDW ME16 ..... 132 C1
Hazelbank *RRTW* TN3 ..... 205 J3
Hazelden Cl *RDART* ME15 ..... 81 F4
Hazel End *SWLY* BR8 ..... 58 B2
Hazel Gv *WALD* ME5 ..... 68 C6
Hazel Rd *DART* DA1 ..... 23 G8
Hazel Shaw *TONN* TN10 ..... 148 C8
The Hazels *RHAM* ME8 ..... 89 J1
Hazel Street Rd *RSIT* ME9 ..... 114 E2
Hazelwood Cl *RTWE/PEM* TN2 ..... 190 D6
Hazelwood Dr *MAIDW* ME16 ..... 132 B2
Hazelwood Hts *OXTED* RH8 ..... 140 E2
Hazelwood Rd *OXTED* RH8 ..... 141 F3
  RSEV TN14 ..... 75 J7
Hazlemere Dr *GILL* ME7 ..... 69 H1
Hazlitt Dr *MAIDW* ME16 ..... 6 A2
Headcorn Rd *HDCN* TN27 ..... 200 D7
  RHAM ME8 ..... 69 J2
  RMAID ME17 ..... 159 J6
  STPH/PW TN12 ..... 198 C2
Headingley Rd *MAIDW* ME16 ..... 110 B8
The Head Race *MAID/BEAR* ME14 ..... 6 A5
Healy Dr *ORP* BR6 ..... 56 A7
Heansill La *HAWK* TN18 ..... 234 E6
Heard Wy *ME10* 94 C1
Hearns Cl *STMC/STPC* BR5 ..... 56 D1
Hearns Rd *STMC/STPC* BR5 ..... 56 D1
Heartenoak Rd *HAWK* TN18 ..... 235 G2
Hearts Delight Rd *RSIT* ME9 ..... 93 G5
Heath Cl *STMC/STPC* BR5 ..... 56 D3
  SWLY BR8 ..... 40 B7
Heathclose Av *DART* DA1 ..... 22 E6
Heathclose Rd *DART* DA1 ..... 22 D7
Heathcote Cl *DIT/AY* ME20 ..... 109 K4
Heathend Rd *BXLY* DA5 ..... 22 B7
Heather Bank *STPH/PW* TN12 ..... 173 K8
Heatherbank Cl *DART* DA1 ..... 22 B5
Heather Cl *SIT* ME10 ..... 94 B3
  WALD ME5 ..... 88 A2
Heather Dr *DART* DA1 ..... 22 D6
  MAID/BEAR ME14 ..... 7 E5
  TENT TN30 ..... 230 B5
Heather End *SWLY* BR8 ..... 58 A2
Heatherside Rd *SCUP* DA14 ..... 38 D1
The Heathers *CRBK* TN17 ..... 225 G3
Heather Wk *TONN* TN10 ..... 148 B8
Heatherwood Cl *RMAID* ME17 ..... 158 C4
Heathfield *RMAID* ME17 ..... 157 G2
Heathfield Av *MAID/BEAR* ME14 ..... 111 J7
Heathfield Cl *HAYES* BR2 ..... 74 B1
  MAID/BEAR ME14 ..... 111 H7
  WALD ME5 ..... 68 C7
Heathfield Rd *HAYES* BR2 ..... 74 B1
  MAID/BEAR ME14 ..... 111 H7
  SEV TN13 ..... 8 B1
Heath Gv *MAIDW* ME16 ..... 132 A4
Heathlands Ri *DART* DA1 ..... 22 E6
Heath La *DART* DA1 ..... 22 E7
Heathlee Rd *DART* DA1 ..... 22 B5
Heathorn St *MAID/BEAR* ME14 ..... 7 E2
Heath Rd *DART* DA1 ..... 22 C5
  MAID/SHEP ME15 ..... 153 J2
  MAIDW ME16 ..... 131 K3
  RMAID ME17 ..... 157 G2
Heathside Av *RMAID* ME17 ..... 154 C2
Heath St *DART* DA1 ..... 23 G6
The Heath *E/WMAL* ME19 ..... 130 C1
Heathview Av *DART* DA1 ..... 22 B5
Heathview Crs *DART* DA1 ..... 22 D6
Heathwood Gdns *SWLY* BR8 ..... 39 K7
Heathwood Wk *BXLY* DA5 ..... 22 B7
Heaverham Rd *RGR/WK* TN15 ..... 103 F4
Hectorage Rd *TON* TN9 ..... 170 C6
Hedge Place Rd *GRH* DA9 ..... 24 D5
The Hedgerows *GVW* DA11 ..... 27 F8
The Hedgerow *MAID/BEAR* ME14 ..... 134 A1
The Hedges *MAID/BEAR* ME14 ..... 111 G7
Hedley St *MAID/BEAR* ME14 ..... 7 D2
Helen Cl *DART* DA1 ..... 22 E6
Helen Thompson Cl *RSIT* ME9 ..... 73 K2
Hellyar Ct *ROCH* ME1 ..... 2 C4
Hempstead La *RSIT* ME9 ..... 95 F3
Hempstead Rd *GILL* ME7 ..... 69 H8
Hempstead Valley Dr *GILL* ME7 ..... 69 H8
Henbane Ct *MAID/BEAR* ME14 ..... 134 A1
Henderson Dr *DART* DA1 ..... 23 K3
Henderson Rd *BH/WHM* TN16 ..... 74 B7
Hendley Dr *CRBK* TN17 ..... 225 J1
Hendy Rd *SNOD* ME6 ..... 86 A6
Henham Gdns *STPH/PW* TN12 ..... 151 J8
Henhurst Rd *MEO* DA13 ..... 46 A7
Heniker La *RMAID* ME17 ..... 179 H1
Henley Cl *RHAM* ME8 ..... 70 A6
  RTWE/PEM TN2 ..... 11 E3
  WALD ME5 ..... 68 B8

Henley Deane *GVW* DA11 ..... 45 F2
Henley Flds *MAID/BEAR* ME14 ..... 112 A8
  TENT TN30 ..... 230 B4
Henley Mdw *TENT* TN30 ..... 230 A4
Henley Rd *STPH/PW* TN12 ..... 173 J7
Henley St *MEO* DA13 ..... 64 C3
Henry St *CHAT* ME4 ..... 4 B5
  RHAM ME8 ..... 70 D5
Henwood Green Rd
  RTWE/PEM TN2 ..... 191 K7
Henwoods Crs *RTWE/PEM* TN2 ..... 191 K8
Henwoods Mt *RTWE/PEM* TN2 ..... 192 A8
Herbert Rd *CHAT* ME4 ..... 4 A5
  RHAM ME8 ..... 70 B6
  SWCM DA10 ..... 26 A5
  SWLY BR8 ..... 40 E4
Herdsdown *HOO/HM* ME3 ..... 50 E1
Hereford Rd *MAID/SHEP* ME15 ..... 133 J7
Heritage Dr *GILL* ME7 ..... 69 G5
Heritage Hl *HAYES* BR2 ..... 74 B1
Heritage Rd *WALD* ME5 ..... 68 B8
Herman Ter *CHAT* ME4 ..... 4 A5
Hermitage Ct *MAIDW* ME16 ..... 131 K1
Hermitage La *DIT/AY* ME20 ..... 109 K7
  MAID/BEAR ME14 ..... 112 D3
  MAIDW ME16 ..... 109 K8
  RMAID ME17 ..... 156 A8
Hermitage Rd *HOO/HM* ME3 ..... 48 B3
Herne Rd *RHAM* ME8 ..... 69 K4
Heron Cl *RSIT* ME9 ..... 72 A3
Heronden Rd *MAID/SHEP* ME15 ..... 156 B2
Herongate Rd *SWLY* BR8 ..... 40 B4
Heron Hill La *MEO* DA13 ..... 83 J2
Heron Rd *DIT/AY* ME20 ..... 108 D5
Herons Wy *RTWE/PEM* TN2 ..... 192 A6
Heron Wy *HOO/HM* ME3 ..... 35 F2
  WALD ME5 ..... 68 B8
Herts Crs *HOO/HM* ME3 ..... 155 F3
Herying Cl *STRD* ME2 ..... 86 A2
Hesiers Hl *WARL* CR6 ..... 96 C4
Hesiers Rd *WARL* CR6 ..... 96 C3
Hesketh Av *RDART* DA2 ..... 24 A7
Heskett Pk *RTWE/PEM* TN2 ..... 192 A8
Hever Av *BGR/WK* TN15 ..... 80 D2
Hever Cl *MAID/SHEP* ME15 ..... 134 B8
Hever Court Rd *GVE* DA12 ..... 45 K4
Hever Cft *STRD* ME2 ..... 66 E1
Hever Gdns *MAIDW* ME16 ..... 6 B4
Hever Pl *SIT* ME10 ..... 93 H3
Hever Rd *BGR/WK* TN15 ..... 80 D2
  EDEN TN8 ..... 165 C7
Hever Wood Rd *BGR/WK* TN15 ..... 80 D3
Hewett Rd *SWLY* BR8 ..... 58 A1
Hewitt Cl *GILL* ME7 ..... 5 F2
Hewitts Rd *ORP* BR6 ..... 77 J1
Hextable Cl *MAIDW* ME16 ..... 110 C7
Hibbs Cl *SWLY* BR8 ..... 40 A7
Hibernia Dr *GVE* DA12 ..... 46 C1
Hickory Dell *GILL* ME7 ..... 89 H1
Higham Cl *MAID/SHEP* ME15 ..... 6 A5
Higham Gdns *TONN* TN10 ..... 171 F1
Higham La *RTON* TN11 ..... 148 E5
  RYE TN31 ..... 244 D8
  TONN TN10 ..... 149 F8
Higham Rd *HOO/HM* ME3 ..... 31 F2
  HOO/HM ME3 ..... 49 H5
Higham School Rd *TONN* TN10 ..... 148 E8
Higham Vw *MAID/BEAR* ME14 ..... 110 E2
High Bank *ROCH* ME1 ..... 3 D6
High Banks *MAID/SHEP* ME15 ..... 155 F1
High Beeches *ORP* BR6 ..... 76 B2
  RTWE/PEM TN2 ..... 11 F1
  SCUP DA14 ..... 39 F3
Highberry *E/WMAL* ME19 ..... 108 C4
Highbourne Pk *RMAID* ME17 ..... 161 J1
High Brooms Rd *STH/RUST* TN4 ..... 190 D6
Highbury La *TENT* TN30 ..... 230 A7
High Cross Rd *BGR/WK* TN15 ..... 126 B5
Highcross Rd *MEO* DA13 ..... 43 J4
High Dewar Rd *RHAM* ME8 ..... 70 D6
High Elms Rd *ORP* BR6 ..... 76 B4
High Elms Rd *ORP* BR6 ..... 75 H4
Highfield Av *ORP* BR6 ..... 76 A2
Highfield Cl *HAWK* TN18 ..... 235 F5
  RHAM ME8 ..... 70 A7
  RTWE/PEM TN2 ..... 191 K8
Highfield Rd *BH/WHM* TN16 ..... 97 G4
  DART DA1 ..... 23 G6
  RHAM ME8 ..... 70 A7
  RSEV TN14 ..... 102 C3
  STH/RUST TN4 ..... 190 C7
  STMC/STPC BR5 ..... 38 A8
Highfield Rd South *DART* DA1 ..... 23 G6
Highfields *EDEN* TN8 ..... 164 C1
High Firs *SWLY* BR8 ..... 58 B1
Highgate Hl *HAWK* TN18 ..... 235 F5
Highgrove *RTWE/PEM* TN2 ..... 207 F6
Highgrove Rd *WALD* ME5 ..... 88 B1
High Halden Rd *HDCN* TN27 ..... 217 K5
High Hilden Cl *RTON* TN11 ..... 170 A2
High House La *RTON* TN11 ..... 149 H5
Highland Rd *MAID/SHEP* ME15 ..... 134 A1
  RSEV TN14 ..... 77 J6
Highlands Cl *STRD* ME2 ..... 48 C8
Highlands Hl *SWLY* BR8 ..... 40 D7

Highlands Pk *BGR/WK* TN15 ..... 102 C8
Highlands Rd *STMC/STPC* BR5 ..... 56 C4
High Meadow *RYE* TN31 ..... 244 D7
High Oak Hl *RSIT* ME9 ..... 72 D6
High Pk *RYE* TN31 ..... 244 D7
High Rdg *CRBK* TN17 ..... 212 C7
Highridge *GILL* ME7 ..... 69 C5
Highridge Cl *MAID/BEAR* ME14 ..... 134 B1
High Rd *RDART* DA2 ..... 40 E1
High Rocks La *RRTW* TN3 ..... 206 B5
Highsted Rd *RSIT* ME9 ..... 94 A7
High St *BGR/WK* TN15 ..... 102 E4
  BGR/WK TN15 ..... 102 D8
  BGR/WK TN15 ..... 105 G3
  BGR/WK TN15 ..... 105 F7
  BH/WHM TN16 ..... 120 C6
  BH/WHM TN16 ..... 121 J3
  CHAT ME4 ..... 3 F4
  CHAT ME4 ..... 4 B3
  CRBK TN17 ..... 212 D6
  CRBK TN17 ..... 225 J2
  CRBK TN17 ..... 238 D3
  DART DA1 ..... 23 H5
  DIT/AY ME20 ..... 109 K3
  E/WMAL ME19 ..... 107 K6
  E/WMAL ME19 ..... 108 E8
  EDEN TN8 ..... 164 C5
  EYN DA4 ..... 59 J3
  EYN DA4 ..... 59 H6
  GILL ME7 ..... 4 C2
  GILL ME7 ..... 4 B3
  GRH DA9 ..... 25 G3
  GVE DA12 ..... 27 J5
  GVW DA11 ..... 26 C5
  HAWK TN18 ..... 234 D4
  HDCN TN27 ..... 200 A1
  HDCN TN27 ..... 202 A5
  HDCN TN27 ..... 217 J3
  HOO/HM ME3 ..... 21 G8
  HOO/HM ME3 ..... 35 F2
  MAID/BEAR ME14 ..... 6 C3
  ORP BR6 ..... 56 B4
  ORP BR6 ..... 75 F6
  ORP BR6 ..... 75 H1
  OXTED RH8 ..... 119 F7
  OXTED RH8 ..... 140 B1
  RDART DA2 ..... 43 G1
  RHAM ME8 ..... 70 C6
  RMAID ME17 ..... 157 G7
  RMAID ME17 ..... 160 D2
  ROCH ME1 ..... 2 C2
  ROCH ME1 ..... 86 B2
  RRTW TN3 ..... 221 J2
  RSEV TN14 ..... 78 C5
  RSEV TN14 ..... 101 J3
  RSIT ME9 ..... 72 A8
  RTON TN11 ..... 150 A6
  RTON TN11 ..... 168 C5
  RTW TN1 ..... 10 C5
  RTWE/PEM TN2 ..... 191 J8
  SCUP DA14 ..... 38 B2
  SEV TN13 ..... 9 E4
  SEV TN13 ..... 122 E1
  SIT ME10 ..... 73 K8
  SNOD ME6 ..... 85 K8
  SOCK/AV MR15 ..... 13 C1
  STH/RUST TN4 ..... 189 C5
  STMC/STPC BR5 ..... 56 D3
  STPH/PW TN12 ..... 176 D8
  STPH/PW TN12 ..... 193 K6
  STPH/PW TN12 ..... 198 B3
  STRD ME2 ..... 2 B1
  STRD ME2 ..... 50 A4
  SWCM DA10 ..... 26 A4
  SWLY BR8 ..... 40 B8
  TENT TN30 ..... 230 A7
  TON TN9 ..... 170 C5
  TONN TN10 ..... 170 C4
  WADH TN5 ..... 233 H3
  WBY/YAL ME18 ..... 152 D5
High Vw *HOO/HM* ME3 ..... 48 B2
Highview *MEO* DA13 ..... 83 J4
Highview Dr *WALD* ME5 ..... 87 J1
Highview Rd *SCUP* DA14 ..... 38 C2
The Highway *ORP* BR6 ..... 76 C1
High Weald Wk *RRTW* TN3 ..... 189 F5
  RTON TN11 ..... 191 J3
  RTWE/PEM TN2 ..... 207 K6
  STH/RUST TN4 ..... 10 B5
  TON TN9 ..... 170 E7
Highwoods Cl *HOO/HM* ME3 ..... 48 B2
High Woods La *RTWE/PEM* TN2 ..... 208 A4
Hilary Gdns *ROCH* ME1 ..... 66 E4
Hilbert Cl *RTW* TN1 ..... 11 E2
Hilborough Wy *ORP* BR6 ..... 75 J1
Hilda May Av *SWLY* BR8 ..... 40 B8
Hilda Rd *CHAT* ME4 ..... 4 A5
Hilden Av *RTON* TN11 ..... 169 K2
Hildenborough Crs *MAIDW* ME16 ..... 110 B7
Hildenborough Rd *RTON* TN11 ..... 147 K2
  RTON TN11 ..... 168 C3
Hilden Park Rd *RTON* TN11 ..... 169 K2
Hilders Cl *EDEN* TN8 ..... 164 B2
Hilders La *EDEN* TN8 ..... 163 K2
Hillary Av *GVW* DA11 ..... 45 F1

Hillary Rd *MAID/BEAR* ME14 .... 111 G7
Hillborough Gv *WALD* ME5 .... 88 B3
Hill Brow *DART* DA1 .... 22 C5
   MAID/BEAR ME14.......................... 134 C1
   SIT ME10 .... 93 J4
Hillbrow Cl *BXLY* DA5 .... 40 A2
Hillbury Gdns *WADH* TN5 .... 232 B5
Hill Cha *WALD* ME5 .... 87 K3
Hill Cl *MEO* DA13 .... 45 F5
Hill Ct *HOO/HM* ME3 .... 50 A2
Hillcrest *EDEN* TN8 .... 165 H1
Hill Crest *SEV* TN13 .... 8 C1
   STH/RUST TN4 .... 190 B6
Hillcrest Dr *GRH* DA9........................... 25 F4
   RTWE/PEM TN2 .... 190 D7
   STRD ME2 .... 48 E5
Hillcrest Rd *BH/WHM* TN16 .... 97 H3
   CHAT ME4 .... 3 F6 🅸
   DART DA1 .... 22 B6
   EDEN TN8 .... 164 C2
   ORP BR6 .... 56 B6
Hillden Shaw *MAID/SHEP* ME15 .... 133 G6
Hill End *ORP* BR6 .... 56 A6
Hill Farm Av *STRD* ME2....................... 48 E5
Hillfield Rd *SEV* TN13 .... 101 G7
Hillgarth *STH/RUST* TN4 .... 190 A6 🅸
Hill Green Rd *RSIT* ME9 .... 91 F6
Hill House Rd *RDART* DA2 .... 24 B6
Hillingdale *BH/WHM* TN16.................. 97 F5
Hillingdon Av *SEV* TN13 .... 102 A8
Hillingdon Ri *SEV* TN13......................... 9 F1
Hillingdon Rd *GVW* DA11 .... 27 J8
Hill Ri *RDART* DA2 .... 42 C3
Hill Rd *DART* DA1 .... 23 H8
   ROCH ME1 .... 2 A6
   ROCH ME1 .... 86 D1
Hill Shaw *HART* DA3 .... 62 A3
Hillshaw Crs *STRD* ME2 .... 66 C1
Hillside *EYN* DA4 .... 59 J4
   RDART DA2 .... 42 D3
   TON TN9 .... 170 A7
Hillside Av *GVE* DA12.......................... 28 A8
   STRD ME2 .... 49 G6
Hillside Ct *SWLY* BR8 .... 58 D1
   WBY/YAL ME18 .... 130 C7
Hillside Dr *GVE* DA12.......................... 28 A8
Hillside Rd *BH/WHM* TN16 .... 97 J6
   CHAT ME4 .... 4 A4 🅸
   DART DA1 .... 22 D5
   RSEV TN14.. 102 D4
   SEV TN13 .... 9 F2
The Hillside *ORP* BR6 .... 76 C4
Hills La *BGR/WK* TN15 .... 80 A7
Hill's Ter *CHAT* ME4 .... 3 F5
Hill St *RTW* TN1 .... 11 D2 🅸
The Hill *CRBK* TN17 .... 225 K2
   GVW DA11... 26 D5
Hill Top *CRBK* TN17 .... 213 K1
Hilltop *MAID/SHEP* ME15 .... 153 H3
   TON TN9 .... 170 B7
Hilltop Gdns *DART* DA1 .... 23 J4
Hilltop Rd *STRD* ME2 .... 49 H5
Hill Vw *BGR/WK* TN15 .... 105 G7
Hill View Cl *BGR/WK* TN15 .... 105 G7
Hill View Rd *HART* DA3 .... 44 C8
   ORP BR6 .... 56 A5
   RTON TN11 .... 169 K1
   STH/RUST TN4 .... 206 B2
Hill View Wy *WALD* ME5 .... 87 K1
Hillydeal Rd *RSEV* TN14 .... 102 A2
Hillyfield Cl *STRD* ME2 .... 48 E5 🅸
Hilton Dr *SIT* ME10 .... 73 G8
Hilton Rd *HOO/HM* ME3 .... 31 G7
Hinksden Rd *CRBK* TN17 .... 236 B3
Hinton Crs *GILL* ME7 .... 69 H8
Hitchen Hatch La *SEV* TN13 .... 8 E1
Hither Chantlers *RRTW* TN3 .... 205 K3
Hive La *GVW* DA11 .... 26 C4
Hoath Cl *GILL* ME7 .... 69 H7
Hoath La *RHAM* ME8............................ 69 J3
Hoath Wy *RHAM* ME8 .... 69 J7 🅸
Hobart Gdns *SIT* ME10 .... 93 H2
Hobbs La *RYE* TN31 .... 246 C8
Hockenden La *SWLY* BR8 .... 39 H8
Hockers Cl *MAID/BEAR* ME14 .... 112 C6
Hockers La *MAID/BEAR* ME14 .... 112 B7
Hodgson Crs *SNOD* ME6 .... 85 K5 🅸
Hodsoll St *BGR/WK* TN15 .... 82 E4
Hodson Crs *STMC/STPC* BR5 .... 56 E2 🅸
Hogbarn La *RMAID* ME17 .... 137 K4
Hoghole La *RRTW* TN3 .... 221 C4
Hog La *MEO* DA13 .... 44 E1
Hognore La *BGR/WK* TN15................. 82 E8
Hogtrough HI *BH/WHM* TN16 .... 121 C1
Holborough Rd *SNOD* ME6 .... 85 K6
Holcombe *BH/WHM* TN16 .... 120 D5
Holcombe Rd *CHAT* ME4 .... 3 F6
   ROCH ME1 .... 66 E1
Holden Cnr *STH/RUST* TN4............... 189 J5
Holden Park Rd *STH/RUST* TN4 ..... 189 K6
Holden Rd *STH/RUST* TN4 .... 189 K5
Holder Cl *WALD* ME5 .... 68 D8
Holding St *RHAM* ME8 .... 70 B5
Hole La *EDEN* TN8 .... 142 A8
Holford St *TON* TN9 .... 170 B5 🅸

Holland Crs *OXTED* RH8 .... 140 E4
Holland La *OXTED* RH8 .... 140 E4
Holland Rd *MAID/BEAR* ME14 .... 7 D2
   OXTED RH8 .... 140 E6
   WALD ME5 .... 87 K2
Hollands Cl *GVE* DA12 .... 47 H3
The Hollies *GVE* DA12 .... 46 A4
   HART DA3 .... 44 D8
Hollin Cl *STH/RUST* TN4 .... 10 B3 🅸
Hollingbourne HI *RMAID* ME17 ...... 136 D2
Hollingbourne Rd *RHAM* ME8............ 69 K3
Hollingworth Rd
   MAID/SHEP ME15........................... 156 B1
Hollingworth Wy
   BH/WHM TN16 .... 120 D5 🅸
Hollow La *RSIT* ME9 .... 91 G1
   SNOD ME6 .... 85 J7
Hollow Trees Dr *RTON* TN11 .... 168 E5
Holly Bank *STPH/PW* TN12 .... 193 K6
Hollybush Cl *SEV* TN13 .... 9 E3
Hollybush La *ORP* BR6 .... 77 H2
Holly Bush La *SEV* TN13 .... 9 E3 🅸
Hollybush Rd *GVE* DA12 .... 27 K8
Holly Cl *GILL* ME7 .... 5 E2
   WALD ME5 .... 68 D5
Hollydene Rd *WADH* TN5 .... 220 B8
Holly Farm *MAID/SHEP* ME15 .... 134 E8
Holly HI *MEO* DA13 .... 84 D4
Holly Rd *DART* DA1 .... 23 G7
   ORP BR6 .... 76 B3
   STRD ME2 .... 48 D8
   STRD ME2 .... 49 J4
Hollyshaw Cl *RTWE/PEM* TN2 .... 11 E5 🅸
Hollytree Av *SWLY* BR8....................... 40 B7
Holly Tree Cl *RMAID* ME17 .... 158 C4
Hollytree Dr *HOO/HM* ME3 .... 48 A3
Hollywood La *BGR/WK* TN15.............. 80 B8
   STRD ME2 .... 49 H4
Holmes Cl *HOO/HM* ME3 .... 33 F3
Holmesdale Cl *MAID/SHEP* ME15 .. 155 F3
Holmesdale HI *EYN* DA4 .... 42 C6
Holmesdale Rd *EYN* DA4 .... 42 B8
Holmewood Rdg *RRTW* TN3 .... 205 J3
Holmewood Rd *STH/RUST* TN4 ...... 190 C7
Holmhurst Cl *STH/RUST* TN4 .... 10 B3 🅸
Holmleigh Av *DART* DA1 .... 23 F3
Holm Mill La *RMAID* ME17 .... 137 F8
Holmoaks *MAID/BEAR* ME14 .... 7 A2
   RHAM ME8 .... 70 B4
Holmsdale Gv *BXLYHN* DA7 .... 22 B1
Holmside *GILL* ME7 .... 5 E6
Holt Wood Av *DIT/AY* ME20 .... 109 H6
Holtwood Cl *RHAM* ME8....................... 90 A1
Holtye Crs *MAID/SHEP* ME15.............. 7 E5
Holyoake Ter *SEV* TN13........................ 8 E5
Holywell La *RSIT* ME9 .... 71 J4
Homedean Rd *SEV* TN13 .... 122 E1
Home Farm Cl *RTON* TN11 .... 168 E3
Home Farm La *RTWE/PEM* TN2 ...... 190 B6
Homefield Cl *STMC/STPC* BR5 .... 56 C1 🅸
   SWLY BR8 .... 40 C8
Homefield Dr *RHAM* ME8 .... 70 E4
Homefield Ri *ORP* BR6 .... 56 B5
Homefield Rd *SEV* TN13........................ 8 A1
Home Gdns *DART* DA1 .... 23 H5
Home HI *SWLY* BR8 .... 40 C5
Home Lea *ORP* BR6 .... 76 A1
Home Mead Cl *GVE* DA12 .... 27 J6
Home Pk *OXTED* RH8 .... 140 E2
Homestead Rd *EDEN* TN8 .... 164 B1
   ORP BR6 .... 76 C3
The Homestead *DART* DA1 .... 23 F5
   RRTW TN3 .... 205 F7 🅸
Homestead Vw *RSIT* ME9 .... 93 G4
Homeview *SIT* ME10 .... 94 C2 🅸
Homewards Rd *HOO/HM* ME3 .... 18 E6
Homewood Av *SIT* ME10 .... 93 J3
Homewood Rd *RRTW* TN3 .... 205 J3
   TENT TN30 .... 230 B5
Hone St *STRD* ME2 .... 49 G6
Honeyball Wk *RSIT* ME9 .... 95 K4
Honey Bee Gld *RHAM* ME8 .... 70 B3 🅸
Honey Cl *GILL* ME7 .... 89 H1
Honeycrock HI *RSIT* ME9 .... 91 J6
Honeyden Rd *SCUP* DA14 .... 39 F4
Honey La *MAID/SHEP* ME15.............. 134 D8
Honeypot Cl *STRD* ME2 .... 49 G6
Honeypot La *BGR/WK* TN15 .... 82 D4
   BGR/WK TN15 .... 103 G6
   LING RH7 .... 163 H2
Honeysuckle Cl *GILL* ME7 .... 89 G2 🅸
Honywood Rd *RMAID* ME17 .... 160 C1
Hoo Common *HOO/HM* ME3 .... 50 B2
Hood Av *STMC/STPC* BR5.................... 56 C2
Hook Cl *WALD* ME5 .... 87 K1
Hookfields *GVW* DA11 .... 45 F1
Hook Green La *RDART* DA2 .... 37 K2
Hook Green Rd *MEO* DA13 .... 44 A5
Hook HI *WADH* TN5 .... 221 J8
Hook La *RMAID* ME17 .... 137 G8
Hook Rd *SNOD* ME6 .... 85 J6
Hook St *RMAID* ME17 .... 161 F6
Hookwood Cnr *OXTED* RH8 .... 119 F7
Hookwood Rd *ORP* BR6....................... 76 D6
Hoopers La *HOO/HM* ME3 .... 34 C1

Hooper's Rd *ROCH* ME1 .... 2 C4 🅸
Hoo Rd *STRD* ME2 .... 49 J3
Hope Av *RTON* TN11 .... 150 A5
Hopehouse La *CRBK* TN17 .... 237 H5
   HAWK TN18 .... 237 G7
Hope Rd *SWCM* DA10 .... 26 A5
Hopes Gv *RASHW* TN26 .... 217 J8
Hope St *CHAT* ME4 .... 4 A5 🅸
   MAID/BEAR ME14 .... 6 C2
Hopewell Dr *GVE* DA12....................... 46 C3
   WALD ME5 .... 68 D6
Hopgarden La *SEV* TN13 .... 123 J7
Hopgarden Rd *TONN* TN10 .... 170 D1
Hop Pocket Cl *CRBK* TN17 .... 215 H6 🅸
Hop Pocket La *STPH/PW* TN12 .... 173 H7
Hopwood Gdns *STH/RUST* TN4....... 10 C1
Horizon Cl *STH/RUST* TN4 .... 190 B6
Hornbeam Av *RTWE/PEM* TN2 .... 190 D5
   WALD ME5 .... 88 C4 🅸
Hornbeam Cl *DIT/AY* ME20 .... 109 F5
   STPH/PW TN12 .... 193 H1 🅸
Hornbeams *MEO* DA13......................... 83 J6
Horn HI *RSIT* ME9 .... 116 E4
Horns La *WBY/YAL* ME18 .... 129 F4
Horns Lodge La *RTON* TN11 .... 148 C6
Horn's Oak Rd *MEO* DA13 .... 63 J8
Horns Rd *HAWK* TN18 .... 234 D6
Horn Yd *GVE* DA12 .... 27 J5 🅸
Horsecroft Cl *ORP* BR6 .... 56 C5 🅸
Horsegrove Av *WADH* TN5 .... 232 D5
Horsell Rd *STMC/STPC* BR5 .... 38 B6
Horseshoe Cl *GILL* ME7 .... 89 G1
   MAID/BEAR ME14 .... 134 A1 🅸
Horseshoes La *RMAID* ME17 .... 157 F2
Horsfield Cl *RDART* DA2 .... 24 B6 🅸
Horsham La *RHAM* ME8 .... 71 G3
Horsley Rd *ROCH* ME1 .... 2 B4
Horsmonden Cl *ORP* BR6.................... 56 A4 🅸
Horsmonden Rd *STPH/PW* TN12 ..... 194 A7
Horsted Av *CHAT* ME4.......................... 67 K5
Horsted Wy *ROCH* ME1........................ 67 J7
Horton Downs *MAID/SHEP* ME15.... 134 B5
Horton Pl *BH/WHM* TN16.................. 120 D5
Horton Rd *EYN* DA4 .... 42 B8
Hortons Cl *CRBK* TN17 .... 227 F7
Hortons Wy *BH/WHM* TN16 .... 120 D5
Horton Wy *EYN* DA4 .... 59 J4
Horwood Cl *ROCH* ME1 .... 67 G6 🅸
Hoselands Vw *HART* DA3 .... 61 K1
Hosey Common La
   BH/WHM TN16 .... 142 E1
Hosey Common Rd
   BH/WHM TN16 .... 120 E8
Hosey HI *BH/WHM* TN16 .... 120 E8
Hoskins Rd *OXTED* RH8 .... 118 C8
Hospital Rd *RMAID* ME17 .... 136 C6
   SEV TN13 .... 98 C1
Hostier Cl *STRD* ME2 .... 86 A2
Hotel Rd *RHAM* ME8 .... 69 H4
Hotham Cl *EYN* DA4 .... 41 K5
   SWLY BR8 .... 40 B7
Hothfield Rd *RHAM* ME8 .... 70 C5
Hottsfield *HART* DA3............................ 43 K8
Houghton Av *GILL* ME7 .... 89 J3
Houselands Rd *TON* TN9 .... 170 B4 🅸
Hovendens *CRBK* TN17 .... 215 H6
Howard Av *ROCH* ME1 .... 3 D5
   SIT ME10 .... 73 J8
Howard Dr *MAIDW* ME16.................. 110 B8
Howard Rd *DART* DA1 .... 23 K5
   E/WMAL ME19 .... 108 D2
Howbury La *ERITH* DA8 .... 22 D1
Howbury Rd *DART* DA1 .... 22 D1
Howells Cl *BGR/WK* TN15 .... 80 D2 🅸
How Green La *EDEN* TN8 .... 165 J5
Howick Cl *DIT/AY* ME20 .... 109 K6
Howland Rd *STPH/PW* TN12 .... 177 F8
Howsmere Cl *STRD* ME2 .... 86 A3
Hubbards HI *RMAID* ME17 .... 161 H1
   SEV TN13 .... 145 K2
Hubbard's La *MAID/SHEP* ME15 ..... 155 G3
Hubble Dr *MAID/SHEP* ME15 .... 134 A7
Huckleberry Cl *WALD* ME5 .... 88 C3 🅸
Hudson Cl *RHAM* ME8.......................... 69 K5
Hughes Dr *STRD* ME2 .... 49 J4
Hugh Price Cl *SIT* ME10 .... 94 D1
Hulsewood Cl *RDART* DA2 .... 40 E1
Humber Crs *STRD* ME2 .... 48 E7
Humber Rd *DART* DA1 .... 23 G4
Humboldt Ct *RTWE/PEM* TN2 .... 11 F2
Hume Av *TIL* RM18 .... 27 J2
Hume Cl *TIL* RM18 .... 27 H2
Hungershall Pk *STH/RUST* TN4 .... 10 A5
Hunsdon Dr *SEV* TN13 .... 9 D2
Hunstanton Cl *RHAM* ME8 .... 90 B3
Hunters Cl *BXLY* DA5 .... 40 B1
Huntersfield Cl *WALD* ME5 .... 88 D5 🅸
Hunters Vw *RSEV* TN14 .... 100 A1
Hunters Wy *GILL* ME7 .... 69 F5
   RTWE/PEM TN2 .... 10 B6
Hunters Wy West *WALD* ME5 .... 5 D6
Huntingdon Wk
   MAID/SHEP ME15........................... 134 A7 🅸
Huntingfield Rd *MEO* DA13 .... 63 H4
Huntington Cl *CRBK* TN17 .... 225 K2 🅸

Huntington Rd *RMAID* ME17 ...... **154** B3
Huntley Av *GVW* DA11 ...... **26** C5
Huntley Mill Rd *WADH* TN5 ...... **232** B3
Huntleys Pk *STH/RUST* TN4 ...... **10** B1
Hunton HI *MAID/SHEP* ME15 ...... **153** K5
Hunton Rd *STPH/PW* TN12 ...... **175** K1
Hunt Rd *GVW* DA11 ...... **45** F1
  TONN TN10 ...... **148** E8
Hunts Farm *La BGR/WK* TN15 ...... **105** C7
Huntsman *La BGR/WK* TN15 ...... **106** A3
  MAID/BEAR ME14 ...... **7** E3
Huntsmans CI *CHAT* ME4 ...... **67** K5 🖪
Hunt St *WBY/YAL* ME18 ...... **152** C2
Hurlfield *RDART* DA2 ...... **41** F1
Huron CI *ROCH* ME1 ...... **76** A2 🖪
Hurricane Rd *E/WMAL* ME19 ...... **129** H3
Hurst CI *STPH/PW* TN12 ...... **198** B2
  TENT TN30 ...... **228** J7
  WALD ME5 ...... **67** K8
Hurst Farm Rd *RSEV* TN14 ...... **145** K3
Hurst Green *La OXTED* RH8 ...... **140** E3
Hurst Green Rd *OXTED* RH8 ...... **140** E3
Hurst HI *WALD* ME5 ...... **87** K4
The Hurstings *MAIDW* ME16 ...... **6** A3
Hurstlands *OXTED* RH8 ...... **140** E3
Hurst La *RSEV* TN14 ...... **145** K4
Hurst PI *RHAM* ME8 ...... **70** C6
The Hurst *RTWE/PEM* TN2 ...... **190** E7
Hurst Wy *MAIDW* ME16 ...... **131** K4
  SEV TN13 ...... **9** E6
Husheath HI *CRBK* TN17 ...... **197** F8
Hutsford CI *RHAM* ME8 ...... **90** A1 🖪
Hyacinth Rd *STRD* ME2 ...... **48** C8
Hybrid CI *ROCH* ME1 ...... **67** J5
Hyde Dr *STMC/STPC* BR5 ...... **56** C1
Hyde Rd *MAIDW* ME16 ...... **110** D7
Hydes Orch *HDCN* TN27 ...... **200** C1 🖪
Hyperion Dr *STRD* ME2 ...... **48** E5 🖪
Hythe CI *STH/RUST* TN4 ...... **190** A5
  STMC/STPC BR5 ...... **56** D1 🖪
Hythe Rd *SIT* ME10 ...... **93** J1
Hythe St *DART* DA1 ...... **23** H4

I

Icehouse Wd *OXTED* RH8 ...... **140** C2
Ide Hill Rd *RSEV* TN14 ...... **144** B3
Iden Crs *STPH/PW* TN12 ...... **198** A4
Iden La *HDCN* TN27 ...... **183** H2
Iden Rd *STRD* ME2 ...... **49** H5
Idenwood *RHAM* ME8 ...... **70** A8
Idleigh Court Rd *HART* DA3 ...... **62** C6
Ifield CI *MAID/SHEP* ME15 ...... **134** B6
Ifield Wy *GVE* DA12 ...... **46** A4
Ightham By-pass *BGR/WK* TN15 ...... **104** C8
Ightham Rd *RTON* TN11 ...... **148** C3
Illustrious CI *WALD* ME5 ...... **88** B1
Impala Gdns *GVW* DA11 ...... **11** D1
Imperial Dr *GVE* DA12 ...... **46** C3
Imperial Rd *GILL* ME7 ...... **4** C5
Impton La *WALD* ME5 ...... **88** A6
Ingleden Park Rd *TENT* TN30 ...... **230** B5
Ingle Rd *CHAT* ME4 ...... **3** F6
Inglewood Rd *BXLYHN* DA7 ...... **22** A3
Ingoldsby Rd *GVE* DA12 ...... **28** B7
Ingram Rd *DART* DA1 ...... **23** H7
  GILL ME7 ...... **23** E3
Institute Rd *CHAT* ME4 ...... **4** A4
Instone Rd *DART* DA1 ...... **23** C6
Invicta Rd *RDART* DA2 ...... **24** D4
Iona CI *WALD* ME5 ...... **88** C5
Iona Rd *MAID/SHEP* ME15 ...... **133** G7
Irene Rd *ORP* BR6 ...... **56** A4
Iris CI *WALD* ME5 ...... **88** B6
Iron Mill La *DART* DA1 ...... **22** C3
Iron Mill PI *DART* DA1 ...... **22** C3
Ironside CI *WALD* ME5 ...... **88** B6
Ironstones *RRTW* TN3 ...... **206** A3 🖪
Irvine Rd *HOO/HM* ME3 ...... **48** A3
Irvine Wy *ORP* BR6 ...... **56** A4
Irving Wy *SWLY* BR8 ...... **40** A7
Island Wy East *CHAT* ME4 ...... **50** C5
Island Wy West *CHAT* ME4 ...... **50** C4
Islingham Rd *HOO/HM* ME3 ...... **49** H3
Ismays Rd *BGR/WK* TN15 ...... **126** B4
Istead Ri *MEO* DA13 ...... **45** G5
Itchingwood Common Rd
  OXTED RH8 ...... **141** G4
Ivens Rd *RMAID* ME17 ...... **137** H3
Iversgate CI *RHAM* ME8 ...... **70** C4
Ives Rd *TON* TN9 ...... **169** K5
Ivy Bower CI *GRH* DA9 ...... **25** G4
Ivy CI *DART* DA1 ...... **23** J5
  GVE DA12 ...... **45** K2
  RMAID ME17 ...... **158** B4
Ivy House La *SEV* TN13 ...... **101** F4
Ivy La *RSEV* TN14 ...... **100** A3

Ivy St *RHAM* ME8 ...... **70** C6

J

Jackass La *HAYES* BR2 ...... **74** A2
Jacklin CI *WALD* ME5 ...... **88** A3
Jackson Av *ROCH* ME1 ...... **67** K6
Jackson CI *GRH* DA9 ...... **24** E4
  RHAM ME8 ...... **69** K5
Jacksons La *TENT* TN30 ...... **230** A7 🖪
Jacob's La *RDART* DA2 ...... **33** J8
Jaggard Wy *STPH/PW* TN12 ...... **198** A3
Jagger CI *RDART* DA2 ...... **24** B6
Jail La *BH/WHM* TN16 ...... **97** H2
James St *DART* DA1 ...... **22** D6
  STRD ME2 ...... **66** A4
James St *CHAT* ME4 ...... **3** F4 🖪
  GILL ME7 ...... **4** C2
  MAID/BEAR ME14 ...... **7** D2
  ROCH ME1 ...... **2** C4
James Whathan Wy
  MAID/BEAR ME14 ...... **6** C2
Japonica CI *WALD* ME5 ...... **88** D1 🖪
Jarrett Av *STRD* ME2 ...... **49** J4 🖪
Jarvis La *CRBK* TN17 ...... **213** F5
Jarvis PI *TENT* TN30 ...... **230** B3 🖪
Jasmine CI *E/WMAL* ME19 ...... **108** D6
Jasmine Rd *E/WMAL* ME19 ...... **108** D6
Jasper Av *ROCH* ME1 ...... **2** C6
Javelin Rd *E/WMAL* ME19 ...... **129** H3
Jefferson Dr *RHAM* ME8 ...... **69** K8
Jeffery St *GILL* ME7 ...... **4** C2
Jeffrey CI *STPH/PW* TN12 ...... **198** A2
Jeffrey St *MAID/BEAR* ME14 ...... **7** D2
Jellicoe Av *GVE* DA12 ...... **45** K1
Jenkins' DI *CHAT* ME4 ...... **3** F5
Jenkins Dr *MAID/SHEP* ME15 ...... **156** A1
Jenner Rd *ROCH* ME1 ...... **2** C4
Jenner Wy *DIT/AY* ME20 ...... **86** E8
Jerome Rd *DIT/AY* ME20 ...... **108** D2
Jersey Rd *STRD* ME2 ...... **49** F6
Jeskyns Rd *MEO* DA13 ...... **46** A7
Jessica Ms *SIT* ME10 ...... **73** K7
Jetty Rd *HOO/HM* ME3 ...... **34** A7
Jewell St *STPH/PW* TN12 ...... **196** D1 🖪
Jeyes Rd *GILL* ME7 ...... **4** C4
Jezreels Rd *GILL* ME7 ...... **5** D5
Jiniwin Rd *ROCH* ME1 ...... **67** J7
Jockey La *CRBK* TN17 ...... **225** K1 🖪
Jodrell Wy *WTHK* RM20 ...... **13** K5
Johns CI *HART* DA3 ...... **62** A2
Johnsdale *OXTED* RH8 ...... **118** D8
Johnson Av *GILL* ME7 ...... **4** C1
Johnson CI *CVW* DA11 ...... **44** E1
Johnson Rd *SIT* ME10 ...... **93** J2
Johnsons Wy *RSEV* TN14 ...... **77** J5
Johnsons Wy *GRH* DA9 ...... **25** H5 🖪
John's Rd *BH/WHM* TN16 ...... **97** H7
  MEO DA13 ...... **63** G2
John St *MAID/BEAR* ME14 ...... **7** D1
  ROCH ME1 ...... **2** C4
  STH/RUST TN4 ...... **10** C2
Joiners St *CHAT* ME4 ...... **4** B6
Jordan CI *MAID/SHEP* ME15 ...... **156** A1
Joslin Rd *PUR* RM19 ...... **13** G5
Joyce CI *CRBK* TN17 ...... **225** J2
Joyce Green La *DART* DA1 ...... **12** B8
Joyden's Wood Rd *BXLY* DA5 ...... **40** A2 🖪
Joy Rd *GVE* DA12 ...... **27** K7
Jubilee CI *GRH* DA9 ...... **25** H5
Jubilee Crs *BGR/WK* TN15 ...... **104** C8
Jubilee Fld *TENT* TN30 ...... **247** K2
Jubilee Ri *BGR/WK* TN15 ...... **102** D5
Jubilee Rd *ORP* BR6 ...... **77** H2
Jubilee St *SIT* ME10 ...... **93** K1
Jubilee Ter *GILL* ME7 ...... **4** C2 🖪
Judd Rd *TON* TN9 ...... **170** B7
Judeth Gdns *GVE* DA12 ...... **46** B3
Judkins CI *WALD* ME5 ...... **68** D3 🖪
Juglans Rd *ORP* BR6 ...... **56** B5
Julian Rd *ORP* BR6 ...... **76** D2
Julians CI *SEV* TN13 ...... **8** C6
Julians Wy *SEV* TN13 ...... **8** A3
Juliette Wy *PUR* RM19 ...... **12** D2
Junction Rd *DART* DA1 ...... **23** G5
  GILL ME7 ...... **5** D4
  RBTBR TN32 ...... **242** B4
Juniper CI *BH/WHM* TN16 ...... **97** J4
  MAIDW ME16 ...... **110** B8
  RTWE/PEM TN2 ...... **190** D5
  WALD ME5 ...... **88** B2
Jury St *GVE* DA12 ...... **27** J5 🖪
Jutland CI *HOO/HM* ME3 ...... **19** G7

K

Katherine Rd *EDEN* TN8 ...... **164** C6
Keary Rd *SWCM* DA10 ...... **26** A6

Keats Gdns *TIL* RM18 ...... **27** J1
Keats Rd *DIT/AY* ME20 ...... **108** D3
Kedleston Dr *STMC/STPC* BR5 ...... **56** A3
Keefe CI *WALD* ME5 ...... **87** J5
Keel Gdns *STH/RUST* TN4 ...... **189** J6
Keith Av *EYN* DA4 ...... **42** A4
Keith Park Crs *BH/WHM* TN16 ...... **74** B7
Kelchers La *RTON* TN11 ...... **172** B1
Kellaway Rd *WALD* ME5 ...... **88** B4
Kelly Dr *GILL* ME7 ...... **4** C1
Kelsey Rd *STMC/STPC* BR5 ...... **38** C7
Kelso Dr *GVE* DA12 ...... **46** C2
Kelvin CI *TONN* TN10 ...... **148** D7
Kelvin Rd *TIL* RM18 ...... **27** H1
Kemble CI *RTWE/PEM* TN2 ...... **190** E7
Kembleside Rd *BH/WHM* TN16 ...... **97** G5 🖪
Kemp CI *WALD* ME5 ...... **87** J2 🖪
Kempton CI *WALD* ME5 ...... **88** D3
Kemsing Rd *BGR/WK* TN15 ...... **104** B4
Kemsley CI *GRH* DA9 ...... **25** C5
  GVW DA11 ...... **45** C2
Kemsley Rd *BH/WHM* TN16 ...... **97** H6
Kemsley Street Rd
  MAID/BEAR ME14 ...... **89** K5
Kendal Dr *TON* TN9 ...... **170** C4
Kendal Pk *STH/RUST* TN4 ...... **10** A2
Kendal Wy *RHAM* ME8 ...... **70** A6
Kenilworth Ct *SIT* ME10 ...... **93** H1
Kenilworth Dr *RHAM* ME8 ...... **70** A8
Kennard CI *ROCH* ME1 ...... **66** E4
Kennedy Gdns *SEV* TN13 ...... **9** E2
Kennel Barn Rd *RSIT* ME9 ...... **115** F2
Kennet La *TONN* TN10 ...... **170** C1
Kennington CI *MAID/SHEP* ME15 ...... **134** B6
  RHAM ME8 ...... **69** J2
Kent Av *MAID/SHEP* ME15 ...... **7** F6
  SIT ME10 ...... **93** J3
Kent CI *ORP* BR6 ...... **75** K2
  ROCH ME1 ...... **67** H6
  STPH/PW TN12 ...... **173** J8
Kent Hatch Rd *OXTED* RH8 ...... **141** C1
Kentish Gdns *RTWE/PEM* TN2 ...... **206** D6
Kent Rd *DART* DA1 ...... **23** C5
  GVW DA11 ...... **27** H7
  HART DA3 ...... **43** J7
  SNOD ME6 ...... **85** K8
  STH/RUST TN4 ...... **10** C1 🖪
  STMC/STPC BR5 ...... **56** C3
  STRD ME2 ...... **65** K8
Kent St *WBY/YAL* ME18 ...... **129** G4
Kent Ter *RHAM* ME8 ...... **71** F4
Kent Vw *SOCK/AV* RM15 ...... **13** G2
Kenward Ct *RTON* TN11 ...... **150** A6 🖪
Kenward Rd *MAIDW* ME16 ...... **132** C1
  WBY/YAL ME18 ...... **152** C3
Kenwood Av *HART* DA3 ...... **44** D8
  WALD ME5 ...... **88** B2
Kenwyn Rd *DART* DA1 ...... **23** C4
Kerry Av *PUR* RM19 ...... **12** D2
Kesteven CI *STRD* ME2 ...... **85** K1
Keston Av *HAYES* BR2 ...... **74** C4
Kestrel CI *SIT* ME10 ...... **94** B4
Kestrel Rd *WALD* ME5 ...... **88** B4
Keswick CI *TON* TN9 ...... **170** C4
Keswick Dr *MAIDW* ME16 ...... **132** C1
Keswick Rd *ORP* BR6 ...... **56** A5
  SIT ME10 ...... **94** B3
Ketridge La *WBY/YAL* ME18 ...... **130** B4
Kettle La *MAID/SHEP* ME15 ...... **131** J8
Kettlewell Ct *SWLY* BR8 ...... **40** C7
Kevington CI *STMC/STPC* BR5 ...... **56** A1 🖪
Kevington Dr *CHST* BR7 ...... **56** A1
Kewlands *MAID/BEAR* ME14 ...... **7** F1 🖪
Keycol HI *RSIT* ME9 ...... **92** D1
Keyes Av *CHAT* ME4 ...... **3** F6
Keyes Gdns *TON* TN9 ...... **169** K7
Keyes Rd *DART* DA1 ...... **23** K3
Keymer CI *BH/WHM* TN16 ...... **97** G5
Key St *SIT* ME10 ...... **93** F1
Keyworth CI *STPH/PW* TN12 ...... **173** H8 🖪
Khartoum Rd *CHAT* ME4 ...... **3** F2
Khyber Rd *GILL* ME7 ...... **4** B1
Kibbles La *STH/RUST* TN4 ...... **189** J6
Killewarren Wy *STMC/STPC* BR5 ...... **56** C4
Killick CI *SEV* TN13 ...... **101** G8
Killick Rd *HOO/HM* ME3 ...... **50** E1
Kiln Barn Rd *DIT/AY* ME20 ...... **109** G6
Kiln CI *SIT* ME10 ...... **94** D7
Kildown *GVE* DA12 ...... **45** K4
Kildown CI *MAIDW* ME16 ...... **110** D7
Kiln Fld *TENT* TN30 ...... **230** C2
Kiln La *RTON* TN11 ...... **168** D5
Kiln Wy *STPH/PW* TN12 ...... **193** J1
Kilnwood *RSEV* TN14 ...... **77** G8
Kimberley Rd *GILL* ME7 ...... **5** D5
Kincraig Dr *SEV* TN13 ...... **8** C2
King Arthur's Dr *STRD* ME2 ...... **49** F5
King Edward Av *DART* DA1 ...... **23** C5
King Edward Rd *CHAT* ME4 ...... **3** F6
  GILL ME7 ...... **5** F2
  GRH DA9 ...... **25** F4
  MAID/SHEP ME15 ...... **7** G3
  ROCH ME1 ...... **2** C3
Kingfisher CI *RSIT* ME9 ...... **73** K2
  STMC/STPC BR5 ...... **56** E1 🖪

Kingfisher Dr *WALD* ME5 .... 68 D7
Kingfisher Rd *DIT/AY* ME20 ...... 108 D4
King George Rd *WALD* ME5 .... 87 K2
King George V HI *RTW* TN1 .... 11 E2
King Henry Ms *ORP* BR6 .... 76 A1
King HI *E/WMAL* ME19 .... 129 J1
Kings Acre *MAID/SHEP* ME15 .... 134 C5 ▣
King's Av *ROCH* ME1 .... 2 C5
King's Bastion *GILL* ME7 .... 4 A3
Kingsdown Cl *GILL* ME7 .... 89 H2
  GVE DA12 .... 28 C7 ▣
  MAIDW ME16 .... 6 B5 ▣
Kingsdown Rd *RSIT* ME9 .... 117 J3
Kings Dr *GVE* DA12 .... 45 J1
Kingsgate Cl *MAIDW* ME16 ...... 132 C2
  STMC/STPC BR5 .... 38 D7
Kingsgate La *TENT* TN30 .... 247 H1
Kings Hill Av *E/WMAL* ME19 ..... 129 J2
Kingshill Dr *HOO/HM* ME3 .... 33 E8
Kingsingfield Cl *BGR/WK* TN15 .. 80 D4
Kingsingfield Rd *BGR/WK* TN15 .. 80 D4
Kingsland Gv *HDCN* TN27 .... 200 B1 ▣
Kingsland La *HDCN* TN27 .... 182 C5
Kings La *STPH/PW* TN12 .... 175 G7
Kingsley Av *DART* DA1 .... 23 K4
Kingsley Rd *MAID/SHEP* ME15 ... 7 D4
  ORP BR6 .... 76 A2
Kingsmead *BH/WHM* TN16 .... 97 H3
Kings Mill Cl *SIT* ME10 .... 93 K1 ▣
Kingsnorth Rd *RHAM* ME8 .... 69 G7
King's Orch *ROCH* ME1 .... 2 C3
Kingsridge Gdns *DART* DA1 .... 23 G5
Kings Rd *BH/WHM* TN16 .... 97 G4
  HDCN TN27 .... 200 A1 ▣
  ORP BR6 .... 56 A8
  TON TN9 .... 170 C7
  WALD ME5 .... 68 E5
Kings Standing Wy
  RTWE/PEM TN2 .... 191 F4
Kings Toll Rd *RTWE/PEM* TN2 .. 192 C8
Kingston Ct *GVW* DA11 .... 26 C5 ▣
Kingston Crs *WALD* ME5 .... 88 C2
Kingston Dr *MAID/SHEP* ME15 .. 133 G6
King St *CHAT* ME4 .... 4 A4
  E/WMAL ME19 .... 107 K6
  GVE DA12 .... 27 J5
  MAID/BEAR ME14 .... 7 D3
  ROCH ME1 .... 2 C4
  SIT ME10 .... 93 K1
Kingsway *GILL* ME7 .... 69 F5
  WALD ME5 .... 68 E5
Kingswear Gdns *STRD* ME2 ...... 2 C1 ▣
Kingswood Av *CHAT* ME4 .... 3 F6 ▣
  SWLY BR8 .... 58 C1
Kingswood Cl *DART* DA1 .... 23 F5
Kingswood Rd *GILL* ME7 .... 5 D2
  ROCH ME1 .... 87 J6
  RTWE/PEM TN2 .... 11 E4
  SEV TN13 .... 101 G8
King William Rd *GILL* ME7 .... 4 C1 ▣
Kinnings Rw *TON* TN9 .... 170 C4 ▣
Kinross Cl *WALD* ME5 .... 68 C7 ▣
Kipling Dr *DIT/AY* ME20 .... 108 D2
Kipling Rd *DART* DA1 .... 24 A4 ▣
Kippington Cl *SEV* TN13 .... 8 B3
Kippington Rd *SEV* TN13 .... 8 C4
Kirby Cl *CRBK* TN17 .... 225 K2
Kirby Rd *HOO/HM* ME3 .... 49 K1
  RDART DA2 .... 24 B6
Kirkdale *MAID/SHEP* ME15 ...... 155 F1
Kirkdale Cl *WALD* ME5 .... 88 C5
Kirkdale Rd *MAID/SHEP* ME15 .. 133 F8 ▣
  RTW TN1 .... 11 D3
Kirkins Cl *STPH/PW* TN12 .... 194 E8 ▣
Kitchener Cl *CHAT* ME4 .... 68 A5
  GVE DA12 .... 45 K2
Kitchener Rd *HOO/HM* ME3 .... 50 A2
  STRD ME2 .... 49 F6
Kite La *STPH/PW* TN12 .... 193 J8
Kit Hill Av *WALD* ME5 .... 87 K3
Knatts La *BGR/WK* TN15 .... 80 D6
Knatts Valley Rd *EYN* DA4 .... 80 B2
Knaves Acre *HDCN* TN27 .... 200 B1
Knave Wood Rd *RSEV* TN14 .... 102 C4
Knight Av *GILL* ME7 .... 5 D2
Knighton Rd *RSEV* TN14 .... 101 H4
Knightrider Ct *MAID/SHEP* ME15 . 7 D4 ▣
Knightrider St *MAID/SHEP* ME15 . 6 C4
Knight St *STRD* ME2 .... 2 A3
  TON TN10 .... 148 E8
Knightsbridge Cl *STH/RUST* TN4 . 10 B2
Knights Cl *HOO/HM* ME3 .... 51 F1
  RTWE/PEM TN2 .... 191 K7
Knights Cft *HART* DA3 .... 62 A7
Knightsfield Rd *SIT* ME10 .... 71 J8
Knights Manor Wy *DART* DA1 ... 23 J5
Knights Pk *RTWE/PEM* TN2 .... 191 F5
Knights Rdg *ORP* BR6 .... 76 C1 ▣
  RTWE/PEM TN2 .... 191 K7 ▣
Knights Rd *HOO/HM* ME3 .... 32 E8
Knight's Wy *HDCN* TN27 .... 200 B1
  RTWE/PEM TN2 .... 191 F6
Knockhall Cha *GRH* DA9 .... 25 H4
Knockhall Rd *GRH* DA9 .... 25 H5

Knockholt Rd *RSEV* TN14 .... 100 B1
Knock Mill La *BGR/WK* TN15 .... 81 F8
Knockwood Rd *TENT* TN30 ...... 230 C5
Knole La *BGR/WK* TN15 .... 9 E5
Knole Rd *DART* DA1 .... 22 D6
  SEV TN13 .... 9 F2
  WALD ME5 .... 88 D4
The Knole *MEO* DA13 .... 45 F5
Knole Wy *BGR/WK* TN15 .... 9 E4
Knoll Ri *ORP* BR6 .... 56 A5
Knoll Rd *SCUP* DA14 .... 38 C3
Knott Ct *MAID/BEAR* ME14 .... 7 D1
Knotts Pl *SEV* TN13 .... 8 C3
Knowle Cl *RRTW* TN3 .... 205 H5
Knowle La *STPH/PW* TN12 .... 194 A2
Knowle Rd *MAID/BEAR* ME14 .... 7 D1
  ROCH ME1 .... 86 B2
  STPH/PW TN12 .... 194 B4
Knowles Gdns *HDCN* TN27 ..... 200 B1 ▣
Knowlton Gdns *MAIDW* ME16 .. 132 B4 ▣
Knowsley Wy *RTON* TN11 .... 147 H8
Koonowla Cl *BH/WHM* TN16 ...... 97 H2
Kyetop Wk *RHAM* ME8 .... 70 C6 ▣
Kynaston Rd *STMC/STPC* BR5 .. 56 C4

Labour-in-vain Rd *BGR/WK* TN15 .. 81 J8
Laburnum Av *DART* DA1 .... 23 F7
  SWLY BR8 .... 40 A8
Laburnum Dr *DIT/AY* ME20 ..... 108 E4
Laburnum Gv *GVW* DA11 .... 26 E6
Laburnum Pl *SIT* ME10 .... 93 K2 ▣
Laburnum Rd *STRD* ME2 .... 66 D1
Lacey Cl *RMAID* ME17 .... 157 G2
Laceys La *RMAID* ME17 .... 154 C7
Lacy Cl *MAIDW* ME16 .... 110 D7 ▣
Ladbrooke Crs *SCUP* DA14 .... 38 E1
Ladds La *SNOD* ME6 .... 85 K4
Ladds Wy *SWLY* BR8 .... 58 A1
Ladham Rd *CRBK* TN17 .... 213 F4
Ladyclose Av *HOO/HM* ME3 ...... 31 F7
Ladycroft Gdns *ORP* BR6 .... 75 H1 ▣
Ladycroft Wy *ORP* BR6 .... 75 H1 ▣
Ladyfields *GVW* DA11 .... 45 G2
  WALD ME5 .... 88 E4 ▣
Ladyfields Cl *RSIT* ME9 .... 92 E1
Lady Oak La *CRBK* TN17 .... 223 G6
Lady's Gift Rd *STH/RUST* TN4 . 189 K6
Ladywood Rd *RDART* DA2 .... 42 D7
  STRD ME2 .... 66 A4
Lagonda Wy *DART* DA1 .... 23 F7
Lake Dr *HOO/HM* ME3 .... 30 B8
Lake Rd *DIT/AY* ME20 .... 109 J6
  STH/RUST TN4 .... 10 A3
Lakeside *EDEN* TN8 .... 166 B2
  SNOD ME6 .... 85 J8
Lakeside Cl *SNOD* ME6 .... 85 K8
Lakes Rd *HAYES* BR2 .... 74 B1
Lakeview *SNOD* ME6 .... 85 K8
Lake View Rd *SEV* TN13 .... 9 E2
Lakewood Dr *RHAM* ME8 .... 69 K8
Lambarde Cl *STRD* ME2 .... 85 K2 ▣
Lambarde Dr *SEV* TN13 .... 8 C2
Lambarde Rd *SEV* TN13 .... 8 C1
Lambardes *HART* DA3 .... 62 A7
Lamb Cl *TIL* RM18 .... 27 K1
Lambden Rd *HDCN* TN27 .... 183 H8
Lamberhurst Rd *STMC/STPC* BR5 . 56 E5 ▣
Lamberhurst Gn *RHAM* ME8 ...... 69 J4
Lamberhurst Rd *STPH/PW* TN12 . 211 F5
Lambersart Rd *RTWE/PEM* TN2 . 190 D5 ▣
Lambert Cl *BH/WHM* TN16 .... 97 H3
Lambert Ms *SNOD* ME6 .... 85 K6 ▣
Lamberts Pl *STPH/PW* TN12 .... 212 A1
Lamberts Rd *RTWE/PEM* TN2 .. 190 D6
Lambert's Yd *TON* TN9 .... 170 B5 ▣
Lambeth Cl *WALD* ME5 .... 88 C2
Lambfrith Gv *GILL* ME7 .... 89 J3
Lambourne Dr *E/WMAL* ME19 .. 129 H4
Lambourne Pl *RHAM* ME8 .... 70 D4
Lambourn Wy *RTWE/PEM* TN2 . 191 H6
  WALD ME5 .... 88 D4
Lambs Bank *TON* TN9 .... 170 B7
Lambsfrith Gv *GILL* ME7 .... 89 J3
Lammas Dr *SIT* ME10 .... 73 K8
Lamorna Av *GVE* DA12 .... 28 A8
Lamorna Cl *ORP* BR6 .... 56 B8 ▣
Lampington Rw *RRTW* TN3 ..... 205 H3 ▣
Lamplighters Cl *DART* DA1 .... 23 J5 ▣
  GILL ME7 .... 89 G2
Lancashire Rd *MAID/SHEP* ME15 . 134 A7
Lancaster Ct *RHAM* ME8 .... 69 K7
Lancaster Wy *E/WMAL* ME19 .. 129 H3
Lancelot Av *STRD* ME2 .... 48 D7
Lancelot Cl *STRD* ME2 .... 48 D8
Lances Cl *MEO* DA13 .... 63 H4 ▣
Lancet La *MAID/SHEP* ME15 .... 133 F8
Lancing Rd *ORP* BR6 .... 56 C6
Landale Gdns *DART* DA1 .... 23 F7

Landau Wy *ERITH* DA8 .... 12 B5
Landor Ct *GILL* ME7 .... 89 H3
Landrail Rd *RSIT* ME9 .... 72 A3
Landseer Av *GVW* DA11 .... 44 E1
Landseer Cl *TONN* TN10 .... 148 E8
Landway *BGR/WK* TN15 .... 102 D7
Land Wy *HOO/HM* ME3 .... 48 C1
The Landway *BGR/WK* TN15 .... 102 E4
  BGR/WK TN15 .... 105 F7
  MAID/BEAR ME14 .... 134 C2 ▣
  STMC/STPC BR5 .... 38 D8
Lanes Av *GVW* DA11 .... 45 G1
The Lane *RRTW* TN3 .... 205 F1
Langafel Cl *HART* DA3 .... 43 K7
Langdale Cl *RHAM* ME8 .... 70 A5
Langdale Ri *MAIDW* ME16 .... 132 C1 ▣
Langdon Rd *ROCH* ME1 .... 2 C4 ▣
Langdon Shaw *SCUP* DA14 .... 38 A3
Langford Pl *SCUP* DA14 .... 38 B1
Langham Gv *MAIDW* ME16 ...... 132 C2
Langholm Rd *RRTW* TN3 .... 205 J3
Langlands Dr *RDART* DA2 .... 42 D3
Langton Cl *MAID/BEAR* ME14 .... 7 F2
Langton Rd *RRTW* TN3 .... 188 E7
Langworth Cl *RDART* DA2 .... 41 G1
Lankester Parker Rd *ROCH* ME1 . 67 H8 ▣
Lansbury Crs *DART* DA1 .... 23 K4
Lansdowne Av *MAID/SHEP* ME15 . 133 J3
Lansdowne Rd *CHAT* ME4 .... 3 E6
  RTW TN1 .... 11 E5 ▣
  SEV TN13 .... 9 F2
  TON TN9 .... 170 B4
  TONN TN10 .... 170 B3
Lansdowne Sq *GVW* DA11 .... 27 G5
  RTW TN1 .... 11 D3 ▣
Lansdown Rd *GVW* DA11 .... 27 G7 ▣
  SCUP DA14 .... 38 C1
  SIT ME10 .... 92 D2
  TIL RM18 .... 27 G1
Lapins La *WBY/YAL* ME18 .... 129 H4
Lapis Cl *GVE* DA12 .... 28 E7
Lapwing Dr *RSIT* ME9 .... 72 A3
Lapwing Rd *HOO/HM* ME3 .... 37 G1
Lapwings *HART* DA3 .... 44 C8
Lapworth Cl *ORP* BR6 .... 56 D6
Larch Cl *DIT/AY* ME20 .... 109 F4
Larch Crs *HOO/HM* ME3 .... 51 F3 ▣▣
  TONN TN10 .... 148 C8
Larchcroft *WALD* ME5 .... 88 D5
The Larches *HOO/HM* ME3 .... 48 B5 ▣
Larch Gv *STPH/PW* TN12 .... 173 H8
Larch Rd *DART* DA1 .... 23 G7
Larch Wood Cl *WALD* ME5 .... 88 E5
Larkfield *STPH/PW* TN12 .... 172 C7
Larkfield Av *GILL* ME7 .... 5 E4
  SIT ME10 .... 73 K8
Larkfield Cl *DIT/AY* ME20 .... 108 E5
Larkfield Rd *DIT/AY* ME20 .... 108 E5
  SCUP DA14 .... 38 A1
  SEV TN13 .... 122 E2
Larkfields *GVW* DA11 .... 45 F1
Larkin Cl *STRD* ME2 .... 49 G4
Larking Dr *MAIDW* ME16 .... 110 D7
Larks Fld *HART* DA3 .... 62 A1
Larkspur Cl *E/WMAL* ME19 .... 108 C5 ▣
  ORP BR6 .... 56 D6 ▣
Larkspur Rd *E/WMAL* ME19 .... 108 D5
  WALD ME5 .... 87 K2
Larkwell La *HART* DA3 .... 62 A1
Laser Quay *STRD* ME2 .... 3 D2
Latham Cl *BH/WHM* TN16 .... 97 G3
Latimer Pl *GILL* ME7 .... 4 C1 ▣
Latona Dr *GVE* DA12 .... 46 C3
Latymers *RTON* TN11 .... 187 K2
Launder Wy *MAID/SHEP* ME15 .. 6 B5
Laura Dr *SWLY* BR8 .... 40 D5
Laura Pl *ROCH* ME1 .... 66 E4 ▣
Laurel Av *GVE* DA12 .... 27 K8
Laurel Bank *STH/RUST* TN4 .... 190 B6
Laurel Cl *DART* DA1 .... 23 F7
  SCUP DA14 .... 38 B1
Laurel Dr *OXTED* RH8 .... 140 D2
Laurel Gv *RMAID* ME17 .... 158 B4
Laurel Rd *GILL* ME7 .... 4 C1
  RTWE/PEM TN2 .... 190 D7
The Laurels *HART* DA3 .... 44 D8
  MAIDW ME16 .... 132 C4 ▣
Laurie Gray Av *WALD* ME5 .... 87 J5
Lavenda Cl *GILL* ME7 .... 89 H2
Lavender Cl *E/WMAL* ME19 .... 108 D6
Lavender Ct *SIT* ME10 .... 94 B3
Lavender Gdns *WADH* TN5 ...... 232 C5 ▣
Lavender HI *SWLY* BR8 .... 40 A8
  TON TN9 .... 170 C6
Lavender Rd *E/WMAL* ME19 .... 108 D6
Lavenders Rd *E/WMAL* ME19 .. 108 A7
Laverstoke Rd *MAIDW* ME16 ... 110 C6
Lavinia Rd *DART* DA1 .... 23 J5
Lawford Gdns *DART* DA1 .... 23 F4
Lawn Cl *CHAT* ME4 .... 3 F6
  SWLY BR8 .... 39 K7
  TENT TN30 .... 229 F7
Lawn Pk *SEV* TN13 .... 9 D6
Lawn Rd *GVW* DA11 .... 26 D5
  TON TN9 .... 170 B6

The Lawns SCUP DA14 ... 38 C2
  STPH/PW TN12 ... 193 K6
Lawrence CI MAID/SHEP ME15 ... 133 G7
Lawrence Dr GVE DA12 ... 64 D1
Lawrence Hill Gdns DART DA1 ... 23 F5
Lawrence Hill DART DA1 ... 23 F5
Lawrence Rd TONN TN10 ... 148 E8
Lawrence St GILL ME7 ... 4 C3
Lawson Gdns DART DA1 ... 23 G4
Lawson Rd DART DA1 ... 23 G3
Laxey Rd ORP BR6 ... 76 A2
The Laxey MAID/SHEP ME15 ... 6 B5
Laxton CI MAID/SHEP ME15 ... 134 B3
Laxton Dr RMAID ME17 ... 156 C5
Laxton Gdns STPH/PW TN12 ... 173 G7
Laxton Wy SIT ME10 ... 73 J8
Layfield Rd GILL ME7 ... 5 F1
Leafield La SCUP DA14 ... 39 G2
Leafy Gln RHAM ME8 ... 69 J8
Leafy Gv HAYES BR2 ... 74 B1
Leafy La MEO DA13 ... 83 H2
Lealands Av RTON TN10 ... 168 C5
Lealands CI RRTW TN3 ... 205 F7
Leaman CI RMAID ME17 ... 33 F2
Leander Dr GVE DA12 ... 46 C2
Leander Rd ROCH ME1 ... 67 H7
Lea Rd SEV TN13 ... 9 E6
Leas Gn CHST BR7 ... 38 A4
The Leas WADH TN5 ... 220 C8
Leather CI EDEN TN8 ... 164 C6
Lea V DART DA1 ... 22 A3
Leaves Green Crs HAYES BR2 ... 74 B6
Leaves Green Rd HAYES BR2 ... 74 B6
Lebanon Gdns BH/WHM TN16 ... 97 H4
Leconfield CI TON TN9 ... 169 K7
Leechcroft Av SWLY BR8 ... 40 C8
Leeds CI ORP BR6 ... 56 E6
Leeds Rd RMAID ME17 ... 157 G3
Leeds Sq RHAM ME8 ... 69 J3
Lee Gn STMC/STPC BR5 ... 56 B2
Lee Green Rd HOO/HM ME3 ... 49 J2
Lee Rd SNOD ME6 ... 85 K6
Leesons Wy STMC/STPC BR5 ... 38 A7
Lees Rd WBY/YAL ME18 ... 152 C7
Leet CI GILL ME7 ... 5 E2
Leeward Rd ROCH ME1 ... 67 H5
Leewood Pl SWLY BR8 ... 58 A1
Legge La E/WMAL ME19 ... 85 G7
Leggs' La RRTW TN3 ... 205 H1
Leicester Dr RTWE/PEM TN2 ... 206 E6
Leicester Rd MAID/SHEP ME15 ... 133 K7
Leigh Av MAID/SHEP ME15 ... 133 H8
Leigh Rd GVW DA11 ... 27 J3
  HOO/HM ME3 ... 49 H3
  RTON TN11 ... 169 H4
Leighton CI STH/RUST TN4 ... 190 A7
Leith HI STMC/STPC BR5 ... 38 B6
Leith Park Rd GVW DA11 ... 27 J7
London Rd BGR/WK TN15 ... 105 F8
Leneda Dr RTWE/PEM TN2 ... 206 D6
Leney Rd WBY/YAL ME18 ... 130 C7
Lenfield Av RMAID/BEAR ME14 ... 7 E3
Lenham Forstal Rd RMAID ME17 ... 161 H6
Lenham Heath Rd RMAID ME17 ... 160 B3
Lenham Rd HDCN TN27 ... 180 E6
  RMAID ME17 ... 158 D4
Lennard Rd SEV TN13 ... 101 C7
Lennox Av GVW DA11 ... 27 H5
Lennox CI GVW DA11 ... 27 G5
Lennox East GVW DA11 ... 27 H6
Lenside Dr MAID/SHEP ME15 ... 134 C4
Leonard Av RSEV TN14 ... 101 K2
  SWCM DA10 ... 25 K6
Leonard CI MAIDW ME16 ... 110 B8
Leonard Rd CHAT ME4 ... 4 B5
Leopold Rd CHAT ME4 ... 4 A5
Lesley CI MEO DA13 ... 45 G6
  SWLY BR8 ... 40 A8
Lesley Pl MAIDW ME16 ... 6 B2
Leslie Crs TENT TN30 ... 230 B1
Leslie Rd GILL ME7 ... 5 D1
Lested La RMAID ME17 ... 156 D4
Lester Rd CHAT ME4 ... 4 B5
Letchworth Av CHAT ME4 ... 68 A5
Le Temple Rd STPH/PW TN12 ... 173 K7
Letter Box La SEV TN13 ... 124 A8
Levett CI HOO/HM ME3 ... 21 G8
Levetts La RBTBR TN32 ... 242 C1
Lewd La HDCN TN27 ... 202 A2
Lewis Av RHAM ME8 ... 69 J4
Lewis Court Dr RMAID ME17 ... 155 H3
Lewis Rd MEO DA13 ... 45 G6
  SCUP DA14 ... 38 D1
  SWCM DA10 ... 25 K5
Leybank RTON TN11 ... 169 J2
Leybourne CI WALD ME5 ... 88 B4
Leybourne Dell CHAT ME4 ... 227 C8
Leybourne Rd STRD ME2 ... 48 E6
Leybourne Wy DIT/AY ME20 ... 108 D2
Leydenhatch La SWLY BR8 ... 40 A6
Leyhill CI SWLY BR8 ... 58 B2
Leyton Av GILL ME7 ... 69 F5
Leyton Cross Rd RDART DA2 ... 40 C1
Leywood Rd MEO DA13 ... 84 A3
Lezayre Rd ORP BR6 ... 76 A2

Lidsing Rd GILL ME7 ... 89 G4
  MAID/BEAR ME14 ... 111 J2
Lilac Crs STRD ME2 ... 48 D5
Lilac Gdns SWLY BR8 ... 40 A8
Lilac Gn E/WMAL ME19 ... 108 E6
Lilac Pl MEO DA13 ... 63 J4
Lilac Rd STRD ME2 ... 66 D1
Lila Pl SWLY BR8 ... 58 B1
Lillechurch Rd HOO/HM ME3 ... 30 E7
Lillieburn E/WMAL ME19 ... 108 B4
Lillie Rd BH/WHM TN16 ... 97 H5
Lime Av GVW DA11 ... 26 E6
Lime CI STPH/PW TN12 ... 176 C8
Lime Ct RHAM ME8 ... 89 K3
Lime Crs E/WMAL ME19 ... 108 E7
Lime Gv SIT ME10 ... 94 B2
Lime Hill Rd RTW TN1 ... 10 C5
Lime Pit La RSEV TN14 ... 100 E4
Lime Rd SWLY BR8 ... 40 A8
Limes CI TENT TN30 ... 230 C7
Limes Gv HAWK TN18 ... 235 F1
Limes Rw ORP BR6 ... 75 G1
The Limes EDEN TN8 ... 164 C5
  PUR RM19 ... 12 E5
Lime Tree Av GRH DA9 ... 29 J5
Lime Tree CI TON TN9 ... 170 C4
Limetree CI WALD ME5 ... 68 C7
Lime Trees STPH/PW TN12 ... 198 A2
Lime Tree Wk SEV TN13 ... 9 D4
Linclon St ERITH DA8 ... 22 C1
Lincoln Green Rd STMC/STPC BR5 ... 56 A2
Lincoln Rd ERITH DA8 ... 22 C1
  MAID/SHEP ME15 ... 133 J6
  SCUP DA14 ... 38 C3
Lincon Rd GILL ME7 ... 5 D1
Linden Av DART DA1 ... 23 F7
Linden Cha SEV TN13 ... 9 D1
Linden CI ORP BR6 ... 76 B1
  PUR RM19 ... 13 G6
  RTWE/PEM TN2 ... 10 B5
  SIT ME10 ... 93 J3
  STPH/PW TN12 ... 173 J8
Linden Gdns RTWE/PEM TN2 ... 10 B6
Linden Park Rd RTWE/PEM TN2 ... 10 B6
Linden Rd GILL ME7 ... 5 E3
  RMAID ME17 ... 154 C2
Linden Sq SEV TN13 ... 8 A1
The Lindens DIT/AY ME20 ... 109 J4
Lindisfarne La GVE DA12 ... 28 B8
Lindridge La STPH/PW TN12 ... 197 J1
Lineacre CI RHAM ME8 ... 70 A8
Lines Ter CHAT ME4 ... 4 A4
Lingfield Av RDART DA2 ... 24 A6
Lingfield Rd BGR/WK TN15 ... 105 G7
  EDEN TN8 ... 164 A6
  GVE DA12 ... 27 J8
Lingley Dr STRD ME2 ... 49 H4
Link Hill La HDCN TN27 ... 182 C4
The Links E/WMAL ME19 ... 107 G4
  WALD ME5 ... 68 C6
Links Vw DART DA1 ... 23 F7
Linkway DIT/AY ME20 ... 109 C5
  RSIT ME9 ... 73 J2
Link Wy RTWE/PEM TN2 ... 190 E6
Linnet Av GVW DA11 ... 27 G5
Linnet Wy PUR RM19 ... 13 F5
Linslade Rd ORP BR6 ... 76 B2
Linton Dann CI HOO/HM ME3 ... 32 E8
Linton Gore RMAID ME17 ... 154 C3
Linton HI RMAID ME17 ... 154 C3
Linton Rd MAID/SHEP ME15 ... 155 F3
Linwood Av STRD ME2 ... 48 D6
Lionel Rd TON TN9 ... 170 A6
Liphook Wy MAIDW ME16 ... 110 C6
Lipscombe Rd RTWE/PEM TN2 ... 11 F1
Liptraps La RTWE/PEM TN2 ... 190 D7
Lipwell HI HOO/HM ME3 ... 32 C2
Lisle CI GVE DA12 ... 28 E8
Lismore CI MAID/SHEP ME15 ... 133 G7
Lister CI E/WMAL ME19 ... 108 D6
Lister Rd TIL RM18 ... 27 H1
Listmas Rd CHAT ME4 ... 4 B5
Little Aly EDEN TN8 ... 184 B1
Little Bounds CI STH/RUST TN4 ... 189 J3
Littlebourne Av RHAM ME8 ... 69 J2
Littlebourne Rd MAID/BEAR ME14 ... 7 F1
Littlebrook Manor Wy DART DA1 ... 23 K4
Little Browns La EDEN TN8 ... 163 J2
Little Buckland Av MAIDW ME16 ... 6 A1
Littlecourt Rd SEV TN13 ... 8 C3
Littlecroft MEO DA13 ... 45 F5
Littlefield Rd RHAM ME8 ... 70 E4
Little Footway RRTW TN3 ... 205 J3
Little Glovers SIT ME10 ... 94 A3
Little John Av WALD ME5 ... 88 A4
Littlejohn Rd STMC/STPC BR5 ... 56 B3
Little Julians HI SEV TN13 ... 8 C6
Little Mallett RRTW TN3 ... 205 J3
Little Market Rw E/WMAL ME19 ... 108 C4
Little Mount Sion RTW TN1 ... 10 C5
Little Oakham Ct HOO/HM ME3 ... 35 F2
Little Orch RMAID ME17 ... 154 D3
Little Oxley DIT/AY ME20 ... 108 C4
Little Queen St DART DA1 ... 23 J6

Little Robhurst RASHW TN26 ... 219 J7
Little Wd SEV TN13 ... 9 E1
Little Wood CI STMC/STPC BR5 ... 38 B6
Livesey St WBY/YAL ME18 ... 130 D4
Livingstone Gdns GVE DA12 ... 46 A3
Livingstone Rd GILL ME7 ... 5 E3
  GVE DA12 ... 46 A3
Lloyds Gn TENT TN30 ... 247 J2
Loampits CI TON TN9 ... 170 D3
Lobelia CI GILL ME7 ... 5 E2
Locarno Av RHAM ME8 ... 69 H4
Lochat Rd HOO/HM ME3 ... 31 K8
Lockesley CI STMC/STPC BR5 ... 56 A3
Lockington CI TON TN9 ... 169 K7
Lockington Gv ROCH ME1 ... 2 C3
Lock La MAIDW ME16 ... 110 D5
Lockside TON TN9 ... 170 C4
Locksley CI WALD ME5 ... 87 K4
Lock St GILL ME7 ... 4 B3
Lockswood MAIDW ME16 ... 110 D7
Lockyer CI PUR RM19 ... 13 G5
Lockyers HI MEO DA13 ... 84 B1
Loddington La RMAID ME17 ... 155 G7
Loder CI RMAID ME17 ... 160 B1
Lodge Av DART DA1 ... 23 F5
Lodge CI ORP BR6 ... 56 C5
  WBY/YAL ME18 ... 130 B6
Lodge Ct GVE DA12 ... 47 H4
Lodge Crs ORP BR6 ... 56 C5
Lodge Gdns RMAID ME17 ... 158 D8
Lodge Hill La HOO/HM ME3 ... 32 A8
Lodge La BH/WHM TN16 ... 120 C6
  GVE DA12 ... 64 E1
Lodge Oak La TON TN9 ... 170 D6
Lodge Rd MAID/BEAR ME14 ... 133 K1
  STPH/PW TN12 ... 198 A1
  TON TN9 ... 170 B4
Lomas La HAWK TN18 ... 244 D1
Lomas Rd SIT ME10 ... 94 E2
Lombard St EYN DA4 ... 60 B1
Lombardy CI GILL ME7 ... 69 H8
Lombardy Dr MAID/BEAR ME14 ... 7 F2
London La CRBK TN17 ... 215 H4
London Rd BGR/WK TN15 ... 81 G5
  BH/WHM TN16 ... 120 D4
  DART DA1 ... 22 A4
  DIT/AY ME20 ... 109 F5
  E/WMAL ME19 ... 106 E5
  EYN DA4 ... 59 G3
  GRH DA9 ... 24 D5
  GVW DA11 ... 26 E5
  RDART DA2 ... 24 B6
  RHAM ME8 ... 70 D6
  RSEV TN14 ... 77 G4
  RSIT ME9 ... 71 J7
  SEV TN13 ... 8 B2
  SIT ME10 ... 93 H1
  SOCK/AV RM15 ... 12 C2
  STH/RUST TN4 ... 10 C4
  STRD ME2 ... 2 A1
  SWCM DA10 ... 25 K4
  SWLY BR8 ... 39 K7
  SWLY BR8 ... 40 B8
  TIL RM18 ... 27 J1
  TONN TN10 ... 170 B3
  WADH TN5 ... 233 H3
London Road Purfleet PUR RM19 ... 13 F6
London Road Rocky HI
  MAIDW ME16 ... 6 B3
London Road West Thurrock
  WTHK RM20 ... 13 K6
Lone Barn Rd RMAID ME17 ... 139 H6
Lonewood Wy RTON TN11 ... 150 B4
Long Acre STMC/STPC BR5 ... 56 E6
Long Barn Rd RSEV TN14 ... 145 K4
Longbury CI STMC/STPC BR5 ... 38 C8
Longbury Dr STMC/STPC BR5 ... 38 C8
Long Catlis Rd RHAM ME8 ... 90 A2
Long Ct PUR RM19 ... 12 E4
Longfellow Rd GILL ME7 ... 4 C5
Longfield TENT TN30 ... 230 A7
Longfield Av HART DA3 ... 44 B7
  HOO/HM ME3 ... 33 F2
Longfield Pl MAID/SHEP ME15 ... 133 H6
Longfield Rd MEO DA13 ... 63 F2
  RTWE/PEM TN2 ... 190 E6
Longfields Dr MAID/BEAR ME14 ... 134 C3
Longford CI RHAM ME8 ... 70 D6
Longham Copse
  MAID/SHEP ME15 ... 134 B5
Longhill Av GILL ME7 ... 4 B5
Longhurst Dr WALD ME5 ... 88 A3
Long La RMAID ME17 ... 177 K1
Longley Rd RHAM ME8 ... 70 C5
  ROCH ME1 ... 42 C6
Longmarsh Vw EYN DA4 ... 42 A6
Longmeadow SEV TN13 ... 101 F8
Long Meads RRTW TN3 ... 206 A3
Long Mead Wy TONN TN10 ... 170 B1
Long Mill La BGR/WK TN15 ... 127 G5
Longparish CI MAID/SHEP ME15 ... 134 B7
Long Rede la RMAID/BEAR ME16 ... 131 K3
Longridge SIT ME10 ... 94 C4
Longshaw Rd MAID/SHEP ME15 ... 156 B2
Long Slip RRTW TN3 ... 205 K3

Longview Wy *RTWE/PEM* TN2 ...... **190** D6
Longwalk *MEO* DA13 .... **45** F6
Longwood *WALD* ME5 .... **88** C5
Lonsdale Crs *RDART* DA2 .... **24** B8
Lonsdale Dr *RHAM* ME8 .... **70** B8
   SIT ME10 .... **93** H1
Lonsdale Gdns *RTW* TN1 .... **10** C4 🗆
Loose Rd *MAID/SHEP* ME15 ...... **133** G8
Lord Chatham's Ride *RSEV* TN14 ... **99** J4
Lords CI *RSIT* ME9 .... **95** F4
Lord St *GVE* DA12 .... **27** J6
Lordswood CI *RDART* DA2 .... **42** D2
Lords Wood CI *WALD* ME5 .... **88** C4
Lords Wood La *WALD* ME5 .... **88** C1
Lorton CI *GVE* DA12 .... **28** B8
Lossenham La *HAWK* TN18 .... **245** G2
Lotus Rd *BH/WHM* TN16 .... **97** K5
Louisville Av *GILL* ME7 .... **5** D4
Louvain Rd *RDART* DA2 .... **24** D6
Lovelace CI *BGR/WK* TN15 .... **80** D2 🗆
   RHAM ME8 .... **90** A1
Love La *HDCN* TN27 .... **200** E1
   ROCH ME1 .... **2** C3
   SOCK/AV RM15 .... **13** G2
   WBY/YAL ME18 .... **130** B7
Lovers La *CRBK* TN17 .... **212** D5
   GRH DA9 .... **25** J3
Low CI *GRH* DA9 .... **25** F4
Lower Bell La *DIT/AY* ME20 .... **109** F4
Lower Bloors La *RHAM* ME8 .... **70** B4
Lower Boxley Rd
   MAID/BEAR ME14 .... **6** C2 🗆
Lower Cft *SWLY* BR8 .... **58** C1
Lower Fant Rd *MAIDW* ME16 .... **6** B4
Lower Farm Rd *RMAID* ME17 ...... **155** H8
Lower Gn *RTON* TN11 .... **168** D5
Lower Green Rd *RRTW* TN3 .... **206** B1
   RTWE/PEM TN2 .... **191** K8
   STH/RUST TN4 .... **206** B2
Lower Hartlip Rd *RSIT* ME9 .... **91** C2
Lower Haysden La *TON* TN9 .... **169** H6
Lower Higham Rd *GVE* DA12 .... **28** C7
Lower Platts *WADH* TN5 .... **232** C5
Lower Rainham Rd *GILL* ME7 .... **69** K1
   RHAM ME8 .... **70** E3
Lower Range Rd *GVE* DA12 .... **28** B6
Lower Rd *GVE* DA12 .... **29** H8
   CVW DA11 .... **26** B3
   MAID/SHEP ME15 .... **7** E4
   MAID/SHEP ME15 .... **131** C2
   RMAID ME17 .... **157** C7
   RSIT ME9 .... **95** G3
   STMC/STPC BR5 .... **56** C3
   SWLY BR8 .... **40** C1
   TENT TN30 .... **241** J8
   TIL RM18 .... **9** J2
Lower Rochester Rd *HOO/HM* ME3... **30** C8
Lower Station Rd *DART* DA1 .... **22** B5
Lower St *RMAID* ME17 .... **135** J7
   RTON TN11 .... **168** E1
Lower Tovil *MAID/SHEP* ME15...... **6** B5
Lower Twydall La *GILL* ME7 .... **69** K2
   RHAM ME8 .... **69** J2
Lower Warren Rd *WALD* ME5 .... **87** K8
Lower Woodlands Rd *GILL* ME7 ...... **5** F2
Lowfield St *DART* DA1 .... **23** H6
Lowlands Rd *SOCK/AV* RM15 .... **13** C5
Low Meadow *STRD* ME2 .... **85** K1
Loxwood CI *STMC/STPC* BR5 .... **56** E6
Lubbock CI *MAID/SHEP* ME15 .... **156** A1 🗆
Luddesdown Rd *MEO* DA13 .... **64** D5
Lughorse La *WBY/YAL* ME18 ...... **152** B4
Lullarook CI *BH/WHM* TN16 .... **97** C3
Lullingstone Av *SWLY* BR8 .... **40** C8
Lullingstone CI *GILL* ME7 .... **89** J3
   STMC/STPC BR5 .... **38** C5 🗆
Lullingstone Crs *STMC/STPC* BR5.... **38** B5
Lullingstone La *EYN* DA4 .... **59** F7
Lullingstone Rd *MAIDW* ME16 ...... **110** C7
Lumsden Ter *CHAT* ME4 .... **3** E4 🗆
Lunar CI *BH/WHM* TN16 .... **97** H3
Lunedale Rd *RDART* DA2 .... **24** B7
Lunsford La *DIT/AY* ME20 .... **108** D4
Lurkins Ri *CRBK* TN17 .... **212** C2
Lushington Rd *MAID/BEAR* ME14... **110** E2
Lustead Hall La *BH/WHM* TN16 ..... **97** C7
Luton High St *WALD* ME5 .... **4** C6
Luton Rd *CHAT* ME4 .... **4** D6
   SCUP DA14 .... **38** D1
Luxon Rd *MEO* DA13 .... **84** B2
Luxted Rd *ORP* BR6 .... **75** F7
Lyall Wy *RHAM* ME8 .... **90** A2
Lychfield Dr *STRD* ME2 .... **49** F5
Lych Gate Rd *ORP* BR6 .... **56** B5
Lydbrook CI *SIT* ME10 .... **93** H2

Lydd Rd *WALD* ME5 .... **88** C1 🗆
Lydens La *EDEN* TN8 .... **165** F8
Lyle CI *STRD* ME2 .... **49** G6
Lyle Ct *MAIDW* ME16 .... **132** C2
Lyle Pk *SEV* TN13 .... **9** D2
Lyminge CI *RHAM* ME8 .... **69** K4
   SCUP DA14 .... **38** A2
Lymington Ct *MAID/SHEP* ME15 .. **156** B2 🗆
Lynden Wy *SWLY* BR8 .... **39** K8
Lyndhurst Av *RHAM* ME8 .... **69** K7
Lyndhurst Dr *SEV* TN13 .... **8** A3
Lyndhurst Gv *SIT* ME10.................. **93** K4
Lyndhurst Rd *MAID/SHEP* ME15 .. **133** J6 🗆
Lyndhurst Wy *MEO* DA13............... **65** F6
Lynette Av *STRD* ME2 .... **49** F5
Lyngs CI *RHAM* ME8 .... **152** D6
Lynmead CI *EDEN* TN8 .... **164** B2 🗆
Lynmouth Ri *STMC/STPC* BR5 ...... **56** C1
Lynne CI *ORP* BR6 .... **76** A2 🗆
Lynors Av *STRD* ME2 .... **49** F4
Lynsted La *RSIT* ME9 .... **95** J7
Lynsted Rd *RHAM* ME8 .... **69** J3
Lynton Av *STMC/STPC* BR5 .... **56** C1
Lynton Dr *WALD* ME5 .... **88** C3
Lynton Rd *GVW* DA11 .... **27** H7
Lynton Rd South *GVW* DA11 .... **27** H7
Lynwood *RRTW* TN3 .... **205** F8
Lyons Crs *TON* TN9 .... **170** C4
Lysander Rd *E/WMAL* ME19........ **129** H3

M

Mabel Rd *SWLY* BR8 .... **40** D4
Mableson Rd *TON* TN9 .... **170** A6
Macaulay CI *DIT/AY* ME20 .... **108** E2
Macdonald Rd *GILL* ME7 .... **5** D2 🗆
Mace La *RSEV* TN14 .... **75** J3
Mackenders CI *DIT/AY* ME20 .... **86** E8
Mackenders La *DIT/AY* ME20......... **87** F8
Mackenzie Wy *GVE* DA12 .... **46** A4
Macklands Wy *RHAM* ME8 .... **70** D4
Madan Rd *BH/WHM* TN16 .... **120** D4
Madden Av *WALD* ME5 .... **87** K1
Madden CI *SWCM* DA10 .... **25** K5 🗆
Maddocks CI *SCUP* DA14 .... **38** E4
Madeira Pk *RTW* TN1 .... **11** D5 🗆
Madginford CI *MAID/SHEP* ME15 .. **134** C4
Madginford Rd *MAID/SHEP* ME15 .. **134** B4
Madison Wy *SEV* TN13 .... **8** B2
Maesmaur Rd *BH/WHM* TN16 .... **97** K8
Mafeking Rd *WALD* ME5.................. **88** A3
Magdalen CI *GILL* ME7 .... **89** H2
Magdalen Gv *ORP* BR6 .... **56** C8
Magnolia Av *RHAM* ME8 .... **89** J1
Magnolia Dr *BH/WHM* TN16 .... **97** F1
Magpie CI *DIT/AY* ME20 .... **108** E5 🗆
Magpie Hall Rd *CHAT* ME4 .... **68** A6
Magpie La *MAID/BEAR* ME14 .... **90** C5
Magwitch CI *ROCH* ME1 .... **2** B4 🗆
Maida CI *CHAT* ME4 .... **4** B6
Maida Vale Rd *DART* DA1 .... **22** D5
Maiden La *DART* DA1 .... **22** D2
Maidstone Rd *BGR/WK* TN15 ...... **125** F1
   CHAT ME4 .... **69** K6
   GILL ME7 .... **89** J4
   HDCN TN27 .... **179** J5
   RHAM ME8 .... **89** K3
   RMAID ME17 .... **157** C4
   ROCH ME1 .... **67** H6
   RSIT ME9 .... **92** C3
   RTON TN11 .... **150** A6
   RTWE/PEM TN2 .... **191** J6
   SCUP DA14 .... **38** E4
   SIT ME10 .... **73** F8
   STPH/PW TN12 .... **176** E7
   SWLY BR8 .... **39** J6
   WALD ME5 .... **87** J5
   WBY/YAL ME18 .... **151** K4
The Mailyns *RHAM* ME8 .... **69** K7
Main Gate Rd *CHAT* ME4.................. **3** F1
Main Rd *BH/WHM* TN16 .... **74** B8
   EDEN TN8 .... **142** C5
   EYN DA4 .... **42** A4
   EYN DA4 .... **59** H3
   HART DA3 .... **43** K7
   HOO/HM ME3 .... **34** A7
   HOO/HM ME3 .... **50** C1
   HOO/HM ME3 .... **50** A2
   RDART DA2 .... **43** H6
   RSEV TN14 .... **99** G5
   STMC/STPC BR5 .... **38** D8
   SWLY BR8 .... **40** C6
   SWLY BR8 .... **57** K3
Main Road Gorse HI *EYN* DA4 .... **60** A5
Main St *RYE* TN31 .... **244** E8
Major York's Rd *STH/RUST* TN4 .... **10** B4
Malan CI *BH/WHM* TN16 .... **97** J4
Malden Dr *MAID/BEAR* ME14 ...... **111** F6
Mallard CI *DART* DA1 .... **23** J4
Mallards Wy *MAID/SHEP* ME15 .... **134** C5
Mallard Wy *HOO/HM* ME3 .... **34** E2
Mallingdene CI *HOO/HM* ME3 .... **31** G6 🗆
Malling Rd *DIT/AY* ME20............... **108** C1

Snod ME6 .... **85** K7
WBY/YAL ME18 .... **129** G5
Mallings Dr *MAID/BEAR* ME14 .... **134** E2
Mallings La *MAID/BEAR* ME14 .... **134** E2
Malling Ter *MAIDW* ME16 .... **132** C2
Mallow CI *GVW* DA11 .... **45** F2 🗆
The Mallows *MAID/BEAR* ME14 .... **110** E7
Mallys PI *EYN* DA4 .... **42** B6 🗆
Malmaynes Hall Rd *HOO/HM* ME3 ... **33** K3
Malta Av *WALD* ME5 .... **68** B7
Malta Rd *TIL* RM18 .... **27** C1
Maltby CI *ORP* BR6 .... **56** B5
Malthouse CI *RMAID* ME17........... **160** D1
Malthouse HI *MAID/SHEP* ME15 .. **155** F2 🗆
Malthouse La *GVE* DA12 .... **47** H3
Malt House La *TENT* TN30 .... **230** A7
Malthouse Rd *BGR/WK* TN15 .... **82** A4
Maltings CI *RTON* TN11 .... **150** A6 🗆
The Maltings *MAID/BEAR* ME14 .. **134** A1 🗆
   ORP BR6 .... **56** A5
   OXTED RH8 .... **140** D2
   RHAM ME8 .... **70** D6
   RMAID ME17 .... **155** H2 🗆
Malton Wy *RTWE/PEM* TN2........ **191** F8
Malus CI *WALD* ME5 .... **88** B5
Malvern Rd *GILL* ME7 .... **5** E6
   ORP BR6 .... **56** C8
Malvina Av *GVE* DA12 .... **27** J8
Malyons Rd *SWLY* BR8 .... **40** C5
Mamignot CI *MAID/BEAR* ME14 ... **134** D1 🗆
Manchester CI *WALD* ME5 .... **68** D8 🗆
Mangravet Av *MAID/SHEP* ME15 .. **133** J7
Manning Rd *STMC/STPC* BR5 .... **56** C1
Manning St *SOCK/AV* RM15 .... **13** G1
Mannock Rd *DART* DA1 .... **23** J2 🗆
Mann Sq *TON* TN9 .... **170** D7
Manor CI *DART* DA1 .... **22** A3
   GVE DA12 .... **28** E3
   MAID/BEAR ME14 .... **134** D3
   RDART DA2 .... **40** D1
   SOCK/AV RM15 .... **13** C1
   STH/RUST TN4 .... **10** A3
Manor Ct *MAID/BEAR* ME14........ **134** D3
   MEO DA13 .... **64** A2
Manor Dr *HART* DA3 .... **62** B3
Manor Fld *GVE* DA12 .... **47** H3
Manorfields CI *CHST* BR7 .... **38** A4
Manor Forstal *HART* DA3 .... **62** A7
Manor Gdns *WALD* ME5 .... **88** A2
Manor Gv *SIT* ME10 .... **93** K3
   TONN TN10 .... **170** C3
Manor House Dr *MAIDW* ME16 .... **6** A4 🗆
Manor House Gdns *EDEN* TN8 .... **164** C5
Manor La *HART* DA3 .... **61** H4
   HART DA3 .... **62** B3
   ROCH ME1 .... **66** E3
Manor Pk *STH/RUST* TN4 .... **10** A4
Manor Ri *MAID/BEAR* ME14 .... **134** D3
Manor Rd *BFN/LL* DA15 .... **38** A1
   BH/WHM TN16 .... **97** J7
   CHAT ME4 .... **3** F4
   DART DA1 .... **22** B3
   EDEN TN8 .... **164** B5
   GVE DA12 .... **27** J5 🗆🗆
   HART DA3 .... **62** D2
   MEO DA13 .... **63** K2
   RSEV TN14 .... **121** K3
   RSIT ME9 .... **117** F5
   STH/RUST TN4 .... **189** J5
   SWCM DA10 .... **25** J5
   TIL RM18 .... **27** H1
Manor St *GILL* ME7 .... **4** A2
Manor Wy *BXLYHN* DA7 .... **22** A2
   GVW DA11 .... **26** D2
   SWCM DA10 .... **25** K3
Mansel Dr *ROCH* ME1 .... **2** A6
Manse Wy *SWLY* BR8 .... **58** D1
Mansfield CI *STMC/STPC* BR5 ...... **56** E4
Mansfield Rd *SWLY* BR8 .... **40** B4
Mansion House CI *HDCN* TN27 .... **217** J4
Mansion Rw *GILL* ME7 .... **4** A2 🗆
The Manwarings
   STPH/PW TN12 .... **194** E8 🗆
Manwood CI *SIT* ME10 .... **94** A4
Maple Av *GILL* ME7 .... **5** D4 🗆
   MAIDW ME16 .... **110** C8
Maple CI *DIT/AY* ME20.................. **108** E4
   SWLY BR8 .... **40** B7 🗆
Maple Rd *DART* DA1 .... **23** F7
   GVE DA12 .... **45** K2
   HOO/HM ME3 .... **51** F5 🗆🗆
   STRD ME2 .... **48** E8
Maplescombe La *EYN* DA4 .... **59** K7
Maplesden CI *MAIDW* ME16 .... **131** K3 🗆
The Maples *HART* DA3 .... **44** C8 🗆
Mapleton Rd *BH/WHM* TN16........ **142** E1
   EDEN TN8 .... **143** G6
Maplins CI *RHAM* ME8 .... **70** C5 🗆
Marathon Paddock *GILL* ME7 .... **5** D4 🗆
Marcet Rd *DART* DA1 .... **23** F4
Marconi Rd *GVW* DA11.................. **44** E1
Marcus Rd *DART* DA1 .... **22** D6
Mardale CI *RHAM* ME8 .... **70** D5
Marden Rd *STPH/PW* TN12 .... **197** G1
   STRD ME2 .... **49** H5

Margate Cl *GILL* ME7 .... 5 E2
Margetts La *ROCH* ME1 .... 86 C5
Margetts Pl *STRD* ME2 .... 50 B3
Marian Sq *STPH/PW* TN12 .. 198 B2
Marina Dr *DART* DA1 .... 23 K7
 GVW DA11 .... 27 C6
Marine Ct *PUR* RM19 .... 12 D4
Marine Dr *HOO/HM* ME3 .... 51 F3
Marine Vw *CHAT* ME4 .... 50 C5
Marion Cl *WALD* ME5 .... 88 B4
Marion Crs *MAID/SHEP* ME15 .. 7 E6
 STMC/STPC BR5 .... 56 C2
Maritime Cl *GRH* DA9 .... 25 G4
 STRD ME2 .... 49 J6
Maritime Wy *CHAT* ME4 .... 50 B6
Market Buildings
 MAID/BEAR ME14 .... 6 C3
Market Meadow
 STMC/STPC BR5 .... 56 D1
Market Pl *DART* DA1 .... 23 H6
Market Sq *BH/WHM* TN16 .. 120 C6
Market St *DART* DA1 .... 23 H6
 MAID/BEAR ME14 .... 6 C3
 RTWE/PEM TN2 .... 10 C5
 STPH/PW TN12 .... 198 B3
Market Wy *BH/WHM* TN16 .. 120 D5
Mark La *GVE* DA12 .... 28 B6
Marks Sq *GVW* DA11 .... 45 G2
Marlborough Cl *ORP* BR6 .. 56 A3
 STH/RUST TN4 .... 10 A3
Marlborough Crs *SEV* TN13 .... 8 A3
Marlborough Rd *DART* DA1 .. 23 F5
 GILL ME7 ....
Marle Place Rd *STPH/PW* TN12 .. 210 E1
Marley La *HDCN* TN27 .... 201 C2
Marley Rd *HOO/HM* ME3 .... 32 E8
 RMAID ME17 .... 137 K8
Marley Wy *ROCH* ME1 .... 2 C6
Marlhurst *EDEN* TN8 .... 164 B2
Marling Wy *GVE* DA12 .... 46 B3
Marlow Av *PUR* RM19 .... 12 E4
Marlow Copse *WALD* ME5 .. 88 A3
Marlowe Rd *DIT/AY* ME20 .. 108 D3
The Marlowes *DART* DA1 .. 22 A3
Marlpit Cl *EDEN* TN8 .... 164 C2
Marquis Dr *GILL* ME7 .... 89 J3
Marriott Rd *DART* DA1 .... 23 K6
Marsden Wy *ORP* BR6 .... 56 A3
Marshall Gdns *RTON* TN11 .. 150 A5
Marshall Rd *RHAM* ME8 .... 69 K5
Marshalls Land *TENT* TN30 .. 230 A3
Marsham Crs *RMAID* ME17 .. 156 D5
Marsham St *MAID/BEAR* ME14 .... 7 D3
Marsham Wy *STRD* ME2 .... 85 K1
Marsh Crs *EDEN* TN8 .... 33 F2
Marsh Green Rd *EDEN* TN8 .. 184 B2
Marshland Vw *HOO/HM* ME3 .. 35 F1
Marsh La *HOO/HM* ME3 .... 15 C8
Marsh Quarter La *HAWK* TN18 .. 243 K2
Marsh Rd *STRD* ME2 .... 86 A1
Marsh St *DART* DA1 .... 23 K2
 STRD ME2 .... 2 B1
Marsh Wy *DIT/AY* ME20 .. 108 E2
Marstan Cl *RSIT* ME9 .... 71 H4
Marston Cl *WALD* ME5 .... 87 K3
Marston Dr *MAID/BEAR* ME14 ...... 7 E2
Martin Ct *GILL* ME7 .... 89 H3
Martindale Av *ORP* BR6 .... 76 B1
Martin Hardie Wy *TONN* TN10 .. 170 E1
Martin Rd *RDART* DA2 .... 41 F1
 SOCK/AV RM15 .... 13 H1
 STRD ME2 .... 49 G2
Martins Cl *HOO/HM* ME3 .... 30 C8
 STMC/STPC BR5 .... 38 E8
 TENT TN30 .... 230 C6
Martins La *STPH/PW* TN12 .. 151 G4
Martin Sq *DIT/AY* ME20 .. 108 E5
Marwell *BH/WHM* TN16 .. 120 B5
Mary Day's *CRBK* TN17 .... 212 D7
Maryfield Cl *BXLY* DA5 .... 40 B1
Maryland Ct *RHAM* ME8 .... 90 B1
Maryland Dr *MAIDW* ME16 .. 131 K4
Maryland Rd *RTWE/PEM* TN2 .. 11 F6
Mascall's Court La *STPH/PW* TN12 .. 193 K2
Mascall's Court Rd
 STPH/PW TN12 .... 193 K2
Mascalls Pk *STPH/PW* TN12 .. 193 H1
Masefield Dr *HOO/HM* ME3 .. 31 C6
Masefield Rd *DART* DA1 .... 24 A4
 GVW DA11 .... 44 E1
Masefield Wy *TON* TN9 .... 169 K6
Master Cl *OXTED* RH8 .... 118 C8
Masters La *E/WMAL* ME19 .. 107 K1
Masthead Cl *GRH* DA9 .... 24 B3
Matfield Crs *MAID/BEAR* ME14 .... 7 F2
Matilda Cl *GILL* ME7 .... 89 K1
Matterdale Gdns *MAIDW* ME16 .. 131 J4
Matthews La *RTON* TN11 .. 150 B3
Mattinson Pl *RSIT* ME9 .... 115 K7
Matts Hill Rd *RSIT* ME9 .... 90 B4
Maude Rd *SWLY* BR8 .... 60 D6
Maunders Cl *WALD* ME5 .... 68 D6
Maximilian Dr *STRD* ME2 .... 86 A2
Maxim Rd *DART* DA1 .... 22 B4

Maxton Cl *MAID/BEAR* ME14 .. 134 B1
Maxwell Dr *MAIDW* ME16 .... 110 B8
Maxwell Gdns *ORP* BR6 .... 56 A7
Maxwell Rd *GILL* ME7 .... 4 A3
May Av *GVW* DA11 .... 27 G7
 STMC/STPC BR5 .... 56 C2
Maybury Av *RDART* DA2 .... 24 B7
Maycotts La *STPH/PW* TN12 .. 193 F5
Mayes Cl *SWLY* BR8 .... 58 D1
Mayfair *STRD* ME2 .... 49 H5
Mayfair Av *MAID/SHEP* ME15 .. 133 G6
Mayfair Rd *DART* DA1 .... 23 G4
Mayfield *SWCM* DA10 .... 25 K5
Mayfield Av *ORP* BR6 .... 56 A5
Mayfield Cl *RHAM* ME8 .... 70 B4
 WALD ME5 .... 88 B5
Mayfield Rd *GVW* DA11 .... 27 G7
 STH/RUST TN4 .... 10 B3
Mayfly Cl *STMC/STPC* BR5 .. 56 E1
Mayford Rd *WALD* ME5 .... 88 E4
Maylands Dr *SCUP* DA14 .... 38 E1
Maynard Pl *WALD* ME5 .... 5 D6
Maynards *STPH/PW* TN12 .. 196 C1
Maynard's La *STPH/PW* TN12 .. 193 G5
Mayplace Av *DART* DA1 .... 22 D3
Maypole Crs *ERITH* DA8 .... 12 B6
Maypole La *CRBK* TN17 .... 212 D6
Maypole Rd *GVE* DA12 .... 28 C7
 ORP BR6 .... 77 G2
May Rd *GILL* ME7 .... 4 B4
 RDART DA2 .... 41 J2
 ROCH ME1 .... 2 C5
May St *SNOD* ME6 .... 86 A6
 STRD ME2 .... 66 A4
May Ter *GILL* ME7 .... 4 A1
Maytham Rd *CRBK* TN17 .... 238 D4
Mayweed Av *WALD* ME5 .... 87 K2
Mcalpine Crs *MAID/SHEP* ME15 .. 155 F3
Mccabe Cl *STPH/PW* TN12 .. 198 A4
Mccudden Rd *DART* DA1 .... 23 J2
Mcdermott Rd *STPH/PW* TN15 .. 105 F7
Mckenzie Cl *DIT/AY* ME20 .. 109 K6
Mc Kenzie Rd *WALD* ME5 .... 88 B3
Mcmillan Cl *GVE* DA12 .... 45 K2
Mead Cl *SWLY* BR8 .... 58 D2
Mead Crs *DART* DA1 .... 23 G7
Meades Cl *STPH/PW* TN12 .. 176 B8
Meadfield Rd *MEO* DA13 .... 63 H6
Meadow Bank *E/WMAL* ME19 .. 108 A6
 RTON TN11 .... 168 D5
Meadow Bank Rd *BGR/WK* TN15 .. 80 E4
Meadowbank Rd *CHAT* ME4 .. 4 A4
Meadowbrook *OXTED* RH8 .. 140 A1
Meadow Cl *RSIT* ME9 .... 73 J2
 SEV TN13 .... 8 C2
 STRD ME2 .... 85 H2
 WALD ME5 .... 88 A1
Meadow Ct *BGR/WK* TN15 .. 105 F3
 RHAM ME8 .... 69 J4
Meadow Crs *STRD* ME2 .... 85 H2
Meadowdown *MAID/BEAR* ME14 .. 134 A2
Meadowdown Cl *GILL* ME7 .. 89 H2
Meadow Hill Rd *RTW* TN1 .. 11 D4
Meadowlands *BGR/WK* TN15 .. 102 D7
 OXTED RH8 .... 140 E5
Meadow La *EDEN* TN8 .... 164 B2
 MEO DA13 .... 83 C5
Meadow Ri *RSIT* ME9 .... 73 J2
Meadow Rd *GVW* DA11 .... 26 D7
 GVW DA11 .... 27 H8
 RRTW TN3 .... 204 E7
 STH/RUST TN4 .... 189 K5
 TON TN9 .... 170 A6
Meadowside *DART* DA1 .... 23 H7
The Meadows *HDCN* TN27 ......
 MAID/SHEP ME15 .... 6 B5
 ORP BR6 .... 76 D2
 RSEV TN14 .... 77 C8
 SIT ME10 .... 94 A4
Meadowsweet View *CHAT* ME4 .. 50 C4
The Meadow *RTWE/PEM* TN2 .. 191 K6
Meadow View Rd *RMAID* ME17 .. 155 H3
Meadow Wk *MAID/SHEP* ME15 ...... 7 E4
 RDART DA2 .... 41 F2
 SNOD ME6 .... 85 J7
Meadow Wy *RDART* DA2 .... 24 B6
 STPH/PW TN12 .... 176 D8
Mead Rd *DART* DA1 .... 23 G7
 EDEN TN8 .... 164 D7
 GVW DA11 .... 27 J8
The Meads Av *SIT* ME10 .... 73 J7
Meadside Wk *WALD* ME5 .... 68 A8
The Meads *CRBK* TN17 .... 225 F5
 RTWE/PEM TN2 .... 11 E5
The Mead *E/WMAL* ME19 .. 108 C4
 HART DA3 .... 61 K6
Mead Wall *HOO/HM* ME3 .. 14 C6
Meadway *RSEV* TN14 .... 77 J7
 RTON TN11 .... 169 J1
The Meadway *ORP* BR6 .... 76 C1
 SEV TN13 .... 8 B1
Meath Cl *STMC/STPC* BR5 .. 56 C2
Medbury Rd *GVE* DA12 .... 28 C7
Medhurst Crs *GVE* DA12 .... 46 C1
Medhurst Gdns *GVE* DA12 .. 46 C1

Medina Rd *DIT/AY* ME20 .... 109 G5
 TONN TN10 .... 148 C8
Medlar Cl *RSIT* ME9 .... 93 F8
Medlar Gv *GILL* ME7 .... 89 H2
The Medlars *MAID/BEAR* ME14 .. 111 K8
 MEO DA13 .... 63 H3
Medway Av *HOO/HM* ME3 .... 33 F2
 WBY/YAL ME18 .... 152 D5
Medway Br *STRD* ME2 .... 66 D3
Medway Cl *SIT* ME10 .... 93 J2
Medway Gdns *CHAT* ME4 ...... 3 F1
Medway Mdw *STPH/PW* TN12 .. 151 J8
Medway Rd *DART* DA1 .... 22 D2
 GILL ME7 ....
 RTW TN1 .... 11 D2
Medway St *CHAT* ME4 .... 6 C3
 MAIDW ME16 .... 6 C3
Medway Valley Wk *DIT/AY* ME20 .. 109 H2
 MAIDW ME16 .... 110 D5
 ROCH ME1 .... 2 C3
 STPH/PW TN12 .... 173 G3
 WBY/YAL ME18 .... 130 E8
Medway Wharf Rd *TON* TN9 .. 170 C5
Meeting House La *CHAT* ME4 ...... 3 F4
Megrims Hl *HAWK* TN18 .... 236 C5
Meirscourt Rd *RHAM* ME8 .... 90 B2
Melbourne Rd *CHAT* ME4 .... 4 A5
Meldrum Cl *OXTED* RH8 .... 140 D3
 STMC/STPC BR5 .... 56 D3
Melford Dr *MAIDW* ME16 .... 132 B2
Melliker La *MEO* DA13 .... 63 C3
Melody Cl *RHAM* ME8 .... 89 K2
Melody Rd *BH/WHM* TN16 ...... 97 F5
Melrose Cl *MAID/SHEP* ME15 .. 133 G7
Melrose Rd *BH/WHM* TN16 .. 97 G3
Melville Rd *MAID/SHEP* ME15 ...... 7 D4
Mercer Dr *RMAID* ME17 .... 137 K8
Mercers *HAWK* TN18 .... 235 C5
 RRTW TN3 .... 205 K3
Mercers Cl *STPH/PW* TN12 .. 173 G3
Mercers Pl *WBY/YAL* ME18 .. 129 J4
Mercer St *RTW* TN1 .... 11 D2
Mercer Wy *RMAID* ME17 .. 156 D5
Merchant Pl *STPH/PW* TN12 .. 176 D8
Mercury Cl *ROCH* ME1 .... 2 A6
Meresborough La *RHAM* ME8 .. 90 D1
Meresborough Rd *RHAM* ME8 .. 90 C2
Mereworth Cl *RHAM* ME8 .... 69 H3
Mereworth Rd *STH/RUST* TN4 .. 10 C1
 WBY/YAL ME18 .... 128 E7
Merivale Gv *WALD* ME5 .... 88 C2
Merle Common Rd *OXTED* RH8 .. 140 E7
Merlin Av *DIT/AY* ME20 .... 108 D4
Merlin Cl *RSIT* ME10 .... 94 B5
 TONN TN10 .... 170 E2
Mermaid Cl *MAID* ME5 .... 89 J1
Mermerus Gdns *GVE* DA12 .. 46 C2
Merrals Wood Rd *STRD* ME2 .. 66 C1
Merrion Cl *STH/RUST* TN4 .. 190 B7
Merrion Wy *STH/RUST* TN4 .. 190 B7
Merry Boys Rd *HOO/HM* ME3 .. 31 C6
Merryfields *STRD* ME2 .... 49 F5
Merryfields Cl *HART* DA3 .... 62 A1
Merryhills Cl *BH/WHM* TN16 .. 97 H3
Merryweather Cl *DART* DA1 .. 23 J5
Mersey Rd *TONN* TN10 .... 170 B1
Merton Av *HART* DA3 .... 61 K1
Merton Cl *WALD* ME5 .... 88 D2
Merton Rd *MAID/SHEP* ME15 .. 134 B4
Mesne Wy *RSEV* TN14 .... 78 C7
Meteor Cl *SIT* ME10 .... 73 K6
Meteor Rd *E/WMAL* ME19 .. 129 H3
Mewsend *BH/WHM* TN16 .... 97 H5
The Mews *RTWE/PEM* TN2 .. 191 J8
 SIT ME10 .... 94 A3
 STRD ME2 .... 48 E7
Micawber Cl *WALD* ME5 .... 88 B5
Michael Gdns *GVE* DA12 .... 46 B4
Michaels La *HART* DA3 .... 61 C6
Mickleham Cl *STMC/STPC* BR5 .. 38 C7
Mickleham Rd *STMC/STPC* BR5 .. 38 A6
Middle Fld *RTWE/PEM* TN2 .. 192 A6
Middlefields *RHAM* ME8 .... 70 D6
Middle Mill Rd *E/WMAL* ME19 .. 108 D7
Middlesex Rd *MAID/SHEP* ME15 .. 133 K7
Middle St *GILL* ME7 .... 4 A2
Middleton Av *SCUP* DA14 .... 38 D4
Middleton Cl *RHAM* ME8 .... 90 B2
Middletune Av *SIT* ME10 .... 73 K7
Middle Wk *RTWE/PEM* TN2 .. 190 E6
Middle Wy *SIT* ME10 .... 94 C3
The Middlings *SEV* TN13 ...... 8 B5
Middlings Wd *SEV* TN13 ...... 8 B4
Midfield Av *SWLY* BR8 .... 40 D4
Midfield Wy *STMC/STPC* BR5 .. 38 C6
Midley Cl *MAIDW* ME16 .... 110 C7
Midsummer Rd *SNOD* ME6 .. 85 H6
The Midway *STH/RUST* TN4 .. 206 C4
Mierscourt Cl *RHAM* ME8 .... 70 D6
Mierscourt Rd *RHAM* ME8 .. 70 C7
Milbourne Gv *SIT* ME10 .... 73 K7
Milburn Rd *GILL* ME7 .... 4 C1
Mildmay Pl *RSEV* TN14 .... 78 C6
Mildred Cl *DART* DA1 .... 23 K5

Milebush La *STPH/PW* TN12 .... 176 E5
Mile La *CRBK* TN17 .... 213 G5
Mile Oak Rd *STPH/PW* TN12 ...... 194 A4
Miles Pl *ROCH* ME1 .... 3 D5 ⓭
Mile Stone Rd *RDART* DA2 .... 24 A5
Milford Cl *MAIDW* ME16 .... 132 C1
Military Rd *CHAT* ME4 .... 3 F5 ⓭
Milk House Cottages *CRBK* TN17 . 215 H6
Milking La *ORP* BR6 .... 76 D7
Mill Bank *HDCN* TN27 .... 180 A8
Millbro *SWLY* BR8 .... 40 D6 ⓭
Millbrook *E/WMAL* ME19 .... 108 B5
Millbrook Cl *MAID/SHEP* ME15 ..... 6 C5
Mill Brook Rd *STMC/STPC* BR5 .. 56 D1
Mill Cl *RMAID* ME17 .... 160 C2
  STRD ME2 .... 49 C5
Mill Crs *TON* TN9 .... 170 D4
Millcroft Rd *HOO/HM* ME3 .... 31 C2
Miller Rd *SIT* ME10 .... 93 K1
Miller Rd *GVE* DA12 .... 28 D8
Millers Wk *MEO* DA13 .... 63 H6
Miller Wy *STRD* ME2 .... 49 H4
Millfield *HART* DA3 .... 61 K6
  RASHW TN26 .... 219 J3 ⓭
  SIT ME10 .... 94 A3
Millfield Dr *GVE* DA11 .... 27 F8
Millfield La *HART* DA3 .... 61 K6
Millfield Rd *BGR/WK* TN15 .... 80 C2
Millfields *WALD* ME5 .... 88 C4
Millfields Cl *STMC/STPC* BR5 .... 56 C1
Millfordhope Rd *STRD* ME2 .... 48 B7
Millhall *DIT/AY* ME20 .... 109 H4
Mill Hall Rd *DIT/AY* ME20 .... 109 F3
Mill HI *EDEN* TN8 .... 164 D7
Mill Hill La *GVE* DA12 .... 47 G3
Millhouse La *E/WMAL* ME19 ..... 107 F3
Mill La *BGR/WK* TN15 .... 126 D1
  BGR/WK TN15 .... 147 F3
  BH/WHM TN16 .... 120 C6
  CRBK TN17 .... 199 G7
  CRBK TN17 .... 215 G6
  EYN DA4 .... 59 H5
  HDCN TN27 .... 201 K4
  ORP BR6 .... 75 F5
  OXTED RH8 .... 140 D3
  OXTED RH8 .... 141 K2
  RMAID ME17 .... 154 D3
  RSEV TN14 .... 78 C5
  RSEV TN14 .... 102 A8
  RSIT ME9 .... 71 H8
  RTON TN11 .... 147 F6
  SNOD ME6 .... 86 A6
  STPH/PW TN12 .... 195 F5
  STPH/PW TN12 .... 198 E5
  TENT TN30 .... 230 B5
  TON TN9 .... 170 C4
  WALD ME5 .... 68 D5
  WALD ME5 .... 87 J5
  WBY/YAL ME18 .... 130 B6
  WBY/YAL ME18 .... 152 E8
Mill Pl *DART* DA1 .... 22 D3
Mill Pond Cl *SEV* TN13 .... 102 B8
Millpond La *HDCN* TN27 .... 229 F4
Mill Pond Rd *DART* DA1 .... 23 H5
Mill Rd *GILL* ME7 .... 4 C2
  GVV DA11 .... 27 F6
  PUR RM19 .... 13 F6
  RDART DA2 .... 41 J2
  SEV TN13 .... 101 G8
  STRD ME2 .... 49 G6
Mills Crs *BGR/WK* TN15 .... 100 D3
Mill Shaw *OXTED* RH8 .... 140 D3
Mills Rd *DIT/AY* ME20 .... 109 J7
Mills Ter *CHAT* ME4 .... 4 A5
Mill Stone Cl *EYN* DA4 .... 42 B7 ⓭
Millstone Ms *EYN* DA4 .... 42 B6
Millstream Cl *RRTW* TN3 .... 204 A4 ⓭
Mill St *BH/WHM* TN16 .... 120 D6
  CRBK TN17 .... 236 E3
  E/WMAL ME19 .... 108 D7
  HAWK TN18 .... 236 D4
  MAID/BEAR ME14 .... 6 A2
  MAID/SHEP ME15 .... 7 D4
  MAID/SHEP ME15 .... 155 F1 ⓭
  SIT ME10 .... 93 K1
  SNOD ME6 .... 86 A6
Mill Vw *RTON* TN11 .... 149 K5
Mill Wk *MAIDW* ME16 .... 132 A3
Millwood Rd *STMC/STPC* BR5 ... 38 D8
Milner Rd *GILL* ME7 .... 5 D1
Milroy Av *GVV* DA11 .... 27 F8
Milstead Cl *MAID/BEAR* ME14 ... 7 F2 ⓭
Milsted Rd *RHAM* ME8 .... 69 K4
Milton Av *GVE* DA12 .... 28 A7
  HOO/HM ME3 .... 31 G6
  RSEV TN14 .... 77 J3
Milton Dr *RTWE/PEM* TN2 ...... 190 D7
Milton Gdns *TON* TN9 .... 169 K7
Milton Hall Rd *GVE* DA12 .... 28 A7
Milton Pl *GVE* DA12 .... 27 K5
Milton Rd *GILL* ME7 .... 27 K5 ⓭
  GVE DA12 .... 27 K5 ⓭
  SEV TN13 .... 101 G8
  SIT ME10 .... 93 K2

SWCM DA10 .... 25 K5
Milton St *MAIDW* ME16 .... 132 C4
  SWCM DA10 .... 25 J5
Mimosa Cl *ORP* BR6 .... 56 D6 ⓭
Mincers Cl *WALD* ME5 .... 88 D4 ⓭
Minerva Av *STRD* ME2 .... 49 F6
Minster Rd *RHAM* ME8 .... 69 K5 ⓭
Minterne Av *SIT* ME10 .... 93 H4
Minters Orch *BGR/WK* TN15 ... 105 H7
Miskin Rd *DART* DA1 .... 23 F6
  HOO/HM ME3 .... 50 E1
Miskin Wy *GVE* DA12 .... 46 A4
Mitchell Av *CHAT* ME4 .... 3 F6
  GVV DA11 .... 26 E8
Mitchell Cl *DART* DA1 .... 23 H8
  RMAID ME17 .... 160 C1
Mitchell Rd *E/WMAL* ME19 ...... 129 H4
  ORP BR6 .... 56 A8
Mitchem Cl *BGR/WK* TN15 .... 80 D5
Mitre Cl *TON* TN9 .... 170 C4
Mitre Rd *ROCH* ME1 .... 2 B4 ⓭
Moat Farm *RTWE/PEM* TN2 ...... 207 F7
Moat Farm Rd *HOO/HM* ME3 ... 17 K8
Moat La *EDEN* TN8 .... 185 K7
Moat Rd *HDCN* TN27 .... 199 K5
Mockbeggar La *CRBK* TN17 ...... 228 A2
Molash Rd *STMC/STPC* BR5 ..... 56 E1
Molescroft Wy *TON* TN9 .... 169 K7
Moles Md *EDEN* TN8 .... 164 C4
Mollison Ri *GVE* DA12 .... 46 B3
Molyneux Park Rd *STH/RUST* TN4 10 B3
Monarch Cl *TIL* RM18 .... 27 J1
  WALD ME5 .... 68 B8
Monckton's Av *MAID/BEAR* ME14 110 E7
Monckton's Dr
  MAID/BEAR ME14 .... 110 E7 ⓭
Monckton's La *MAID/BEAR* ME14 110 E7
Moncrif Cl *MAID/BEAR* ME14 ... 134 D2
Monkdown *MAID/SHEP* ME15 .. 134 C5 ⓭
Monks La *OXTED* RH8 .... 141 H8
  WADH TN5 .... 220 D7
Monks Orch *DART* DA1 .... 23 F8
Monks Wk *MEO* DA13 .... 44 B4
Monks Wy *RYE* TN31 .... 244 E6
Monkton Rd *BGR/WK* TN15 .... 105 F7
Monkwood Cl *ROCH* ME1 .... 67 G6 ⓭
Monmouth Cl *RHAM* ME8 .... 70 A4
Monson Rd *RTW* TN1 .... 11 J3 ⓭
Monson Wy *RTW* TN1 .... 11 J3 ⓭
Montacute Gdns
  RTWE/PEM TN2 .... 10 B5 ⓭
Montacute Rd *RTWE/PEM* TN2 .. 10 C6
Montague Cl *SWLY* BR8 .... 58 C1 ⓭
Montbretia Cl *STMC/STPC* BR5 . 56 D1 ⓭
Monteith Cl *RRTW* TN3 .... 205 K3
Montfort Dr *WBY/YAL* ME18 .... 129 J4
Montfort Rd *RSEV* TN14 .... 102 C4
  STRD ME2 .... 2 A1
  WALD ME5 .... 87 K4
Montgomery Av *WALD* ME5 ...... 68 B7
Montgomery Rd *EYN* DA4 .... 42 C6
  GILL ME7 .... 5 K8
  STH/RUST TN4 .... 190 B7
Montpelier Ga *MAIDW* ME16 ... 132 B1 ⓭
Montreal Cl *SEV* TN13 .... 8 A2
  TIL RM18 .... 27 H2
Montrose Av *WALD* ME5 .... 5 E6
Mont St Aignan Wy *EDEN* TN8 . 164 C5
Monypenny *CRBK* TN17 .... 238 D3
Moonstone Dr *WALD* ME5 .... 88 C4 ⓭
Moorden La *RTON* TN11 .... 167 J5
Moore Av *TIL* RM18 .... 27 J1
Moore St *SWCM* DA10 .... 25 K5
Moore St *STRD* ME2 .... 49 F6
Moorfield Rd *ORP* BR6 .... 56 B4
Moor HI *HAWK* TN18 .... 235 G3
Moorhouse Rd *OXTED* RH8 ..... 141 K1
Mooring Rd *ROCH* ME1 .... 67 J5
Moor Park Cl *RHAM* ME8 .... 70 D6
The Moor Rd *RSEV* TN14 .... 101 K7
Moor St *RHAM* ME8 .... 70 E6
The Moor *HAWK* TN18 .... 235 F6
Morants Court Rd *RSEV* TN14 .. 100 E5
Morden St *ROCH* ME1 .... 2 C4 ⓭
Morel Ct *SEV* TN13 .... 9 D1
Morello Cl *RSIT* ME9 .... 95 K4 ⓭
  SWLY BR8 .... 58 A1
Morement Rd *HOO/HM* ME3 ... 32 E8
Moreton Ct *DART* DA1 .... 22 B2
Morewood Cl *SEV* TN13 .... 8 B2
Morgan Dr *RDART* DA2 .... 24 D6
Morgan Rd *STRD* ME2 .... 49 F6 ⓭
Morhen Cl *SNOD* ME6 .... 85 H7
Morland Av *DART* DA1 .... 22 E4
Morland Dr *RRTW* TN3 .... 221 K1
  STRD ME2 .... 49 F5
Morley Dr *STPH/PW* TN12 ...... 194 D8
Morley Rd *TON* TN9 .... 170 D5
Morley's Rd *RSEV* TN14 .... 146 B4
Mornington Cr *BXLY* DA5 .... 22 A7
Morris Cl *E/WMAL* ME19 .... 108 D5 ⓭
Morris Court Cl *RSIT* ME9 .... 94 E3
Morris Gdns *DART* DA1 .... 23 K4

Morry La *RMAID* ME17 .... 158 B6
Mortimer Rd *BH/WHM* TN16 ... 74 B7
  ORP BR6 .... 56 B5 ⓭
Mortimers Av *HOO/HM* ME3 ... 31 F6
Moselle Rd *BH/WHM* TN16 ...... 97 J5
Mosquito Rd *E/WMAL* ME19 ... 129 H3 ⓭
Mossbank *WALD* ME5 .... 88 B3 ⓭
Moss Wy *RDART* DA2 .... 42 C3
Mossy Gld *RHAM* ME8 .... 70 B8
Mostyn Dr *MAID/BEAR* ME14 ..... 7 F3
Mosyer Dr *STMC/STPC* BR5 ..... 56 E6
Mote Av *MAID/SHEP* ME15 .... 7 E4
  MAID/SHEP ME15 .... 133 K3
Mote Rd *BGR/WK* TN15 .... 126 A7
  MAID/SHEP ME15 .... 7 D4
Motney Hill Rd *RHAM* ME8 .... 70 D2
Mouchotte Cl *BH/WHM* TN16 .. 74 A7
Moultain HI *SWLY* BR8 .... 58 D1
Mount Av *WBY/YAL* ME18 ...... 152 E5
Mountbatten Av *HOO/HM* ME3 . 48 B2
  WALD ME5 .... 68 B7
Mount Castle La *RMAID* ME17 . 161 F5 ⓭
Mount Cl *SEV* TN13 .... 8 B2
Mount Culver Av *SCUP* DA14 ... 38 E4
Mount Dr *MAID/BEAR* ME14 ... 134 D2 ⓭
Mount Edgcumbe Rd
  STH/RUST TN4 .... 10 C4
Mount Ephraim *RTW* TN1 .... 10 C3
Mount Ephraim Rd *RTW* TN1 ... 10 C3 ⓭
Mountfield *BGR/WK* TN15 .... 105 G7
Mountfield Cl *MEO* DA13 .... 83 F4
Mountfield Gdns *RTWE/PEM* TN2 ... 11 D4
Mountfield Pk *TON* TN9 .... 170 C6
Mountfield Rd *RTWE/PEM* TN2 . 11 D4
Mountfield Wy *STMC/STPC* BR5 56 D1
Mount Harry Rd *SEV* TN13 .... 9 D2
Mount La *MAID/BEAR* ME14 ... 134 D2
  RSIT ME9 .... 91 G2
Mount Pleasant *BH/WHM* TN16 97 H4
  DIT/AY ME20 .... 110 A3
  RTON TN11 .... 147 H8
  STPH/PW TN12 .... 173 H8 ⓭
  TENT TN30 .... 230 C6 ⓭
Mount Pleasant Av
  RTWE/PEM TN2 .... 11 D4 ⓭
Mount Pleasant Dr
  MAID/BEAR ME14 .... 134 C1
Mount Pleasant La *RRTW* TN3 . 210 C8
Mount Pleasant Rd *DART* DA1 ... 23 J5
  RSEV TN14 .... 145 K4
  RTW TN1 .... 10 C4
Mount Rd *CHAT* ME4 .... 3 F5
  DART DA1 .... 22 C5
  ROCH ME1 .... 2 A6
Mountsfield Cl *MAIDW* ME16 ...... 6 A2
Mounts HI *CRBK* TN17 .... 226 C7
Mount Sion *RTW* TN1 .... 10 C5
Mounts La *CRBK* TN17 .... 238 E4
Mounts Rd *GRH* DA9 .... 25 G5
Mountview *RSIT* ME9 .... 93 G4
Mountview Rd *ORP* BR6 .... 56 B4
Moyle Cl *RHAM* ME8 .... 90 A2
Mozart Ct *CHAT* ME4 .... 3 E5 ⓭
Muir Rd *MAID/SHEP* ME15 .... 7 D4
Mulberry Cl *GILL* ME7 .... 89 H2
  MEO DA13 .... 63 J3
  RTWE/PEM TN2 .... 190 D5
Mulberry La *PUR* RM19 .... 12 D4
Mulberry Rd *GVW* DA11 .... 45 F2
Mulberry Wy *BGR/WK* TN15 .... 80 D2
Multon Rd *BGR/WK* TN15 .... 80 D2
Munday Bois Rd *HDCN* TN27 .. 182 E5
Munford Dr *SWCM* DA10 .... 26 A6
Mungo Park Rd *GVE* DA12 .... 46 A3
Mungo Park Wy *STMC/STPC* BR5 .. 56 D4
Munn's La *RSIT* ME9 .... 71 H8
Munsgore La *RSIT* ME9 .... 92 D4
Murrain Dr *MAID/SHEP* ME15 . 134 C5
Murray Rd *STMC/STPC* BR5 .... 38 C8
  STRD ME2 .... 49 H6 ⓭
Murston Rd *SIT* ME10 .... 94 C3
Murton-neale Cl *HAWK* TN18 .. 235 G4 ⓭
Museum St *MAID/BEAR* ME14 ..... 6 C3 ⓭
Musket La *RMAID* ME17 .... 135 J4
Mussenden La *EYN* DA4 .... 60 C3
Mustang Rd *E/WMAL* ME19 .... 129 H3 ⓭
Mynn Crs *MAID/BEAR* ME14 ... 134 C1
Myrtle Crs *WALD* ME5 .... 88 A1
Myrtle Gv *SOCK/AV* RM15 .... 13 G2
Myrtle Pl *RDART* DA2 .... 24 C7
Myrtle Rd *DART* DA1 .... 23 G8

N

Nag's Head La *ROCH* ME1 .... 3 D4
Nansen Rd *GVE* DA12 .... 46 A2
Napier Cl *SIT* ME10 .... 93 H2
Napier Rd *GILL* ME7 .... 5 D4
  GVV DA11 .... 27 G3
  RTWE/PEM TN2 .... 11 F5
Napoleon Dr *STPH/PW* TN12 .. 196 D1 ⓭
Napwood Cl *RHAM* ME8 .... 70 A8 ⓭
Nares Rd *RHAM* ME8 .... 90 A2
Nash Bank *MEO* DA13 .... 45 G7

Nash Cl WALD ME5 .... 88 D4
Nash Cft MEO DA13 .... 45 F2
Nashenden La ROCH ME1 .... 66 E4
Nash St MEO DA13 .... 45 H7
Natal Rd CHAT ME4 .... 4 A6
Nativity Cl SIT ME10 .... 93 K2
Neale St CHAT ME4 .... 3 F6
Neal Rd BGR/WK TN15 .... 80 C2
Neb La OXTED RH8 .... 140 A2
Neills Rd RRTW TN3 .... 221 F4
Nellington Rd RRTW TN3 .... 206 A2
Nelson Av TON TN9 .... 170 A5
Nelson Cl BH/WHM TN16 .... 97 J4
Nelson Pl SCUP DA14 .... 38 B2
Nelson Rd DART DA1 .... 23 F5
  GILL ME7 .... 5 D4
  GVW DA11 .... 27 G8
  ROCH ME1 .... 86 B2
  RTWE/PEM TN2 .... 11 F5
  SCUP DA14 .... 38 B2 🔟
Nelson Ter WALD ME5 .... 68 D5
Nepicar La BGR/WK TN15 .... 105 J2
Neptune Cl STRD ME2 .... 3 E1
Neptune Wy STRD ME2 .... 3 D1
Nestor Ct WBY/YAL ME18 .... 130 E6
Netley Cl MAID/BEAR ME14 .... 111 K8 🔟
Nettlestead La WBY/YAL ME18 .... 129 J8
Nevill Ct E/WMAL ME19 .... 108 A5
Neville Cl BFN/LL DA15 .... 38 A2
  MAID/BEAR ME14 .... 111 H6
Neville Rd CHAT ME4 .... 3 E6
Nevill Ga RTWE/PEM TN2 .... 11 D6
Nevill Pk STH/RUST TN4 .... 10 A4
Nevill Pl SNOD ME6 .... 85 K7 🔟
Nevill Rdg STH/RUST TN4 .... 206 C3
Nevill Rd SNOD ME6 .... 85 K7
Nevill St RTWE/PEM TN2 .... 10 C5
Nevill Ter RTWE/PEM TN2 .... 10 B5 🔟
Newark Yd STRD ME2 .... 2 B1
Newbarn La RSEV TN14 .... 98 D3
New Barn Rd HART DA3 .... 44 C8
  MEO DA13 .... 44 D5
  RMAID ME17 .... 179 C4
  SWLY BR8 .... 80 B6
New Barns Rd MAID/BEAR ME14 ... 111 K8 🔟
Newbridge Av SIT ME10 .... 73 K7
Newbury Av MAID ME16 .... 6 A1
Newbury Cl HOO/HM ME3 .... 31 G6 🔟
Newbury La WADH TN5 .... 220 E6
Newchurch Rd MAID/SHEP ME15......... 7 D6
Newcomen Rd STH/RUST TN4 .... 10 C2
Newland Green La HDCN TN27 .... 182 D6
Newlands RRTW TN3 .... 205 K2
Newlands Av SIT ME10 .... 93 G2
Newlands Farm La HOO/HM ME3 .... 33 J1
Newlands La MEO DA13 .... 83 G5
Newlands Ri STH/RUST TN4 .... 10 C1 🔟
Newlands Rd CRBK TN17 .... 11 D1
Newlands Wy STH/RUST TN4 .... 190 B7 🔟
New Lodge Dr OXTED RH8..................... 118 D7
Newlyn Dr STPH/PW TN12..................... 198 B1
Newman's Rd GVW DA11 .... 27 G8
New Mill Rd STMC/STPC BR5................... 38 D6
Newnham Cl RHAM ME8 .... 69 K4 🔟
Newnham St CHAT ME4 .... 4 A5
New Pond Rd CRBK TN17 .... 226 E8
Newports SWLY BR8 .... 58 A4
New Pound La WBY/YAL ME18 .... 128 C4
New Rd CHAT ME4.. 3 F5
  CRBK TN17 .... 225 H2
  DIT/AY ME20 .... 109 G3
  E/WMAL ME19 .... 108 E5
  EYN DA4 .... 27 J5
  GVW DA11 .... 27 H5 🔟
  GVW DA11 .... 27 G8
  HDCN TN27 .... 183 G4
  HDCN TN27 .... 200 B1
  HOO/HM ME3 .... 31 F2
  MEO DA13 .... 63 G2
  ORP BR6 .... 56 B4
  OXTED RH8 .... 141 F1
  RMAID ME17 .... 156 E1
  ROCH ME1 .... 8 D4
  ROCH ME1 .... 86 D6
  RSEV TN14 .... 121 K3
  RTON TN11 .... 187 J5
  STPH/PW TN12 .... 173 J8
  SWLY BR8 .... 40 C8
  SWLY BR8 .... 40 C5
New Road Av CHAT ME4.............................. 3 E4
New Road Hl HAYES BR2 .... 74 D4
New Stairs CHAT ME4 .... 3 F2
New St BGR/WK TN15................................ 82 E2

BH/WHM TN16 .... 120 C6
CHAT ME4 .... 3 E5
New Street Rd BGR/WK TN15 .... 62 D7
New Swan Yd GVE DA12 .... 27 J5 🔟
Newton Abbot Rd GVW DA11 .... 27 G8
Newton Av TONN TN10 .... 148 D1
Newton Cl MAIDW ME16 .... 6 B4
  WALD ME5 .... 88 D4 🔟
Newton Gdns STPH/PW TN12 .... 173 H7 🔟
Newton Rd RTW TN1 .... 11 D3 🔟
  TIL RM18 .... 27 H1
Newton's Ct GRH DA9 .... 24 C3
Newton Willows RRTW TN3 .... 205 F7
New Wharf Rd TON TN9 .... 170 B4
New Years La RSEV TN14 .... 99 F2
Nicholas Cl MAIDW ME16 .... 132 A3 🔟
Nicklaus Dr WALD ME5 .... 88 A3
Nickleby Cl ROCH ME1 .... 2 C6
Nickleby Rd GVE DA12 .... 28 D7
Nicolson Rd STMC/STPC BR5................... 56 D4
Nightingale Cl BH/WHM TN16.............. 97 G2
  DIT/AY ME20 .... 108 D4
  GVW DA11 .... 27 G8
  RHAM ME8 .... 70 C7 🔟
Nightingale La RSEV TN14 .... 144 D1
Nightingale Rd RSEV TN14 .... 102 B4
The Nightingales CRBK TN17 .... 216 C6
Nightingale Wy SWLY BR8 .... 40 B8
Nile Rd GILL ME7 .... 4 C4
Nine Acres Rd STRD ME2 .... 65 K3
Nine Elms Gv GVW DA11 .... 27 H6
Ninehams Rd BH/WHM TN16 .... 97 H8
Nineveh La HAWK TN18 .... 226 A8
Niven Cl HOO/HM ME3 .... 49 H3
Nizels La RTON TN11 .... 146 D7
Noah's Ark BGR/WK TN15 .... 103 F5
Nobel Cl RSIT ME9 .... 95 K4
Noble Tree Rd RTON TN11 .... 147 F8
The Nook WBY/YAL ME18 .... 152 D4
Norah La HOO/HM ME3 .... 48 A2
Nore Cl GILL ME7 .... 69 F5
Norfield Rd RDART DA2 .... 39 K2
Norfolk Cl DART DA1 .... 23 K5
  WALD ME5 .... 88 D3
Norfolk Rd GVE DA12 .... 28 A5
  MAID/SHEP ME15 .... 133 J6
  RTW TN1 .... 11 D5 🔟
  TON TN9 .... 170 A5
Norheads La BH/WHM TN16 .... 96 E5
Norman Cl MAID/BEAR ME14 .... 7 E1
  RHAM ME8 .... 89 J2
  RSEV TN14... 102 B4
  STRD ME2 .... 66 E2
Normanhurst Rd BGR/WK TN15 .... 105 C7
  STMC/STPC BR5 .... 38 C7
Norman Ri CRBK TN17 .... 225 K2 🔟
Norman Rd DART DA1 .... 23 H7
  E/WMAL ME19 .... 107 J5
  RTW TN1 .... 11 D2 🔟
  SNOD ME6 .... 85 K8
Normans Cl GVW DA11 .... 27 H6
Normans La EDEN TN8 .... 163 J6
Norman St RSEV TN14 .... 144 A1
Norreys Rd RHAM ME8............................. 70 B7
Norrington Rd MAID/SHEP ME15 .... 133 G8
Norris Wy DART DA1 .... 22 C2
Norstead Gdns STH/RUST TN4 .... 190 B7
Norsted La ORP BR6 .... 76 C6
North Ash Rd HART DA3......................... 62 A7
North Bank Cl STRD ME2 .... 66 E1
Northbourne Rd RHAM ME8 .... 69 J2
Northcote Rd GVW DA11 .... 27 G7
  STRD ME2 .... 2 A1
  TON TN9 .... 170 B5 🔟
North Cray Rd SCUP DA14 .... 39 F4
North Crs RMAID ME17 .... 154 D2
North Dane Wy WALD ME5 .... 88 D1
North Down STPH/PW TN12 .... 198 A2
Northdown Cl MAID/BEAR ME14 .... 111 H7
  STPH/PW TN12 .... 173 H8 🔟
Northdown Rd HART DA3........................ 43 K7
  RSEV TN14 .... 102 C4
North Downs Wy BGR/WK TN15 .... 104 E2
  MAID/BEAR ME14 .... 112 A2
  OXTED RH8 .... 117 H8
  RMAID ME17 .... 114 B8
  RMAID ME17 .... 138 D7
  RMAID ME17 .... 161 K2
  SEV TN13 .... 101 F5
  STRD ME2 .... 65 J5
Northdown Vw RMAID ME17 .... 137 K8
North End La ORP BR6 .... 75 D7
North Farm La RTWE/PEM TN2 .... 190 D6
North Farm Rd STH/RUST TN4 .... 190 C7
Northfield MAID DA3 .... 44 A8
Northfield Av STMC/STPC BR5 .... 56 D3
Northfields MAIDW ME16 .... 131 K4
  RRTW TN3 .... 188 E6
Northfleet Cl MAID/BEAR ME14 .... 74 F2 🔟
North Folly Rd MAID/SHEP ME15 ..... 153 K3
Northgate ROCH ME1 .... 2 C2 🔟
Northgrove Rd HAWK TN18 .... 235 F4 🔟
North Hill RMAID ME17............................. 234 C5
North Kent Av GVW DA11 .... 26 C5
North Kent Aveune GVW DA11 .... 26 D5

Northleigh Cl MAID/SHEP ME15 .... 133 G8
North Meadow E/WMAL ME19 .... 107 F7
North Pasley Rd CHAT ME4 .... 4 B1
North Pole Rd WBY/YAL ME18 .... 131 F4
Northridge RYE TN31 .... 244 D8
Northridge Rd GVE DA12 .... 45 K1
North Riding DART DA3 .... 44 E8
North Rd CHAT ME4 .... 50 C6
  CRBK TN17 .... 212 D5
  DART DA1 .... 22 C5
  GILL ME7 .... 4 A1
  HOO/HM ME3 .... 15 G8
  MAID ME17 .... 19 G4
  PUR RM19 .... 13 G4
North St DART DA1 .... 23 G6
  EDEN TN8 .... 185 G8
  GVE DA12 .... 27 J6 🔟
  HDCN TN27 .... 200 A1
  HDCN TN27 .... 217 K4
  MAIDW ME16 .... 131 J4
  RMAID ME17 .... 157 C7
  RTWE/PEM TN2 .... 11 E4
  SIT ME10 .... 73 K7
  STRD ME2 .... 2 B1
North Ter HOO/HM ME3 .... 32 A7
Northumberland Av RHAM ME8 .... 70 B5
Northumberland Rd
  MAID/SHEP ME15 .... 133 J7
  MEO DA13 .... 45 C5
North Vw MAID/SHEP ME15 .... 7 E6
Northview SWLY BR8 .... 40 B7
North View Rd SEV TN13 .... 102 A3
North Wy MAID/BEAR ME14 .... 111 H7
Northwood Av HOO/HM ME3 .... 33 F7
Northwood Dr SIT ME10 .... 94 A5
Northwood Rd TONN TN10 .... 148 B8
Norton Crs TONN TN10 .... 148 B7
Norton Gv WALD ME5 .... 87 K2
Norton Rd RMAID ME17 .... 156 C5
  STH/RUST TN4 .... 190 A5 🔟
Nortons La TENT TN30 .... 229 J1
Nortons Wy STPH/PW TN12 .... 172 C7
Norwich Av TONN TN10 .... 170 D1
Norwich Cl STRD ME2 .... 48 C8 🔟
Norwood Cl HOO/HM ME3...................... 31 G2
Norwood La MEO DA13 .... 63 J2
Nottidge Rd STH/RUST TN4 .... 206 C5 🔟
Nottingham Av
  MAID/SHEP ME15 .... 133 K8 🔟
Novar Cl ORP BR6 .... 56 A4
The Nower RSEV TN14 .... 99 F7
Nuffield Rd SWLY BR8 .... 40 D4
Nunappleton Wy OXTED RH8 .... 140 E8 🔟
Nunnery La RTON TN11 .... 187 H6
Nursery Av MAID/BEAR ME14 .... 134 C3
  MAIDW ME16 .... 110 B8
Nursery Cl ORP BR6 .... 56 A4
  RDART DA2 .... 24 B6
  SEV TN13 .... 9 E1
  SWLY BR8 .... 39 K7 🔟
  TONN TN10 .... 170 E2
  WADH TN5 .... 233 F3
Nursery Gdns HOO/HM ME3 .... 51 F1 🔟
Nursery Pl SEV TN13 .... 123 F1
Nursery Rd DIT/AY ME20 .... 109 G5
  MEO DA13 .... 63 H2
  RHAM ME8 .... 70 A6
  STH/RUST TN4 .... 190 A6
  STPH/PW TN12 .... 173 H6
Nurstead Av HART DA3 .... 44 E8
Nurstead Church La MEO DA13 .... 63 H1
Nurstead La HART DA3............................. 62 E1
Nutfield Cl MAID ME15 .... 68 C6
Nutfields BGR/WK TN15 .... 126 B2
  SIT ME10 .... 94 C3
Nuthatch HART DA3 .... 44 C8
Nutley Cl WALD ME5 .... 88 C6
Nut Tree Cl ORP BR6 .... 56 C7
Nutwood Cl MAID/BEAR ME14 ... 134 A2 🔟

Oakapple La MAIDW ME16................... 132 A3
Oak Av GILL ME7 .... 5 E2
  SEV TN13 .... 123 K7
Oak Cl DART DA1 .... 22 B3
  HOO/HM ME3 .... 51 F3 🔟
Oakdale La EDEN TN8 .... 142 C4
Oakdale Rd STH/RUST TN4 .... 10 B3
Oakdene Rd SEV TN13 .... 8 C1
  STMC/STPC BR5 .... 56 B3
Oak Dr DIT/AY ME20 .... 108 E4
  HOO/HM ME3 .... 48 A3
Oak End Cl STH/RUST TN4 .... 190 A4
Oakenden La EDEN TN8 .... 186 D5
Oakenden Rd MEO DA13 .... 64 B5
Oak Farm Gdns HDCN TN27 .... 180 B8
Oak Farm La BGR/WK TN15.................... 83 F5
Oakfield HAWK TN18 .... 235 F4
Oakfield Court Rd
  RTWE/PEM TN2 .... 11 E4 🔟
Oakfield La RDART DA2 .... 22 D8
Oakfield Park Rd DART DA1 .... 23 G4
Oakfield Pl DART DA1 .... 23 G3

Oakfield Rd *EDEN* TN8 .... 164 B2
  STPH/PW TN12 .... 193 F6
Oakfields *SEV* TN13 .... 9 D5
  SIT ME10 .... 93 H3 ▣
Oakhill Rd *ORP* BR6.......... 56 A6
  PUR RM19 .... 13 F5
Oak Hill Rd *SEV* TN13 .... 8 C4
Oakhurst Cl *WALD* ME5.......... 88 A3
Oaklands Cl *BGR/WK* TN15.......... 80 D2
Oaklands La *BH/WHM* TN16 .... 97 G2
Oaklands Rd *GVW* DA11 .... 45 G2
  HAWK TN18 .... 235 D5
  RDART DA2 .... 24 A7
  RRTW TN3 .... 204 E8
Oaklands Wy *RTON* TN11 .... 169 K2
Oak La *HDCN* TN27 .... 200 B1
  RSIT ME9 .... 71 G5
  SEV TN13 .... 8 C6
  SIT ME10 .... 123 H8
Oaklea Rd *STPH/PW* TN12 .... 173 H8
Oakleigh Cl *SWLY* BR8.......... 40 B8
  WALD ME5.......... 87 K4
Oak Lodge La *BH/WHM* TN16 .... 120 D4
Oakmead *MEO* DA13 .... 63 H6 ▣
  TONN TN10 .... 148 C8
Oakmore Gdns *STMC/STPC* BR5 .... 56 D1
Oak Rd *BH/WHM* TN16 .... 120 D4
  GRH DA9 .... 24 D5
  GVE DA12.......... 45 J1
  HOO/HM ME3 .... 51 F3 ▣▣
  ORP BR6 .... 76 B3
  RTWE/PEM TN2 .... 190 D7
  SIT ME10 .... 94 D1
  STPH/PW TN12 .... 172 D7
  STRD ME2 .... 48 D8
Oaks Dene *WALD* ME5 .... 88 A5
Oaks Forstal *HAWK* TN18 .... 243 K1
Oakshaw *OXTED* RH8 .... 118 B6
Oaks Rd *TENT* TN30.......... 230 B7
The Oaks *DIT/AY* ME20 .... 109 J5
  SWLY BR8 .... 40 B7
Oak Tree Auenue *GRH* DA9 .... 24 E6
Oak Tree Av *MAID/SHEP* ME15 .... 133 F4
Oak Tree Cl *RTW* TN1 .... 10 C6
  STPH/PW TN12 .... 196 D1 ▣
Oakum Ct *CHAT* ME4.......... 4 B6
Oak Vw *EDEN* TN8.......... 164 B4
Oakwood Cl *DART* DA1 .... 24 A7
Oakwood Cl *MAIDW* ME16.......... 6 A4
Oakwood Ri *HART* DA3 .... 43 K8
  RTWE/PEM TN2 .... 190 E7
Oast Cl *RTWE/PEM* TN2 .... 190 D7
Oast Ct *SIT* ME10 .... 93 K4
  WBY/YAL ME18 .... 152 D5
Oast House Wy *STMC/STPC* BR5.......... 56 C1
Oast La *RTON* TN11 .... 170 A2
Oast Rd *OXTED* RH8 .... 140 D2
Oastview *RHAM* ME8 .... 70 D6
Oast Vw *STPH/PW* TN12.......... 194 E8
Oast Wy *HART* DA3 .... 61 K3
Oatfield Cl *CRBK* TN17 .... 225 J1
Oatfield Dr *CRBK* TN17 .... 225 J1
Oatfield Rd *ORP* BR6 .... 56 A5
Ocelot Ct *CHAT* ME4 .... 4 B5 ▣
Ockham Dr *STMC/STPC* BR5 .... 38 B5 ▣
Ockley La *HAWK* TN18.......... 235 G2
Ockley Rd *HAWK* TN18 .... 235 G4
Octavia Ct *WALD* ME5 .... 88 C3 ▣
Odiham Dr *MAIDW* ME16 .... 110 C7
Offen's Dr *STPH/PW* TN12 .... 198 A3
Offham Rd *E/WMAL* ME19 .... 107 J7
Officers Ter *CHAT* ME4 .... 3 F1
Old Ashford Rd *RMAID* ME17 .... 160 F2
The Old Bailey *RMAID* ME17 .... 137 J8 ▣
Old Barn Cl *BGR/WK* TN15 .... 102 E4
  GILL ME7 .... 69 G8
  TON TN9 .... 169 K6
Old Barn Rd *E/WMAL* ME19 .... 108 D6
Old Barn Wy *BXLYHN* DA7 .... 22 A3
Old Bexley La *BXLY* DA5.......... 22 A8
Oldbury Cl *STMC/STPC* BR5.......... 56 E1
Oldbury La *BGR/WK* TN15 .... 126 B1
The Old Carriageway *GILL* ME7.......... 89 G3
  SEV TN13 .... 122 E2
Old Chapel Rd *SWLY* BR8 .... 57 K4
Old Chatham Rd *DIT/AY* ME20 .... 87 J8
  MAID/BEAR 110 E5
Old Church La *WBY/YAL* ME18.......... 151 C1
Old Church Rd *ROCH* ME1 .... 86 C5
  RTWE/PEM TN2 .... 191 K5
  WBY/YAL ME18.......... 151 F1
Old Coach Rd *BGR/WK* TN15 .... 104 E1
Old Dartford Rd *EYN* DA4 .... 59 J3
Old Downs *HART* DA3 .... 61 K2
Old Dr *MAID/SHEP* ME15 .... 133 F8
Old Farm Gdns *SWLY* BR8 .... 40 C8 ▣
Old Ferry Rd *RSIT* ME9 .... 55 K8
Oldfield Cl *MAID/SHEP* ME15.......... 134 A5
  RHAM ME8 .... 70 A6
Old Forge La *RSIT* ME9 .... 114 D2
Old Forge Wy *SCUP* DA14 .... 38 C2
Old Gardens Cl *RTWE/PEM* TN2 .... 207 C6
The Old Gdn *SEV* TN13 .... 123 F2
Old Hadlow Rd *TONN* TN10 .... 170 E2

Old Ham La *RMAID* ME17 .... 160 B2
Old Hl *ORP* BR6.......... 75 K2
Old House La *RRTW* TN3 .... 205 G1
Old House Rd *RSIT* ME9 .... 91 H2
Old Kent Rd *STPH/PW* TN12 .... 173 H8
Old Lain *RMAID* ME17 .... 137 K8
Old La *BGR/WK* TN15.......... 126 B2
  BH/WHM TN16 .... 97 H8
  OXTED RH8 .... 140 D1
Old Lenham Rd *RSIT* ME9.......... 139 K1
Old London Rd *BGR/WK* TN15 .... 105 F2
  RSEV TN14.......... 77 H5
  TONN TN10 .... 170 C3 ▣
Old Loose Hl *MAID/SHEP* ME15.......... 155 F2
Old Maidstone Rd *SCUP* DA14.......... 39 G5
Old Manor Wy *BXLYHN* DA7.......... 22 A1
Old Mill Cl *EYN* DA4 .... 59 H5
Old Mill La *DIT/AY* ME20 .... 110 C3
Old Mill Rd *RMAID* ME17 .... 135 H6
Old Orch *HAWK* TN18 .... 243 J1
Old Orchard La *E/WMAL* ME19 .... 108 D5
The Old Orch *RHAM* ME8 .... 70 D5
Old Otford Rd *RSEV* TN14 .... 101 K5
Old Pattens La *ROCH* ME1 .... 3 D6
Old Perry St *GVW* DA11 .... 27 F8
Old Regent Dr *CRBK* TN17 .... 238 C3
Old Rd *CHAT* ME4 .... 3 F4
  DART DA1 .... 22 A3
  STPH/PW TN12 .... 151 H8
  WBY/YAL ME18 .... 129 K7
Old Rd East *GVE* DA12 .... 28 A7
Old Rd West *GVW* DA11 .... 27 G7
Old School Cl *RMAID* ME17 .... 160 D2
Old School Ct *HDCN* TN27 .... 183 F3
  HOO/HM ME3 .... 50 A2 ▣
Old School La *E/WMAL* ME19 .... 107 H2
Old Soar Rd *BGR/WK* TN15 .... 127 H6
Old Station Rd *WADH* TN5 .... 220 A8
Old Tannery Cl *TENT* TN30 .... 229 K7 ▣
Old Terry's Lodge Rd
  BGR/WK TN15.......... 103 K3
Old Tovil Rd *MAID/SHEP* ME15.......... 6 C5
Old Trafford Cl *MAIDW* ME16 .... 110 B8
Old Tree La *RMAID* ME17 .... 155 J3
Old Tye Av *BH/WHM* TN16 .... 97 J3
The Old Wk *RSEV* TN14.......... 101 K4
Old Wardsdown *WADH* TN5 .... 233 F3
Old Watling St *STRD* ME2.......... 48 A6
The Old Yews *HART* DA3 .... 44 C8
Oleander Cl *ORP* BR6 .... 75 J1
Oliver Cl *CHAT* ME4 .... 4 B6
  WTHK RM20.......... 13 K7
Oliver Crs *EYN* DA4 .... 59 J4
Olive Rd *DART* DA1 .... 23 G7
Oliver Rd *STPH/PW* TN12 .... 198 A3
  SWLY BR8 .... 40 A8
  WTHK RM20.......... 13 K8
Oliver Twist Cl *ROCH* ME1 .... 2 B1
Olivine Cl *WALD* ME5 .... 88 B6
Olliffe Cl *WALD* ME5 .... 88 A4 ▣
Onslow Dr *SCUP* DA14 .... 38 E1
Onslow Rd *ROCH* ME1 .... 3 D5
Orache Dr *MAID/BEAR* ME14 .... 134 A1
Orange Court La *ORP* BR6.......... 75 F4
Orange Ter *ROCH* ME1 .... 3 D3
Orbit Cl *WALD* ME5 .... 88 B6
Orchard Av *DART* DA1 .... 22 E6
  DIT/AY ME20 .... 109 J5
  GVW DA11 .... 45 J3
  STRD ME2 .... 48 E5 ▣
Orchard Cl *EDEN* TN8 .... 164 B4
  HART DA3 .... 44 C7
  RMAID ME17 .... 154 C3
  RMAID ME17 .... 157 G2
  RSEV TN14.......... 102 A8
  RTWE/PEM TN2 .... 190 D7
  STPH/PW TN12 .... 194 D8
Orchard Crs *STPH/PW* TN12 .... 194 E8
Orchard Dr *EDEN* TN8.......... 164 B4
  MEO DA13 .... 63 G2
  RSIT ME9 .... 91 K1
  TONN TN10 .... 170 C3
Orchard Gld *HDCN* TN27.......... 200 C8
Orchard Gv *DIT/AY* ME20 .... 109 F4
  ORP BR6.......... 56 A6
Orchard Hl *DART* DA1 .... 22 B4
Orchard Pl *MAIDW* ME16 .... 6 B4
  SIT ME10 .... 94 B3
Orchard Ri *RRTW* TN3.......... 204 E7
Orchard Rd *GVW* DA11 .... 26 D8
  MAID/BEAR ME14 .... 134 A2
  ORP BR6 .... 75 G1
  ORP BR6 .... 76 D4
  RSEV TN14.......... 101 K3
  SEV TN13 .... 8 A1
  STPH/PW TN12 .... 151 J8
  SWCM DA10 .... 25 K4
  TENT TN30.......... 230 A3
Orchard St *DART* DA1 .... 23 H5
  MAID/SHEP ME15.......... 7 D4
  RSIT ME9 .... 91 K1
The Orchard *MAID/BEAR* ME14 .... 134 D2
  SEV TN13 .... 101 G8 ▣
  SWLY BR8 .... 40 A7 ▣
Orchard Vw *MAID/BEAR* ME14 .... 112 C6

RSIT ME9 .... 95 K3
  TENT TN30 .... 230 C7
Orchard Wy *BGR/WK* TN15 .... 102 E4
  CRBK TN17 .... 225 H2
  OXTED RH8 .... 140 E4
  RDART DA2 .... 41 G1
  SNOD ME6 .... 85 J7
  STPH/PW TN12 .... 194 E8
Orchid Cl *STRD* ME2 .... 48 B8
Orchidhurst *RTWE/PEM* TN2 .... 190 D7 ▣
Ordnance Rd *GVE* DA12 .... 27 K5
Ordnance St *CHAT* ME4 .... 3 E5
Ordnance Ter *CHAT* ME4 .... 3 E4 ▣
Oriole Wy *DIT/AY* ME20 .... 108 C4
Orion Rd *ROCH* ME1 .... 67 H7
Orlestone Gdns *ORP* BR6 .... 77 F3
Orlick Rd *GVE* DA12 .... 28 E8
The Orpines *WBY/YAL* ME18 .... 130 D7
Orpington By-pass *RSEV* TN14 .... 77 H4
Orwell Cl *DIT/AY* ME20 .... 108 D5
Orwell Spike *E/WMAL* ME19 .... 129 J1
Osborne Rd *GILL* ME7 .... 5 D3
Osbourne Rd *RDART* DA2 .... 24 A5
Osgood Av *ORP* BR6.......... 76 A1
Osgood Gdns *ORP* BR6.......... 76 A1
Osmers Hl *WADH* TN5 .... 220 B7
Osney Wy *GVE* DA12 .... 28 C8
Osprey Av *WALD* ME5 .... 5 E6
Osprey Ct *SIT* ME10 .... 94 B3
Osprey Wk *DIT/AY* ME20 .... 108 C5
Ospringe Pl *RTWE/PEM* TN2 .... 191 F8
Osterberg Rd *DART* DA1 .... 23 J3
Ostlers Ct *SNOD* ME6 .... 85 K6 ▣
Otford La *RSEV* TN14 .... 77 G8
Otford Rd *RSEV* TN14 .... 101 K8
Otham La *MAID/SHEP* ME15 .... 134 E4
Otham St *MAID/SHEP* ME15 .... 134 D7
Otlinge Cl *STMC/STPC* BR5 .... 56 E1 ▣
Ottawa Rd *TIL* RM18 .... 27 H1
Otterbourne Pl
  MAID/SHEP ME15 .... 134 A5 ▣
Otterham Quay La *RHAM* ME8 .... 70 E6
Otteridge Rd *MAID/BEAR* ME14 .... 134 C3
Otters Cl *STMC/STPC* BR5 .... 56 E1 ▣
Otway St *CHAT* ME4 .... 4 A5
Otway Ter *CHAT* ME4 .... 4 A5
The Oval *HART* DA3 .... 44 D8
Ovenden Rd *RSEV* TN14 .... 99 K7
Overcliffe *GVW* DA11 .... 27 H5
Overdale *RSEV* TN14 .... 145 K4
Overmead *SWLY* BR8 .... 58 B2 ▣
Over Minnis *HART* DA3 .... 62 A7
Overy St *DART* DA1 .... 23 H6
Owen Cl *E/WMAL* ME19 .... 108 D6 ▣
Owens Wy *GILL* ME7 .... 51 H8
Oxenden Wood Rd *ORP* BR6.......... 76 C2
Oxenhill Rd *RSEV* TN14 .... 102 C4
Oxenhoath Rd *RTON* TN11 .... 149 J2
Oxford Cl *GVE* DA12 .... 28 C8 ▣
Oxford Rd *GILL* ME7 .... 5 D5
  MAID/SHEP ME15.......... 133 K5
  SCUP DA14 .... 39 G5
Oxford St *SNOD* ME6 .... 85 K6
Ox La *TENT* TN30 .... 230 B4
Ox Lea *RRTW* TN3 .... 205 K3
Oxley Shaw La *E/WMAL* ME19 .... 108 C4
Oyster Cl *SIT* ME10 .... 73 K8 ▣

P

Packer Pl *WALD* ME5.......... 68 B6
Packham Rd *GVW* DA11 .... 45 G1
Packhorse Rd *SEV* TN13.......... 122 E2
Padbrook *OXTED* RH8 .... 118 E8
Paddlesworth Rd *SNOD* ME6 .... 85 F5
Paddock Cl *BGR/WK* TN15 .... 105 J8
  EYN DA4 .... 42 B6
  OXTED RH8 .... 140 D2
  RRTW TN3 .... 204 E1
Paddocks Cl *STMC/STPC* BR5 .... 56 E6
The Paddocks *EDEN* TN8 .... 185 H7
  GILL ME7 .... 89 H7
  STPH/PW TN12 .... 151 C8 ▣
The Paddock *BH/WHM* TN16 .... 120 C5
  CHAT ME4 .... 3 F4
  MEO DA13 .... 83 G7
  RTON TN11 .... 150 A5
  RTWE/PEM TN2 .... 191 J8
  RYE TN31 .... 244 E7
Paddock Wy *OXTED* RH8 .... 140 D2
Pad's Hl *MAID/SHEP* ME15 .... 7 D3 ▣
Page Cl *RDART* DA2.......... 43 H1
Pagehurst Rd *STPH/PW* TN12 .... 197 J3
Paget St *GILL* ME7 .... 4 C3
Pagitt St *CHAT* ME4 .... 3 E6
Paiges Farm Cl *RSEV* TN14 .... 146 A4
Pains Hl *OXTED* RH8 .... 141 G3
Painters Ash La *GVW* DA11 .... 44 E1
Palace Av *MAID/SHEP* ME15 .... 7 D3
Palace Rd *BH/WHM* TN16 .... 98 A8
Palewell Cl *STMC/STPC* BR5.......... 38 C7
Palmar Rd *MAIDW* ME16 .... 6 A1
Palmarsh Cl *STMC/STPC* BR5 .... 56 E1 ▣

Palm Av SCUP DA14 ... 38 E4
Palmer Av GVE DA12 ... 46 A2
Palmers Brook RTON TN11 ... 150 B4
Palmers Green La STPH/PW TN12 ... 194 B5
Palmers Orch CHAT ME4 ... 78 C6
Palmerston Rd CHAT ME4 ... 68 A5
Pankhurst Rd HOO/HM ME3 ... 32 E8
Pannell Rd HOO/HM ME3 ... 21 F8
Panteny La RSIT ME9 ... 95 F4
Panter's SWLY BR8 ... 40 C5
The Pantiles RTWE/PEM TN2 ... 10 C5
Panton Cl WALD ME5 ... 88 D2
Papion Gv WALD ME5 ... 87 K4
The Parade STRD ME2 ... 48 D6
Parham Rd CHAT ME4 ... 3 F6
Park Av EDEN TN8 ... 164 B4
  GILL ME7 ... 5 D6
  GVE DA12 ... 27 K7
  GVW DA11 ... 27 F7
  MAID/BEAR ME14 ... 7 E1
  ORP BR6 ... 56 B7
  RMAID ME17 ... 154 E4
  RTON TN11 ... 169 K1
  SIT ME10 ... 93 J5
Park Barn Rd RMAID ME17 ... 157 K1
Park Cl STH/RUST TN4 ... 10 A5
Park Corner Rd MEO DA13 ... 26 B8
Park Crs CHAT ME4 ... 68 A6
Park Dr HART DA3 ... 43 K8
  SIT ME10 ... 93 J5
Parker Cl RHAM ME8 ... 90 B1
Park Farm Rd E/WMAL ME19 ... 84 B7
Parkfield BGR/WK TN15 ... 124 D2
Parkfield Rd RHAM ME8 ... 70 C4
Parkfields STRD ME2 ... 48 B7
Parkgate Rd ORP BR6 ... 57 K8
Park HI MEO DA13 ... 63 F1
Park Hill Rd RSEV TN14 ... 102 C4
Park House Gdns STH/RUST TN4 ... 190 A5
Parkland Cl SEV TN13 ... 124 A8
Parklands OXTED RH8 ... 140 C2
Park La BGR/WK TN15 ... 102 E5
  BGR/WK TN15 ... 124 D2
  HAWK TN18 ... 224 D7
  MAID/BEAR ME14 ... 111 F7
  RMAID ME17 ... 155 K4
  SEV TN13 ... 9 E3
  SOCK/AV RM15 ... 13 H1
  SWLY BR8 ... 41 F7
Park Pl GVE DA12 ... 27 K5
  SEV TN13 ... 123 F2
Park Rd DART DA1 ... 23 K6
  E/WMAL ME19 ... 106 E3
  E/WMAL ME19 ... 108 B3
  GVW DA11 ... 27 J8
  LING RH7 ... 162 C5
  OXTED RH8 ... 118 D7
  RTON TN11 ... 149 J1
  SIT ME10 ... 93 K3
  STH/RUST TN4 ... 11 D2
  STMC/STPC BR5 ... 56 D3
  STPH/PW TN12 ... 197 G3
  SWCM DA10 ... 25 K5
  SWLY BR8 ... 41 F7
  WBY/YAL ME18 ... 151 H1
Parkside HOO/HM ME3 ... 31 G7
  RSEV TN14 ... 77 F8
Parkside Av BXLYHN DA7 ... 22 A1
  TIL RM18 ... 27 J1
Parkside Cross BXLYHN DA7 ... 22 C2
Park St RTWE/PEM TN2 ... 11 E4
Park Ter GRH DA9 ... 25 G4
The Park SCUP DA14 ... 38 A5
Park Vw RYE TN31 ... 244 D8
  SOCK/AV RM15 ... 13 H1
Park View Cl EDEN TN8 ... 164 B4
Park Wall GVW DA11 ... 26 C4
Park Wy BXLY DA5 ... 40 C1
  MAID/SHEP ME15 ... 7 E6
  RMAID ME17 ... 154 C3
Parkway TONN TN10 ... 170 D1
Parkwood Cl RTWE/PEM TN2 ... 11 E1
Park Wood La STPH/PW TN12 ... 198 E4
Parkwood Rd BH/WHM TN16 ... 97 J8
Parr Av GILL ME7 ... 5 D2
Parrock Av GVE DA12 ... 27 K7
Parrock Rd GVE DA12 ... 27 K7
Parrock St GVE DA12 ... 27 J5
Parrs Haed Ms ROCH ME1 ... 2 C2
Parsonage La STH/RUST TN4 ... 206 A1
Parsonage La EYN DA4 ... 42 A4
  RRTW TN3 ... 210 E8
  RSIT ME9 ... 73 F6
  SCUP DA14 ... 39 G2
  STRD ME2 ... 49 H6
Parsonage Rd STH/RUST TN4 ... 206 A1
Parsons La BGR/WK TN15 ... 81 K5
  RDART DA2 ... 40 E1
Partridge Av DIT/AY ME20 ... 108 D3
Partridge Dr CHAT ME4 ... 50 C5
Pasley Rd GILL ME7 ... 4 A1
Pasley Rd East CHAT ME4 ... 4 A1
Pastens Rd OXTED RH8 ... 141 G2
Pastime Cl SIT ME10 ... 75 K6
The Patch SEV TN13 ... 8 A1

Patrixbourne Av RHAM ME8 ... 69 K4
Pattenden Gdns STPH/PW TN12 ... 151 J7
Pattenden La STPH/PW TN12 ... 176 B6
Pattens La CHAT ME4 ... 67 K5
Patterdale Rd RDART DA2 ... 24 B7
Paulinus Cl STMC/STPC BR5 ... 38 D7
The Pavement TENT TN30 ... 230 A3
Pavilion La WBY/YAL ME18 ... 129 J6
Payden St RMAID ME17 ... 139 K6
  RSIT ME9 ... 139 J4
Paynesfield Rd BH/WHM TN16 ... 97 C7
Payne's La MAID/SHEP ME15 ... 133 C7
Peach Cft GVW DA11 ... 45 F1
Peacock St GVE DA12 ... 27 K6
Peal Cl HOO/HM ME3 ... 51 F1
Pearman Cl RHAM ME8 ... 70 D5
Pearse Pl RRTW TN3 ... 221 J1
Pearsons Green Rd
  STPH/PW TN12 ... 194 A1
  STPH/PW TN12 ... 194 C2
Pearson Wy DART DA1 ... 23 J8
Pear Tree La DIT/AY ME20 ... 109 C6
Pear Tree Cl CRBK TN17 ... 225 K3
  SWLY BR8 ... 40 A7
Pear Tree La GILL ME7 ... 69 F7
  MAID/SHEP ME15 ... 133 H8
Peartree La STRD ME2 ... 47 K4
Pease Hl BGR/WK TN15 ... 82 A2
Peasley La CRBK TN17 ... 212 C8
Peat Wy HOO/HM ME3 ... 20 C7
Peckham Cl STRD ME2 ... 49 H6
Peel Dr SIT ME10 ... 94 D2
Peel St MAID/BEAR ME14 ... 7 D1
Peens La RMAID ME17 ... 155 J7
Pegasus Ct GVE DA12 ... 45 K1
Peggoty Cl HOO/HM ME3 ... 48 A3
Pelham Rd GVW DA11 ... 27 G6
Pelham Rd South GVW DA11 ... 27 G7
Pelican Cl STRD ME2 ... 48 B8
Pell Cl WADH TN5 ... 220 C8
Pells La BGR/WK TN15 ... 81 F6
Pemberton Gdns SWLY BR8 ... 40 B8
Pemble Cl STPH/PW TN12 ... 172 C7
Pembroke CHAT ME4 ... 50 B6
Pembroke Gdns RHAM ME8 ... 90 B2
Pembroke Pl EYN DA4 ... 42 A6
Pembroke Rd RMAID ME17 ... 154 C3
  TON TN9 ... 170 A5
Pembury Cl RTWE/PEM TN2 ... 191 K7
Pembury Gdns MAIDW ME16 ... 6 A4
Pembury Gra RTWE/PEM TN2 ... 191 G8
Pembury Gv TON TN9 ... 170 C6
Pembury Hall Rd RTWE/PEM TN2 ... 191 J3
Pembury Rd RTON TN11 ... 191 G3
  RTWE/PEM TN2 ... 11 E4
  TON TN9 ... 170 B6
Pembury St SIT ME10 ... 93 K2
Pembury Wks RTON TN11 ... 191 H4
Pembury Wy RHAM ME8 ... 70 B4
Pencroft Dr DART DA1 ... 23 F6
Pendennis Rd ORP BR6 ... 56 F5
Penderel Ms TENT TN30 ... 230 B6
Penenden HART DA3 ... 62 A6
Penenden Heath Rd
  MAID/BEAR ME14 ... 111 H7
Penenden St MAID/BEAR ME14 ... 7 D1
Penfield La RSIT ME9 ... 117 G2
Penfold Cl MAID/SHEP ME15 ... 134 A8
  WALD ME5 ... 68 C7
Penfold HI RMAID ME17 ... 135 K6
Penfolds Cl TONN TN10 ... 170 C1
Penfold Wy MAID/SHEP ME15 ... 133 F8
Penguin Cl STRD ME2 ... 48 C8
Penhurst Cl MAID/BEAR ME14 ... 134 B1
Penlee Cl EDEN TN8 ... 164 C4
Pennant Rd ROCH ME1 ... 67 H7
Penn Cl SIT ME10 ... 94 C4
Penney Cl DART DA1 ... 23 G6
Pennine Wy GVW DA11 ... 45 F1
  MAID/SHEP ME15 ... 134 C5
Pennington Pl STH/RUST TN4 ... 190 B4
Pennington Rd STH/RUST TN4 ... 190 A4
Penns La RSEV TN14 ... 122 A6
Penns Yd RTWE/PEM TN2 ... 191 J8
Pennyfields CRBK TN17 ... 225 K2
Penshurst Cl BGR/WK TN15 ... 80 D2
  HART DA3 ... 44 E7
  RHAM ME8 ... 70 A4
Penshurst Rd RTON TN11 ... 167 K6
  RTON TN11 ... 188 B4
Penshurst Wy STMC/STPC BR5 ... 56 D1
The Penstocks MAIDW ME16 ... 6 A5
Pen Wy TONN TN10 ... 170 E1
Pepingstraw Cl E/WMAL ME19 ... 107 F7
Pepper HI GVW DA11 ... 44 D1
Pepys Cl GVW DA11 ... 44 E1
Pepys Ri ORP BR6 ... 56 A5
Pepy's Wy STRD ME2 ... 48 E6
Perch La RRTW TN3 ... 210 A5
Peregrine Dr SIT ME10 ... 94 B3
Peregrine Rd WBY/YAL ME18 ... 129 J4
Perimeter Rd DIT/AY ME20 ... 109 C3
Periwinkle Cl SIT ME10 ... 93 K1

Perkins Cl GRH DA9 ... 24 E4
Perran Cl HART DA3 ... 62 A1
Perryfield St MAID/BEAR ME14 ... 6 C1
Perry Gv DART DA1 ... 23 K3
Perry Hall Cl ORP BR6 ... 56 B4
Perry Hall Rd ORP BR6 ... 56 A5
Perry Hl HOO/HM ME3 ... 31 H5
Perrys La ORP BR6 ... 76 C8
Perry St CHAT ME4 ... 3 E5
  CHST BR7 ... 38 A4
  DART DA1 ... 22 B2
  GVW DA11 ... 27 F7
  MAID/BEAR ME14 ... 6 C2
Perth Gdns SIT ME10 ... 93 H2
Pescot Av HART DA3 ... 44 B8
Pested Bars Rd RMAID ME17 ... 155 J1
Peter Av OXTED RH8 ... 118 B8
Petersfield RTWE/PEM TN2 ... 192 A7
Petersham Dr STMC/STPC BR5 ... 38 A7
Petersham Gdns
  STMC/STPC BR5 ... 38 A7
Petham Gn RHAM ME8 ... 69 K4
Petten Cl STMC/STPC BR5 ... 56 E5
Petter Gv STMC/STPC BR5 ... 56 D5
Petteridge La STPH/PW TN12 ... 193 G8
Pett La RSIT ME9 ... 91 K6
Peverel Dr MAID/BEAR ME14 ... 134 D2
Pheasant La MAID/SHEP ME15 ... 133 H7
Pheasant Rd CHAT ME4 ... 4 C6
Phelps Cl BGR/WK TN15 ... 80 D2
Phillip Av SWLY BR8 ... 58 A1
Phillippa Ct SIT ME10 ... 73 K7
Phillips Cl DART DA1 ... 22 E5
Phillips Ct RHAM ME8 ... 69 J4
Philpots La RTON TN11 ... 146 C5
Phoenix Dr WBY/YAL ME18 ... 130 C8
Phoenix Pl DART DA1 ... 23 G6
Phoenix Rd WALD ME5 ... 88 C4
Pickering St MAID/SHEP ME15 ... 133 G8
Pickforde La WADH TN5 ... 232 C5
Pickle's Wy HOO/HM ME3 ... 15 F8
Pickwick Crs ROCH ME1 ... 2 C6
Pickwick Gdns GVW DA11 ... 44 E1
Pier Approach Rd GILL ME7 ... 5 D1
Pierce Mill La RTON TN11 ... 172 D1
Pier Rd GILL ME7 ... 5 D1
  GRH DA9 ... 25 G3
  GVW DA11 ... 27 G5
Pigdown La EDEN TN8 ... 185 K2
Pigsdean Rd MEO DA13 ... 64 E4
Pikefish La STPH/PW TN12 ... 174 C5
Pikes La LING RH7 ... 162 C5
Pikey La E/WMAL ME19 ... 130 B1
Pile La STPH/PW TN12 ... 198 C2
Pilgrims Ct DART DA1 ... 23 K4
Pilgrims Lakes RMAID ME17 ... 137 J8
Pilgrims La OXTED RH8 ... 119 C3
Pilgrims Rd STRD ME2 ... 65 J7
  SWCM DA10 ... 25 K3
Pilgrims Vw GRH DA9 ... 25 H5
  MAID/BEAR ME14 ... 110 E3
Pilgrims Wy BGR/WK TN15 ... 105 F2
  DART DA1 ... 24 A7
  DIT/AY ME20 ... 87 G8
  E/WMAL ME19 ... 111 J2
  MAID/BEAR ME14 ... 111 J2
  RMAID ME17 ... 136 D3
  RMAID ME17 ... 137 K7
  ROCH ME1 ... 86 D2
  RSEV TN14 ... 102 C3
  SNOD ME6 ... 84 E5
  STRD ME2 ... 66 B3
  STRD ME2 ... 85 G3
Pilgrims Wy East RSEV TN14 ... 102 A3
Pilgrims Wy West RSEV TN14 ... 101 H3
Pillar Box La RTON TN11 ... 149 K1
Pillar Box Rd BGR/WK TN15 ... 125 J1
Pilot Rd ROCH ME1 ... 67 H6
Pilots Pl GVE DA12 ... 27 K5
Pimpernel Cl MAID/BEAR ME14 ... 134 D2
Pimpernel Wy WALD ME5 ... 87 K2
Pinchbeck Rd ORP BR6 ... 76 A2
Pincroft Wd HART DA3 ... 62 D1
Pine Av GVE DA12 ... 28 A7
Pine Cl DIT/AY ME20 ... 108 E4
  SWLY BR8 ... 58 C1
Pine Gv EDEN TN8 ... 164 B4
  GILL ME7 ... 89 H1
  MAID/BEAR ME14 ... 7 E1
Pinehurst RSEV TN14 ... 102 C8
Pineneedle La SEV TN13 ... 9 D2
Pine Pl MAID/SHEP ME15 ... 6 B6
Pine Rdg TONN TN10 ... 148 B8
Pine Ri MEO DA13 ... 63 H3
Pine Rd STRD ME2 ... 48 E8
Pinesfield La E/WMAL ME19 ... 83 J8
Pine Tree La BGR/WK TN15 ... 126 A4
Pine Vw BGR/WK TN15 ... 105 J7
Pinewood Av SEV TN13 ... 102 B8
Pinewood Cl STPH/PW TN12 ... 173 H8
Pinewood Dr MAID/BEAR ME14 ... 88 E6
  ORP BR6 ... 75 K1
Pinewood Gdns STH/RUST TN4 ... 190 A5
Pinewood Rd RTWE/PEM TN2 ... 11 F2
Pinkham STPH/PW TN12 ... 173 J1

Pinks Hl SWLY BR8.....58 B2
Pinnock La STPH/PW TN12.....198 A5
Pinnock's Av GVW DA11.....21 J7
Pintail Cl HOO/HM ME3.....21 G8
The Pintails CHAT ME4.....50 C5
Pioneer Wy SWLY BR8.....40 B8
Piper's Green Rd BH/WHM TN16.....121 G7
Pipers La BH/WHM TN16.....121 H6
Pippin Cl RMAID ME17.....154 B4
   SIT ME10.....73 J8
Pippin Cft GILL ME7.....69 H8
Pippin Rd STPH/PW TN12.....151 H8
The Pippins MEO DA13.....63 H3
Pippin Wy WBY/YAL ME18.....129 J4
Pirbright Cl WALD ME5.....88 E4
Pirrip Cl GVE DA12.....28 C7
Pitchfont La OXTED RH8.....118 E5
Pitfield HART DA3.....62 A1
Pitfield Dr MEO DA13.....63 G7
Pit La EDEN TN8.....164 C2
Pitstock Rd RSIT ME9.....117 H2
Pittlesden TENT TN30.....230 H7
Pitt Rd MAIDW ME16.....132 B5
   RMAID ME17.....157 J4
Pivington La HDCN TN27.....183 H4
Pixot Hl STPH/PW TN12.....193 K5
Pix's La CRBK TN17.....238 D3
Pizien Well Rd WBY/YAL ME18.....129 J8
Place La RSIT ME9.....91 G1
Plain Rd STPH/PW TN12.....196 C3
Plains Av MAID/SHEP ME15.....7 E6
Plane Av GVW DA11.....26 E6
Plane Wk TONN TN10.....148 C7
Plantation Dr STMC/STPC BR5.....56 E5
Plantation La MAID/BEAR ME14.....134 C2
Plantation Rd GILL ME7.....40 D5
   SWLY BR8.....40 D5
Platt Common BGR/WK TN15.....105 J5
The Platters RHAM ME8.....69 K6
The Plat EDEN TN8.....164 D5
   RYE TN31.....244 E8
Platt House La BGR/WK TN15.....82 D8
The Platt RMAID ME17.....157 G7
Plaxdale Green Rd BGR/WK TN15.....81 J7
Plaxtol La BGR/WK TN15.....126 C6
Playstool Cl RSIT ME9.....72 A8
Playstool Rd RSIT ME9.....71 K8
Pleasance Rd TONN TN10.....149 F8
Pleasant Valley La
   MAID/SHEP ME15.....154 B2
Pleasant Vw ORP BR6.....75 H1
Pleasure House Rd RMAID ME17.....157 J7
Plomley Cl RHAM ME8.....90 A2
Plough Hl BGR/WK TN15.....127 F2
Ploughmans Wy RHAM ME8.....70 B8
   WALD ME5.....88 B5
Plough Wents Rd RMAID ME17.....156 H4
Plover Cl WALD ME5.....88 B5
Plover Rd DIT/AY ME20.....108 C3
Plowenders Cl E/WMAL ME19.....107 F3
Pluckley Cl RHAM ME8.....69 K3
Pluckley Rd HDCN TN27.....202 B4
Plug La MEO DA13.....84 A1
Plummer La TENT TN30.....229 K8
Plumtree Gv GILL ME7.....89 H2
Plum Tree La RSIT ME9.....90 E6
Plumtree Rd HDCN TN27.....179 J6
Plumtrees MAID/BEAR ME14.....132 A4
Plymouth Dr BGR/WK TN15.....9 E3
Plymouth Pk BGR/WK TN15.....9 E3
Poachers La WALD ME5.....88 D1
Podkin Wd WALD ME5.....88 A6
Polesden Rd RTWE/PEM TN2.....11 F5
Polesteeple Hl BH/WHM TN16.....97 H4
The Poles RSIT ME9.....71 H2
Polhill RSEV TN14.....100 C2
Polhill Dr WALD ME5.....88 A4
Police Station Rd E/WMAL ME19.....108 A6
Pollards Oak Crs OXTED RH8.....140 E3
Pollards Oak La OXTED RH8.....140 E3
Pollards Wood Hl OXTED RH8.....140 E1
Pollards Wood Rd OXTED RH8.....141 F1
Polley Cl RTWE/PEM TN2.....191 J7
Pollyhaugh EYN DA4.....59 H7
Polperro Cl ORP BR6.....56 A3
Pond Dr SIT ME10.....94 B4
Pond Farm Rd RMAID ME17.....114 B5
   RSIT ME9.....92 E5
Pondfield La GVE DA12.....47 H5
Pond Hl HOO/HM ME3.....15 C8
Pond La BGR/WK TN15.....125 J4
Pook La HDCN TN27.....218 B2
Poona Rd RTWE/PEM TN2.....11 D5
Pootings Rd EDEN TN8.....142 D6
Poot La RSIT ME9.....53 H8
Pope Dr STPH/PW TN12.....198 A2
Pope House La TENT TN30.....230 B2
Popes La OXTED RH8.....140 D6
Popes St MAIDW ME16.....132 C4
Poplar Av GVE DA12.....45 K2
Poplar Cl HOO/HM ME3.....51 F3
   STRD DA2.....66 E1
Poplar Gv MAIDW ME16.....132 C1
Poplar Rd STRD DA2.....66 D1
   TENT TN30.....247 J2

Poplars Cl HART DA3.....44 D8
Poplar Wk MEO DA13.....63 J3
Policans Rd STRD ME2.....66 A3
Poppy Cl GILL ME7.....5 E3
   MAIDW ME16.....6 A4
Porchester Rd HART DA3.....62 A1
   MAID/SHEP ME15.....133 G8
Porchfield Cl GVE DA12.....27 K8
Port Av GRH DA9.....25 G5
Port Cl MAID/BEAR ME14.....134 B1
   WALD ME5.....88 C3
Porters Rd STPH/PW TN12.....193 H8
Porters Wk RMAID ME17.....157 G2
Port Hl ORP BR6.....76 C7
Portland Av GVE DA12.....27 J8
   SIT ME10.....94 D2
Portland Pl SNOD ME6.....85 K6
Portland Rd GILL ME7.....26 E5
   GVW DA11.....26 E5
   ROCH ME1.....86 B2
Portland St CHAT ME4.....4 B6
Portman Cl BXLY DA5.....22 B7
Portman Pk TON TN9.....170 C3
Port Ri CHAT ME4.....3 F5
Portsdown Cl MAIDW ME16.....132 B4
Portsmouth Cl STRD ME2.....48 C8
Port Victoria Rd HOO/HM ME3.....37 H3
Portway Rd HOO/HM ME3.....31 G6
Post Barn Rd CHAT ME4.....3 F6
Postern La TON TN9.....170 D4
   TON TN9.....171 F6
Postley Rd MAID/SHEP ME15.....7 D6
Postmill Dr MAID/SHEP ME15.....6 C6
Post Office Rd HAWK TN18.....235 F4
Potash La BGR/WK TN15.....105 J8
Pot Kiln La RASHW TN26.....219 J3
Potter's La HAWK TN18.....225 G8
Pottery Rd HOO/HM ME3.....50 E1
Poulters Wd HAYES BR2.....74 C1
Pound Bank Cl BGR/WK TN15.....80 E4
Poundfield Rd HAWK TN18.....243 J1
Pound La RSEV TN14.....99 K2
   SEV TN13.....9 E3
Pound Rd STPH/PW TN12.....151 G8
Poundsbridge Hl RRTW TN3.....188 B8
Pounsley Rd SEV TN13.....101 G3
Pout Rd SNOD ME6.....85 J7
Poverest Rd STMC/STPC BR5.....56 A2
Povey Av STRD ME2.....49 H4
Powdermill Cl RTWE/PEM TN2.....190 C6
Powder Mill La DART DA1.....23 H8
   RTON TN11.....168 E4
   STH/RUST TN4.....190 B7
Powell Cl DIT/AY ME20.....110 A3
Powerscroft Rd SCUP DA14.....38 D4
Powlett Rd STRD ME2.....49 H5
Poynings Cl ORP BR6.....56 D6
Poyntell Rd STPH/PW TN12.....198 B2
Prall's La STPH/PW TN12.....193 C4
Pratling St DIT/AY ME20.....110 B3
Premier Cl DIT/AY ME20.....109 J5
Prentis Cl SIT ME10.....93 H1
Prentis Quay SIT ME10.....93 K1
Prestley Dr TONN TN10.....148 D7
Preston Av GILL ME7.....69 F5
Preston Rd GVW DA11.....27 F7
   TON TN9.....170 A5
Pretoria Rd CHAT ME4.....3 F6
   GILL ME7.....5 D5
Prettymans La EDEN TN8.....165 G3
Pridmore Rd SNOD ME6.....85 J6
Priestfield Rd GILL ME7.....5 E3
Priestfields ROCH ME1.....2 B6
Priest Hl OXTED RH8.....119 F8
Priestlands Park Rd BFN/LL DA15.....38 A1
Priestley Dr DIT/AY ME20.....108 D2
Priestwood Rd MEO DA13.....83 J2
Primrose Av RHAM ME8.....89 J1
Primrose Cl ROCH ME1.....67 K7
Primrose Dr DIT/AY ME20.....109 H6
Primrose La RSIT ME9.....93 F8
Primrose Rd STRD ME2.....85 H1
Primrose Wy STPH/PW TN12.....193 J1
Prince Arthur Rd GILL ME7.....4 B2
Prince Charles Av EYN DA4.....42 C7
   WALD ME5.....94 C4
   WALD ME5.....88 C2
Princes Av RDART DA2.....24 A7
   WALD ME5.....68 D7
Princes Cl SCUP DA14.....38 E1
Princes Rd DART DA1.....22 E6
   GVE DA12.....45 K2
   RDART DA2.....24 B7
   SWLY BR8.....40 D4
Princess Mary Av CHAT ME4.....4 B1
Princes St GVW DA11.....27 J5
   MAID/BEAR ME14.....7 D2
   ROCH ME1.....2 C5
   RTWE/PEM TN2.....11 E4
Princes Vw DART DA1.....23 K7
Princes Wy MAID/BEAR ME14.....112 C5
Prinys Dr RHAM ME8.....89 K2
Priorsdean Cl MAIDW ME16.....131 J5
Priorsford Av STMC/STPC BR5.....56 B1
Prior's Wy EDEN TN8.....185 G8

Priory Cl DART DA1.....23 F4
   MAID/SHEP ME15.....132 B6
Priory Flds EYN DA4.....59 J6
Priory Gdns DART DA1.....23 G4
Priory Gv DIT/AY ME20.....109 H5
   TON TN9.....170 B6
Priory Hl DART DA1.....23 G5
Priory La EYN DA4.....59 J5
Priory Pl DART DA1.....23 G5
Priory Rd DART DA1.....23 G3
   MAID/SHEP ME15.....7 D4
   RHAM ME8.....69 H4
   STRD ME2.....2 A2
   TON TN9.....170 C6
Priory St TON TN9.....170 B6
Priory Wk TON TN9.....170 C6
Priory Wy TENT TN30.....230 C7
Pristling La STPH/PW TN12.....197 H6
Prospect Av STRD ME2.....49 G6
Prospect Gv GVE DA12.....28 A6
Prospect Pk STH/RUST TN4.....189 K5
Prospect Pl DART DA1.....23 H5
   GVE DA12.....28 A6
   MAIDW ME16.....6 B4
Prospect Rd RTWE/PEM TN2.....11 D4
   SEV TN13.....9 E2
   STH/RUST TN4.....189 K5
Prospect Rw CHAT ME4.....4 A5
   GILL ME7.....4 A2
Provender Wy MAID/BEAR ME14.....134 A2
Providence La ROCH ME1.....2 C3
Providence St GRH DA9.....25 F4
Puddingcake La CRBK TN17.....239 G1
Pudding La MAID/BEAR ME14.....6 C3
Pudding Rd RHAM ME8.....70 C6
Puddledock La BH/WHM TN16.....143 C3
   RDART DA2.....A0 B3
Puffin Rd HOO/HM ME3.....37 G1
Pump Cl E/WMAL ME19.....108 B5
Pump La GILL ME7.....70 A3
   RHAM ME8.....69 K4
Punch Cft HART DA3.....61 K7
Purbeck Rd CHAT ME4.....3 E6
Purcell Av TONN TN10.....149 F8
Purfleet By-pass PUR RM19.....13 G5
Purfleet Rd SOCK/AV RM15.....13 F1
Purser Wy GILL ME7.....4 C1
Puttenden La RTON TN11.....149 F4
Pyrus Cl WALD ME5.....88 B6

Q

The Quadrant PUR RM19.....13 G4
Quaker Cl SEV TN13.....9 F2
Quaker Dr CRBK TN17.....214 E8
Quaker La CRBK TN17.....214 E8
Quakers Cl HART DA3.....44 A8
Quantock Cl RTWE/PEM TN2.....11 F2
Quantock Dr BXLYHN DA7.....22 B1
Quarry Bank TON TN9.....170 A7
Quarry Cl OXTED RH8.....140 C1
Quarry Hl BGR/WK TN15.....9 F2
Quarry Hill Rd BGR/WK TN15.....104 E8
   STH/RUST TN4.....170 A7
   TON TN9.....170 A7
Quarry Ms PUR RM19.....12 E4
Quarry Ri TON TN9.....170 A7
Quarry Rd MAID/SHEP ME15.....7 D5
   OXTED RH8.....140 C1
   RMAID ME17.....155 J2
   RTW TN1.....11 D2
Quarry Sq MAID/BEAR ME14.....7 D2
Quarry Wy WTHK ME20.....13 K6
Quay La GRH DA9.....25 G3
Quayside CHAT ME4.....50 C6
Quebec Av BH/WHM TN16.....120 D5
Quebec Rd TIL RM18.....27 H1
Quebec Sq BH/WHM TN16.....120 D5
Queen Anne Rd MAID/BEAR ME14.....7 E3
Queendown Av RHAM ME8.....90 A1
Queen Elizabeth Ii Br GRH DA9.....24 D1
Queen Elizabeth Sq
   MAID/SHEP ME15.....133 K8
The Queen Mother Ct ROCH ME1.....2 B4
Queen's Av HAWK TN18.....6 A2
   SNOD ME6.....85 K6
Queens Ct HAWK TN18.....235 F4
Queen's Dr RSEV TN14.....102 A7
Queen's Farm Rd GVE DA12.....29 H8
Queens Gdns RDART DA2.....24 A7
   STH/RUST TN4.....11 D1
Queen's Rd GILL ME7.....4 C4
   GVE DA12.....45 K1
   HAWK TN18.....235 G4
   MAIDW ME16.....132 B3
   SNOD ME6.....85 K6
   STH/RUST TN4.....11 D1
   WALD ME5.....68 E5
Queen St CHAT ME4.....4 A4
   GVE DA12.....27 J3
   HAWK TN18.....236 D8
   ROCH ME1.....2 C4

STPH/PW TN12 ...... 194 A1
Queensway HOO/HM ME3 ...... 19 G5
Queens Wy MAID/BEAR ME14 ...... 112 C5
Queenswood Rd DIT/AY ME20 ...... 87 J7
The Quern MAID/SHEP ME15 ...... 6 B6
Quested Wy RMAID ME17 ...... 137 G8
Quickbourne La RYE TN31 ...... 245 F7
Quickrells Av HOO/HM ME3 ...... 31 G1
Quickthorn Crs WALD ME5 ...... 87 K1
Quilter Rd STMC/STPC BR5 ...... 56 D5
Quincewood Gdns TONN TN10 ...... 148 B7
Quinion Cl WALD ME5 ...... 88 A6
Quinnell St RHAM ME8 ...... 70 B5
Quinton Rd RSIT ME9 ...... 73 H7
Quixote Crs STRD ME2 ...... 49 G5

R

Rabbits Rd EYN DA4 ...... 42 E7
Racefield Cl GVE DA12 ...... 47 H4
Radleigh Gdns CHAT ME4 ...... 67 K5
Raeburn Av DART DA1 ...... 22 E4
Raeburn Cl TONN TN10 ...... 148 E8
Ragge Wy BGR/WK ME15 ...... 102 D7
Rag Hill Rd BH/WHM TN16 ...... 97 H8
Ragpole Ct DIT/AY ME20 ...... 109 G6
Ragstone Rd MAID/SHEP ME15 ...... 134 C4
Railway Ap TON TN9 ...... 170 B6
Railway Pl GVE DA12 ...... 27 J5
Railway St CHAT ME4 ...... 3 F4
 GILL ME7 ...... 5 D3
 GVW DA11 ...... 26 B4
Railway Ter BH/WHM TN16 ...... 120 D4
Rainham Rd GILL ME7 ...... 4 C5
Raleigh Cl WALD ME5 ...... 68 B8
Raleigh Ms ORP BR6 ...... 76 A1
Ramillies Cl WALD ME5 ...... 88 B1
Rammell Ms CRBK TN17 ...... 225 K2
Rampion Cl MAID/BEAR ME14 ...... 134 A1
Ramsden Cl STMC/STPC BR5 ...... 56 D5
Ramsden La CRBK TN17 ...... 237 H3
Ramsden Rd ORP BR6 ...... 56 C4
 STMC/STPC BR5 ...... 56 D5
Ramslye Rd STH/RUST TN4 ...... 206 C5
Ramus Wood Av ORP BR6 ...... 75 K1
Randall Hill Rd BGR/WK TN15 ...... 105 F3
Randall Rd CHAT ME4 ...... 67 K5
Randall St MAID/BEAR ME14 ...... 6 C2
Randle's La ORP BR6 ...... 99 K1
Randolph Rd GILL ME7 ...... 4 C3
Ranelagh Gdns GVW DA11 ...... 27 G6
Range Rd GVE DA12 ...... 28 A6
Rangeworth Pl BFN/LL DA15 ...... 38 A1
Rankine Rd RTWE/PEM TN2 ...... 190 D7
Ranmore Pth STMC/STPC BR5 ...... 56 B1
Ranscombe Cl STRD ME2 ...... 66 C1
Ranters La CRBK TN17 ...... 222 E2
Ranworth Cl ERITH DA8 ...... 22 B1
Raphael Rd GVE DA12 ...... 28 A6
Rapier Cl PUR RM19 ...... 12 D4
Rashleigh Wy EYN DA4 ...... 60 B1
Raspberry Hill La RSIT ME9 ...... 55 H8
Ratcliffe Hwy HOO/HM ME3 ...... 33 H4
Rathmore Rd GVW DA11 ...... 27 H6
Raven Cl DIT/AY ME20 ...... 108 E5
Ravensbourne Rd DART DA1 ...... 22 D2
Ravensbury Rd STMC/STPC BR5 ...... 56 A1
Ravenscourt Rd STMC/STPC BR5 ...... 38 B8
Ravens Dane Cl
 MAID/SHEP ME15 ...... 134 C5
Ravensdale Av SNOD ME6 ...... 85 K6
 STRD ME2 ...... 49 G6
Rawdon Rd MAID/SHEP ME15 ...... 7 D4
Rawlings Cl ORP BR6 ...... 76 A1
Rawling St RSIT ME9 ...... 117 F2
Rayfield Ct SNOD ME6 ...... 85 K5
Rayford Cl DART DA1 ...... 23 F4
Rayleigh Cl MAIDW ME16 ...... 110 D7
Raymer Rd MAID/BEAR ME14 ...... 111 H6
Rayners Hl RMAID ME17 ...... 139 J8
Rays Hl EYN DA4 ...... 60 B1
Reader's Bridge Rd TENT TN30 ...... 229 K2
Reading St TENT TN30 ...... 241 H3
Readscroft Rd RHAM ME8 ...... 90 A1
Read Wy GVE DA12 ...... 46 A3
Recreation Av SNOD ME6 ...... 85 K6
Recreation Cl MAID/BEAR ME14 ...... 7 E1
Recreation Ground Rd TENT TN30 230
Rectory Cl DART DA1 ...... 22 B3
 ROCH ME1 ...... 86 B1
 SCUP DA14 ...... 38 C2
 SNOD ME6 ...... 85 K6
Rectory Dr STH/RUST TN4 ...... 189 G3
Rectory Flds CRBK TN17 ...... 225 K1
Rectory Gra ROCH ME1 ...... 2 C6
Rectory La BGR/WK TN15 ...... 126 C1
 BH/WHM TN16 ...... 119 J2
 BH/WHM TN16 ...... 121 J3
 MAIDW ME16 ...... 132 A5
 RMAID ME17 ...... 156 E8
 RMAID ME17 ...... 157 G7
 RMAID ME17 ...... 159 J1

SCUP DA14 ...... 38 C2
SEV TN13 ...... 9 D5
Rectory La North E/WMAL ME19 ...... 108 B4
Rectory La South E/WMAL ME19 ...... 108 A4
Rectory Meadow MEO DA13 ...... 44 B4
Rectory Park Rd STPH/PW TN12 ...... 211 K4
Rectory Rd BGR/WK TN15 ...... 82 D1
 HAYES BR2 ...... 74 C3
 HOO/HM ME3 ...... 31 F4
 SIT ME10 ...... 94 C3
 SWCM DA10 ...... 25 K6
Redbank E/WMAL ME19 ...... 108 C4
Redbridge Cl MAID/BEAR ME14 ...... 88 D1
Redcliffe La MAID/BEAR ME14 ...... 111 H7
Redding Cl RDART DA2 ...... 24 D8
Rede Court Rd STRD ME2 ...... 48 D6
Rede Wood Rd MAIDW ME16 ...... 131 J3
Redfern Av GILL ME7 ...... 5 E3
Red Hl WBY/YAL ME18 ...... 130 C6
Redhill Rd BGR/WK TN15 ...... 61 K8
Redhill Wd HART DA3 ...... 62 B8
Red House Gdns WBY/YAL ME18 ...... 130 B7
Redhouse Rd BH/WHM TN16 ...... 97 G8
Redland Shaw CHAT ME4 ...... 67 K5
Redlands Rd SEV TN13 ...... 8 B3
Red La OXTED RH8 ...... 141 F7
Redleaf Cl RTWE/PEM TN2 ...... 11 F1
Red Lion Cl STMC/STPC BR5 ...... 56 D3
Red Lodge Crs BXLY DA5 ...... 40 A1
Red Lodge Rd BXLY DA5 ...... 40 A1
Redmans La RSEV TN14 ...... 78 C2
Red Oak HAWK TN18 ...... 234 E6
Redpoll Wk STPH/PW TN12 ...... 193 J1
Redsells Cl MAID/SHEP ME15 ...... 134 C5
Redshank Rd CHAT ME4 ...... 50 B5
Red St MEO DA13 ...... 44 C4
Redvers Rd CHAT ME4 ...... 4 A6
Redwall La RMAID ME17 ...... 154 B7
Redwell La BGR/WK TN15 ...... 126 B2
Redwing Rd WALD ME5 ...... 68 C8
Redwings La RTWE/PEM TN2 ...... 191 K4
Redwood Cl WALD ME5 ...... 88 C4
Redwood Pk RTON TN11 ...... 192 C1
Reedham Crs HOO/HM ME3 ...... 31 H3
Reeds La RTON TN11 ...... 148 E1
Reed St HOO/HM ME3 ...... 15 G8
Reeves Cl STPH/PW TN12 ...... 198 A2
Reeves Ct STMC/STPC BR5 ...... 56 C4
Reeves Cresent SWLY BR8 ...... 40 A8
Reeves Ter WADH TN5 ...... 232 C5
Reform Rd CHAT ME4 ...... 4 B5
Regency Ct SIT ME10 ...... 93 J2
Regency Ct BGR/WK TN15 ...... 80 D2
Regent Dr MAID/BEAR ME14 ...... 133 G6
Regent St GILL ME7 ...... 4 B4
Regents Dr HAYES BR2 ...... 74 C1
Regent St CRBK TN17 ...... 238 C3
Reginald Av STRD ME2 ...... 66 B3
Reginald Rd MAIDW ME16 ...... 6 B4
Reinden Gv MAID/SHEP ME15 ...... 134 B5
Rembrandt Cl TONN TN10 ...... 148 E8
Rembrandt Dr GVW DA11 ...... 44 E1
Renown Rd WALD ME5 ...... 88 D4
Renton Dr STMC/STPC BR5 ...... 56 E4
Repton Rd ORP BR6 ...... 56 B8
Repton Wy WALD ME5 ...... 88 A2
Resolution Cl WALD ME5 ...... 88 B1
Restharrow Wy MAID/BEAR ME14 ...... 134 A1
The Retreat ORP BR6 ...... 76 C2
Revenge Rd MAID/BEAR ME14 ...... 88 D4
 WALD ME5 ...... 88 D5
Reynolds Cl TONN TN10 ...... 148 E8
Reynolds Flds HOO/HM ME3 ...... 30 B8
Reynolds La STH/RUST TN4 ...... 10 B1
Rhode St CHAT ME4 ...... 3 F4
Rhodewood Rd MAID/SHEP ME15 ...... 134 C5
Rhododendron Av MEO DA13 ...... 83 H3
Ribblesdale Rd RDART DA2 ...... 24 B7
Ribston Gdns STPH/PW TN12 ...... 173 G7
Richard's Cl RTON TN11 ...... 167 H4
Richardson Cl GRH DA9 ...... 24 E1
Richardson Rd STH/RUST TN4 ...... 10 C1
Richard St CHAT ME4 ...... 3 F4
 ROCH ME1 ...... 3 H6
Richborough Cl STMC/STPC BR5 ...... 56 E1
Richborough Dr STRD ME2 ...... 49 F5
Richmond Cl BH/WHM TN16 ...... 97 F6
 STRD ME2 ...... 50 A5
 WALD ME5 ...... 88 C2
Richmond Dr SIT ME10 ...... 73 K7
Richmond Rd GILL ME7 ...... 4 C2
Richmond Wy MAID/SHEP ME15 ...... 133 G6
Ricketts Hill Rd BH/WHM TN16 ...... 97 H5
Riddlesdale Av STH/RUST TN4 ...... 10 C1
Riddles Rd SIT ME10 ...... 93 H3
Ridge Av DART DA1 ...... 22 C5
Ridgelands RRTW TN3 ...... 189 G2
Ridge La MEO DA13 ...... 83 H3
The Ridge CTHM CR3 ...... 118 C4
Ridge Wy DART DA1 ...... 22 C5
 EDEN TN8 ...... 164 C2
Ridgeway RDART DA2 ...... 42 D3
 RTWE/PEM TN2 ...... 191 K7
Ridgeway Av GVE DA12 ...... 45 J1

Ridgeway Crs TONN TN10 ...... 170 D2
The Ridgewaye STH/RUST TN4 ...... 190 A5
The Ridgeway CHAT ME4 ...... 67 K7
 GILL ME7 ...... 4 C1
 GVE DA12 ...... 47 H5
 TON TN9 ...... 170 D2
Ridgewood MEO DA13 ...... 44 D6
Ridgway MAIDW ME16 ...... 132 B4
Riding La RTON TN11 ...... 147 H7
Riding Pk RTON TN11 ...... 147 H7
The Ridings BH/WHM TN16 ...... 97 J4
 RTWE/PEM TN2 ...... 191 F8
 STPH/PW TN12 ...... 173 J7
Ridlands Gv OXTED RH8 ...... 141 J1
Ridlands La OXTED RH8 ...... 141 J1
Ridlands Ri OXTED RH8 ...... 141 J1
Ridley Rd ROCH ME1 ...... 2 B4
Ringden Av STPH/PW TN12 ...... 193 G1
Ringlestone Crs
 MAID/BEAR ME14 ...... 111 F6
Ringlestone Rd RMAID ME17 ...... 137 G2
Ringshall Rd CHST BR7 ...... 38 B8
Rings Hl RTON TN11 ...... 168 E2
Ringwood Av ORP BR6 ...... 76 D5
Ringwood Rd RHAM ME8 ...... 70 A6
Ringwood Rd MAID/SHEP ME15 ...... 133 J6
Ripon Cl RHAM ME8 ...... 70 A3
Risden La HAWK TN18 ...... 235 J7
The Rise DART DA1 ...... 22 C3
 GILL ME7 ...... 89 H3
 GVE DA12 ...... 46 B2
 ROCH ME1 ...... 3 D5
 RSIT ME9 ...... 93 G4
 SEV TN13 ...... 124 A7
Ritch Rd SNOD ME6 ...... 85 J6
River Cl MAID/SHEP ME15 ...... 132 A7
River Dr STRD ME2 ...... 48 D7
Riverhead Cl MAIDW ME16 ...... 6 A1
 SIT ME10 ...... 93 H3
Riverhill SEV TN13 ...... 146 C2
River Lawn Rd TON TN9 ...... 170 B5
River Park Vw ORP BR6 ...... 56 C4
Rivers Cl WBY/YAL ME18 ...... 130 C7
Riversdale GVW DA11 ...... 27 F8
Riverside EDEN TN8 ...... 164 C5
 EYN DA4 ...... 59 G6
Riverside Cl STMC/STPC BR5 ...... 38 D7
Riverside Rd SCUP DA14 ...... 39 F1
Riverside Wy DART DA1 ...... 23 H4
River St GILL ME7 ...... 4 A2
River Vw GILL ME7 ...... 70 A3
 MAID/SHEP ME15 ...... 6 C5
Riverview Rd GRH DA9 ...... 25 F4
River Wk TON TN9 ...... 170 B5
River Wy DIT/AY ME20 ...... 108 E2
Roach St STRD ME2 ...... 2 A1
Roan Ct STRD ME2 ...... 48 E6
Roberts Cl SIT ME10 ...... 73 J7
 STMC/STPC BR5 ...... 56 D2
Roberts Orchard Rd
 MAIDW ME16 ...... 131 J3
Roberts Rd RHAM ME8 ...... 70 B6
 SNOD ME6 ...... 85 J6
Robin Hood Gn STMC/STPC BR5 ...... 56 B2
Robin Hood La WALD ME5 ...... 87 J5
Robin Hood Lane (Lower)
 WALD ME5 ...... 87 K5
Robin Hood Lane (Upper)
 WALD ME5 ...... 87 K5
Robinia Av GVW DA11 ...... 26 E6
Robins Av RMAID ME17 ...... 160 C2
Robins Cl RMAID ME17 ...... 160 C2
Robin Wy STMC/STPC BR5 ...... 38 C5
Robson Dr DIT/AY ME20 ...... 109 H4
 HOO/HM ME3 ...... 50 E1
Robyns Cft GVW DA11 ...... 45 F1
Robyns Wy EDEN TN8 ...... 164 D6
 SEV TN13 ...... 8 B1
Rocfort Rd SNOD ME6 ...... 85 K6
Rochdale Rd RTW TN1 ...... 11 E1
Rochester Av ROCH ME1 ...... 2 C4
Rochester Crs HOO/HM ME3 ...... 32 E8
Rochester Rd DART DA1 ...... 23 K6
 DIT/AY ME20 ...... 110 A3
 GVE DA12 ...... 28 C8
 ROCH ME1 ...... 86 D3
 STRD ME2 ...... 66 C3
 TONN TN10 ...... 170 D2
 WALD ME5 ...... 87 H2
Rochester St CHAT ME4 ...... 3 E6
Rochester Wy DART DA1 ...... 22 B6
Rock Av GILL ME7 ...... 4 C5
Rockfield Cl OXTED RH8 ...... 140 D2
Rockfield Rd OXTED RH8 ...... 140 D1
Rock Hl ORP BR6 ...... 77 J2
Rock Hill Rd HDCN TN27 ...... 182 E4
Rock Rd BGR/WK TN15 ...... 105 F3
 MAID/BEAR ME14 ...... 6 C5
 SIT ME10 ...... 93 K2
Rocks Cl E/WMAL ME19 ...... 108 E8
Rocks Hl CRBK TN17 ...... 215 C5
The Rocks Rd E/WMAL ME19 ...... 108 E8
Rock Villa Rd RTW TN1 ...... 10 C3
Rodmell Rd RTWE/PEM TN2 ...... 10 C6
Rodney Av TONN TN10 ...... 170 E2

Roebuck Rd *ROCH* ME1 .... 2 C3
Roedean Cl *ORP* BR6 .... 56 C8
Roedean Rd *RTWE/PEM* TN2 .... 10 C6
Roehampton Cl *GVE* DA12 .... 28 B6
Roffen Rd *ROCH* ME1 .... 2 C6
Rogers Ct *SIT* ME10 .... 93 K3
Rogersmead *TENT* TN30 .... 229 K7
Rogers Rough Rd *CRBK* TN17 .... 222 E3
Rogers Wood La *BGR/WK* TN15 ...... 61 F8
Rogues Hl *RTON* TN11 .... 187 K2
Rollo Rd *SWLY* BR8 .... 40 C5
Rolvenden Av *RHAM* ME8 .... 69 K3
Rolvenden Dr *SIT* ME10 .... 93 K1
Rolvenden Hl *CRBK* TN17 .... 239 F1
Rolvenden Rd *STRD* ME2 .... 49 H4
Roman Cl *WALD* ME5 .... 87 J5
Roman Hts *MAID/BEAR* ME14 .... 111 J7
Roman Wy *DART* DA1 .... 22 B4
  STRD ME2 .... 66 E2
Romany Rd *RHAM* ME8 .... 69 J4
Romden Rd *HDCN* TN27 .... 202 E4
Romford Rd *RTWE/PEM* TN2 .... 192 A7
Romney Cl *MAID/SHEP* ME15 .... 134 C3
Romney Ct *SIT* ME10 .... 93 J1
Romney Pl *MAID/SHEP* ME15 .... 7 D3
Romney Rd *GVW* DA11 .... 45 F1
  WALD ME5 .... 88 C1
Romney Wy *TONN* TN10 .... 170 E1
Romsey Cl *STRD* ME2 .... 48 D6
Ronfearn Av *STMC/STPC* BR5 .... 56 E2
Roodlands La *EDEN* TN8 .... 143 K8
Rookery Cl *RSIT* ME9 .... 93 F8
Rookery Crs *HOO/HM* ME3 .... 15 G8
Rookery Gdns *STMC/STPC* BR5 ...... 56 D2
Rookery Rd *ORP* BR6 .... 74 E5
Rookesley Rd *STMC/STPC* BR5 ...... 56 E4
Rook La *RSIT* ME9 .... 72 E8
Rookley Cl *RTWE/PEM* TN2 .... 11 F5 ▣
Rooks Hl *BGR/WK* TN15 .... 125 G8
Roonagh Ct *SIT* ME10 .... 93 K4
Ropers *RRTW* TN3 .... 188 E7
Roosevelt Av *WALD* ME5 .... 68 A7
Ropemakers Ct *CHAT* ME4 .... 4 B5
Roper Cl *RHAM* ME8 .... 89 K3
Roper's Green La *HOO/HM* ME3 ...... 33 H6
Roper's La *HOO/HM* ME3 .... 33 G6
Rope Wk *CHAT* ME4 .... 4 A4 ▣
Ropewalk *CRBK* TN17 .... 225 J1
The Rope Wk *HAWK* TN18 .... 243 F7
Roseacre *OXTED* RH8 .... 140 E4
Roseacre Gdns
  MAID/BEAR ME14 .... 134 C3 ▣
Roseacre La *MAID/BEAR* ME14 ..... 134 C3
Rose Av *GVE* DA12 .... 28 B7
Rose Bank Cl *MAID/SHEP* ME15 ...... 7 E3
Rosebank Gdns *GVW* DA11 .... 27 F7
Rosebery Cl *SIT* ME10 .... 94 E2
Rosebery Gdns *GVW* DA11 .... 27 G7
Rosebery Rd *CHAT* ME4 .... 3 E6
  GILL ME7 .... 5 D1
Rosecroft Cl *BH/WHM* TN16 .... 97 K5 ▣
  STMC/STPC BR5 .... 56 D3
Rosedale Cl *RDART* DA2 .... 24 A6
Rosedene Cl *DART* DA1 .... 23 F6
Rosefield *SEV* TN13 .... 8 C3
Rosegarth *MEO* DA13 .... 45 F6
Rosehill Wk *RTW* TN1 .... 10 C4 ▣
Roseholme *MAIDW* ME16 .... 6 A5
Rose La *RMAID* ME17 .... 161 H5
Roselare Cl *BH/WHM* TN16 .... 120 C4
Roseleigh Av *MAIDW* ME16 .... 132 C2
Roseleigh Rd *SIT* ME10 .... 93 J5
Rosemary Cl *OXTED* RH8 .... 140 E4 ▣
Rosemary La *BGR/WK* TN15 .... 82 C3
  HDCN TN27 .... 201 J1
  WADH TN5 .... 232 E1
Rosemary Rd *E/WMAL* ME19 .... 108 D5
  MAID/SHEP ME15 .... 134 C3 ▣
Rosemount Cl *MAID/SHEP* ME15 .. 155 F2
Rosemount Ct *STRD* ME2 .... 49 F5 ▣
Roseneath Cl *ORP* BR6 .... 76 C3
Rose St *GVW* DA11 .... 26 C5
  ROCH ME1 .... 3 D5
  TON TN9 .... 170 C6
Rosewood *RDART* DA2 .... 40 B2
Rosewood Cl *SCUP* DA14 .... 38 D1 ▣
Rose Yd *MAID/BEAR* ME14 .... 7 D3 ▣
Rosherville Wy *GVW* DA11 .... 27 F6
Rossdale *RTWE/PEM* TN2 .... 11 E2
Rossell Rd *TIL* RM18 .... 27 C1 ▣
Rosslyn Gn *MAIDW* ME16 .... 132 B1 ▣
Ross Rd *DART* DA1 .... 22 D5
Ross St *ROCH* ME1 .... 3 D4
Rothermere Ct *CRBK* TN17 .... 227 C8
Rother Rd *TONN* TN10 .... 170 B1
Rother V *WALD* ME5 .... 88 D2
Rothley Cl *TENT* TN30 .... 230 B6

Rouge La *GVE* DA12 .... 27 J7
Roughetts Rd *E/WMAL* ME19 .... 107 H3
Roughway La *RTON* TN11 .... 127 H8
Round Ash Wy *HART* DA3 .... 61 K3
The Roundel *SIT* ME10 .... 93 K4
Roundel Wy *STPH/PW* TN12 .... 196 C1
Roundhay *E/WMAL* ME19 .... 108 B5
Roundhill Rd *RTWE/PEM* TN2 ...... 11 F6
Roundlyn Gdns *STMC/STPC* BR5 ... 56 C1
Round St *MEO* DA13 .... 45 K8
Roundwell *MAID/BEAR* ME14 .... 135 F2
Round Wood Cl *WALD* ME5 .... 88 B5
Rover Rd *WALD* ME5 .... 88 C4
Rowan Cl *DIT/AY* ME20 .... 109 J5 ▣
  MEO DA13 .... 63 J3
  STPH/PW TN12 .... 193 H1
Rowan Crs *DART* DA1 .... 23 F7
Rowan Lea *WALD* ME5 .... 68 C6
Rowan Rd *SWLY* BR8 .... 40 A8
Rowans Cl *HART* DA3 .... 43 J7
Rowan Shaw *TONN* TN10 .... 148 D8
The Rowans *SOCK/AV* RM15 .... 13 G1 ▣
Rowan Tree Rd *RTWE/PEM* TN2 .... 10 A6 ▣
Rowbrocke Cl *RHAM* ME8 .... 90 A3
Rowdow La *RSEV* TN14 .... 102 B3
Rowhill Rd *RDART* DA2 .... 40 D3
Rowland Av *GILL* ME7 .... 69 F5
Rowland Cl *WALD* ME5 .... 69 F5
Rowlatt Cl *RDART* DA2 .... 41 F2
Rowley Hl *RTWE/PEM* TN2 .... 191 K5
Rowmarsh Cl *GVW* DA11 .... 44 E1
Rowzill Rd *SWLY* BR8 .... 40 C4
Royal Av *TON* TN9 .... 170 C6
Royal Cha *STH/RUST* TN4 .... 10 B3
Royal Eagle Cl *STRD* ME2 .... 3 E1
Royal Engineers' Rd
  MAID/BEAR ME14 .... 6 C1
Royal Pier Rd *GVE* DA12 .... 27 J5
Royal Rd *RDART* DA2 .... 41 K3
  SCUP DA14 .... 38 E1
Royal Sovereign Av *CHAT* ME4 .... 4 B1
Royal West Kent Av *TONN* TN10 .. 170 D2
Roydon Hall Rd *WBY/YAL* ME18 ... 151 G1
Royston Rd *DART* DA1 .... 22 C5
  MAID/SHEP ME15 .... 134 C3
Roystons Cl *RHAM* ME8 .... 70 C4
Royton Av *RMAID* ME17 .... 160 D1
Ruckinge Wy *RHAM* ME8 .... 69 K3
Ruck La *STPH/PW* TN12 .... 211 H3
Rudge Cl *WALD* ME5 .... 88 E4
Rugby Cl *WALD* ME5 .... 88 E4
Ruggles Cl *HOO/HM* ME3 .... 33 F3
Ruins Barn Rd *RSIT* ME9 .... 116 C2
  SIT ME10 .... 93 K6
Rumstead La *MAID/BEAR* ME14 .. 114 A4
  RSIT ME9 .... 114 B1
Rumstead Rd *RSIT* ME9 .... 114 B2
Runciman Cl *ORP* BR6 .... 76 D5
Runham La *RMAID* ME17 .... 159 J3
Rural V *GVW* DA11 .... 27 F6
Ruscombe Av *STH/RUST* TN4 ...... 189 H4 ▣
Rush Cl *WALD* ME5 .... 88 B3
Rushdean Rd *STRD* ME2 .... 66 C1
Rushdene Wk *BH/WHM* TN16 .... 97 H4
Rushet Rd *STMC/STPC* BR5 .... 38 B7
Rushetts *RRTW* TN3 .... 205 J2
Rushetts Rd *BGR/WK* TN15 .... 80 C5
Rushford Cl *HDCN* TN27 .... 200 A1
Rushfords *LING* RH7 .... 62 C8
Rushmead Dr *MAID/SHEP* ME15 .. 133 G7
Rushmere Ct *MAID/BEAR* ME14 .. 104 D7
Rushmore Hl *ORP* BR6 .... 76 D7
  RSEV TN14 .... 99 K1
Rushymead *BGR/WK* TN15 .... 102 E5
Ruskin Cl *E/WMAL* ME19 .... 108 D6 ▣
Ruskin Gv *DART* DA1 .... 23 K4
Russell Cl *DART* DA1 .... 22 D2
  SIT ME10 .... 93 H3
Russell Ct *CHAT* ME4 .... 4 B5
Russell Pl *EYN* DA4 .... 41 K6
Russell Rd *DIT/AY* ME20 .... 87 H7
  GVE DA12 .... 28 A5
Russells Av *RHAM* ME8 .... 70 D6
Russet Cl *STRD* ME2 .... 48 D6
The Russets *MAIDW* ME16 .... 132 B1 ▣
  MEO DA13 .... 63 H3
Russett Cl *DIT/AY* ME20 .... 109 J6
  ORP BR6 .... 76 C1
Russett Rd *STPH/PW* TN12 .... 151 H8
Russett Wy *SWLY* BR8 .... 40 B8
Russet Wy *E/WMAL* ME19 .... 129 H4
Rusthall Gra *STH/RUST* TN4 .... 206 C2 ▣
Rusthall High St *STH/RUST* TN4 .. 206 A2
Rusthall Pk *STH/RUST* TN4 .... 206 C2
Rusthall Rd *STH/RUST* TN4 .... 206 C3
Rustwick *STH/RUST* TN4 .... 206 C2
Rutherford Wy *TONN* TN10 .... 148 D7
Rutland Cl *DART* DA1 .... 23 G6 ▣
Rutland Pl *RHAM* ME8 .... 89 K3
Rutland Rd *MAID/SHEP* ME15 ..... 134 A6
  STMC/STPC BR5 .... 56 D3
Ruxley Cl *SCUP* DA14 .... 38 E4
Ruxton Cl *SWLY* BR8 .... 40 B8
Ruxton Ct *SWLY* BR8 .... 40 B8 ▣
Ryan Dr *MAID/SHEP* ME15 .... 134 C4

Ryarsh La *E/WMAL* ME19 .... 107 K5
Ryarsh Rd *E/WMAL* ME19 .... 107 K1
Rycault Cl *MAIDW* ME16 .... 6 B4 ▣
Rycault La *RHAM* ME8 .... 90 A3
Rycroft La *RSEV* TN14 .... 145 G1
Rydal Cl *STH/RUST* TN4 .... 10 A2
Rydal Dr *STH/RUST* TN4 .... 10 A2
Ryde Cl *WALD* ME5 .... 68 C6
Ryders *RRTW* TN3 .... 205 K3
Rye Crs *STMC/STPC* BR5 .... 56 D5
Ryecroft *GVE* DA12 .... 46 B3 ▣
  HART DA3 .... 62 E1
Ryecroft Rd *RSEV* TN14 .... 101 J4
Ryedale Ct *SEV* TN13 .... 101 G8
Ryegrass Cl *WALD* ME5 .... 68 D8 ▣
Rye La *RSEV* TN14 .... 101 H6
Rye Rd *HAWK* TN18 .... 235 K6
Rymers Cl *RTWE/PEM* TN2 .... 190 D7
Rysted La *BH/WHM* TN16 .... 120 C5

Sackville Cl *SEV* TN13 .... 9 D1
Sackville Rd *DART* DA1 .... 23 G8
Saddington St *GVE* DA12 .... 27 J6
Saddlers Cl *MAID/BEAR* ME14 .... 134 A1
Saddler's Pk *EYN* DA4 .... 59 G7
Sadlers Cl *WALD* ME5 .... 87 J4
Sage Rd *ROCH* ME1 .... 2 A5
Sailmakers Ct *CHAT* ME4 .... 4 B6
St Aidan's Wy *GVE* DA12 .... 46 B1
St Albans Cl *GILL* ME7 .... 5 E1
  GVE DA12 .... 46 A1
St Alban's Gdns *GVE* DA12 .... 46 A1
St Alban's Rd *DART* DA1 .... 23 J5
  STRD ME2 .... 48 B8
St Andrew Rd *GILL* ME7 .... 5 E1
St Andrew's La *MAIDW* ME16 ...... 132 A4
  STPH/PW TN12 .... 173 J8 ▣
St Andrews Cl *STH/RUST* TN4 .... 190 A5 ▣
St Andrews Dr *ORP* BR6 .... 56 C3
St Andrews Park Rd
  STH/RUST TN4 .... 190 A5
St Andrew's Rd *GVE* DA12 .... 27 J6 ▣
  MAIDW ME16 .... 132 A4
  SCUP DA14 .... 38 E1
  STPH/PW TN12 .... 173 J8 ▣
  TIL RM18 .... 27 F1
St Andrews Wy *OXTED* RH8 .... 141 J2
St Anne Ct *MAIDW* ME16 .... 6 B3
St Ann's Green La *STPH/PW* TN12 .. 177 F6
St Aubyns Cl *ORP* BR6 .... 56 A7
St Aubyns Gdns *ORP* BR6 .... 56 A6
St Barnabas Cl *GILL* ME7 .... 5 D5
  MAIDW ME16 .... 110 C6
  RTW TN1 .... 11 D2 ▣
St Bartholomew's La *CHAT* ME4 .... 3 E4 ▣
St Bartholomew's Ter *ROCH* ME1 .. 3 E4 ▣
St Benedict Rd *SNOD* ME6 .... 85 H6
St Benedict's Av *GVE* DA12 .... 46 B1
St Benets Wy *TENT* TN30 .... 230 B6
St Benjamins Dr *ORP* BR6 .... 76 D4
St Bernards Wy *TONN* TN10 .... 148 D6
St Botolph Rd *GVW* DA11 .... 44 E1
St Botolph's Av *SEV* TN13 .... 8 C3
St Botolph's Rd *SEV* TN13 .... 9 D3
St Chad's Dr *GVE* DA12 .... 46 B1
St Clair Cl *OXTED* RH8 .... 140 A1
St Clements Cl *GVW* DA11 .... 45 G1 ▣
St Clements Ct *PUR* RM19 .... 12 E4 ▣
St Clere Hill Rd *BGR/WK* TN15 ..... 80 E7
St Columba's Cl *GVE* DA12 .... 46 B1
St David's Crs *GVE* DA12 .... 46 A2
St David's Rd *HOO/HM* ME3 .... 19 G6
  SWLY BR8 .... 40 C4
St Dunstan's Dr *GVE* DA12 .... 46 B1
St Edith's Rd *BGR/WK* TN15 .... 102 E5
St Edmunds Rd *DART* DA1 .... 23 J3
St Faith's La *MAID/BEAR* ME14 ... 134 D2
St Faith's St *MAID/BEAR* ME14 ...... 6 C3 ▣
St Francis Av *GVE* DA12 .... 46 B2
St Francis Rd *MEO* DA13 .... 83 J3
St George's Ct *BGR/WK* TN15 .... 105 F3 ▣
St George's Crs *GVE* DA12 .... 46 A2
St Georges Ms *TON* TN9 .... 170 B6 ▣
St George's Pk *RTWE/PEM* TN2 .. 206 E6
St George's Rd *GILL* ME7 .... 4 C2
  SCUP DA14 .... 38 E4
  SEV TN13 .... 9 D1
  SWLY BR8 .... 58 C1 ▣
St George's Sq *MAIDW* ME16 .... 6 A4
St Giles Cl *ORP* BR6 .... 75 J1
St Gregory's Crs *GVE* DA12 .... 28 B3
St Helens La *MAID/SHEP* ME15 ... 131 J6
St Helens Rd *HOO/HM* ME3 .... 31 G1
St Hellier's Cl *MAIDW* ME16 .... 132 B4
St Hildas Ct *BGR/WK* TN15 .... 127 F6
St Hilda's Wy *GVE* DA12 .... 46 A2
St James' La *RDART* DA2 .... 24 D6
St James' Pk *RTW* TN1 .... 11 E2
  RTWE/PEM TN2 .... 11 E2
St James Pl *DART* DA1 .... 23 G5 ▣

St James Rd *HOO/HM* ME3 ..... 21 G8
RTW TN1 ..... 11 E2
St James' Rd *RTW* TN1 ..... 11 E3
St James's Av *GVW* DA11 ..... 27 H6
St James's Rd *GVW* DA11 ..... 27 H6
SEV TN13 ..... 9 D1
St James's St *GVW* DA11 ..... 27 H5 🖫
St James Wy *SCUP* DA14 ..... 39 F3
St John's Av *SIT* ME10 ..... 94 C3
St John's Cl *HOO/HM* ME3 ..... 48 B3
St John's Hl *SEV* TN13 ..... 9 E2
St John's La *HART* DA3 ..... 62 A3
St John's Pk *STH/RUST* TN4 ..... 190 A6
St John's Rd *GILL* ME7 ..... 4 C5
GVE DA12 ..... 28 A6
HOO/HM ME3 ..... 32 E8
HOO/HM ME3 ..... 48 B2
RDART DA2 ..... 24 B6
SCUP DA14 ..... 38 C2
SEV TN13 ..... 9 D1
STH/RUST TN4 ..... 190 A7
St Johns Wy *ROCH* ME1 ..... 2 A6
St Josephs Cl *ORP* BR6 ..... 56 A8 🖫
St Justin Cl *STMC/STPC* BR5 ..... 38 E8
St Katherine's La *SNOD* ME6 ..... 85 J7
St Kilda Rd *ORP* BR6 ..... 56 A5
St Laurence Av *DIT/AY* ME20 ..... 110 B6
St Laurence Cl *RSIT* ME9 ..... 94 E4
STMC/STPC BR5 ..... 38 E8
St Lawrence Av *STH/RUST* TN4 ..... 189 H3
St Leonards Av *CHAT* ME4 ..... 3 F6
St Leonards Rd *MAIDW* ME16 ..... 110 C6
St Leonard's St *E/WMAL* ME19 ..... 107 K7
St Luke's Av *MAID/BEAR* ME14 ..... 7 E2
St Lukes Cl *RDART* DA2 ..... 42 D3
SWLY BR8 ..... 40 A7 🖫
St Luke's Rd *MAID/BEAR* ME14 ..... 7 E2
STH/RUST TN4 ..... 11 D1
St Luke's Wy *HOO/HM* ME3 ..... 19 G6
St Margarets Cl *MAIDW* ME16 ..... 132 B4 🖫
ORP BR6 ..... 56 C8 🖫
RDART DA2 ..... 24 C8
St Margaret's Crs *GVE* DA12 ..... 46 B1
St Margarets Dr *RHAM* ME8 ..... 89 K1
St Margaret's Ms *ROCH* ME1 ..... 2 C3 🖫
St Margaret's Rd *DIT/AY* ME20 ..... 42 D5
St Margaret's St *ROCH* ME1 ..... 2 B4
St Mark's Av *GVW* DA11 ..... 27 G7
St Mark's Ct *DIT/AY* ME20 ..... 86 E8 🖫
St Mark's Rd *RTWE/PEM* TN2 ..... 206 E7
St Martin's Cl *MAID/BEAR* ME14 ..... 112 C5
St Martins Dr *EYN* DA4 ..... 59 G7
St Martins Meadow
BH/WHM TN16 ..... 121 J2
St Martin's Rd *DART* DA1 ..... 23 J5
St Mary's Church Rd *RSEV* TN14 ..... 122 A4
St Mary's Cl *BGR/WK* TN15 ..... 105 J7
GVE DA12 ..... 27 K8
OXTED RH8 ..... 118 C8
STMC/STPC BR5 ..... 38 C7
WADH TN5 ..... 232 B5
WBY/YAL ME18 ..... 174 C2
St Mary's Ct *BH/WHM* TN16 ..... 120 D5
St Mary's Dr *SEV* TN13 ..... 8 A2
St Mary's Gdns *CHAT* ME4 ..... 4 B1
St Mary's Gn *BH/WHM* TN16 ..... 97 G5
St Mary's Gv *BH/WHM* TN16 ..... 97 G5
St Mary's La *RRTW* TN3 ..... 188 E6
WADH TN5 ..... 232 B5
St Marys Rd *BGR/WK* TN15 ..... 105 G4
GILL ME7 ..... 4 C2
GRH DA9 ..... 24 D4
STRD ME2 ..... 2 B1
SWLY BR8 ..... 58 A1
TON TN9 ..... 170 B7
St Mary's Vw *RSIT* ME9 ..... 72 B8
St Marys Wy *HART* DA3 ..... 43 K8
St Matthews Dr *ROCH* ME1 ..... 2 A6
St Matthew's Wy *HOO/HM* ME3 ..... 19 G6 🖫
DIT/AY ME20 ..... 110 C3
St Michael's Cl *CHAT* ME4 ..... 3 F5
St Michaels Ct *STRD* ME2 ..... 49 G6 🖫
St Michaels Dr *RSEV* TN14 ..... 102 B3
St Michael's Rd *MAIDW* ME16 ..... 6 A4
SIT ME10 ..... 93 K2
STH/RUST TN4 ..... 190 B7
St Mildred's Cl *TENT* TN30 ..... 230 A7 🖫
St Nicholas Gdns *STRD* ME2 ..... 48 E6
St Patrick's Gdns *GVE* DA12 ..... 46 A2
St Paul's Cl *STRD* ME2 ..... 66 C1 🖫
SWCM DA10 ..... 25 K6
TONN TN10 ..... 170 D1
St Paul's St *SIT* ME10 ..... 93 K1 🖫
STH/RUST TN4 ..... 206 B2
St Peters Cl *DIT/AY* ME20 ..... 109 F5
SWCM DA10 ..... 26 A6
St Peters Pl *DIT/AY* ME20 ..... 86 E8
St Peters Rd *DIT/AY* ME20 ..... 109 F5
St Peters Rw *RRTW* TN3 ..... 204 E1
St Peters St *MAIDW* ME16 ..... 6 C3 🖫
RTWE/PEM TN2 ..... 11 E4 🖫
St Peter St *ROCH* ME1 ..... 3 D4
St Philip's Av *MAID/SHEP* ME15 ..... 7 E4
St Ronan's Cl *MAID/SHEP* ME15 ... 133 J7 🖫
St Saviours Rd *MAID/SHEP* ME15 ... 133 K8

Saints Hl *RTON* TN11 ..... 187 J5
St Stephen's Sq *MAID/SHEP* ME15 ... 6 B5 🖫
St Stephen's St *TON* TN9 ..... 170 B6
St Stephens Ct *RTW* TN1 ..... 11 D2 🖫
St Thomas Rd *GVW* DA11 ..... 27 F7 🖫
St Thomas's Av *GVW* DA11 ..... 27 J8
St Vincents La *E/WMAL* ME19 ..... 106 D4
St Vincents Rd *DART* DA1 ..... 23 K5
St Welcume's Wy *RMAID* ME17 ..... 137 J8
St Werburgh Crs *MAID/HM* ME3 ..... 50 E1
St William's Wy *ROCH* ME1 ..... 3 D5
St Winifred's Rd *BH/WHM* TN16.. 97 K5
Saladin Dr *PUR* RM19 ..... 12 E4
Salcote Rd *GVE* DA12 ..... 46 B3 🖫
Salem Pl *GVW* DA11 ..... 26 E6 🖫
Salem St *MAID/SHEP* ME15 ..... 7 D4 🖫
Salisbury Av *RHAM* ME8 ..... 70 A6
SWLY BR8 ..... 58 D1
Salisbury Cl *SIT* ME10 ..... 94 D2
TONN TN10 ..... 170 D1
Salisbury Rd *CHAT* ME4 ..... 4 A5
DIT/AY ME20 ..... 87 H6
GVW DA11 ..... 27 G7
MAID/BEAR ME14.. ..... 7 D1
RDART DA2 ..... 24 B7
RRTW TN3 ..... 205 J3
STH/RUST TN4 ..... 190 C6
TONN TN10 ..... 170 D2
Sallows Shaw *MEO* DA13 ..... 63 K2
Sally Port *GILL* ME7 ..... 4 A2
Sally Port Gdns *GILL* ME7 ..... 4 A2
Salmon Rd *DART* DA1 ..... 23 J2
Saltbox Hl *BH/WHM* TN16 ..... 74 A8
Saltings Rd *SNOD* ME6 ..... 85 K7
Salt La *HOO/HM* ME3 ..... 30 E2
Salt's Av *MAID/SHEP* ME15 ..... 155 F3
Salts La *MAID/SHEP* ME15 ..... 155 G2
Saltwood Cl *ORP* BR6 ..... 56 D8
Saltwood Rd *MAID/SHEP* ME15 ..... 6 C6
Samara *WALD* ME5 ..... 88 B5
Samphire Cl *MAID/BEAR* ME14 ..... 134 A2
Sanctuary Cl *DART* DA1 ..... 23 F5
Sanctuary Rd *RHAM* ME8 ..... 69 H3
Sandbanks Hl *RDART* DA2 ..... 43 H4
Sandbourne Dr *MAID/BEAR* ME14.. 111 F5
Sanderson Av *RSEV* TN14 ..... 77 H5 🖫
Sanderson Wy *TON* TN9 ..... 170 E5
Sandersted Rd *STMC/STPC* BR5 .. 56 C3 🖫
Sandfield Rd *RTON* TN11 ..... 187 H7
Sandford Rd *SIT* ME10 ..... 93 K1
Sandgate Cl *RHAM* ME8 ..... 90 C2
Sandhill La *HOO/HM* ME3 ..... 30 C8
Sandhurst Cl *RHAM* ME8 ..... 69 K3 🖫
RTWE/PEM TN2 ..... 190 C2
Sandhurst Pk *RTWE/PEM* TN2 ..... 11 F1
Sandhurst Rd *BFN/LL* DA15.. ..... 38 A1
CRBK TN17 ..... 237 K5
ORP BR6 ..... 56 B7
RTWE/PEM TN2 ..... 190 D7
TIL RM18 ..... 27 K1
Sandilands *SEV* TN13 ..... 123 F1
Sand La *CRBK* TN17 ..... 199 J8
Sandling La *MAID/BEAR* ME14.. 110 E5
Sandling Rd *MAID/BEAR* ME14 ..... 6 C1
Sandling Wy *CHAT* ME4 ..... 50 C5
Sandown Cl *RTWE/PEM* TN2 ..... 191 F8
Sandown Dr *RHAM* ME8.. ..... 70 A7
Sandown Gv *RTWE/PEM* TN2 ..... 191 F8
Sandown Pk *RTWE/PEM* TN2 ..... 208 A1
Sandown Rd *E/WMAL* ME19 ..... 107 K6
GVE DA12.. ..... 45 K3
Sandpiper Rd *WALD* ME5 ..... 88 D4
The Sandpipers *GVE* DA12 ..... 28 A8
Sandpiper Wy *STMC/STPC* BR5.. ..... 56 E1
Sandringham Rd *RHAM* ME8 ..... 90 B2
Sand Rd *RRTW* TN3 ..... 221 J2
Sandrock Rd *RTWE/PEM* TN2 ..... 11 E3
Sandstone Dr *SIT* ME10 ..... 73 K6
Sandstone Ri *MAID/BEAR* ME14 .. 88 D6 🖫
Sandway Rd *RMAID* ME17 ..... 160 A3
STMC/STPC BR5.. ..... 56 D1
Sandy Bank Rd *GVE* DA12 ..... 46 C3
Sandy Rdg *BGR/WK* TN15 ..... 105 G7
Sandycroft Rd *STRD* ME2 ..... 48 E5 🖫
Sandy Dell *GILL* ME7 ..... 89 H3
Sandy La *BGR/WK* TN15 ..... 106 B5
BGR/WK TN15.. ..... 126 B4
BH/WHM TN16.. ..... 120 D4
E/WMAL ME19 ..... 107 J3
MAID/BEAR ME14.. ..... 111 J3
MAID/BEAR ME14.. ..... 134 D1
MEO DA13 ..... 43 K2
ORP BR6 ..... 56 B4
OXTED RH8 ..... 118 A8
OXTED RH8 ..... 119 F6
RDART DA2 ..... 43 J1
SEV TN13 ..... 9 E2
SNOD ME6 ..... 85 H8
STMC/STPC BR5.. ..... 38 E5
TENT TN30.. ..... 230 B7
Sandy Mt *MAID/BEAR* ME14 ..... 134 D1
Sapho Pk *GVE* DA12 ..... 46 C2
Saphora Cl *ORP* BR6 ..... 75 J1 🖫
Saracen Cl *GILL* ME7 ..... 69 H5

Saracen Flds *WALD* ME5 ..... 88 C6
Sara Crs *GRH* DA9 ..... 25 F3
Sara Pk *GVE* DA12 ..... 46 B2 🖫
Sarsen Hts *WALD* ME5 ..... 88 A5
Sarsens Cl *GVE* DA12 ..... 46 C8 🖫
Sassoon Cl *DIT/AY* ME20.. ..... 108 E2
Satis Av *SIT* ME10 ..... 73 K7
Saunders Cl *GVW* DA11.. ..... 27 F8
Saunders Rd *STH/RUST* TN4 ..... 10 A6
Saunders St *GILL* ME7 ..... 4 C2
Saunders Wy *DART* DA1 ..... 23 J8
Savage Rd *WALD* ME5 ..... 88 C3
Savoy Rd *DART* DA1 ..... 23 F4
Sawpit Rd *RSIT* ME9 ..... 117 G3
Sawyers Ct *CHAT* ME4 ..... 4 B6
Saxbys Rd *BGR/WK* TN15 ..... 125 H1
Saxby Wd *RTON* TN11 ..... 168 D5
Saxon Cl *GVW* DA11 ..... 44 D1
RSEV TN14.. ..... 101 H4
STRD ME2 ..... 48 E5
WBY/YAL ME18 ..... 129 H4
Saxon Pl *EYN* DA4 ..... 60 B2
Saxon Rd *RDART* DA2 ..... 41 H2
Saxons Dr *MAID/BEAR* ME14 ..... 7 E1
Saxon Shore Wy *GILL* ME7 ..... 51 K8
GVE DA12.. ..... 27 K5
HOO/HM ME3 ..... 29 K3
ROCH ME1 ..... 3 D4
RSIT ME9 ..... 55 H5
STRD ME2 ..... 49 K6
Saxton St *GILL* ME7 ..... 4 C3
Saxville Rd *STMC/STPC* BR5.. ..... 38 C8
Sayer Cl *GRH* DA9 ..... 25 F4
Sayes Court Rd *STMC/STPC* BR5.. ..... 38 B8
Scabharbour Rd *RSEV* TN14 ..... 146 A4
Scadbury Gdns *STMC/STPC* BR5.. ..... 38 B7
Scads Hill Cl *ORP* BR6 ..... 56 A3
Scarborough Cl *BH/WHM* TN16 ..... 97 G5
Scarborough La *ROCH* ME1.. ..... 86 C5
Scarlet Cl *STMC/STPC* BR5 ..... 56 C1 🖫
Scholars Ri *STRD* ME2 ..... 48 B7
Scholey Cl *STRD* ME2 ..... 86 A2
School Ap *BGR/WK* TN15 ..... 105 F7
School Av *GILL* ME7 ..... 5 E4
School Cl *DART* DA1 ..... 22 C5
MEO DA13 ..... 63 H4 🖫
School Fld *EDEN* TN8 ..... 164 C4
School Hl *RRTW* TN3 ..... 210 E8
School House La *STPH/PW* TN12 ... 195 H2
School La *BGR/WK* TN15 ..... 80 E6
BGR/WK TN15.. ..... 102 D8
E/WMAL ME19 ..... 106 C1
EYN DA4 ..... 60 E3
HOO/HM ME3 ..... 30 B8
HOO/HM ME3 ..... 48 B2
MAID/SHEP ME15.. ..... 134 A5
MEO DA13 ..... 83 H4
RDART DA2 ..... 43 H1
RMAID ME17 ..... 157 J2
RMAID ME17 ..... 159 K4
ROCH ME1 ..... 86 C1
RSIT ME9 ..... 72 A4
RSIT ME9 ..... 72 A7
RSIT ME9 ..... 73 H3
RSIT ME9 ..... 92 E3
RSIT ME9 ..... 94 A3
RTON TN11 ..... 126 E8
RTON TN11 ..... 150 A6
SWLY BR8 ..... 40 E5
School Ri *RTWE/PEM* TN2 ..... 10 B6 🖫
School Rd *GVE* DA12 ..... 45 K1
SIT ME10 ..... 94 C3
School Ter *HAWK* TN18 ..... 235 F4
Schooner Ct *GRH* DA9 ..... 24 B3
Scimitar Cl *GILL* ME7 ..... 69 H5
Scords La *BH/WHM* TN16.. ..... 143 J3
Scotby Av *WALD* ME5 ..... 88 C2
Scotland La *GVE* DA12 ..... 46 C5
Scotshall La *WARL* CR6 ..... 96 A2
Scott Av *RHAM* ME8 ..... 70 D6
Scott Cl *DIT/AY* ME20 ..... 109 G6
Scotteswood Av *CHAT* ME4 ..... 3 F6
Scott Rd *GVE* DA12 ..... 46 A3
TON TN9 ..... 169 K6 🖫
Scott's Ter *CHAT* ME4 ..... 3 F5
Scott St *MAID/BEAR* ME14 ..... 6 C1
Scotts Wy *RTWE/PEM* TN2 ..... 206 D6
SEV TN13 ..... 8 A1
Scragged Oak Rd
MAID/BEAR ME14.. ..... 89 J8
Scraps Hl *RSIT* ME9 ..... 95 F2
Scratchers La *EYN* DA4.. ..... 60 C7
Scratton Flds *GVE* DA12 ..... 64 A2
Scudders Hl *HART* DA3 ..... 61 H3
Seabrook Rd *RTON* TN11 ..... 170 A3
Seagull Rd *STRD* ME2 ..... 48 C8
Seal Dr *BGR/WK* TN15 ..... 102 D8
Seal Hollow Rd *SEV* TN13.. ..... 9 E3
Seal Rd *SEV* TN13 ..... 102 B8
Seaton Rd *DART* DA1 ..... 22 D6
GILL ME7 ..... 5 E5
Seaview *HOO/HM* ME3.. ..... 37 C1
Seaview Rd *GILL* ME7 ..... 4 C4
Second Av *GILL* ME7 ..... 5 E5
WALD ME5 ..... 68 D5

Secretan Rd *ROCH* ME1 .... 67 G5
Sedcombe Cl *SCUP* DA14 .... 38 D2 ⓫
Sedge Crs *WALD* ME5 .... 87 K2
Sedley La *MEO* DA13 .... 44 B3
Sedley Cl *DIT/AY* ME20 .... 109 J4
  HOO/HM ME3 .... 31 H7
  RHAM ME8 .... 89 K3
Sefton Cl *RTWE/PEM* BR5 .... 56 A1
Sefton Rd *STMC/STPC* BR5 .... 56 A1
Selah Dr *SWLY* BR8 .... 39 K6
Selborne La *SCUP* DA14 .... 38 C3
Selbourne Cl *HART* DA3 .... 62 E1
Selbourne Rd *GILL* ME7 .... 5 D1
Selbourne Wk *MAID/SHEP* ME15 ..... 134 B8
Selby Rd *MAID/SHEP* ME15 .... 156 B2
Selstead Cl *RHAM* ME8 .... 69 J5
Selwyn La *TIL* RM18 .... 27 C1
Senacre La *MAID/SHEP* ME15 .... 134 A8
Senacre Sq *MAID/SHEP* ME15 .... 134 B7
Sequoia Gdns *ORP* BR6 .... 56 A4 ⓫
Sermon Dr *SWLY* BR8 .... 39 K8
Serpentine Rd *SEV* TN13 .... 9 E2
Setford Rd *WALD* ME5 .... 68 D8
Settington Av *WALD* ME5 .... 68 D5
Seven Acres *SWLY* BR8 .... 58 A3
Seven Mile La *BGR/WK* TN15 ..... 106 B6
  RTON TN11 .... 151 C2
Sevenoaks By-pass *SEV* TN13 .... 8 A5
Sevenoaks Rd *BGR/WK* TN15 ..... 104 C7
  ORP BR6 .... 56 A8
  RSEV TN14 .... 77 C4
Sevenoaks Wy *STMC/STPC* BR5 .... 38 D7
Severn Cl *TONN* TN10 .... 170 C1
Severn Rd *WALD* ME5 .... 88 D1
Sevington Pk *MAID/SHEP* ME15 ..... 133 F8
Seymour Rd *GVW* DA11 .... 27 C7
  RHAM ME8 .... 71 F6
  WALD ME5 .... 4 B5
Seymour Wk *SWCM* DA10 .... 25 K6
Shacklands Rd *RSEV* TN14 .... 77 K6
Shackleton Cl *WALD* ME5 .... 68 C3 ⓫
The Shades *STRD* ME2 .... 48 A7
Shaftesbury Cl *E/WMAL* ME19 ..... 108 D5 ⓫
Shaftesbury Dr *MAIDW* ME16 .... 132 C2
Shaftesbury La *DART* DA1 .... 24 A3
Shaftesbury Rd *STH/RUST* TN4 .... 10 C1
Shakespeare Av *TIL* RM18 .... 27 J1
Shakespeare Farm Rd
  HOO/HM ME3 .... 18 C2
Shakespeare Rd *DART* DA1 .... 23 K3
  GILL ME7 .... 4 C5
  SIT ME10 .... 94 B2
  TON TN9 .... 169 K6
Shamrock Cl *GVE* DA12 .... 28 B6
Shandon Cl *RTWE/PEM* TN2 .... 11 E3
Shanklin Cl *WALD* ME5 .... 68 D6
Sharfleet Dr *STRD* ME2 .... 48 A7
Sharland Rd *GVE* DA12 .... 27 K8
Sharman Ct *SCUP* DA14 .... 38 B2
Sharnal La *SNOD* ME6 .... 85 K7
Sharnal St *HOO/HM* ME3 .... 33 H5
Sharon Crs *WALD* ME5 .... 88 A2
Sharp's Fld *HDCN* TN27 .... 200 C1
Sharps Gn *GILL* ME7 .... 70 A1
Sharp Wy *DART* DA1 .... 23 J2
Sharsted Wy *GILL* ME7 .... 89 H3
  MAID/BEAR ME14 .... 134 D1 ⓫
Shaw Cl *HOO/HM* ME3 .... 31 C7
Shaw Rd *BH/WHM* TN16 .... 97 C7
Shawstead Rd *WALD* ME5 .... 68 D7
Shaws Wy *ROCH* ME1 .... 2 E5
The Shaw *RTWE/PEM* TN2 .... 11 E5
Sheafe Dr *CRBK* TN17 .... 225 J1
Sheal's Crs *MAID/SHEP* ME15 .... 7 D5
Shearers Cl *MAID/BEAR* ME14 .... 134 A2
Shearwater *HART* DA3 .... 44 C8
  MAIDW ME16 .... 132 B1 ⓫
Shearwater Cl *STRD* ME2 .... 48 B7 ⓫
Shearwood Cresent *DART* DA1 .... 22 C2
Sheen Rd *STMC/STPC* BR5 .... 56 A1
Sheepcote La *RTWE/PEM* TN2 .... 57 H1
Sheephurst La *STPH/PW* TN12 .... 195 H1
Sheerstone *RSIT* ME9 .... 73 J3
Sheet Hl *BGR/WK* TN15 .... 126 D5
Sheffield Rd *STH/RUST* TN4 .... 189 K4
The Sheilings *BGR/WK* TN15 .... 102 C5
Shelbury Cl *SCUP* DA14 .... 38 B1
Shelden Dr *RHAM* ME8 .... 70 C6
Sheldon Wy *DIT/AY* ME20 .... 108 E3
Shellbank La *RDART* DA2 .... 43 C5
Shelldrake Cl *HOO/HM* ME3 .... 37 C1 ⓫
Shelley Rd *MAIDW* ME16 .... 132 C4
Shelleys La *RSEV* TN14 .... 99 C3
Shelton Cl *TONN* TN10 .... 170 C1
Shenden Cl *SEV* TN13 .... 124 A3
Shenden Wy *SEV* TN13 .... 124 A7
Shenley Gv *MAID/BEAR* ME14 .... 111 F4
Shenley Rd *DART* DA1 .... 23 K5
Shepherds Cl *ORP* BR6 .... 56 A7 ⓫
Shepherds Ga *GILL* ME7 .... 89 C1
Shepherds Gate Dr
  MAID/BEAR ME14 .... 134 A1
Shepherds La *DART* DA1 .... 22 D7
Shepherd St *GVW* DA11 .... 26 E6
Shepherds Wk *RTWE/PEM* TN2 ..... 11 F3 ⓫

Shepherds Wy *HOO/HM* ME3 .... 35 F2
  RMAID ME17 .... 157 G2
Shepperton Cl *WALD* ME5 .... 88 D2 ⓫
Sheppey Rd *MAID/SHEP* ME15 .... 135 F7
Sheppey Wy *SIT* ME10 .... 93 F1
Sheppy Pl *GVE* DA12 .... 27 J6
Sheraton Cl *WALD* ME5 .... 88 A5
Sherborne Rd *STMC/STPC* BR5 .... 56 A2
Sherbourne Cl *BGR/WK* TN15 .... 80 D2
Sherbourne Dr *MAIDW* ME16 .... 132 B4
  STRD ME2 .... 49 F5 ⓫
Sherenden La *STPH/PW* TN12 ..... 196 C6
Sherenden Rd *RTON* TN11 .... 171 J5
Sheridan Cl *MAID/BEAR* ME14 ..... 110 E6
  WALD ME5 .... 68 D7
Sheridan Ct *DART* DA1 .... 23 K3
Sheriff Dr *WALD* ME5 .... 88 B4
Sherman Cl *GILL* ME7 .... 69 J5
Shernden La *EDEN* TN8 .... 184 C1
Shernolds *MAID/SHEP* ME15 .... 133 H7
Sherway Cl *HDCN* TN27 .... 200 C1
Sherway Rd *HDCN* TN27 .... 181 H7
Sherwood Av *WALD* ME5 .... 88 B4
Sherwood Pl *RRTW* TN3 .... 205 H3 ⓫
Sherwood Rd *RTWE/PEM* TN2 ..... 11 F3 ⓫
  RTWE/PEM TN2 .... 11 F1
Sherwood Wy *RTWE/PEM* TN2... 11 F1
The Shieling *MEO* DA13 .... 83 C5
Shillinghield Cl *MAID/BEAR* ME14 ..... 134 B1
Shingle Barn La *WBY/YAL* ME18 ..... 153 F2
Shipbourne Rd *RTON* TN11 .... 148 D4
  TON TN9 .... 170 C2
Ship Field Cl *BH/WHM* TN16 ..... 97 G8
Ship Hl *BH/WHM* TN16 .... 97 H8
Ship La *EYN* DA4 .... 41 H6
  ROCH ME1 .... 3 E4
  SOCK/AV RM15 .... 13 H2
  SWLY BR8 .... 41 G6
Shipley Hills Rd *MEO* DA13 .... 63 G5
Shipwrights Av *CHAT* ME4 .... 4 A6
Shire La *ORP* BR6 .... 74 E3
The Shires *STPH/PW* TN12 .... 173 J7
Shirley La *DART* DA1 .... 23 F3
  GVE DA12 .... 28 E8 ⓫
Shirley Gdns *STH/RUST* TN4 ..... 206 B2 ⓫
Shirley Gv *STH/RUST* TN4 .... 206 C1
Shirley Wy *MAID/SHEP* ME15 ..... 134 C3
Sholden Gdns *STMC/STPC* BR5 ..... 56 D2
Sholden Rd *STRD* ME2 .... 49 F6
Shorefields *RHAM* ME8 .... 70 D4
Shoregate La *RSIT* ME9 .... 53 J8
Shoreham La *ORP* BR6 .... 77 H2
  RSEV TN14 .... 77 H7
  SEV TN13 .... 8 B1
  TENT TN30 .... 230 A3
Shoreham Pl *RSEV* TN14 .... 78 D7
Shoreham Rd *RSEV* TN14 .... 101 K2
  STMC/STPC BR5 .... 38 C6
Shorehill La *BGR/WK* TN15 .... 102 E2
The Shore *GVW* DA11 .... 26 D4
Shorne Cl *STMC/STPC* BR5 .... 56 E1
Shorne Ifield Rd *GVE* DA12 .... 46 E4
Shortlands Rd *SIT* ME10 .... 94 B2
Short La *OXTED* RH8 .... 141 F1
Short St *CHAT* ME4 .... 4 B5 ⓫
Shorts Wy *ROCH* ME1 .... 2 A6
Shottenden Rd *GILL* ME7 .... 5 D1
Showfields Rd *RTWE/PEM* TN2 ..... 10 B6
Shropshire Ter *MAID/SHEP* ME15 ..... 134 A7
Shrubbery Rd *EYN* DA4 .... 42 C6
  GVE DA12 .... 27 J7
Shrubcote *TENT* TN30 .... 230 C7 ⓫
Shrubsole Dr *MAID/BEAR* ME14 ..... 110 E3
Shurland Av *SIT* ME10 .... 94 A5
Shurlock Av *SWLY* BR8 .... 40 A7
Shuttle Rd *DART* DA1 .... 22 D2
Sidcup Hl *SCUP* DA14 .... 38 C3
Sidcup Pl *SCUP* DA14 .... 38 B3
Sidmouth Rd *STMC/STPC* BR5 ..... 56 C2 ⓫
Sidney Cl *RTWE/PEM* TN2 .... 206 D6
Sidney Gdns *RSEV* TN14 .... 102 A3
Sidney Rd *GILL* ME7 .... 4 C1
  ROCH ME1 .... 2 A6
Sidney St *MAIDW* ME16 .... 132 C4
Silchester Ct *MAID/BEAR* ME14... 111 J7
Silkham Rd *OXTED* RH8 .... 118 B6
Silk Mills Cl *RSEV* TN14 .... 102 A8
Silver Bank *WALD* ME5 .... 68 B8
Silver Birch Av *MEO* DA13 .... 83 G5
Silver Birch Cl *RDART* DA2 .... 40 B2
Silver Birches *WALD* ME5 .... 88 B3
Silver Cl *TON* TN9... .... 170 B8
Silverdale *HART* DA3 .... 62 A1 ⓫
  MAIDW ME16 .... 131 K4
Silverdale Dr *RHAM* ME8 .... 70 B7
Silverdale Gv *SIT* ME10 .... 93 H3
Silverdale La *HAWK* TN18 .... 243 G2
  STH/RUST TN4 .... 11 D1
Silverdale Rd *STH/RUST* TN4 .... 11 D1
  STMC/STPC BR5 .... 38 B8
Silver Hl *CHAT* ME4 .... 3 F5
  ROCH ME1 .... 66 E4 ⓫
  TENT TN30... .... 230 B5
Silver Hill Gdns *CHAT* ME4 .... 3 F5 ⓫

Silverhurst Dr *TONN* TN10 .... 148 C8
Silver Rd *GVE* DA12 .... 28 B8
Silverspot Cl *RHAM* ME8... .... 70 C7
Silversted La *BH/WHM* TN16 .... 98 E7
Silver St *RSIT* ME9 .... 115 K1
Silver Tree *WALD* ME5 .... 88 B5
Silverweed Rd *WALD* ME5 .... 88 A1
Silwood Cl *RTWE/PEM* TN2 .... 190 E7
Simmonds La *MAID/SHEP* ME15 ..... 134 D8
Simpson Rd *SIT* ME10 .... 93 H1
  SNOD ME6 .... 85 K8
Sinclair Cl *RHAM* ME8 .... 90 B1 ⓫
Sinclair Wy *RDART* DA2 .... 42 C2
Singapore Dr *GILL* ME7 .... 4 B2 ⓫
Single's Cross La *RSEV* TN14 .... 99 J2
Single St *BH/WHM* TN16 .... 98 B2
Singlewell Rd *GVW* DA11 .... 45 J1
Sirdar Strd *GVE* DA12 .... 46 C3
Sir David's Pk *STH/RUST* TN4 .... 189 J5
Sir Evelyn Rd *ROCH* ME1 .... 67 G6
Sir John Hawkins Wy *CHAT* ME4... 3 F4 ⓫
Sir Thomas Longley Rd *STRD* ME2... 3 F1
Siskin Gdns *STPH/PW* TN12 .... 193 J1
Sissinghurst Dr *MAIDW* ME16 .... 132 B2
Sissinghurst Rd *CRBK* TN17 .... 216 A6
  RENT TN17 .... 216 E4
Sittingbourne Rd
  MAID/BEAR ME14... .... 7 E2
Six Fields Pth *TENT* TN30 .... 230 A7
Six Penny Cl *EDEN* TN8 .... 164 C6
Skeet Hill La *STMC/STPC* BR5 .... 57 G6
Skene Cl *RHAM* ME8 .... 70 D5
Skeynes Rd *EDEN* TN8 .... 164 B5
Skibbs La *ORP* BR6 .... 57 F7
Skid Hill La *WARL* CR6 .... 96 D2
Skinner Gdns *CRBK* TN17 .... 215 H6
Skinners Cl *DIT/AY* ME20 .... 87 F8
Skinners La *EDEN* TN8 .... 164 C4
Skinner St *CHAT* ME4 .... 3 F5
  GILL ME7 .... 4 C2
Skinner's Wy *RMAID* ME17... .... 157 G2
Skinney La *EYN* DA4 .... 42 C8
Skippers Cl *GRH* DA9 .... 25 G4 ⓫
Skye Cl *MAID/SHEP* ME15... .... 133 C7
Slade Cl *WALD* ME5 .... 88 C4
Slade Rd *RMAID* ME17 .... 139 K6
The Slade *RRTW* TN3... .... 221 J3
  TON TN9 .... 170 B4
Slaney Rd *STPH/PW* TN12 .... 198 B2
Slatin Rd *STRD* ME2... .... 49 F6
Sleepers Stile Rd *WADH* TN5 .... 220 E5
Slicketts Hl *CHAT* ME4 .... 4 A4 ⓫
Slip Mill Rd *HAWK* TN18 .... 234 E4
The Slip *BH/WHM* TN16 .... 120 C5
Slough Rd *RSIT* ME9 .... 117 G2
Small Bridge Rd *STPH/PW* TN12... 212 A4
Small Grains *HART* DA3 .... 61 G7
Smallhythe Rd *TENT* TN30 .... 229 K7 ⓫
Small Profits *WBY/YAL* ME18 ..... 152 E2
Smarden Rd *HDCN* TN27 .... 200 C2
  HDCN TN27 .... 203 G1
  HDCN TN27 .... 217 K2
Smarts Hl *RTON* TN11 .... 187 J5
Smarts Rd *GVE* DA12 .... 45 J1
Smeed Cl *SIT* ME10 .... 94 C2 ⓫
Smetham Gdns *STRD* ME2 .... 49 C5 ⓫
Smithers La *STPH/PW* TN12 .... 151 J7
Smithfield Rd *HOO/HM* ME3 .... 37 H1
Smith Rd *WALD* ME5 .... 88 C3
Smith's *MAID/SHEP* ME15 .... 153 G2
Smiths La *EDEN* TN8 .... 142 C4
Smiths Orch *RSIT* ME9 .... 115 K1
Smith St *STRD* ME2 .... 2 A2
Smugglers Ms *HAWK* TN18 .... 235 G5
Smugglers Whf *GRH* DA9 .... 25 G4
Smythe Cl *STH/RUST* TN4 .... 189 J3
Smythe Rd *EYN* DA4 .... 41 K6 ⓫
Snag La *RSEV* TN14 .... 75 J7
Snatts Hl *OXTED* RH8 .... 118 D8
Snelling Av *GVW* DA11 .... 27 G8
Snipe Cl *RTWE/PEM* TN2 .... 192 A6
Snoad La *STPH/PW* TN12 .... 197 G6
Snodhurst Av *WALD* ME5 .... 87 K1
Snodland Rd *E/WMAL* ME19 .... 85 G7
Snoll Hatch Rd *STPH/PW* TN12... 173 H1
Snowdon Av *MAID/BEAR* ME14 ..... 7 E2
Snowdon Cl *WALD* ME5 .... 68 C7 ⓫
Snowdown La *HDCN* TN27 .... 201 G6
Solefields Rd *SEV* TN13 .... 123 K7
Soleoak Dr *SEV* TN13 .... 9 D5
Sole St *MEO* DA13 .... 64 A2
Solomon Rd *RHAM* ME8 .... 70 C5
Solomons Rd *CHAT* ME4 .... 3 F4
Somerden Rd *STMC/STPC* BR5 ..... 56 C4
Somerfield Cl *MAIDW* ME16 .... 6 A3 ⓫
Somerfield La *MAIDW* ME16 .... 6 A2
Somerfield Rd *MAIDW* ME16 .... 6 A3
Somerhill Rd *TON* TN9 .... 170 D6
Somerset Cl *SIT* ME10 .... 93 H2
  WALD ME5 .... 68 D6
Somerset Rd *DART* DA1 .... 22 E5
  MAID/SHEP ME15... .... 133 J6
  ORP BR6 .... 56 B4
  STH/RUST TN4 .... 10 C1

Somerville Gdns *STH/RUST* TN4 .... 10 B3
Somerville Rd *DART* DA1 .... 23 J5 ☒
Somner Wk *MAID/SHEP* ME15 .. 156 B2 ☒
Soper's La *HAWK* TN18 .... 234 D2
Sophurst La *STPH/PW* TN12 ...... 209 K1
Sopwith Cl *BH/WHM* TN16 .... 97 H3
Sorrell Rd *WALD* ME5 .... 88 A2
Sorrell Wy *GVW* DA11 .... 45 F2 ☒
Sortmill Rd *SNOD* ME6 .... 86 A7
Sounds Ldg *SWLY* BR8 .... 57 K3 ☒
South Ash Rd *BGR/WK* TN15 ...... 81 K2
South Av *RHAM* ME8 .... 69 H4
  SIT ME10 .... 94 B3
South Bank *BH/WHM* TN16 .... 120 D5
  HOO/HM ME3 .... 31 G4
  RMAID ME17 .... 157 C7
  STPH/PW TN12 .... 198 A4
Southbourne Gv *WALD* ME5 ...... 88 B2 ☒
South Bush La *RHAM* ME8 .... 70 E8
South Crs *RMAID* ME17 .... 154 C3
Southdene *RSEV* TN14 .... 77 G8
South Dr *ORP* BR6 .... 75 K1
South Eastern Rd *STRD* ME2 ...... 2 C1 ☒
Southernden Rd *HDCN* TN27 .... 181 G5
Southern Pl *SWLY* BR8 .... 58 A1 ☒
Southey Wy *DIT/AY* ME20 .... 108 D2
Southfield *CHST* BR7 .... 38 A3
  STH/RUST TN4 .... 10 C1
Southfields *ROCH* ME1 .... 2 B5
  RRTW TN3 .... 188 E7
  WADH TN5 .... 220 B8
Southfield Shaw *MEO* DA13 .... 83 J5
Southfields Rd *BGR/WK* TN15 .... 80 E3
Southfields Wy *STH/RUST* TN4 .. 190 B6
Southfleet Av *HART* DA3 .... 44 C7
Southfleet Rd *GVW* DA11 .... 27 G7 ☒
  RDART DA2 .... 43 H2
  SWCM DA10 .... 26 B6
South Ga *PUR* RM19 .... 13 G4
Southgate La *TENT* TN30 .... 230 C7
South Green La *RSIT* ME9 .... 91 J7
South Gv *RTW* TN1 .... 10 C5 ☒
South Hall Cl *EYN* DA4 .... 59 J4
South Hill Rd *GVE* DA12 .... 27 J7
Southhill Rd *CHAT* ME4 .... 3 F5
South Kent Av *GVW* DA11 .... 26 D5
South La *RMAID* ME17 .... 157 G8
Southlees La *RSIT* ME9 .... 114 D4
South Pk *SEV* TN13 .... 9 D4
South Park Rd *MAID/SHEP* ME15 .. 7 E6
South Rd *GILL* ME7 .... 4 A1
  STPH/PW TN12 .... 176 E8
South St *GVE* DA12 .... 27 J6
  MAIDW ME16 .... 131 J6
  MEO DA13 .... 63 G8
South Street Rd *RSIT* ME9 .... 91 H6
Southview Cl *SWLY* BR8 .... 58 D1 ☒
South View Rd *RDART* DA2 .... 41 G1
  STH/RUST TN4 .... 190 B6
  WADH TN5 .... 220 B8
Southwark Rd *STRD* ME2 .... 48 C8
South Wy *PUR* RM19 .... 13 J3
Southways *RMAID* ME17 .... 157 G7 ☒
Southwell Rd *STRD* ME2 .... 48 B8
Southwood *MAIDW* ME16 .... 131 K4
Southwood Av *STH/RUST* TN4 .... 10 C1
Southwood Rd *STH/RUST* TN4 .. 206 A1
Sovereign Bvd *GILL* ME7 .... 5 E6
Sovereigns Wy *STPH/PW* TN12 .. 176 B8
Sovereign Wy *TON* TN9 .... 170 C5
Spade La *RSIT* ME9 .... 71 F8
Spar Cl *RTON* TN11 .... 150 B5
Sparepenny La *EYN* DA4 .... 59 H4
Sparkeswood Av *CRBK* TN17 .... 238 C2
Spearhead Rd *MAID/BEAR* ME14 .. 111 F7
Speedgate HI *HART* DA3 .... 61 F6
Speedwell Av *WALD* ME5 .... 87 K2
Speedwell Cl *GILL* ME7 .... 5 E3
  MAID/BEAR ME14 .... 134 A1 ☒
Spekes Rd *GILL* ME7 .... 69 H8
Speldhurst HI *RRTW* TN3 .... 189 F6
Speldhurst Rd *RRTW* TN3 .... 205 J1
  STH/RUST TN4 .... 189 K6
Spelmonden Rd *STPH/PW* TN12 .. 211 J2
Spencer Cl *WALD* ME5 .... 88 B1
Spencer St *GVW* DA11 .... 27 H6
Spencer Wk *TIL* RM18 .... 27 H1
Spenlow Dr *WALD* ME5 .... 88 B6 ☒
Spenny La *STPH/PW* TN12 .... 175 G8
Speyside *TONN* TN10 .... 170 B1 ☒
Spielman Rd *DART* DA1 .... 27 J1
The Spillway *MAID/SHEP* ME15 .. 6 A5 ☒
Spindle Gld *MAID/BEAR* ME14 .... 7 F2
Spindlewood Cl *WALD* ME5 ...... 88 C3 ☒
Spinners Cl *HDCN* TN27 .... 217 J4
The Spinney *MAID/SHEP* ME15 .. 7 E5 ☒
  SCUP DA14 .... 39 F3
  SWLY BR8 .... 40 B7
  TON TN9 .... 170 A7
  WALD ME5 .... 88 C5 ☒
Spinney Wy *RSEV* TN14 .... 75 J6
Spire Cl *GVE* DA12 .... 27 J7 ☒
The Spires *DART* DA1 .... 23 G8
  MAIDW ME16 .... 6 A3

Spital St *DART* DA1 .... 23 G5
Spitfire Cl *WALD* ME5 .... 68 C8
Spitfire Rd *E/WMAL* ME19 .... 129 H3
Spode La *EDEN* TN8 .... 185 G6
Sponden La *HAWK* TN18 .... 236 B6
Spongs La *CRBK* TN17 .... 215 H5
Sportsfield *MAID/BEAR* ME14 ...... 7 E2
Spot La *MAID/SHEP* ME15 .... 134 C4
Spout La *EDEN* TN8 .... 142 C5
  STPH/PW TN12 .... 210 E1
Spray HI *RRTW* TN3 .... 221 K2
The Sprig *MAID/BEAR* ME14 ..... 134 C2
Springcroft *HART* DA3 .... 62 B3
Spring Cross *HART* DA3 .... 62 B7
Springett Cl *DIT/AY* ME20 .... 86 E8
Springett Wy *RMAID* ME17 .... 154 D2
Springfield *OXTED* RH8 .... 140 B1
Springfield Av *MAID/BEAR* ME14 .. 6 B1
  SWLY BR8 .... 58 C1 ☒
  TENT TN30 .... 230 B4
Springfield Rd *DIT/AY* ME20 ..... 108 D2
  EDEN TN8 .... 164 B5
  GILL ME7 .... 5 E2
  RRTW TN3 .... 205 F7
  SIT ME10 .... 93 J1
  STH/RUST TN4 .... 189 K5
Springfields *WADH* TN5 .... 232 C5
Springfields Wy *STMC/STPC* BR5 .. 38 D8
Spring Gdns *BH/WHM* TN16 ...... 97 G5
  RSEV TN14 .... 76 C2
Spring Gv *GVE* DA12 .... 27 J7
Springhead *RTWE/PEM* TN2 ...... 11 F2
Spring Head Rd *BGR/WK* TN15 .. 102 D4
Springhead Rd *GVW* DA11 .... 26 D6
Spring HI *RTON* TN11 .... 187 J8
  RYE TN31 .... 244 E7
Springholm Cl *BH/WHM* TN16 .... 97 G5
Spring La *BGR/WK* TN15 .... 126 B1
  OXTED RH8 .... 140 B2
  STH/RUST TN4 .... 189 H3
Spring Shaw Rd *STMC/STPC* BR5 .. 38 B6
Spring V *GRH* DA9 .... 25 H5
  MAIDW ME16 .... 6 B3
Springvale *RHAM* ME8 .... 69 K8
  RSIT ME9 .... 73 J2
Spring Vale Cl *SWLY* BR8 .... 40 C5
Spring V North *DART* DA1 .... 23 G5 ☒
Spring V South *DART* DA1 .... 23 G6 ☒
Springwell Rd *TON* TN9 .... 170 B6
Springwood Rd *MAIDW* ME16 ... 132 A5
Sprotshill Cl *SIT* ME10 .... 73 K8
Spruce Cl *DIT/AY* ME20 .... 108 E4
Sprucedale Cl *SWLY* BR8 .... 40 B7
Spruce Rd *BH/WHM* TN16 .... 97 H3
Spurrell Av *RDART* DA2 .... 40 A2
Spur Rd *ORP* BR6 .... 56 B6
Spurway *MAID/BEAR* ME14 ...... 134 C2
Square HI *MAID/BEAR* ME14 .... 7 E3
Square Hill Rd *MAID/SHEP* ME15 .. 7 E4
The Square *BH/WHM* TN16 .... 97 G8
  RMAID ME17 .... 160 D1
  RTON TN11 .... 150 A6
Squerryes Mede
  BH/WHM TN16 .... 120 C6 ☒
Squires Cl *STRD* ME2 .... 48 A7
Squires Fld *SWLY* BR8 .... 40 D5
Squires Wy *RDART* DA2 .... 40 A2
Squirrel Wy *RTWE/PEM* TN2 .... 207 K1
Stable Cl *WALD* ME5 .... 88 D1
Stabledene Wy *RTWE/PEM* TN2 .. 191 K8 ☒
Stace Cl *TENT* TN30 .... 230 C6
Stacey Cl *GVE* DA12 .... 46 B3
Stacey Rd *RTON* TN11 .... 170 A3
Stacklands Cl *BGR/WK* TN15 .... 80 D2 ☒
Stack La *HART* DA3 .... 62 A2
Stack Rd *EYN* DA4 .... 60 C1
Stadium Wy *DART* DA1 .... 22 B5
Staffa Rd *MAID/SHEP* ME15 .... 133 C7
Staffhurst Wood Rd *OXTED* RH8 .. 141 D8
Stafford Cl *GRH* DA9 .... 24 E4 ☒
Stafford Rd *RTWE/PEM* TN2 .... 207 K2
  TON TN9 .... 170 B4
Stafford St *GILL* ME7 .... 4 C3
Stafford Wy *SEV* TN13 .... 85 J6
Stag Rd *RTWE/PEM* TN2 .... 190 D5
  WALD ME5 .... 88 C1
Stagshaw Cl *MAID/SHEP* ME15 .... 7 D5
Stainer Rd *TONN* TN10 .... 149 F8
Stairfoot La *SEV* TN13 .... 122 E1
Stair Rd *TON* TN9 .... 171 F2
Stake La *STRD* ME2 .... 65 K8
Staleys Rd *BGR/WK* TN15 .... 104 E7
Stalham Ct *GILL* ME7 .... 89 J2 ☒
Stalin Av *WALD* ME5 .... 68 C6
The Stampers *MAID/SHEP* ME15 .. 6 A5 ☒
Stanam Rd *RTWE/PEM* TN2 ...... 209 H1
Stanbridge Rd *EDEN* TN8 .... 164 B4
Stanbrook Rd *GVW* DA11 .... 27 G7
Standard Rd *ORP* BR6 .... 75 F5
Standen Cl *RHAM* ME8 .... 90 B2
Standen St *CRBK* TN17 .... 237 F4
Stanford Dr *MAIDW* ME16 .... 132 C3 ☒

Stanford Gdns *SOCK/AV* RM15 .... 13 J1
Stanford La *RTON* TN11 .... 150 E4
Stanford Wy *STRD* ME2 .... 66 B4
Stangate Rd *E/WMAL* ME19 .... 84 E6
  STRD ME2 .... 48 B7
Stangrove Rd *EDEN* TN8 .... 164 C5
Stanham Pl *DART* DA1 .... 22 D3
Stanham Rd *DART* DA1 .... 23 F4
Stanhope Av *SIT* ME10 .... 94 B3
Stanhope Cl *MAID/BEAR* ME14 .. 110 E7
Stanhope HI *BFN/LL* DA15 .... 38 B2
  RTW TN1 .... 11 E2 ☒
  STRD ME2 .... 2 A1 ☒
  SWCM DA10 .... 26 A4
Stanhopes *OXTED* RH8 .... 119 F7
Stanhope Wy *SEV* TN13 .... 123 F1
Stan La *WBY/YAL* ME18 .... 128 C5
Stanley Cl *GRH* DA9 .... 24 D4
  STPH/PW TN12 .... 197 K2
Stanley Crs *GVE* DA12 .... 46 A3
Stanley Rd *GILL* ME7 .... 4 C2 ☒
  ORP BR6 .... 56 A5
  RTW TN1 .... 11 D2
  SCUP DA14 .... 38 B1
  SWCM DA10 .... 26 A5
  WALD ME5 .... 68 D8
Stanley Wy *STMC/STPC* BR5 .... 56 C2
Stansted Cl *MAID* ME16 .... 110 C7
Stansted Rd *BGR/WK* TN15 .... 82 B5
Stansted La *BGR/WK* TN15 .... 81 G5
Stanton Cl *STMC/STPC* BR5 .... 56 D4
Staple Cl *BXLY* DA5 .... 40 A1
  SIT ME10 .... 73 K8
Staple Dr *STPH/PW* TN12 .... 198 B3
Staplehurst Rd *RHAM* ME8 .... 69 J3
  SIT ME10 .... 73 H8
  STPH/PW TN12 .... 177 H3
Staplers Ct *MAID/BEAR* ME14 .. 111 H6 ☒
Stapleton Rd *ORP* BR6 .... 56 A7
Starboard Av *GRH* DA9 .... 25 G5 ☒
Star HI *DART* DA1 .... 22 B4
  ROCH ME1 .... 3 D3
Star Hill Rd *RSEV* TN14 .... 100 B3
Star La *GILL* ME7 .... 69 G6
  STMC/STPC BR5 .... 56 E1
Starling Cl *HART* DA3 .... 44 C8
Star Mill La *WALD* ME5 .... 5 D6
Starts Hill Av *ORP* BR6 .... 75 H1 ☒
Starveacre La *HART* DA3 .... 93 H4
Station Ap *BGR/WK* TN15 .... 105 F7 ☒
  DART DA1 .... 23 H5
  EDEN TN8 .... 164 C5
  MAIDW ME16 .... 6 C4
  ORP BR6 .... 56 A6
  ORP BR6 .... 76 C1
  OXTED RH8 .... 118 C8
  RSEV TN14 .... 102 A3
  STMC/STPC BR5 .... 56 C1
  STPH/PW TN12 .... 173 J7 ☒
  STPH/PW TN12 .... 198 A1
  STRD ME2 .... 85 K1 ☒
  SWLY BR8 .... 58 B1
Station Approach Rd *TIL* RM18 .... 27 H3
Station Ct *BGR/WK* TN15 .... 105 F7
Station HI *RTON* TN11 .... 167 H5
Station Rd *BGR/WK* TN15 .... 105 F7
  BH/WHM TN16 .... 121 H2
  CRBK TN17 .... 212 B7
  DART DA1 .... 22 C5
  DIT/AY ME20 .... 109 G5
  DIT/AY ME20 .... 109 K4
  EDEN TN8 .... 142 B6
  EDEN TN8 .... 164 C3
  EYN DA4 .... 42 A7
  EYN DA4 .... 59 G8 ☒
  GRH DA9 .... 25 F4
  GVW DA11 .... 26 C5
  HART DA3 .... 43 K8
  HDCN TN27 .... 200 B1
  HDCN TN27 .... 203 J2
  HOO/HM ME3 .... 31 F3
  MAID/BEAR ME14 .... 6 C2 ☒
  MAID/SHEP ME15 .... 132 A7
  MEO DA13 .... 44 A2
  MEO DA13 .... 63 H2
  ORP BR6 .... 56 A6
  RHAM ME8 .... 70 D4
  RMAID ME17 .... 137 H8
  RRTW TN3 .... 205 F7
  RSEV TN14 .... 100 B3
  RSEV TN14 .... 70 D6
  RSEV TN14 .... 101 K5
  RSIT ME9 .... 72 A3
  RSIT ME9 .... 95 K4
  RYE TN31 .... 244 E6
  SCUP DA14 .... 38 B1
  SEV TN13 .... 101 C7
  STMC/STPC BR5 .... 56 D1 ☒
  STPH/PW TN12 .... 173 H7
  STPH/PW TN12 .... 198 B1
  STRD ME2 .... 2 B1
  STRD ME2 .... 66 B8
  SWLY BR8 .... 58 B1
  TENT TN30 .... 230 A7
  WBY/YAL ME18 .... 152 A5

Station Rd East OXTED RH8 .... 118 C8
Station Rd West OXTED RH8 .... 118 C8
Station St SIT ME10 .... 94 A2
Steadman Cl HOO/HM ME3 .... 48 B1
Stede Hl RMAID ME17 .... 137 K6
Stedman Cl BXLY DA5 .... 40 B1
Steele Av GRH DA9 .... 25 F4
Steele St SIT ME2 .... 88 B5
Steele St WADH TN5 .... 49 F6
Steellands Ri WADH TN5 .... 232 C5
Steep Cl ORP BR6 .... 76 A2
Steeple Heights Dr BH/WHM TN16 .. 97 H4
Steerforth Cl ROCH ME1 .... 2 C6 🔢
Steers Pl RTON TN11 .... 150 A4
Stella Cl STPH/PW TN12 .... 196 E1 🔢
Stephen Cl ORP BR6 .... 56 A7
Stephen's Rd STH/RUST TN4 .... 10 C1
Stepneyford La CRBK TN17 .... 228 A5
Steps Hill Rd RSIT ME9 .... 91 G8
Step Style SIT ME10 .... 94 C4 🔢
Sterling Av MAIDW ME16 .... 132 C1
Sterling Rd SIT ME10 .... 93 J5
Sterndale Rd DART DA1 .... 23 J6 🔢
Stevens Cl BXLY DA5 .... 40 A2
    HDCN TN27 .... 183 F3
    RDART DA2 .... 42 D3
    SNOD ME6 .... 85 K6 🔢
Stevenson Cl MAID/SHEP ME15 .... 6 C4 🔢
Stevenson Wy DIT/AY ME20 .... 108 D2
Stevens Rd DIT/AY ME20 .... 86 E8
Stewart Rd STH/RUST TN4 .... 190 C7
Stickens La E/WMAL ME19 .... 108 C2
Stickfast La RMAID ME17 .... 180 B2
    RSIT ME9 .... 73 F5
Stilebridge La RMAID ME17 .... 177 G1
    STPH/PW TN12 .... 176 E3
Still La STH/RUST TN4 .... 189 K4 🔢
Stirling Cl RHAM ME8 .... 90 B2
    ROCH ME1 2
Stirling Dr ORP BR6 .... 76 C1
Stirling Rd E/WMAL ME19 .... 129 H3
Stisted Wy HDCN TN27 .... 183 F3
Stockbury Dr MAIDW ME16 .... 110 D7
Stockenbury STPH/PW TN12 .... 151 H8
Stockers Brow RSIT ME9 .... 94 B7
Stockers Hl RSIT ME9 .... 94 B7
Stockett La RMAID ME17 .... 154 C3
Stock Hl BH/WHM TN16 .... 97 H3
Stockland Green Rd RRTW TN3 .... 189 G6
Stock La RDART DA2 .... 41 F2
Stocks Green Rd RTON TN11 .... 150 A4
Stocks La TENT TN30 .... 247 K3
Stockton Cl MAID/BEAR ME14... .... 111 H6
Stoke Rd HOO/HM ME3 .... 33 J7
    HOO/HM ME3 .... 35 F1
Stoneacre Cl RHAM ME8 .... 90 A1
Stoneacre La MAID/SHEP ME15 .... 134 D8
Stonebridge Green Rd
    HDCN TN27 .... 183 G2
Stonebridge Rd GVW DA11 .... 26 B4
Stone Court La RTWE/PEM TN2 .... 192 B4
Stonecroft MAID DA13 .... 83 H6 🔢
Stonecross Lea WALD ME5 .... 68 C5
Stonegate Cl STMC/STPC BR5 .... 38 D8 🔢
Stone Hill Rd HDCN TN27 .... 183 F4
Stonehorse La HOO/HM ME3 .... 49 F3
Stonehouse La ORP BR6 .... 76 E4
    PUR RM19 .... 13 J5
Stonehouse Rd ORP BR6 .... 76 E4
Stoneings La RSEV TN14 .... 99 F5
Stoneleigh Av OXTED RH8 .... 141 J1
Stone Pit La HAWK TN18 .... 244 B1
Stone Place Rd GRH DA9 .... 24 D4
Stones Cross Rd SWLY BR8 .... 57 K2
Stonestile Rd HDCN TN27 .... 179 J7
Stone St CRBK TN17 .... 225 K1
    GVE DA12 .... 27 J5
    RTW TN1 .... 11 D3
Stone Street Rd BGR/WK TN15... .... 125 G3
Stoneswood Rd OXTED RH8 .... 141 K5
Stonewall Park Rd RRTW TN3 .... 205 J3
Stonewood RDART DA2 .... 43 H1
Stoney Bank MEO ME7 .... 69 G5
Stony Cnr HART DA3 .... 63 F1
Stony La ROCH ME1 .... 87 C1
Stopford Rd GILL ME7 .... 5 D4
Stornaway Std GVE DA12 .... 46 C2
Stour Cl STRD ME2 .... 48 E7
    TONN TN10 .... 170 B1
Stour Rd DART DA1 .... 22 D2
Stour Valley Wk RMAID ME17 .... 160 D2
Stowe Rd ORP BR6 .... 56 C2
Strand Approach Rd GILL ME7 .... 5 E1
Strand Cl MEO DA13 .... 63 H4
Stratford Av RHAM ME8 .... 70 C6
Stratford La RHAM ME8 .... 70 C6
Stratford Rd E/WMAL ME19 .... 107 J6
Stratford St RTW TN1 .... 11 E2
Stratton Ter BH/WHM TN16 .... 120 C6 🔢
Strawberry Cl RHAM ME8 .... 206 D6
Strawberry Flds RYE TN31 .... 244 D3
    SWLY BR8 .... 40 B7 🔢
Strawberry V TON TN9 .... 170 C5 🔢
Straw Mill Hl MAID/SHEP ME15... .... 6 B6
Stream La HAWK TN18 .... 235 F7

Stream Pit La HAWK TN18 .... 243 J1
Streamside DIT/AY ME20 .... 109 F5
Stream Side TONN TN10 .... 148 D7
The Stream DIT/AY ME20 .... 109 F5
Streatfield EDEN TN8 .... 164 D5
Street End Rd WALD ME5 .... 68 C6
Streetfield RMAID ME17 .... 158 D7
Streetfield Rd RHAM ME8 .... 70 C5 🔢
The Street BGR/WK TN15 .... 81 K1
    CRBK TN17 .... 199 C3
    CRBK TN17 .... 215 H6
    CRBK TN17 .... 227 F8
    E/WMAL ME19 .... 106 C1
    E/WMAL ME19 .... 107 H2
    EYN DA4 .... 60 A1
    GILL ME7 .... 89 J5
    GVE DA12 .... 47 H3
    GVE DA12... .... 64 D1
    HDCN TN27 .... 183 K7
    HDCN TN27 .... 183 F3
    HOO/HM ME3 .... 33 F3
    MAID/BEAR ME14 .... 111 J3
    MAID/BEAR ME14 .... 112 C5
    MAID/BEAR ME14 .... 134 E2
    MEO DA13 .... 63 H5
    RMAID ME17 .... 158 D7
    RSIT ME9 .... 71 H2
    RSIT ME9 .... 72 A3
    RSIT ME9 .... 73 K2
    RSIT ME9 .... 91 G2
    RSIT ME9 .... 93 F4
    RSIT ME9 .... 95 H8
    RSIT ME9 .... 95 F3
    RSIT ME9 .... 115 K7
    RSIT ME9 .... 115 K1
    STRD ME2 .... 85 H1
    TENT TN30 .... 247 J4
    WBY/YAL TN18 .... 129 F6
    WBY/YAL TN18 .... 130 E7
Strettitt Gdns STPH/PW TN12... .... 173 H1
Strickland Av DART DA1 .... 23 J5
Strickland Wy ORP BR6 .... 56 A3 🔢
Strover St GILL ME7 .... 4 C1
Strumer Ct WBY/YAL TN18 .... 129 J4
Struttons Av GVW DA11 .... 27 G8
Stuart Cl MAID/BEAR ME14 .... 7 E1
    RTWE/PEM TN2 .... 206 E6
    SWLY BR8 .... 40 C5
Stuart Rd GILL ME7 .... 5 D5
    GVW DA11 .... 27 H5
Stubbs Hl ORP BR6 .... 76 D8
Studland Cl BFN/LL DA15 .... 38 A1 🔢
Studley Cl SCUP DA14 .... 38 C3
Studley Crs HART DA3 .... 44 D7
Sturdee Av GILL ME7 .... 5 E4
Sturla Rd CHAT ME4 .... 4 A6
Sturry Wy RHAM ME8 .... 69 K4
Styants Bottom Rd BGR/WK TN15.. .... 125 K1
Style Cl RHAM ME8 .... 90 B2
Styles Cl EDEN TN8 .... 165 H1
Suffolk Av RHAM ME8 .... 70 C5
Suffolk Cl DART DA1 .... 23 H5
    GVE DA12... .... 28 A5
    MAID/SHEP ME15 .... 133 K6
    SCUP DA14 .... 38 D4
Suffolk Wy BGR/WK TN15 .... 9 E4
Sullivan Cl DART DA1 .... 22 E5
Sullivan Rd TONN TN10 .... 170 E1
Sultan Rd MAID ME7 .... 88 D4
Summer Cl TENT TN30 .... 230 C5
Summerhill HDCN TN27 .... 179 J8
Summerhill Av STH/RUST TN4 .... 189 K5 🔢
Summerhill Rd DART DA1 .... 23 G6
    STPH/PW TN12 .... 177 H6
Summerhouse Dr RDART DA2... .... 40 A3
Summervale Rd STH/RUST TN4 .... 206 C5
Sunburst Cl STPH/PW TN12 .... 196 D1 🔢
Sun Ct ERITH DA8 .... 22 C1
Sunderland Cl RHAM ME8 .... 70 A8 🔢
Sunderland Dr RHAM ME8... .... 70 D6
Sundridge Cl DART DA1 .... 23 K5
Sundridge Dr WALD ME5 .... 88 B2
Sundridge Hl RSEV TN14 .... 99 J5
    STRD ME2 .... 66 B4
Sundridge La RSEV TN14 .... 99 H4
Sundridge Rd RSEV TN14... .... 100 C2
Sun Hl HART DA3 .... 61 F6
Sun La GVE DA12 .... 27 K8
Sunningdale Cl RHAM ME8 .... 70 A8 🔢
Sunningdale Dr RHAM ME8 .... 70 A8
Sunninghill GVW DA11 .... 27 F8 🔢
Sunningvale Av BH/WHM TN16 .... 97 G4
Sunningvale Cl BH/WHM TN16 .... 97 H3
Sunny Bank SIT ME10 .... 94 C1
Sunnyfields Cl RHAM ME8 .... 70 B6
Sunnymead Av GILL ME7 .... 5 E3
Sunnyside Rd STH/RUST TN4 .... 206 B2
Sun Rd SWCM DA10 .... 26 A5
Superior Dr ORP BR6 .... 76 A2 🔢
Surrenden Rd STPH/PW TN12... .... 198 A3
Surrey Cl RTWE/PEM TN2 .... 206 E6
Surrey Rd MAID/SHEP ME15 .... 133 K6
Susan's Hl RASHW TN26 .... 231 K4
Sussex Border Pth EDEN TN8 .... 184 C6

    HAWK TN18 .... 235 G8
    RRTW TN3 .... 204 A2
    TENT TN30 .... 247 J7
    WADH TN5 .... 232 E2
Sussex Cl RTWE/PEM TN2 .... 11 E6
Sussex Dr WALD ME5 .... 88 B2
Sussex Ms RTWE/PEM TN2 .... 10 C5 🔢
Sussex Rd DART DA1 .... 23 K6
    MAID/SHEP ME15 .... 133 K5
    SCUP DA14 .... 38 C3
    STMC/STPC BR5 .... 56 D3
    TON TN9 .... 170 A6
Sutherland Av BH/WHM TN16 .... 97 H4
    STMC/STPC BR5 .... 56 A3
Sutherland Cl GVE DA12 .... 28 E8 🔢
Sutherland Rd RTW TN1 .... 11 D5
Sutton Baron Rd RSIT ME9 .... 92 E6
Sutton Cl RHAM ME8 .... 70 D6
Sutton Ct STPH/PW TN12 .... 196 C1
Sutton Forge STPH/PW TN12 .... 196 D1
Sutton Rd MAID/SHEP ME15 .... 133 H6
    RMAID ME17 .... 156 E2
Sutton St MAID/BEAR ME14 .... 135 F3
Swadelands Cl RMAID ME17 .... 160 C1
Swaffield Rd SEV TN13 .... 9 E1
Swain Cl STRD ME2 .... 48 E6
Swain Rd RHAM ME8 .... 69 J8
    TENT TN30 .... 230 B3
Swaisland Rd DART DA1... .... 22 E4
Swaislands Dr DART DA1 .... 22 C4
Swaledale Rd RDART DA2 .... 24 B7
Swale Rd DART DA1 .... 22 D2
    STRD ME2 .... 48 B7
Swallow Cl GRH DA9 .... 24 E4
Swallow Dr RTWE/PEM TN2 .... 191 F8
Swallow Ri WALD ME5 .... 88 B1
Swallow Rd DIT/AY ME20... .... 108 D4
Swallowtail Cl STMC/STPC BR5 .... 56 E1 🔢
Swan Cl SIT ME10 .... 94 C2
    STMC/STPC BR5 .... 38 B8
Swan Cottages TENT TN30 .... 247 J3
Swanland Dr TON TN9 .... 169 K7
Swan La CRBK TN17 .... 212 E3
    DART DA1 .... 22 E4
    EDEN TN8 .... 164 C2
Swanley La SWLY BR8 .... 40 C8
Swanley Village Rd SWLY BR8 .... 40 E6
Swanmead Wy TON TN9 .... 170 D4
Swan Rdg EDEN TN8 .... 164 D2
Swanscombe St SWCM DA10 .... 26 C5
Swanstree Av SIT ME10 .... 94 C4
Swan St E/WMAL ME19 .... 108 A6
    TENT TN30... .... 247 J3
Swanton Rd WBY/YAL ME18 .... 128 B7
Swanzy Rd RSEV TN14 .... 102 A7
Sward Rd STMC/STPC BR5... .... 56 B3
Swattenden La CRBK TN17 .... 225 H4
Swaynesland Rd OXTED RH8 .... 141 K5
Sweeps Hill Cl RTWE/PEM TN2 .... 191 K7 🔢
Sweeps La STMC/STPC BR5 .... 56 E2
Sweetings La RRTW TN3 .... 221 F5
Sweets La E/WMAL ME19... .... 130 E2
Sweyne Rd SWCM DA10 .... 25 K5
Swievelands Rd BH/WHM TN16 .... 97 F6
Swift Cl DIT/AY ME20 .... 108 E4
Swift Crs WALD ME5 .... 68 C8
Swifts Vw CRBK TN17 .... 214 E3
Swiller's La GVE DA12 .... 47 H3
Swinburne Gdns TIL RM18... .... 27 J1
Swingate Av HOO/HM ME3 .... 31 C1
Swingate Cl WALD ME5 .... 88 C1
Swinton Av HOO/HM ME3 .... 50 A1
Sycamore Cl GVE DA12 .... 28 A6 🔢
Sycamore Crs MAIDW ME16 .... 132 C1
Sycamore Dr DIT/AY ME20 .... 109 J3
    SWLY BR8 .... 40 B8
Sycamore Gdns STPH/PW TN12 .. 193 H1 🔢
Sycamore Rd DART DA1 .... 23 G6
    STRD ME2 .... 66 D2
Sychem La RTON TN11 .... 192 C1
Sychem Pl STPH/PW TN12 .... 172 C7
Sydney Av SIT ME10 .... 93 H7
Sydney Rd CHAT ME4 .... 4 A5
    TIL RM18 .... 27 H1
Sylewood Cl ROCH ME1 .... 67 G6 🔢
Sylvan Cl OXTED RH8 .... 119 F8
Sylvan Gld WALD ME5 .... 88 B6
Sylvan Rd RHAM ME8 .... 69 K6
Sylvestre Cl STRD ME2 .... 85 K2 🔢
Symmonds Dr SIT ME10 .... 94 B1
Symonds Cl BGR/WK TN15... .... 80 B7
Symonds La WBY/YAL ME18 .... 152 C7
Symonds Rd HOO/HM ME3 .... 31 F3
Symons Av CHAT ME4 .... 3 F6

T

Tadburn Gn WALD ME5 .... 88 C2
Taddington Wood La WALD ME5 .... 87 K4
The Tail Race MAID/SHEP ME15 .... 6 B6
Tainter Rd RTON TN11 .... 149 K5
Talbot Pk RTWE/PEM TN2 .... 11 F2
Talbot Rd HAWK TN18 .... 235 F6

MAIDW ME16 .... 110 C8
Tallents Cl EYN DA4 .... 42 A5
Tall Trees Cl RMAID ME17 ..... 158 B4
Tally Rd OXTED RH8 .... 141 J2
Talus Cl RAIN RM19 .... 13 H4
Tamar Dr STRD ME2 .... 48 E8
Tamarind Cl GILL ME7 .... 89 H2
Tamar Rd TONN TN10 .... 170 B1
Tamesis Strd GVE DA12 .... 46 B3
Tangier La RRTW TN3 .... 207 G8
Tanglewood Cl RHAM ME8 ...... 69 K8
Tangmere Cl GILL ME7 .... 5 F3
Tanhouse Rd OXTED RH8 .... 140 B3
Tanker Hl RHAM ME8 .... 70 A8
Tank Hill Rd PUR RM19 .... 12 E4
Tank La PUR RM19 .... 12 E4
Tanners Md EDEN TN8 .... 164 C5
Tannery Rd TON TN9 .... 170 C5
Tanyard HAWK TN18 .... 243 J1
Tanyard Hl GVE DA12 .... 47 H4
Tanyard La STH/RUST TN4 ...... 189 K5
The Tanyard CRBK TN17 .... 225 K2
Tarling Cl SCUP DA14 .... 38 C1
Tarragon Rd MAIDW ME16 .... 132 B3
Tasker Cl MAID/SHEP ME15 ..... 134 D3
Tassell Cl E/WMAL ME19 .... 108 C5
Taswell Rd RHAM ME8 .... 70 D5
Tates HAWK TN18 .... 235 G5
Tates Orch HART DA3 .... 62 A3
Tatler Cl MAID ME 88 E4
Tatsfield La BH/WHM TN16 ..... 97 K8
Tattlebury La CRBK TN17 ...... 212 E6
Tattlebury Rd HDCN TN27 ...... 179 K7
Taunton Cl BXLYHN DA7 .... 22 A2
MAID/SHEP ME15 .... 134 B8
Taunton Rd GVW DA11 .... 26 B4
Taunton V GVE DA12 .... 46 A1
Taveners Rd RHAM ME8 .... 70 A7
Tavern Cl BGR/WK TN15 .... 105 F7
Tavistock Cl RHAM ME8 .... 70 B7
SIT ME10 .... 93 J2
WALD ME5 .... 88 A5
Tay Cl WALD ME5 .... 88 C1
Taylor Cl ORP BR6 .... 56 A8
RMAID ME17 .... 137 H8
Taylor Rd SNOD ME6 .... 85 J7
Taylor Rw RDART DA2 .... 41 F1
Taylors Cl SCUP DA14 .... 38 A2
Taylors La E/WMAL ME19 .... 83 G8
HOO/HM ME3 .... 48 A3
HOO/HM ME3 .... 48 A1
STRD ME2 .... 2 B1
Taylor St STH/RUST TN4 .... 189 K6
Tea Garden La RRTW TN3 .... 206 A5
Teal Av STMC/STPC BR5 .... 56 E1
Teal Cl HOO/HM ME3 .... 37 G1
Teapot La DIT/AY ME20 .... 109 J4
Teasaucer Hl MAID/SHEP ME15 .. 133 F6
Teasel Cl MAID/BEAR ME14 ..... 134 B2
Teasel Rd MAID ME5 .... 48 A4
Tebbs Wy BGR/WK TN15 .... 126 C3
Tedder Av WALD ME5 .... 68 B7
Tedder Rd STH/RUST TN4 .... 190 B7
Teesdale Rd RDART DA2 .... 24 B7
Telegraph Hl HOO/HM ME3 ...... 48 B3
Telston La RSEV TN14 .... 101 H4
SEV TN13 .... 101 G4
Tempest Rd E/WMAL ME19 .... 129 H3
Templar Dr GVW DA11 .... 45 H3
Temple Gdns SIT ME10 .... 94 C3
Temple Hl DART DA1 .... 23 J4
Temple Hill Sq DART DA1 ...... 23 J4
Temple Wy E/WMAL ME19 .... 108 D6
Ten Acre Wy RHAM ME8 .... 70 E5
Tenchley's La OXTED RH8 ...... 141 H4
Tennyson Av HOO/HM ME3 .... 31 G7
Tennyson Rd DART DA1 .... 23 K4
GILL ME7 .... 4 C5
Tennyson Wk GVW DA11 .... 44 E1
TIL RM18 .... 27 J1
Tensing Av GVW DA11 .... 45 F1
Tenterden Rd CRBK TN17 .... 238 D2
HDCN TN27 .... 217 K6
WALD ME5 .... 88 C1
Terence Cl CHAT ME4 .... 4 A6
GVE DA12 .... 28 C8
Terminus Rd MAIDW ME16 .... 132 A4
Tern Crs STRD ME2 .... 48 B8
Terrace Rd MAIDW ME16 .... 6 B3
SIT ME10 .... 94 C3
The Terraces RDART DA2 .... 24 B6
Terrace St GVE DA12 .... 27 J5
The Terrace GVE DA12 .... 27 J5
ROCH ME1 .... 2 C3
SEV TN13 .... 123 F1
Terry's Lodge Rd BGR/WK TN15 . 104 C5
Terry Wk DIT/AY ME20 .... 108 C4
Testers Cl OXTED RH8 .... 141 F2
Teston La MAID/SHEP ME15 ..... 131 G7
Teston Rd E/WMAL ME19 .... 106 D6
E/WMAL ME19 .... 129 K1
Teynham Gn RHAM ME8 .... 69 H2
Thackeray Rd DIT/AY ME20 ..... 108 C3
Thames Av HOO/HM ME3 .... 33 F2
RHAM ME8 .... 70 B6

Thames Ga DART DA1 .... 23 K4
Thames Rd DART DA1 .... 22 D2
TONN TN10 .... 170 C1
Thames Vw HOO/HM ME3 .... 31 H7
Thames Wy GVE DA12 .... 26 E7
Thamley PUR RM19 .... 12 E4
Thatch Barn Rd HDCN TN27 ..... 180 B8
Thatcher Rd STPH/PW TN12 ..... 198 A2
Thatchers La HOO/HM ME3 ...... 31 G1
The Thatchers MAIDW ME16 ..... 132 B3
Thelma Cl GVE DA12 .... 46 C3
Theobalds HAWK TN18 .... 235 F4
Theodore Cl RTWE/PEM TN2 ..... 190 E7
Theodore Pl GILL ME7 .... 4 C3
Third Av CHAT ME4 .... 68 D5
GILL ME7 .... 5 E5
Third St RRTW TN3 .... 205 J3
Thirlemere Cl MAIDW ME16 ..... 110 D6
Thirlmere Cl GILL ME7 .... 69 H1
STRD ME2 .... 49 H5
Thirlmere Rd STH/RUST TN4 .... 206 C1
Thirza Rd DART DA1 .... 23 J5
Thistlebank WALD ME5 .... 88 B3
Thistledown MAID/BEAR ME14 ... 134 B2
Thistledown Cl GILL ME7 ...... 89 H2
Thistle Rd GVE DA12 .... 28 B6
Thomas Dr GVE DA12 .... 28 A8
Thomas Rd SIT ME10 .... 94 C2
Thomas St ROCH ME1 .... 2 C5
STH/RUST TN4 .... 10 C2
Thompson Cl RHAM ME8 .... 70 D6
Thomson Cl SNOD ME6 .... 85 K5
Thong La BGR/WK TN15 .... 126 E1
GVE DA12 .... 28 D8
Thorn Cl WALD ME5 .... 87 J5
Thorndale Cl WALD ME5 .... 87 J5
Thorndon La CRBK TN17 .... 238 E6
Thorndike Cl CHAT ME4 .... 68 A6
Thorndon Cl STMC/STPC BR5 .... 38 A7
Thorndon Rd STMC/STPC BR5 .... 38 A7
The Thorn Est HDCN TN27 ...... 183 H8
Thornfield Gdns RTWE/PEM TN2 . 208 A1
Thornham Rd RHAM ME8 .... 69 K3
Thornhill Pl MAID/BEAR ME14 .. 7 D1
Thorn Rd STPH/PW TN12 .... 197 F3
Thorn's Meadow BH/WHM TN16 ... 121 J2
Thorold Rd CHAT ME4 .... 4 B5
Thorpe Av TONN TN10 .... 170 C1
Thorpe Wk RHAM ME8 .... 89 K3
Thrale Wy RHAM ME8 .... 90 B2
Three Elm La TONN TN10 .... 149 H8
Three Gates Rd HART DA3 ...... 61 F4
Three Leg Cross Rd WADH TN5 .. 232 B3
Threshers Dr MAID/BEAR ME14 .. 133 K1
The Thrift RDART DA2 .... 43 H1
Thrush Cl WALD ME5 .... 68 C7
Thursland Rd SCUP DA14 .... 39 F3
Thurston Dr STRD ME2 .... 48 C7
Thyssel La RYE TN31 .... 248 E8
Tibbs Court La STPH/PW TN12 .. 193 H7
Ticehurst Cl STMC/STPC BR5 ... 38 B5
Tichborne Cl MAIDW ME16 ...... 110 C8
The Tideway ROCH ME1 .... 67 H6
Tilbury Cl STMC/STPC BR5 ..... 38 C7
Tilbury Gdns TIL RM18 .... 27 H3
Tilbury Rd RHAM ME8 .... 70 D4
Tilden Cl RASHW TN26 .... 219 J7
Tilden Gill Rd TENT TN30 ..... 230 C7
Tilden La STPH/PW TN12 .... 176 C6
Tilden Rd HDCN TN27 .... 180 C4
Tilebarn Cnr TONN TN10 .... 170 E2
Tile Flds RMAID ME17 .... 136 B4
Tile Kiln La BXLY DA5 .... 22 A8
Tile Lodge Rd HDCN TN27 ...... 161 K7
Tilghman Wy SNOD ME6 .... 86 A5
Till Av EYN DA4 .... 59 J3
Tillingbourne Gn
STMC/STPC BR5 .... 56 B1
Tilmans Md DART DA1 .... 59 J4
Tilsden La CRBK TN17 .... 226 A3
Tilton Rd BGR/WK TN15 .... 105 F7
Timber Bank MEO DA13 .... 83 G6
Timberbank WALD ME5 .... 68 B8
Timbertop Rd BH/WHM TN16 ..... 97 G5
Timber Tops WALD ME5 .... 88 E6
Tinker Pot La BGR/WK TN15 .... 80 D8
Tinkerpot Ri BGR/WK TN15 ..... 103 G1
Tinkers La WADH TN5 .... 232 B3
Tintagel Gdns STRD ME2 .... 48 E7
Tintagel Rd STMC/STPC BR5 .... 56 D6
Tintern Rd MAIDW ME16 .... 110 C7
Titchfield Rd MAID/SHEP ME15 . 134 B8
Titsey Hl OXTED RH8 .... 119 F3
WARL CR6 .... 118 D3
Titsey Rd OXTED RH8 .... 119 F6
Tobruk Wy WALD ME5 .... 68 A8
Toby Gdns RTON TN11 .... 150 A6
Toddington Crs WALD ME5 ...... 87 J5
Tolgate La STRD ME2 .... 2 B1
Tolgate Wy MAID/BEAR ME14 .... 134 C1
Tolhurst Rd STPH/PW TN12 ..... 172 C7
Toll GRH DA9 .... 24 B3
Tollgate Ms BGR/WK TN15 ...... 105 G7
Tollgate Pl HDCN TN27 .... 200 C1
Tollgate Rd RDART DA2 .... 24 C6

Tolsey Md BGR/WK TN15 .... 105 G6
Tom Joyce Cl SNOD ME6 .... 85 J7
Tomlin Cl SNOD ME6 .... 85 K6
STPH/PW TN12 .... 198 A2
Tonbridge By-pass RSEV TN14 .. 146 C4
RTON TN11 .... 146 E6
Tonbridge Rd BGR/WK TN15 ..... 126 C4
MAIDW ME16 .... 131 K4
RTON TN11 .... 147 H8
RTWE/PEM TN2 .... 191 H7
SEV TN13 .... 9 E6
WBY/YAL ME18 .... 129 G6
Tonge Rd SIT ME10 .... 94 C2
Tong La STPH/PW TN12 .... 210 E3
Tong Rd STPH/PW TN12 .... 210 E1
Tongswood Dr HAWK TN18 .... 235 J5
Tooley St GVW DA11 .... 26 E6
Top Dartford Rd SWLY BR8 ..... 40 D4
Toplands Av SOCK/AV RM15 ..... 13 F1
Torbay Rd STPH/PW TN12 .... 173 K1
Toronto Rd GILL ME7 .... 5 E4
TIL RM18 .... 27 H1
Torrens Wk GVE DA12 .... 46 B3
Torrington Cl WBY/YAL ME18 ... 129 F6
Tovil Gn MAID/SHEP ME15 ...... 6 B5
Tovil Hl MAID/SHEP ME15 ...... 6 B6
Tovil Rd MAID/SHEP ME15 ...... 6 C5
Tower Cl GVE DA12 .... 46 B3
ORP BR6 .... 56 A6
Tower Cft EYN DA4 .... 59 H6
Tower Gdns MAID/BEAR ME14 .... 134 D3
Tower Hl E/WMAL ME19 .... 107 F7
Tower La MAID/BEAR ME14 ...... 134 C2
Tower Rd DART DA1 .... 23 F6
ORP BR6 .... 56 A6
Towers Wd EYN DA4 .... 59 J6
Tower Vw E/WMAL ME19 .... 129 K2
Town Acres TON TN9 .... 170 C2
Townfield Cnr GVE DA12 .... 27 K7
Town Hl E/WMAL ME19 .... 108 A5
RRTW TN3 .... 221 J2
Town Hill Cl E/WMAL ME19 ..... 108 A5
Townland Cl HDCN TN27 .... 217 K5
Town Rd HOO/HM ME3 .... 31 H9
Townsend Rd SNOD ME6 .... 85 H5
Townshead Cl SCUP DA14 .... 38 C4
Toy's Hl BH/WHM TN16 .... 143 J2
EDEN TN8 .... 143 J7
The Tracies RSIT ME9 .... 72 B8
Tradescant Dr MEO DA13 .... 63 J3
Trafalgar Rd DART DA1 .... 23 H8
GVW DA11 .... 27 H6
ROCH ME1 .... 86 B2
Trafalgar St GILL ME7 .... 4 C3
Tramways CHAT ME4 .... 4 C6
Transfesa Rd STPH/PW TN12 .... 173 J7
Trapfield Cl MAID/BEAR ME14 .. 134 E2
Trapfield La MAID/BEAR ME14 .. 134 E2
Trapham Rd MAIDW ME16 .... 6 A2
Travers Gdns RSIT ME9 .... 115 K1
Travertine Rd WALD ME5 .... 88 C5
Trebble Rd SWCM DA10 .... 25 K5
Trebilco Cl RTWE/PEM TN2 ..... 190 D7
Tredegar Rd RDART DA2 .... 40 D1
Treebourne Rd BH/WHM TN16 .... 97 G4
Tree La BGR/WK TN15 .... 126 E6
Treetops BGR/WK TN15 .... 102 E4
GVE DA12 .... 45 J3
TON TN9 .... 170 B7
Trelawn Crs WALD ME5 .... 88 C4
Trellyn Cl MAIDW ME16 .... 131 K4
Trench Rd TONN TN10 .... 148 B8
Trentham Dr STMC/STPC BR5 .... 56 B1
Trenton Cl MAIDW ME16 .... 110 B7
Trent Rd WALD ME5 .... 88 C1
Trevale Rd ROCH ME1 .... 67 G5
Trevelyan Cl DART DA1 .... 23 J3
Trevereux Hl OXTED RH8 .... 142 A3
Trevino Dr WALD ME5 .... 88 A4
Trevithick Dr DART DA1 .... 23 J3
Trevor Dr MAIDW ME16 .... 132 B1
Trewin Cl DIT/AY ME20 .... 109 H3
Trident Cl STRD ME2 .... 3 E1
Trinity Cl RTWE/PEM TN2 ...... 11 F3
Trinity Gdns DART DA1 .... 23 G5
Trinity Rd GILL ME7 .... 4 C2
GVE DA12 .... 27 K6
Tristan Gdns STH/RUST TN4 .... 206 C2
Trivett Cl GRH DA9 .... 25 F4
Trolling Down Hl RDART DA2 ... 24 A8
Troodos Hl MAID/BEAR ME14 .... 111 F6
Trosley Av GVW DA11 .... 27 J8
Trottiscliffe Rd E/WMAL ME19 . 106 E3
Trotts La BH/WHM TN16 .... 120 C6
Trotwood Cl WALD ME5 .... 88 B6
Troy La EDEN TN8 .... 163 K2
Troys Md RMAID ME17 .... 136 B4
Trubridge Rd HOO/HM ME3 ...... 50 E1
Truro Cl RHAM ME8 .... 70 A3
Truro Rd GVE DA12 .... 46 A4
Truro Wk TONN TN10 .... 170 D1
Trycewell La BGR/WK TN15 ..... 104 D8
Tubbenden La South ORP BR6 ... 75 J1
Tubs Hl SEV TN13 .... 8 C3
Tudeley La RTON TN11 .... 171 H6

TON TN9 .... 170 D7
Tudeley Rd *TON* TN9 .... 170 E7
Tudor Av *MAID/BEAR* ME14 .... 7 E1
Tudor Cl *DART* DA1 .... 22 E5
  GVW DA11 .... 27 F7
Tudor Ct *RTWE/PEM* TN2 .... 10 A6 ▣
  SWLY BR8 .... 57 K4
Tudor Crs *RSEV* TN14 .... 102 A4
Tudor Dr *RSEV* TN14 .... 102 A3
Tudor Gv *HOO/HM* ME3 .... 50 A2
  RHAM ME8 .... 70 B6
Tufa Cl *WALD* ME5 .... 88 C5
Tufnail Rd *DART* DA1 .... 23 J5
Tufton Rd *RHAM* ME8 .... 70 C5
Tufton St *MAID/BEAR* ME14 .... 7 D3
Tulip Tree Cl *TON* TN9 .... 170 A6
Tumblefield Rd *BGR/WK* TN15 .. 82 A6
Tumblers Hl *RMAID* ME17 ...... 157 H7
Tunbury Av *WALD* ME5 .... 88 A3
Tunbury Av South *WALD* ME5 .. 88 A5
Tunnel Rd *RTW* TN1 .... 11 D2
Tunstall Rd *RSIT* ME9 .... 93 H6
Tupman Cl *ROCH* ME1 .... 2 B4
Turgis Cl *RMAID* ME17 .... 157 G2
Turnbull Rd *RDART* DA2 .... 24 D6
Turnden Rd *CRBK* TN17 .... 225 G3
Turner Av *CRBK* TN17 .... 225 K3
Turner Ct *DART* DA1 .... 23 F4
Turner Rd *BH/WHM* TN16 .... 74 B7
  RDART DA2 .... 43 G1
  TONN TN10 .... 170 E1
Turners Av *TENT* TN30 .... 230 B6
Turners Gdns *SEV* TN13 .... 124 A7
Turners Green La *WADH* TN5 .... 220 B8
Turners Green Rd *WADH* TN5 .... 220 B7
Turner's Oak Shaw *HART* DA3 .. 61 K6
Turner St *GILL* ME7 .... 31 C1
Turnpike Dr *ORP* BR6 .... 76 D4
Turnstone Rd *WALD* ME5 .... 88 D4
The Turnstones *GVE* DA12 .... 28 A8
Tuscan Dr *WALD* ME5 .... 88 D5
Tutsham Wy *STPH/PW* TN12 .... 173 H8
Tuxford Rd *STH/RUST* TN4 ...... 206 A1
Tweed Rd *TONN* TN10 .... 170 C1
Twisden Rd *E/WMAL* ME19 ...... 108 D6
Twisleton Ct *DART* DA1 .... 23 G5
Twitton La *RSEV* TN14 .... 101 C3
Twitton Mdw *RSEV* TN14 .... 101 G3
Two Gates Hl *HOO/HM* ME3 .... 48 C3
Twydall Gn *RHAM* ME8 .... 69 J3
Twydall Rd *RHAM* ME8 .... 69 J4
Twyford Cl *RHAM* ME8 .... 70 D4 ▣
Twyford Rd *RTON* TN11 .... 150 A5
Tydeman Rd *MAID/SHEP* ME15 .. 134 B4
Tye La *ORP* BR6 .... 75 H1
Tyland La *MAID/BEAR* ME14 .... 111 F3
Tyler Cl *E/WMAL* ME19 .... 108 D6
Tyler Dr *RHAM* ME8 .... 90 B2
Tylers Green Rd *SWLY* BR8 ...... 57 K3
Tyne Cl *WALD* ME5 .... 88 C1
Tynedale Cl *RDART* DA2 .... 24 C7 ▣
Tyne Rd *TONN* TN10 .... 170 B1
Typhoon Rd *E/WMAL* ME19 ...... 129 H3

U

Uckfield La *EDEN* TN8 .... 185 J1
Ufton Cl *MAID/SHEP* ME15 ...... 134 A5
Ufton La *SIT* ME10 .... 93 K3
Ulcombe Hl *RMAID* ME17 ...... 158 D5
Ulcombe Rd *HDCN* TN27 .... 180 A8
  RMAID ME17 .... 157 J7
Underdown Av *CHAT* ME4 ...... 68 A5 ▣
Underlyn La *STPH/PW* TN12 .... 176 D3
Underriver House Rd *RTON* TN11 .. 147 G3
Underwood Cl *MAID/SHEP* ME15 .. 6 C5 ▣
Unicorn Wy *GRH* DA9 .... 24 E4 ▣
Unicumes La *MAIDW* ME16 ...... 132 C4
Union St *CHAT* ME4 .... 4 A4 ▣
  MAID/BEAR ME14 .... 7 D2
  ROCH ME1 .... 2 C3 ▣
Unity St *SIT* ME10 .... 93 K3
University Wy *DART* DA1 .... 23 G2
Unwin Cl *DIT/AY* ME20 .... 110 A3 ▣
Upbury Wy *CHAT* ME4 .... 4 A4
Upchat Rd *HOO/HM* ME3 .... 49 K2
Updale Rd *SCUP* DA14 .... 38 A2
Uplands *STRD* ME2 .... 48 C8 ▣
Uplands Rd *ORP* BR6 .... 56 C5
Uplands Wy *SEV* TN13 .... 8 B2
Upnor Rd *STRD* ME2 .... 49 J6
Upper Austin Lodge Rd *EYN* DA4 .. 79 C1
Upper Av *MEO* DA13 .... 45 F6
Upper Barn Hl *MAID/SHEP* ME15 .. 153 J3
Upper Britton Pl *GILL* ME7 ...... 4 B3 ▣
Upper Bush Rd *STRD* ME2 ...... 65 J4
Upper Cumberland Wk *RTW* TN1 .. 11 D5
Upper Dr *BH/WHM* TN16 .... 97 C5
Upper Dunstan Rd *STH/RUST* TN4 .. 11 D1
Upper Fant Rd *MAIDW* ME16 .... 132 C4
Upper Field Rd *SIT* ME10 .... 94 C1
Upper Green Rd *RTON* TN11 .... 148 C1

Upper Grosvenor Rd
  STH/RUST TN4 .... 11 D2
Upper Haysden La *STH/RUST* TN4 .. 169 H8
Upper Hunton Hl
  MAID/SHEP ME15 .... 154 A3
Upper Luton Rd *WALD* ME5 .... 4 B5
Upper Ml *WBY/YAL* ME18 ...... 130 B6
Upper Nellington *RRTW* TN3 .... 206 A2
Upper Profit *RRTW* TN3 .... 205 K3
Upper Rd *MAID/SHEP* ME15 .... 7 E5
Upper Spring La *BGR/WK* TN15 .. 126 B1
Upper Stephens *RRTW* TN3 ...... 205 K3
Upper Stone St *MAID/SHEP* ME15 .. 7 D4
Upper St *RMAID* ME17 .... 136 C3
  RMAID ME17 .... 157 H1
Upperton Rd *SCUP* DA14 .... 38 A3
Upton Quarry *RRTW* TN3 ...... 205 J3 ▣
Uptons *HDCN* TN27 .... 180 A8
Uridge Crs *TONN* TN10 .... 170 C2 ▣
Uridge Rd *TONN* TN10 .... 170 C2
Urquhart Cl *WALD* ME5 .... 88 B1 ▣
Usborne Cl *STPH/PW* TN12 ...... 198 A3
Uvedale Rd *OXTED* RH8 .... 118 D8

V

Vale Av *RTW* TN1 .... 10 C4 ▣
  STH/RUST TN4 .... 189 K5
Vale Dr *WALD* ME5 .... 87 J1
Valenciennes Rd *SIT* ME10 ...... 93 K3
Valentine Cl *GILL* ME7 .... 69 H5
Valentine Dr *HOO/HM* ME3 ...... 33 F3
Valentine Rd *MAID/SHEP* ME15 .. 134 A7 ▣
Valerian Cl *WALD* ME5 .... 87 K2
Vale Ri *TON* TN9 .... 170 D5
Vale Rd *DART* DA1 .... 22 E7
  GVW DA11 .... 26 E6
  HAWK TN18 .... 235 F3
  MAID/SHEP ME15 .... 154 C2
  RTW TN1 .... 10 C4
  STH/RUST TN4 .... 189 K5
  TON TN9 .... 170 B5 ▣
  TON TN9 .... 170 D5
Valetta Wy *ROCH* ME1 .... 2 B4
Valiant Rd *WALD* ME5 .... 88 D4
The Vallance *RSIT* ME9 .... 95 H4
Valley Cl *DART* DA1 .... 22 C5
Valley Dr *GVE* DA12 .... 46 A2
  MAID/SHEP ME15 .... 133 F8
  RTON TN11 .... 150 D4
  SEV TN13 .... 9 H3
Valley Forge Cl *TONN* TN10 .... 171 F2
Valley Gdns *GRH* DA9 .... 25 G5
Valley La *BGR/WK* TN15 .... 82 D4
  MEO DA13 .... 83 H4
Valley Ri *WALD* ME5 .... 88 A4
Valley Rd *DART* DA1 .... 22 C5
  GILL ME7 .... 5 E4
  HART DA3 .... 61 G5
  STH/RUST TN4 .... 206 C2
  STMC/STPC BR5 .... 38 C6
The Valley *RMAID* ME17 .... 154 D3
Valley Vw *BH/WHM* TN16 ...... 97 G5
  GRH DA9 .... 25 G5
  STH/RUST TN4 .... 190 A4
Valley View Rd *ROCH* ME1 ...... 67 G5
Vancouver Dr *RHAM* ME8 ...... 69 K5
Vanessa Wk *GVE* DA12 .... 46 C3
Vanessa Wy *BXLY* DA5 .... 40 A1
Vange Cottage Ms *ROCH* ME1 .. 2 B4 ▣
Vanguard Wy *EDEN* TN8 .... 142 A5
  LING RH7 .... 184 A6
  OXTED RH8 .... 118 D4
Vanity La *RMAID* ME17 .... 154 D6
Vanquisher Wk *GVE* DA12 ...... 46 C1
Varnes St *DIT/AY* ME20 .... 86 E8
Vaughan Av *TONN* TN10 .... 148 E8
Vauxhall Cl *GVW* DA11 .... 27 G6
Vauxhall Crs *SNOD* ME6 .... 85 K8
Vauxhall Gdns *SNOD* ME6 ...... 85 K8
Vauxhall La *RTON* TN11 .... 170 D8
  STH/RUST TN4 .... 189 K3
Vauxhall Pl *DART* DA1 .... 23 H6
Veles Rd *SNOD* ME6 .... 85 J6
Venners Cl *BXLYHN* DA7 .... 22 B1
Ventnor Cl *WALD* ME5 .... 88 D4
Vermont Rd *STH/RUST* TN4 .... 206 B2 ▣
Vernon Cl *BGR/WK* TN15 .... 80 E4
  STMC/STPC BR5 .... 38 C8
Vernon Rd *RTW* TN1 .... 11 E1
  SWCM DA10 .... 26 A5
Verona Gdns *GVE* DA12 .... 46 B2
Veryan Ct *STMC/STPC* BR5 ...... 56 D1
Vesper Ct *HDCN* TN27 .... 202 A5
Vestry Rd *RSEV* TN14 .... 102 A6
Vexil Cl *PUR* RM19 .... 13 H4
Via Romana *GVE* DA12 .... 28 E7
Vicarage Cl *DIT/AY* ME20 ...... 109 K3
  HOO/HM ME3 .... 34 D3
  STRD ME2 .... 85 H1
Vicarage Dr *GVW* DA11 .... 26 D5 ▣
Vicarage Hl *BH/WHM* TN16 ...... 120 B5
Vicarage La *GVE* DA12 .... 28 D8

  HOO/HM ME3 .... 51 F2
  MAID/SHEP ME15 .... 132 B7
  RSIT ME9 .... 72 B3
Vicarage Rd *GILL* ME7 .... 4 C3
  SIT ME10 .... 73 J7
  STH/RUST TN4 .... 189 K4
  STRD ME2 .... 2 B1
  STRD ME2 .... 85 H1
  WBY/YAL ME18 .... 152 E5
Vicary Wy *MAIDW* ME16 .... 6 A2
Victoria Cl *RMAID* ME17 .... 159 J7
  WALD ME5 .... 87 J4 ▣
Victoria Dr *EYN* DA4 .... 42 C7
  WBY/YAL ME18 .... 129 H4
Victoria Gdns *BH/WHM* TN16 .... 97 G2
Victoria Hill Rd *SWLY* BR8 ...... 40 C6
Victoria Rd *BFN/LL* DA15 ...... 38 A1
  CHAT ME4 .... 4 B6
  DART DA1 .... 23 G4
  EDEN TN8 .... 144 C6
  GVW DA11 .... 27 G7
  RTON TN11 .... 150 B8
  RTW TN1 .... 11 D3 ▣
  SIT ME10 .... 93 J2
  STH/RUST TN4 .... 189 J5
  WALD ME5 .... 87 K4
Victoria St *DIT/AY* ME20 .... 86 E8
  GILL ME7 .... 5 D2
  MAIDW ME16 .... 6 B3
  ROCH ME1 .... 2 C3
  STRD ME2 .... 2 B1
Victoria Ter *ROCH* ME1 .... 2 A6
Victory Wy *GRH* DA9 .... 24 B3
Vidgeon Av *HOO/HM* ME3 ...... 32 E8
View Cl *BH/WHM* TN16 .... 97 G3
Viewlands Av *BH/WHM* TN16 .... 98 E7
View Rd *HOO/HM* ME3 .... 31 G7
Vigilant Wy *GVE* DA12 .... 46 C3
Vigo Rd *BGR/WK* TN15 .... 82 E7
Viking Av *GVW* DA11 .... 44 D1
Viking Wy *BGR/WK* TN15 .... 80 D1
Villa Cl *GVE* DA12 .... 28 E8
Village Green Av *BH/WHM* TN16 .. 97 J4
Village Green Rd *DART* DA1 ...... 22 D3
Village Green Wy *BH/WHM* TN16 .. 97 J4
Villa Rd *HOO/HM* ME3 .... 48 A3
Vincent Cl *DIT/AY* ME20 .... 87 H7
  SIT ME10 .... 94 D3
Vincent Sq *BH/WHM* TN16 ...... 74 B8
Vine Av *SEV* TN13 .... 9 D3
Vine Court Rd *SEV* TN13 .... 9 E3
The Vineries *GILL* ME7 .... 5 E3
Vine Rd *ORP* BR6 .... 76 A2
Viners Cl *SIT* ME10 .... 93 K5
Vines La *ROCH* ME1 .... 2 C3
  RTON TN11 .... 147 G5
The Vine *SEV* TN13 .... 9 E3
Vine Wk *STPH/PW* TN12 .... 198 A3
Vineyard Crs *RHAM* ME8 .... 70 E5 ▣
Viney's Gdns *TENT* TN30 .... 230 C5
Vinson Cl *ORP* BR6 .... 56 B5
Vinters Rd *MAID/BEAR* ME14 .... 7 E5
Vintners Wy *MAID/BEAR* ME14 .. 134 A2 ▣
Violet Cl *WALD* ME5 .... 88 B6
Virginia Rd *GILL* ME7 .... 4 C1 ▣
Vixen Cl *WALD* ME5 .... 68 C8
Volante Dr *SIT* ME10 .... 73 K7
Volante Wy *GVE* DA12 .... 46 B2
Vulcan Cl *WALD* ME5 .... 68 C7

W

Wade Av *STMC/STPC* BR5 ...... 56 E4
Wadham Pl *SIT* ME10 .... 94 C4
Wadlands Rd *HOO/HM* ME3 .... 31 G1
Waghorn Rd *SNOD* ME6 .... 85 K6 ▣
Waghorn St *CHAT* ME4 .... 4 B6 ▣
Wagoners Cl *MAID/BEAR* ME14 .. 134 A2 ▣
Wagon La *STPH/PW* TN12 ...... 174 A5
Wagtail Wy *STMC/STPC* BR5 .... 56 E1
Waid Cl *DART* DA1 .... 23 J5
Wainscott Rd *STRD* ME2 .... 49 J4
Wainscott Wk *STRD* ME2 .... 49 J3
Wakefield Rd *GRH* DA9 .... 25 H4
Wakehurst Cl *RMAID* ME17 ...... 154 B3 ▣
Wakeley Rd *RHAM* ME8 .... 70 D5
Wakely Cl *BH/WHM* TN16 ...... 97 G5
Wake Rd *ROCH* ME1 .... 67 H6
Waldeck Rd *DART* DA1 .... 23 J6
Waldenhurst Rd *STMC/STPC* BR5 .. 56 E4
Waldens Cl *STMC/STPC* BR5 .... 56 E4
Waldens Rd *STMC/STPC* BR5 .... 57 F3
The Waldens *RMAID* ME17 ...... 158 C4
Walderslade Rd *CHAT* ME4 ...... 68 A7
  WALD ME5 .... 68 A8 ▣
  WALD ME5 .... 88 A3
Walderslade Woods *WALD* ME5 .. 87 J4
Waldron Dr *MAID/SHEP* ME15 .... 133 F8
The Waldrons *OXTED* RH8 ...... 140 D2
Walker Cl *DART* DA1 .... 22 C2
Walkhurst Rd *CRBK* TN17 ...... 227 G7
Walkley Rd *DART* DA1 .... 22 E4
Wallace Cl *RTWE/PEM* TN2 ...... 207 F6

Wallace Gdns SWCM DA10 ...... 25 K5
Wallace Rd ROCH ME1 ...... 67 K6
Wallbridge La RHAM ME8 ...... 71 G3
Wall Cl HOO/HM ME3 ...... 32 E7
Waller Hl CRBK TN17 ...... 215 J1
Wallers RRTW TN3 ...... 188 J7
Wallhouse Rd ERITH DA8 ...... 12 A7
Wallis Av MAID/SHEP ME15 ...... 156 A1
Wallis Cl RDART DA2 ...... 40 D1
The Wall SIT ME10 ...... 93 K1
Walmer Gdns SIT ME10 ...... 93 J1
Walmers Av HOO/HM ME3 ...... 47 K2
Walnut Cl STPH/PW TN12 ...... 173 J8
  WALD ME5 ...... 68 C6
Walnut Hill Rd MEO DA13 ...... 45 F8
Walnuts Rd ORP BR6 ...... 56 B5
Walnut Tree Av DART DA1 ...... 23 H8
  MAID/SHEP ME15 ...... 155 G1
Walnut Tree Cl SIT ME10 ...... 109 F5
Walnut Tree Dr SIT ME10 ...... 93 J2
Walnut Tree La MAID/SHEP ME15 ...... 155 G1
Walnut Tree Wy MEO DA13 ...... 63 H3
Walnut Wy RTWE/PEM TN2 ...... 190 D6
  SWLY BR8 ...... 40 A7
Walpole Cl E/WMAL ME19 ...... 108 D6
Walsham Rd WALD ME5 ...... 88 A5
Walsingham Cl WALD ME8 ...... 88 A6
Walsingham Rd STMC/STPC BR5 ...... 38 C6
Walter Burke Av ROCH ME1 ...... 86 B1
Walter's Farm Rd TON TN9 ...... 170 C5
Walters Green Rd RTON TN11 ...... 187 G8
Walters Rd HOO/HM ME3 ...... 33 F8
Waltham Cl DART DA1 ...... 22 D5
  STMC/STPC BR5 ...... 56 E5
Waltham Rd RHAM ME8 ...... 69 J3
Walton Rd SCUP DA14 ...... 38 C1
  TONN TN10 ...... 149 F8
Wanden La HDCN TN27 ...... 182 B5
Wansbury Wy SWLY BR8 ...... 58 D2
Warblers Cl STRD ME2 ...... 2 A1
Warden Cl MAIDW ME16 ...... 132 C2
Warden Mill Cl WBY/YAL ME18 ...... 130 B7
Warden Rd ROCH ME1 ...... 2 C5
Wardsbrook Rd WADH TN5 ...... 232 B7
Wardwell La RSIT ME9 ...... 72 B4
Ware St MAID/BEAR ME14 ...... 134 C1
Warham Rd RTN4 ...... 101 K3
Waring Cl ORP BR6 ...... 76 A2
Waring Dr ORP BR6 ...... 76 A2
Waring Rd SCUP DA14 ...... 38 D4
Warland Rd BGR/WK TN15 ...... 80 E4
Warlingham Cl RHAM ME8 ...... 70 D5
Warmlake Rd MAID/SHEP ME17 ...... 156 D5
Warner St CHAT ME4 ...... 3 F5
Warnford Gdns
  MAID/SHEP ME15 ...... 133 G6
Warnford Rd ORP BR6 ...... 76 A1
Warren Av ORP BR6 ...... 76 A1
Warren Cl SIT ME10 ...... 94 C4
Warren Ct BGR/WK TN15 ...... 9 E4
Warren Dr ORP BR6 ...... 76 C1
Warren Gdns ORP BR6 ...... 76 B1
Warren La OXTED RH8 ...... 140 E5
  RSIT ME9 ...... 91 F3
Warren Rd DART DA1 ...... 41 H1
  MEO DA13 ...... 44 C3
  MEO DA13 ...... 65 F3
  ORP BR6 ...... 76 A1
  SCUP DA14 ...... 38 D1
Warren Vw GVE DA12 ...... 47 H4
Warren Wood Rd ROCH ME1 ...... 67 J7
Warrington Rd STPH/PW TN12 ...... 173 H8
Warrior Av GVE DA12 ...... 45 K2
Warwick Cl ORP BR6 ...... 56 B7
Warwick Crs ROCH ME1 ...... 66 E4
  SIT ME10 ...... 93 H1
Warwick Gdns MEO DA13 ...... 63 H6
Warwick Pk RTWE/PEM TN2 ...... 11 D6
Warwick Pl GVW DA11 ...... 26 C4
  MAIDW ME16 ...... 6 B3
Warwick Rd RTW TN1 ...... 10 C5
  SCUP DA14 ...... 38 C3
Washneys Rd ORP BR6 ...... 76 B8
Washpond La WARL CR6 ...... 96 A5
Wassall La CRBK TN17 ...... 238 C7
Watchmans Ter WALD ME5 ...... 4 C6
Watercress Dr RSEV TN14 ...... 102 A7
Watercroft Rd RSEV TN14 ...... 77 G5
Waterdales GVW DA11 ...... 26 E7
Waterditch La RMAID ME17 ...... 139 K8
Waterdown Rd STH/RUST TN4 ...... 206 C5
Waterfield RTWE/PEM TN2 ...... 207 F7
Wateringbury Cl STMC/STPC BR5 ...... 38 E8
Wateringbury Rd E/WMAL ME19 ...... 130 D3
Waterlakes EDEN TN8 ...... 164 C6
Water La E/WMAL ME19 ...... 108 A6
  EDEN TN8 ...... 163 H7
  HAWK TN18 ...... 225 G7
  HDCN TN27 ...... 199 J2

HDCN TN27 ...... 201 J4
MAID/BEAR ME14 ...... 135 C1
MAID/SHEP ME15 ...... 153 H8
OXTED RH8 ...... 118 E5
PUR RM19 ...... 12 E4
RMAID ME17 ...... 158 D5
RSEV TN14 ...... 78 C7
SCUP DA14 ...... 39 C1
Waterloo Pl TON TN9 ...... 170 B6
Waterloo Rd CRBK TN17 ...... 225 K1
  GILL ME7 ...... 4 C4
  SIT ME10 ...... 93 J1
  TON TN9 ...... 170 B6
Waterloo St GVE DA12 ...... 27 K6
  MAID/SHEP ME15 ...... 7 D4
Waterlow Rd MAID/BEAR ME14 ...... 7 D1
  MEO DA13 ...... 83 H7
Waterman's La STPH/PW TN12 ...... 193 K3
Watermeadow Cl GILL ME7 ...... 69 G8
Watermill Cl MAIDW ME16 ...... 132 B1
  STRD ME2 ...... 49 H6
Watermint Cl STMC/STPC BR5 ...... 56 E1
Waters Edge MAID/SHEP ME15 ...... 6 C5
Waterside DART DA1 ...... 22 B4
  MAID/BEAR ME14 ...... 6 C2
Waterside La GILL ME7 ...... 5 F1
Waterside Ms WBY/YAL ME18 ...... 130 B8
Water Slippe RTON TN11 ...... 149 K5
Waters Pl GILL ME7 ...... 69 H8
Waterton Av GVE DA12 ...... 28 B6
Watery La BGR/WK TN15 ...... 103 H7
  SCUP DA14 ...... 38 C4
Watkins Cl STPH/PW TN12 ...... 198 A1
Watling Av WALD ME5 ...... 5 D6
Watling Pl SIT ME10 ...... 94 B3
Watling St DART DA1 ...... 24 A6
  GVE DA12 ...... 46 D6
  GVW DA11 ...... 45 J3
  MEO DA13 ...... 44 C1
  STRD ME2 ...... 2 A1
  WALD ME5 ...... 5 D6
Watson Av WALD ME5 ...... 87 J1
Watson's Hl SIT ME10 ...... 93 K1
Watts' Av ROCH ME1 ...... 2 C4
Watts Cl SNOD ME6 ...... 86 A6
Watts Crs PUR TN4 ...... 13 C4
Watt's Cross Rd RTON TN11 ...... 169 F1
Watts' St CHAT ME4 ...... 3 E5
Wat Tyler Wy MAID/SHEP ME15 ...... 7 D4
Waveney Rd TONN TN10 ...... 170 B1
Waverley Cl RMAID ME17 ...... 154 C4
  WALD ME5 ...... 88 E4
Waverley Dr RTWE/PEM TN2 ...... 191 F8
Wayfield Rd WALD ME5 ...... 68 A7
Waylands SWLY BR8 ...... 58 C1
Waylands Cl RSEV TN14 ...... 100 A2
Wayne Cl ORP BR6 ...... 56 A7
Wayside TENT TN30 ...... 230 B4
Wayside Av TENT TN30 ...... 230 B3
Wayside Dr EDEN TN8 ...... 164 D3
Wayville Rd DART DA1 ...... 24 A6
Weald Cl MAID/SHEP ME15 ...... 133 J8
  MEO DA13 ...... 45 F5
  RSEV TN14 ...... 145 K4
Weald Ct RTON TN11 ...... 147 H8
  SIT ME10 ...... 93 J4
Wealden Av TENT TN30 ...... 230 B4
Wealden Cl RTON TN11 ...... 169 J1
Wealden Wy DIT/AY ME20 ...... 109 J6
Weald Rd SEV TN13 ...... 123 K7
Weald Vw STPH/PW TN12 ...... 194 B5
  WADH TN5 ...... 220 B8
Weald View Rd TON TN9 ...... 170 B7
Wealdway BGR/WK TN15 ...... 105 K8
  MEO DA13 ...... 45 J6
  RRTW TN3 ...... 188 B3
  STPH/PW TN12 ...... 151 F4
  WBY/YAL ME18 ...... 127 K4
  WBY/YAL ME18 ...... 150 D1
Weardale Av RDART DA2 ...... 24 B8
Weare Rd STH/RUST TN4 ...... 190 C6
Weatherly Cl ROCH ME1 ...... 2 C4
Weavering Cl STRD ME2 ...... 49 G4
Weavering St MAID/BEAR ME14 ...... 134 A2
Weavers Cl GVW DA11 ...... 27 H7
  STPH/PW TN12 ...... 198 B2
Weavers La RSEV TN14 ...... 102 A8
The Weavers HDCN TN27 ...... 217 K5
  MAIDW ME16 ...... 132 B2
Webb Cl HOO/HM ME3 ...... 32 E8
Webster Rd RHAM ME8 ...... 70 C5
Wedgewood Cl MAIDW ME16 ...... 132 B1
Wedgewood Dr WALD ME5 ...... 68 B7
Wedgwoods BH/WHM TN16 ...... 97 G8
Weeds Wood Rd WALD ME5 ...... 88 A2
Weeks La HDCN TN27 ...... 217 K1
Week St MAID/BEAR ME14 ...... 6 C2
Weird Wd HART DA3 ...... 44 D8
Welbeck Av STH/RUST TN4 ...... 190 C6
Weld Cl STPH/PW TN12 ...... 198 B2
Welland Rd TONN TN10 ...... 170 C1
Well Cl RTON TN11 ...... 168 D5
Wellcome Av DART DA1 ...... 23 H3
Weller Av ROCH ME1 ...... 3 D6

Weller Rd STH/RUST TN4 ...... 206 B2
Wellers Cl BH/WHM TN16 ...... 120 C6
Well Fld HART DA3 ...... 62 A1
Well Hl ORP BR6 ...... 77 J3
Well Hill La ORP BR6 ...... 77 J3
Wellington Cottages HAWK TN18 ...... 234 E2
Wellingtonia Wy EDEN TN8 ...... 164 C4
Wellington Pl MAID/BEAR ME14 ...... 6 C1
Wellington Rd DART DA1 ...... 23 F5
  GILL ME7 ...... 4 C4
  SIT ME10 ...... 93 G1
  STMC/STPC BR5 ...... 56 C3
  TIL RM18 ...... 27 H2
Wellington St GVE DA12 ...... 27 K6
Wellington Wy E/WMAL ME19 ...... 129 H3
Wellmeade Dr SEV TN13 ...... 9 D6
Well Penn Rd HOO/HM ME3 ...... 31 G2
Well Rd MAID/BEAR ME14 ...... 7 D2
  RSEV TN14 ...... 102 A4
Wells Cl RTW TN1 ...... 10 C4
  TENT TN30 ...... 230 A6
  TON TN9 ...... 170 D2
Wells Rd STRD ME2 ...... 66 C1
Well St E/WMAL ME19 ...... 108 C6
  MAID/SHEP ME15 ...... 154 E2
Well Winch Rd SIT ME10 ...... 93 J1
Welton Cl TON TN9 ...... 169 K7
Wemmick Cl ROCH ME1 ...... 67 J7
Wendover Cl STRD ME2 ...... 86 A1
Wendover Wy ORP BR6 ...... 56 B3
Wents Wd MAID/BEAR ME14 ...... 134 B3
Wentworth Cl GVW DA11 ...... 45 H3
  ORP BR6 ...... 75 K1
Wentworth Dr DART DA1 ...... 22 D6
  HOO/HM ME3 ...... 31 G6
  RHAM ME8 ...... 70 B7
  SIT ME10 ...... 93 H1
Wesley Cl MAIDW ME16 ...... 131 K3
  STMC/STPC BR5 ...... 38 D8
Wessex Dr ERITH DA8 ...... 22 B1
Westbourne St SIT ME10 ...... 93 K1
Westbrook Dr STMC/STPC BR5 ...... 56 E5
Westbrooke Cl CHAT ME4 ...... 4 A6
Westbury Ter BH/WHM TN16 ...... 120 C5
Westcott Av GVW DA11 ...... 45 H1
Westcourt St GILL ME7 ...... 5 J1
West Crescent Rd GVE DA12 ...... 27 J5
West Cross TENT TN30 ...... 229 K7
West Cross Gdns TENT TN30 ...... 229 K7
West Dr RMAID ME17 ...... 157 K7
  WALD ME5 ...... 87 J1
Wested La SWLY BR8 ...... 58 C4
West End BGR/WK TN15 ...... 102 D4
  BH/WHM TN16 ...... 121 H4
Westergate Rd STRD ME2 ...... 48 E6
Westerham Cl RHAM ME8 ...... 69 J2
Westerham Hl BH/WHM TN16 ...... 120 B1
Westerham Rd BH/WHM TN16 ...... 121 G4
  HAYES BR2 ...... 74 C2
  OXTED RH8 ...... 118 E5
  RSEV TN14 ...... 122 C2
  SEV TN13 ...... 122 E2
  SIT ME10 ...... 93 H3
Westerhill Rd RMAID ME17 ...... 154 C5
Western Av HAWK TN18 ...... 235 F4
Western Cross Cl GRH DA9 ...... 15 H5
Western Rd BGR/WK TN15 ...... 105 F7
  HAWK TN18 ...... 235 F4
  MAIDW ME16 ...... 132 C3
  RTW TN1 ...... 11 E2
  STH/RUST TN4 ...... 189 K5
  TON TN9 ...... 220 B8
Westfield SEV TN13 ...... 9 E1
Westfield Cl GVE DA12 ...... 45 K4
Westfields HDCN TN27 ...... 183 K5
Westfield Sole Rd
  MAID/BEAR ME14 ...... 88 E6
Westfield Ter CRBK TN17 ...... 225 F5
Westgate Rd DART DA1 ...... 23 G5
Westharold SWLY BR8 ...... 40 A8
West Heath Cl DART DA1 ...... 22 C5
West Heath La SEV TN13 ...... 123 K7
West Heath Rd DART DA1 ...... 22 C5
West Hl DART DA1 ...... 23 G5
  ORP BR6 ...... 74 E7
  OXTED RH8 ...... 140 B1
West Hill Bank OXTED RH8 ...... 140 B1
Westhill Cl GVE DA12 ...... 27 J7
West Hill Dr DART DA1 ...... 23 F5
West Hill Rd DART DA1 ...... 23 G5
West Kent Av GVW DA11 ...... 26 D5
Westlands Av SIT ME10 ...... 93 G2
Westlands Wy OXTED RH8 ...... 118 B6
West La HOO/HM ME3 ...... 21 F8
  SIT ME10 ...... 94 B2
Westmarsh Cl MAID/SHEP ME15 ...... 134 B7
Westmead DIT/AY ME20 ...... 109 G2
West Mill Rd DIT/AY ME20 ...... 109 G2
Westmoreland Dr RSIT ME9 ...... 72 A3
Westmore Rd BH/WHM TN16 ...... 97 G8
Westmorland Cl
  MAID/SHEP ME15 ...... 134 A7
Westmorland Gn
  MAID/SHEP ME15 ...... 134 A7

Westmorland Rd
MAID/SHEP ME15 .... **134** A7
West Motney Wy *RHAM* ME8 .... **70** C3
Westmount Av *CHAT* ME4 .... **3** F5
Weston Av *WTHK* RM20 .... **13** K4
Weston Rd *STRD* ME2 .... **2** A1
West Park Av *STH/RUST* TN4 .... **190** A5
West Park Rd *MAID/SHEP* ME15 .... **7** E5
Westree Rd *MAID* ME16 .... **6** B4
West Rdg *SIT* ME10 .... **93** J4
Westrise *TON* TN9 .... **170** A7
West Rd *CRBK* TN17 .... **212** D6
GILL ME7 .... **4** A1
West Shaw *HART* DA3 .... **43** J7
West St *BGR/WK* TN15 .... **105** F3
E/WMAL ME19 .... **107** K6
GILL ME7 .... **5** D2
GVW DA11 .... **27** H5
MAID/SHEP ME15 .... **153** J6
RMAID ME17 .... **137** C8
RMAID ME17 .... **138** E6
SIT ME10 .... **93** K2
STRD ME2 .... **49** G5
West View Rd *DART* DA1 .... **23** J5
SWLY BR8 .... **58** A3 🔲
West Wk *MAIDW* ME16 .... **132** B3
Westway *RMAID* ME16 .... **154** C3
RTWE/PEM TN2 .... **191** K7
Westways *BH/WHM* TN16 .... **120** C5
EDEN TN8 .... **164** C4
Westwell Cl *STMC/STPC* BR5 .... **56** E5
Westwell Ct *TENT* TN30 .... **229** K7
Westwood Rd *MAID/SHEP* ME15 ... **133** C7
MEO DA13 .... **43** K3
West Wood Rd *RSIT* ME9 .... **90** E7
Westwood Rd *STH/RUST* TN4 .... **206** A1
STPH/PW TN12 .... **151** C8
Wetheral Dr *WALD* ME5 .... **88** C2
Weybridge Cl *WALD* ME5 .... **88** D2
Wey Cl *WALD* ME5 .... **88** D1
Weyhill Cl *MAID/BEAR* ME14 .... **7** F1
Wharfedale Rd *RDART* DA2 .... **24** B7 🔲
Wharf La *HOO/HM* ME3 .... **15** G8
Wharf Rd *GILL* ME7 .... **4** C1 🔲
GVE DA12 .... **28** B5
MAID/SHEP ME15 .... **6** B5
Whatman Cl *MAID/BEAR* ME14 .... **7** F1 🔲
Wheatcroft Cl *SIT* ME10 .... **94** C2
Wheatcroft Gv *RHAM* ME8 .... **70** C7
Wheatear Wy *WALD* ME5 .... **68** C7 🔲
Wheatfield *E/WMAL* ME19 .... **108** C5
Wheatfield Cl *CRBK* TN17 .... **225** J1
Wheatfield Dr *CRBK* TN17 .... **225** J1
Wheatfield Lea *CRBK* TN17 .... **225** J1
Wheatfields *MAID/BEAR* ME14 ... **133** K2 🔲
WALD ME5 .... **88** C4
Wheatfield Wy *CRBK* TN17 .... **225** J1
Wheatley Cl *GRH* DA9 .... **25** F4 🔲
Wheatsheaf Cl *MAID/SHEP* ME15 .. **133** H6
RSEV TN14 .... **77** C3
Wheatsheaf Hl *RSEV* TN14 .... **77** C3
RSEV TN14 .... **144** B2
Wheatsheaf Wy *TONN* TN10 .... **148** D8
Wheeler Av *OXTED* RH8 .... **118** B8
Wheeler's La *RMAID* ME17 .... **154** D6
The Wheelers *RHAM* ME8 .... **69** J8
Wheeler St *HDCN* TN27 .... **200** B1
MAID/BEAR ME14 .... **7** D2 🔲
Whetsted Rd *STPH/PW* TN12 .... **172** E6
Whiffen's Av *CHAT* ME4 .... **3** F3
Whiffen's Avenue W *CHAT* ME4 ...... **3** F3 🔲
Whimbrel Av *DIT/AY* ME20 .... **108** C4
The Whimbrels *CHAT* ME4 .... **50** C5 🔲
Whinfell Wy *GVE* DA12 .... **46** C2
Whippendell Cl *STMC/STPC* BR5 ..... **38** B6
Whippendell Wy *STMC/STPC* BR5 .. **38** C5
Whistler Rd *TONN* TN10 .... **148** D7
Whitby Cl *BH/WHM* TN16 .... **97** F6
GRH DA9 .... **25** F4
Whitchurch Cl *MAIDW* ME16 .... **6** B3
Whitcombe Cl *WALD* ME5 .... **88** D4
White Av *GVW* DA11 .... **45** C1
Whitebeam Dr *RMAID* ME17 .... **154** B3
White Bear Pas *STH/RUST* TN4 ..... **10** C5 🔲
Whitebine Gdns *STPH/PW* TN12 ... **151** J8
Whitebread La *RYE* TN31 .... **245** C6
White Cottage Rd *TONN* TN10 ...... **148** C8
Whitecroft *SWLY* BR8 .... **40** B7 🔲
Whitefield Cl *STMC/STPC* BR5 .... **38** D8 🔲
Whitefield Rd *STH/RUST* TN4 .... **10** C1
White Friars *SEV* TN13 .... **8** C6
Whitegate Cl *RMAID* ME17 .... **189** K6
Whitegates Av *BGR/WK* TN15 .... **80** D2 🔲
Whitehall Dr *RMAID* ME17 .... **158** B3
Whitehall La *ERITH* DA8 .... **22** C1
Whitehall Rd *MAID/BEAR* ME14 .... **113** J8 🔲
SIT ME10 .... **93** K4
White Hart Cl *SEV* TN13 .... **124** A7
White Hart Rd *ORP* BR6 .... **56** B4
White Hart Wd *SEV* TN13 .... **124** A8
Whitehead La *RDART* DA2 .... **41** F1
Whiteheads La *MAID/BEAR* ME14 .. **134** D2
Whitehill *BGR/WK* TN15 .... **105** H3
Whitehill La *GVE* DA12 .... **46** A1
Whitehill Pde *GVE* DA12 .... **45** K1
White Hill Rd *MAID/BEAR* ME14 ..... **90** A5

Whitehill Rd *DART* DA1 .... **22** D4
GVE DA12 .... **27** K8
HART DA3 .... **43** J7
MEO DA13 .... **43** J5
MEO DA13 .... **63** J7
Whitehorse Hl *WALD* ME5 .... **4** B5 🔲
White Horse La *MAID/SHEP* ME15 . **134** C7
White Horse Rd *MEO* DA13 .... **84** A5
Whitehouse Cl *HOO/HM* ME3 .... **51** F2 🔲
Whitehouse Crs *ROCH* ME1 .... **87** F6
White House Rd *RSEV* TN14 .... **145** H1
Whitelake Rd *TONN* TN10 .... **170** C1
White La *BH/WHM* TN16 .... **119** F2
Whiteleaves Ri *STRD* ME2 .... **66** A4
White Lodge Cl *SEV* TN13 .... **9** D2
White Oak Cl *TON* TN9 .... **170** B7 🔲
White Post Hl *EYN* DA4 .... **59** K4
White Post La *MEO* DA13 .... **63** J1
Whitepost La *MAID* DA13 .... **83** G4
White Rd *CHAT* ME4 .... **68** B5
White Rock Ct *MAIDW* ME16 .... **6** B4 🔲
White Rock Pl *MAIDW* ME16 .... **6** B4
Whites Cl *GRH* DA9 .... **25** H5
White's La *HAWK* TN18 .... **235** H4
Whitewall Rd *STRD* ME2 .... **49** J6
Whitewall Wy *STRD* ME2 .... **3** J1
Whitewebbs Wy *STMC/STPC* BR5 ... **38** A6
Whitewood Cottages
BH/WHM TN16 .... **97** G7
Whitmore St *MAIDW* ME16 .... **132** C4
Whitney Wk *SCUP* DA14 .... **39** F4
Whybourne Crest *RTWE/PEM* TN2 . **11** F6
Whyman Av *CHAT* ME4 .... **68** B5
Wichling Cl *STMC/STPC* BR5 .... **56** E5 🔲
Wickenden Rd *SEV* TN13 .... **9** E1
Wickham Cl *RSIT* ME9 .... **72** A8
Wickham Gdns *STH/RUST* TN4 ..... **206** C1
Wickham St *ROCH* ME1 .... **3** D5
Wickhams Wy *HART* DA3 .... **62** A3 🔲
Wickhurst Rd *RSEV* TN14 .... **145** H3
Wicksteed Cl *BXLY* DA5 .... **40** A1
Widbury Cl *RRTW* TN3 .... **205** J3 🔲
Widgeon Rd *STRD* ME2 .... **48** C8
Wierton Hl *RMAID* ME17 .... **155** K7
Wierton La *RMAID* ME17 .... **156** A4
Wierton Rd *RMAID* ME17 .... **156** A5
Wigmore Rd *RHAM* ME8 .... **89** J1
Wihtred Rd *RSIT* ME9 .... **94** E4
Wilberforce Rd *RMAID* ME17 .... **154** D3
Wilberforce Wy *GVE* DA12 .... **46** A3
Wilde Cl *TIL* RM18 .... **27** J1
Wilderness Av *BGR/WK* TN15 ...... **124** D1
Wilderness Mt *SEV* TN13 .... **9** F1
Wilderness Gdns *RYE* TN31 .... **244** D7
Wilderness Rd *OXTED* RH8 .... **140** C1
Wildfell Cl *MAID/BEAR* ME14 .... **88** D6
Wildman Cl *RHAM* ME8 .... **90** A3
Wildwood Cl *RMAID* ME17 .... **158** C4
Wildwood Gld *GILL* ME7 .... **89** H1
Wilfred St *GVE* DA12 .... **27** J5 🔲🔲
Wilks Av *DART* DA1 .... **23** J8
Wilks Cl *RHAM* ME8 .... **70** E4
Will Adams Wy *GILL* ME7 .... **69** G5
Willelsey Gdns *CRBK* TN17 .... **214** E8 🔲
William Judge Cl *TENT* TN30 .... **230** D7
William Luck Cl *STPH/PW* TN12 .... **151** C8 🔲
William Rd *STRD* ME2 .... **66** B4 🔲
William St *GVE* DA12 .... **27** J6
RHAM ME8 .... **70** D4
SIT ME10 .... **93** K3
STH/RUST TN4 .... **10** C2
Willington Gn *MAID/SHEP* ME15 ... **134** A7
Willington St *MAID/SHEP* ME15 ... **134** A7
SWLY BR8 .... **58** C1
Willow Av *HOO/HM* ME3 .... **51** F6 🔲
Willowbank Dr *HOO/HM* ME3 .... **33** F2
Willowby Gdns *RHAM* ME8 .... **90** B2
Willow Cl *STMC/STPC* BR5 .... **56** C5
Willow Crs *STPH/PW* TN12 .... **172** C7
STPH/PW TN12 .... **198** B1
Willow La *STPH/PW* TN12 .... **174** C6
Willow Lea *TONN* TN10 .... **148** C7
Willowmead *DIT/AY* ME20 .... **108** C4
Willow Pk *RSEV* TN14 .... **101** H4
Willow Rd *MAID/SHEP* ME15 .... **134** B5
Willow Rd *DART* DA1 .... **23** F7
DIT/AY ME20 .... **108** D3
STRD ME2 .... **48** D8
Willowside *SNOD* ME6 .... **85** K5
The Willows *RHAM* ME8 .... **70** B4
RSIT ME9 .... **72** A8
Willow Tree Rd *RTWE/PEM* TN2 ... **10** A6
Willow Wk *MEO* DA13 .... **83** G3
RTWE/PEM TN2 .... **190** E6
Willow Wy *MAID/SHEP* ME15 .... **7** E3
Willow Wents *WBY/AY.ME18*........ **128** C5
Willow Wood Rd *MEO* DA13 .... **83** G4
Wilman Rd *STH/RUST* TN4 .... **190** A7
Wilmar Wy *BGR/WK* TN15 .... **102** D7
Wilmington Av *ORP* BR6 .... **56** D6
Wilmington Court Rd *RDART* DA2 .. **40** D1
Wilmington Wy *RHAM* ME8 .... **69** J4
Wilmot Rd *DART* DA1 .... **22** E4
Wilson Av *ROCH* ME1 .... **67** J5

Wilson Cl *MAID/SHEP* ME15 .... **134** A7
RTON TN11 .... **169** J1
Wilson La *EYN* DA4 .... **42** E7
Wilson Rd *TONN* TN10 .... **170** E1
Wilsons La *MAID/SHEP* ME15 ...... **154** A2
Wilsons Wy *MEO* DA13 .... **83** G3
Wilton Dr *DIT/AY* ME20 .... **109** F6
Wiltshire Cl *RDART* DA2 .... **24** C6
WALD ME5 .... **68** D6
Wiltshire Rd *ORP* BR6 .... **56** B4
Wiltshire Wy *MAID/SHEP* ME15 .. **134** A7 🔲
RTWE/PEM TN2 .... **190** D7
Wimborne Av *STMC/STPC* BR5 ..... **38** A8
Wimbourne Dr *RHAM* ME8 .... **70** A8
Winch Cl *CRBK* TN17 .... **225** K3
Winchelsea Rd *WALD* ME5 .... **88** C1
Winchester Av *WALD* ME5 .... **88** A2
Winchester Crs *GVE* DA12 .... **46** A1
Winchester Rd *HAWK* TN18 .... **235** G4
ORP BR6 .... **56** D8
TONN TN10 .... **170** D2
Winchester Wy *RHAM* ME8 .... **70** D5
Winch's Garth *STPH/PW* TN12 ..... **198** B1 🔲
Wincliff Rd *TON* TN9 .... **170** B6
Windermere Cl *DART* DA1 .... **22** E7
Windermere Dr *RHAM* ME8 .... **70** A7
Windermere Gv *SIT* ME10 .... **93** J3
Windhover Wy *GVE* DA12 .... **46** B2
Windmill Cl *STRD* ME2 .... **49** G5
Windmill Ct *RMAID* ME17 .... **155** H3 🔲
Windmill Hts *MAID/BEAR* ME14 ... **134** D2
Windmill Hl *BGR/WK* TN15 .... **106** A7
RMAID ME17 .... **159** F6
STPH/PW TN12 .... **193** K5
Windmill La *BGR/WK* TN15 .... **106** A6
WADH TN5 .... **220** E6
Windmill La East *E/WMAL* ME19 ... **107** K8
Windmill La West *E/WMAL* ME19 .. **107** J8
Windmill Pk *BGR/WK* TN15 .... **105** K7
Windmill Rd *GILL* ME7 .... **4** C5 🔲
SEV TN13 .... **145** K1
SIT ME10 .... **73** J8
Windmill St *GVE* DA12 .... **27** J6
RTWE/PEM TN2 .... **11** F4 🔲
STRD ME2 .... **49** G5
Windsor Av *CHAT* ME4 .... **3** F6
Windsor Cl *MAID/BEAR* ME14 .... **7** E1
ORP BR6 .... **76** B2
SIT ME10 .... **93** J4
Windsor Rd *GILL* ME7 .... **5** D3
GVE DA12 .... **45** J2
Windward Rd *ROCH* ME1 .... **67** H5
Windyridge *GILL* ME7 .... **69** F5
Winfield La *BGR/WK* TN15 .... **126** E4
Winford Ms *ROCH* ME1 .... **2** A6
Wingate Rd *SCUP* DA14 .... **38** D3
Wingfield Rd *GVW* DA11 .... **27** J6
Wingham Cl *MAID/SHEP* ME15 ..... **134** B7
RHAM ME8 .... **69** K3
Wingrove Dr *MAID/BEAR* ME14 .... **134** A1
STRD ME2 .... **2** C1
Winifred Rd *DART* DA1 .... **22** E4
MAID/SHEP ME15 .... **134** B5
Winnipeg Dr *ORP* BR6 .... **76** A2
Winser Rd *CRBK* TN17 .... **238** E5
Winston Cl *GRH* DA9 .... **24** E5
Winston Dr *STRD* ME2 .... **49** J4
Winstone Scott Av *RRTW* TN3 ... **205** H2 🔲
Winston Rd *STRD* ME2 .... **66** C1
Winterfield La *E/WMAL* ME19 ...... **108** C6
Wireless Rd *BH/WHM* TN16 .... **97** H2
The Wirrals *WALD* ME5 .... **88** B2
Wisecarre *RRTW* TN3 .... **221** J3
Wise's La *BGR/WK* TN15 .... **81** K5 🔲
RSIT ME9 .... **93** F3
Wisley Rd *STMC/STPC* BR5 .... **38** B5
Wisteria Gdns *SWLY* BR8 .... **40** A7
Witches La *SEV* TN13 .... **123** F2
Witham Wy *STRD* ME2 .... **48** E7
Withens Cl *STMC/STPC* BR5 .... **56** D1 🔲
Withyham Rd *RRTW* TN3 .... **204** D8
Wittersham Rd *CRBK* TN17 .... **246** C2
TENT TN30 .... **247** C1
Wivenhoe Cl *RHAM* ME8 .... **70** D4
Wodehouse Cl *DIT/AY* ME20 ...... **108** D2 🔲
Wodehouse Rd *DART* DA1 .... **23** K3
Wolfe Rd *MAIDW* ME16 .... **132** B4
Wolf's Hl *OXTED* RH8 .... **140** E2
Wolf's Rd *OXTED* RH8 .... **141** F1
Wolfs Wd *OXTED* RH8 .... **140** E3
Wollaston Cl *RHAM* ME8 .... **90** A3
Wolseley Rd *STH/RUST* TN4 .... **190** C1
Wolsey Ms *ORP* BR6 .... **76** A1
Wolsley Cl *DART* DA1 .... **22** B4
Wombwell Gdns *GVW* DA11 .... **26** E8
Wood Av *PUR* RM19 .... **13** C4
Woodberry Dr *SIT* ME10 .... **94** C3
Woodberry Gv *BXLY* DA5 .... **40** A1
Woodbridge Dr *MAID/SHEP* ME15 ... **6** B6
Woodbury Cl *BH/WHM* TN16 .... **97** K5
Woodbury La *TENT* TN30 .... **230** A7
Woodbury Park Gdns
STH/RUST TN4 .... **11** D2

Index - featured places

Arden Business Centre
STRD ME2 .... **3** E1
Arden Business Park
STRD ME2 .... **3** D1
Arden Junior School
GILL ME7 .... **5** D1
The Artisan Gallery
GRH DA9 .... **24** E6
Ascot Hever Golf Club
EDEN TN8 .... **165** K5
Ashford Borough Council
TENT TN30 .... **230** B6
The Ashworth Practice
ORP BR6 .... **56** C4
Assembly Hall Theatre
RTWE/PEM TN2 .... **11** D4
Astor of Hever School
MAIDW ME16 .... **132** C3
The Atman Clinic
STH/RUST TN4 .... **10** C1
Aveley Primary School
SOCK/AV RM15 .... **13** J1
Avenue Theatre
SIT ME10 .... **94** A3
Avicenna Medical Centre
E/WMAL ME19 .... **108** C4
Axton Chase School
HART DA3 .... **44** A8
Aylesford CP School
DIT/AY ME20 .... **109** H5
Aylesford St Marks
C of E Primary School
DIT/AY ME20 .... **86** E8
Aylesford St Peters
C of E Primary School
DIT/AY ME20 .... **110** A3
Aylesford Secondary School
DIT/AY ME20 .... **109** H5
Bad Apple Theatre Co
RTW TN1 .... **11** E3
Balfour CP Infant School
CHAT ME4 .... **67** K5
Balfour Junior School
CHAT ME4 .... **3** E6
Ballard Business Park
STRD ME2 .... **66** E1
Ballater Surgery
ORP BR6 .... **56** A4
Balmoral Clinic
GILL ME7 .... **4** C3
The Bank Street Gallery
BGR/WK TN15 .... **9** E4
Bapchild & Tonge
C of E Primary School
SIT ME10 .... **94** E3
Barming CP School
MAIDW ME16 .... **131** K4
Barnes Cray Primary School
DART DA1 .... **22** D3
Barnsole CP Infant School
GILL ME7 .... **5** E4
Barnsole Junior School
GILL ME7 .... **5** E4
Barrow Grove CP School
SIT ME10 .... **93** J2
The Barry School
STH/RUST TN4 .... **10** C1
Beacon Hill Industrial Estate
PUR RM19 .... **13** F4
Bean Primary School
RDART DA2 .... **43** H2
Bearsted CP School
MAID/BEAR ME14 .... **134** D1
Bearsted Green Business Centre
MAID/BEAR ME14 .... **134** E1
Bedensfield Clinic
SCUP DA14 .... **39** F3
Bedgebury Junior School
CRBK TN17 .... **223** J5
Beechcroft Farm
Industrial Estate
BGR/WK TN15 .... **61** J7
Beechings Industrial Centre
RHAM ME8 .... **69** H2
Bell Shopping Centre
SIT ME10 .... **94** A2
Bell Wood CP Infant School
MAID/SHEP ME15 .... **156** A1
Bellwood CP Junior School
MAID/SHEP ME15 .... **156** A1
Benenden C of E Primary School
CRBK TN17 .... **227** F8

Benenden Girls School
CRBK TN17 .... **227** F6
Benenden Hospital
CRBK TN17 .... **228** A3
Benenden School
CRBK TN17 .... **226** E6
Bennett Memorial
Diocesan School
STH/RUST TN4 .... **10** A1
Bentley Street Industrial Estate
GVE DA12 .... **27** K5
Bethany School
CRBK TN17 .... **213** G1
Bexley Hospital
BXLY DA5 .... **22** B8
Bidborough Primary School
STH/RUST TN4 .... **189** H3
Biddenden Club House
HDCN TN27 .... **217** K5
Biggin Hill Business Park
BH/WHM TN16 .... **97** H2
Biggin Hill Junior School
BH/WHM TN16 .... **97** J3
Birchwood County
Primary School
SWLY BR8 .... **40** A6
Birkbeck Primary School
SCUP DA14 .... **38** C1
Bishops Down CP School
STH/RUST TN4 .... **10** A2
Blacklands County Junior School
E/WMAL ME19 .... **108** D7
Black Lion Leisure Centre
GILL ME7 .... **4** B2
Blackthorn Medical Centre
MAIDW ME16 .... **132** A3
Blenheim Junior & Infant School
ORP BR6 .... **56** D6
Bligh Way CP School
STRD ME2 .... **48** B7
Blubery House Cranbrook School
CRBK TN17 .... **225** K1
Bobbing CP School
RSIT ME9 .... **73** G7
Bodiam Castle (NT)
RBTBR TN32 .... **243** G6
Bodiam Manor School
RBTBR TN32 .... **243** F6
Bodiam Primary School
RBTBR TN32 .... **243** F6
Borden C of E Primary School
RSIT ME9 .... **92** E3
Borden Grammar School
SIT ME10 .... **94** A3
Borough Green Medical Centre
BGR/WK TN15 .... **105** F7
Borough Green Primary School
BGR/WK TN15 .... **105** G7
Borstal Manor County
Junior School
ROCH ME1 .... **66** E4
Borstal Village Surgery
ROCH ME1 .... **66** E4
Bough Beech Sailing Club
EDEN TN8 .... **166** D2
Boughton Monchelsea
County Primary School
RMAID ME17 .... **155** H4
Bower Grove School
MAIDW ME16 .... **132** B4
The Bower Mount Clinic
MAIDW ME16 .... **6** A3
Bowes Industrial Centre
MEO DA13 .... **63** G8
Bowls Centre
MAID/BEAR ME14 .... **7** D3
Boxmend Industrial Estate
RMAID ME17 .... **156** B3
Boyd Business Centre
STRD ME2 .... **3** D1
Bradbourne School
RSEV TN14 .... **101** J8
Bradfields School
WALD ME5 .... **68** B8
Braeside Surgery
EYN DA4 .... **59** K4
Branbridges Industrial Estate
STPH/PW TN12 .... **173** J1
Brasted Surgery
BH/WHM TN16 .... **121** J4
Brattle Farm Museum
STPH/PW TN12 .... **197** K5

Bredgar C of E Primary School
RSIT ME9 .... **116** A1
Bredhurst C of E School
GILL ME7 .... **89** J5
Brenchley & Matfield
C of E Primary School
STPH/PW TN12 .... **193** J6
Brent CP School
RDART DA2 .... **24** B6
Bridge Industrial Centre
MAIDW ME16 .... **6** B5
Brittania Business Park
DIT/AY ME20 .... **109** J6
Broadwater CP School
RTWE/PEM TN2 .... **206** E6
Broadway Shopping Centre
MAIDW ME16 .... **6** C3
Bromley Hospitals N H S Trust
ORP BR6 .... **56** A8
Bromley Museum
ORP BR6 .... **56** C4
Brompton Medical Centre
GILL ME7 .... **4** A2
Brompton Westbrook CP School
GILL ME7 .... **4** A3
Brookfield County Infant School
DIT/AY ME20 .... **108** E4
Brookfield CP Junior School
DIT/AY ME20 .... **108** D4
Brookhurst Surgery
ORP BR6 .... **56** B6
The Brook Theatre Arts &
Entertainment Ltd
CHAT ME4 .... **3** F3
Broomhill Bank School
RRTW TN3 .... **189** G8
Brunswick House Clinic
MAIDW ME16 .... **6** B2
Brunswick House CP School
MAIDW ME16 .... **6** B2
Bryony School
RHAM ME8 .... **69** K7
Bryony School
RHAM ME8 .... **90** C1
Burnham Trading Estate
DART DA1 .... **23** G3
Burrswood Medical Centre
RRTW TN3 .... **204** D6
Burwood School
ORP BR6 .... **56** E6
Business Centre
WBY/YAL ME18 .... **131** F6
The Butts County Infants School
SIT ME10 .... **73** K8
Byron CP School
GILL ME7 .... **5** D5
Byron House Surgery
GILL ME7 .... **4** C5
Cage Green County
Primary School
TONN TN10 .... **170** D1
Canal Industrial Park
GVE DA12 .... **28** A5
Cannock House School
ORP BR6 .... **77** G1
Canterbury Road CP School
SIT ME10 .... **94** C3
Capel CP School
RTON TN11 .... **172** B7
Cascades Leisure Centre
GVE DA12 .... **46** D2
Castle View Business Centre
ROCH ME1 .... **3** D2
Cecil Road County Primary School
GVW DA11 .... **27** G7
The Cedans School
ROCH ME1 .... **2** C4
Central Business Park
STRD ME2 .... **3** E1
Central Theatre
CHAT ME4 .... **3** F4
Chalklin Business Park
RTWE/PEM TN2 .... **190** E6
Chantry Medical Practice
SEV TN13 .... **9** D4
Chapter School
STRD ME2 .... **48** C7
Charles Darwin School
BH/WHM TN16 .... **97** K2
Chart Hills Golf Club
HDCN TN27 .... **200** E8

Chatham Grammar
School for Boys
CHAT ME4 .... 68 A5
Chatham Grammar
School for Girls
WALD ME5 .... 4 C6
Chatham South School
CHAT ME4 .... 68 A6
Chaucer Business Park
BGR/WK TN15 .... 103 H6
Chelsfield Park Hospital
ORP BR6 .... 77 G1
Chelsfield Primary School
ORP BR6 .... 77 F1
Chequers Shopping Centre
MAID/BEAR ME14 .... 7 D3
Chevening Primary School
RSEV TN14 .... 122 D1
Chiddingstone C of E School
EDEN TN8 .... 166 E7
Child Health Centre
STRD ME2 .... 48 D8
Chinese Medical Centre
DART DA1 .... 23 H5
Church House Surgery
TON TN9 .... 170 C4
Churchill Business Park
BH/WHM TN16 .... 120 D5
Churchill Clinic
WALD ME5 .... 68 B7
Churchill Gallery
BH/WHM TN16 .... 120 C6
Churchill School
BH/WHM TN16 .... 120 C4
Cinema
MAID/SHEP ME15 .... 7 D3
Civic Centre
DART DA1 .... 23 H5
Civic Centre
GVW DA11 .... 27 J6
Clanricarde Medical Centre
RTW TN1 .... 10 C4
Claremont CP School
RTWE/PEM TN2 .... 11 D5
Clearways Industrial Estate
BGR/WK TN15 .... 80 D3
Cleeve Park School
SCUP DA14 .... 38 D1
Cliffe Woods County
Primary School
HOO/HM ME3 .... 31 H6
Cliffe Woods Surgery
HOO/HM ME3 .... 31 G6
The Clinic
GVE DA12 .... 45 K1
Clock House Gallery
TON TN9 .... 170 C3
The Club House
MAID/BEAR ME14 .... 7 E2
Cobham CP School
GVE DA12 .... 64 D1
Cobtree Medical Centre
RMAID ME17 .... 157 F6
Colebrook Industrial Estate
RTWE/PEM TN2 .... 190 E5
Colebrook Industrial Estate
RTWE/PEM TN2 .... 191 F5
College
SIT ME10 .... 93 H3
The College Practice
MAID/SHEP ME15 .... 6 C4
Colliers Green Primary School
CRBK TN17 .... 214 A4
Collingwood Industrial Estate
RMAID ME17 .... 157 G4
Combe Bank School
RSEV TN14 .... 122 A2
Compass Centre
CHAT ME4 .... 50 C6
The Computer Surgery
MAIDW ME16 .... 110 C7
Connections Business Park
RSEV TN14 .... 101 K7
Conquest Industrial Estate
STRD ME2 .... 66 E1
Copperfields Shopping Centre
DART DA1 .... 23 H5
Corinthian Sports Club
HART DA3 .... 61 J3
Cornwallis School
MAID/SHEP ME15 .... 155 F3
Cottage Industrial Estate
DIT/AY ME20 .... 110 B4

Council Offices
CRBK TN17 .... 225 J1
Council Offices
SEV TN13 .... 9 D4
County Hall
MAID/BEAR ME14 .... 7 D2
County Primary Infant School
RHAM ME8 .... 70 B6
Court View Surgery
STRD ME2 .... 48 E7
Coxheath CP School
RMAID ME17 .... 154 C3
Cranbrook Clinic
CRBK TN17 .... 225 K1
Cranbrook Golf Club
CRBK TN17 .... 227 F2
Cranbrook Primary School
CRBK TN17 .... 214 E8
Cranbrook Rugby Football Club
CRBK TN17 .... 214 E8
Cranbrook School
CRBK TN17 .... 225 K1
The Crane Surgery
CRBK TN17 .... 225 K1
Crayfield Industrial Park
STMC/STPC BR5 .... 38 D7
Crayfields Business Park
STMC/STPC BR5 .... 56 D7
Crayford Industrial Estate
DART DA1 .... 22 C4
Crayford Leisure Centre &
Greyhound Stadium
DART DA1 .... 22 B5
Crayford Medical Centre
DART DA1 .... 22 C4
Crayside Industrial Estate
DART DA1 .... 22 D2
Crayside Industrial Estate
DART DA1 .... 22 E2
Crescent Surgery
STMC/STPC BR5 .... 56 C1
Crest Industrial Estate
STPH/PW TN12 .... 176 C8
Crockenhill CP School
SWLY BR8 .... 57 K3
Crockham Hill
C of E Primary School
EDEN TN8 .... 142 C4
Crosshall Surgery
STMC/STPC BR5 .... 56 D1
Crowden House
Cranbrook School
CRBK TN17 .... 226 A1
Crown & County Courts
MAIDW ME16 .... 6 C4
Crown Court Clinic
ROCH ME1 .... 3 D3
Cudham School
BH/WHM TN16 .... 98 A3
Culverstone Gm Primary School
MEO DA13 .... 83 F3
Cuxton County Infant School
STRD ME2 .... 66 A4
Cuxton CP Junior School
STRD ME2 .... 66 A4
Cuxton Industrial Estate
STRD ME2 .... 66 B4
Cygnet Leisure Centre
GVW DA11 .... 27 F8
Dajen Business Park
CHAT ME4 .... 68 D5
Dale Hill Hotel & Golf Club
WADH TN5 .... 232 H3
Danecourt School
RHAM ME8 .... 69 H4
Darenth CP School
RDART DA2 .... 42 C4
Dartford Borough Council
DART DA1 .... 23 G7
Dartford County Court
DART DA1 .... 23 H5
Dartford FC
EYN DA4 .... 41 K6
Dartford FC
RDART DA2 .... 24 A7
Dartford Golf Club
DART DA1 .... 22 E8
Dartford Grammar School
DART DA1 .... 23 F5
Dartford Grammar
School for Girls
DART DA1 .... 23 F6

Dartford Hospital School
HART DA3 .... 44 B8
Dartford Magistrates Court
DART DA1 .... 23 G5
Dartford Natural Health Centre
DART DA1 .... 23 H6
Dartford West Boys School
DART DA1 .... 23 G6
Dartford West Health Centre
DART DA1 .... 23 F5
Dartford West High
School for Girls
DART DA1 .... 23 F6
Deacon Industrial Estate
DIT/AY ME20 .... 110 A4
Deacon Trading Centre
STRD ME2 .... 2 A3
Delce Junior School
ROCH ME1 .... 2 C6
Detling C of E Primary School
MAID/BEAR ME14 .... 112 C5
Ditton C of E Junior School
DIT/AY ME20 .... 109 G5
Ditton Infant School
DIT/AY ME20 .... 109 G5
Dolphin Yard Sailing Barge
Museum
SIT ME10 .... 94 B1
Dorton College of Further
Education
BGR/WK TN15 .... 124 C1
Douglas Moat Practice
STH/RUST TN4 .... 10 C5
Dover Road Primary School
GVW DA11 .... 27 F7
Downe Primary School
ORP BR6 .... 75 F6
Down Ho
ORP BR6 .... 75 F7
Downsview Junior School
SWLY BR8 .... 40 D8
Downs Way School
OXTED RH8 .... 118 C5
Dr Ali Surgery
CHAT ME4 .... 3 F4
Dulwich College
Preparatory School
CRBK TN17 .... 226 C2
Dunton Green County
Primary School
SEV TN13 .... 101 G7
East Borough CP School
MAID/BEAR ME14 .... 7 E2
East Farleigh CP School
MAID/SHEP ME15 .... 132 A8
East Peckham Primary School
STPH/PW TN12 .... 151 H7
Edenbridge CP School
EDEN TN8 .... 164 C5
Edenbridge & District
War Memorial Hospital
EDEN TN8 .... 164 C7
Edenbridge Golf & Country Club
EDEN TN8 .... 164 A4
Edenbridge Leisure Centre
EDEN TN8 .... 164 B4
The Edenbridge Medical Centre
EDEN TN8 .... 164 C5
Eden Valley School
EDEN TN8 .... 164 C4
Education Centre
MAID/BEAR ME14 .... 6 C7
Egerton CP School
HDCN TN27 .... 183 F3
Elaine CP School
STRD ME2 .... 48 D7
Elm House Gallery
EDEN TN8 .... 165 H1
The Elms Medical Centre
HOO/HM ME3 .... 50 E1
The Elms Medical Practice
HOO/HM ME3 .... 19 G5
English Martyrs Catholic
Primary School
STRD ME2 .... 49 G6
Essex County Council
TIL RM18 .... 27 H1
Eurolink Industrial Centre
SIT ME10 .... 94 B1
Eurolink Industrial Centre
SIT ME10 .... 94 B2
Eurolink Industrial Centre
SIT ME10 .... 94 C2

Eurolink Industrial Estate
SIT ME10 .... **94** C1

Eye Hospital
MAID/BEAR ME14 .... **7** D3

Eynsford Castle
EYN DA4 .... **59** H6

Eynsford Cricket Club
EYN DA4 .... **59** H6

Fairfax Gallery
RTW TN1 .... **10** C5

Fairfield Pool & Leisure Centre
DART DA1 .... **23** H6

Fairview Industrial Estate
OXTED RH8 .... **140** E4

Fairview Schools
RHAM ME8 .... **89** K1

The Family Medical Centre
WALD ME5 .... **88** D4

Farnborough Primary School
ORP BR6 .... **75** J1

Fawkham Manor Hospital
HART DA3 .... **61** H5

Fawkham Primary School
HART DA3 .... **61** F5

Featherby CP School
RHAM ME8 .... **69** H3

Featherby Junior School
RHAM ME8 .... **69** H3

Fleetdown Infants School
RDART DA2 .... **24** B7

Fleetdown Junior School
RDART DA2 .... **24** B8

Fleetway Sports Club
GVE DA12 .... **27** K7

Fondu Sports Club
PUR RM19 .... **13** G4

Fordcombe C of E Primary School
RRTW TN3 .... **204** E1

Forge Lane CP School
GILL ME7 .... **5** E2

Fort Luton Museum
CHAT ME4 .... **68** B5

Fort Pitt Grammar School
ROCH ME1 .... **3** E4

Fossebank New School
RTON TN11 .... **147** J7

Four Elms CP School
EDEN TN8 .... **165** H1

Friends of Orpington Hospital
ORP BR6 .... **75** K2

Frittenden Primary School
CRBK TN17 .... **199** G8

Fulston Manor School
SIT ME10 .... **94** A4

Furness School
SWLY BR8 .... **40** C4

Furness Swanley Football Club
SWLY BR8 .... **58** A1

Gads Hill House School
STRD ME2 .... **48** B4

The Gallery
CRBK TN17 .... **225** K1

The Gallery
MAID/SHEP ME15 .... **7** D3

The Gallery
ORP BR6 .... **56** B4

The Gallery
STH/RUST TN4 .... **190** A4

Galley Hill Industrial Estate
SWCM DA10 .... **25** K4

Gaza Trading Estate
RTON TN11 .... **146** B7

Geoffrey Whitworth Theatre
DART DA1 .... **22** C3

The Gillingham College
GILL ME7 .... **5** F4

Gillingham Football Club
GILL ME7 .... **5** E3

Gillingham Golf Club Ltd
GILL ME7 .... **5** E6

Gillingham Medical Centre
GILL ME7 .... **5** F4

The Glade Business Centre
WTHK RM20 .... **13** K5

Glencoe CP Junior School
CHAT ME4 .... **4** A6

Godden Green Clinic
BGR/WK TN15 .... **125** F4

Goldsmiths College Sports Ground
SCUP DA14 .... **39** G1

Golf Centre
STMC/STPC BR5 .... **38** E6

Gordon CP Junior School
STRD ME2 .... **49** F6

Gore Court Cricket Club
SIT ME10 .... **93** G1

Goudhurst & Kilndown C of E Primary School
CRBK TN17 .... **212** E6

Graham Gallery
STH/RUST TN4 .... **10** C4

Grange Park College
E/WMAL ME19 .... **108** A4

The Granville School
SEV TN13 .... **8** C2

Gravesend County Court
GVE DA12 .... **27** J5

Gravesend Cricket Club
GVW DA11 .... **27** H6

Gravesend Grammar School for Boys
GVE DA12 .... **28** A6

Gravesend Grammar School for Girls
GVW DA11 .... **27** H7

Gravesend Museum
GVW DA11 .... **27** J5

Gravesend & Northfleet Football Club Ltd
GVW DA11 .... **26** D5

Gravesend & North Kent Hospital
GVW DA11 .... **27** H5

Gravesend Rowing Club
GVE DA12 .... **27** K5

Gravesend Yacht Club
GVE DA12 .... **28** A5

Gravesham Borough Council
GVW DA11 .... **26** D7

Gravesham Borough Council
GVW DA11 .... **27** J6

Grays Farm Primary School
STMC/STPC BR5 .... **38** C6

Great Comp Garden
BGR/WK TN15 .... **106** A8

Great Hollenden Business Centre
RTON TN11 .... **147** G4

Greenacres Dental Health Centre
DIT/AY ME20 .... **109** J5

Greenhithe Health Clinic
GRH DA9 .... **25** G4

Green Street Primary School
ORP BR6 .... **76** A2

Greenvale Infant School
CHAT ME4 .... **4** A6

Grosvenor Medical Centre
RTW TN1 .... **10** C3

Grove Dairy Farm Business Centre
RSIT ME9 .... **73** F8

Grovehurst Surgery
SIT ME10 .... **73** K5

Grove Park CP School
SIT ME10 .... **73** G8

Guardian Industrial Estate
STPH/PW TN12 .... **176** C7

Guelder Rose Medical Centre
STPH/PW TN12 .... **198** B2

The Guildhall Museum
ROCH ME1 .... **2** B2

Guru Nanak Sports Club
GVE DA12 .... **27** K6

Hadlow College
RTON TN11 .... **149** K6

Hadlow CP School
RTON TN11 .... **150** A6

Halling County Primary School
STRD ME2 .... **86** A3

Halstead Place School
RSEV TN14 .... **77** F7

Halstead Primary School
RSEV TN14 .... **77** G7

Harenc School
SCUP DA14 .... **38** D3

Harrietsham Primary School
RMAID ME17 .... **137** J8

Hartley CP School
HART DA3 .... **61** K3

Haslemere Industrial Estate
MAID/SHEP ME15 .... **156** B1

Haslemere Trading Estate
MAID/SHEP ME15 .... **156** B1

Hawkhurst C of E Primary School
HAWK TN18 .... **235** F6

Hawkhurst Squash Club
HAWK TN18 .... **234** E4

Hawkwell Business Centre
RTWE/PEM TN2 .... **192** B4

Hayesbrook School
TON TN9 .... **170** A6

Hazelwood School
OXTED RH8 .... **140** E2

Hazlitt Theatre
MAID/BEAR ME14 .... **7** D3

Headcorn CP School
HDCN TN27 .... **180** A8

The Headcorn Gallery
HDCN TN27 .... **200** A1

Heath Farm School
HDCN TN27 .... **161** K7

Heathfield College
HAYES BR2 .... **74** B2

Helen Alison School
MEO DA13 .... **63** H4

Hempstead Infant School
GILL ME7 .... **89** H1

Hempstead Junior School
GILL ME7 .... **89** H2

Henley Business Park
STRD ME2 .... **3** D1

Herton Court School
SCUP DA14 .... **38** D2

Hever C of E Primary School
EDEN TN8 .... **165** K8

Hever Golf Club
EDEN TN8 .... **165** K5

Hever Golf Clubhouse
EDEN TN8 .... **165** K5

Hextable Comprehensive School
SWLY BR8 .... **40** C6

Hextable CP School
SWLY BR8 .... **40** C4

Higham CP School
HOO/HM ME3 .... **48** B1

High Elms Golf Course
ORP BR6 .... **75** H3

High Firs CP School
SWLY BR8 .... **58** C1

High Halden C of E Primary School
RASHW TN26 .... **219** K7

High Halstow Primary School
HOO/HM ME3 .... **32** E3

Highsted School for Girls
SIT ME10 .... **94** A4

The Highways Primary School
ORP BR6 .... **76** D1

Hildenborough Primary School
RTON TN11 .... **147** G8

Hilden Oaks School
TONN TN10 .... **170** B2

Hill School
BH/WHM TN16 .... **120** B2

Hills Surgery
RHAM ME8 .... **70** A8

Hilltop Primary School
STRD ME2 .... **49** H5

Hillyfields Junior School
GILL ME7 .... **5** D2

Historical Society Museum
CHAT ME4 .... **3** F3

Historic Vehicles Collection
CRBK TN17 .... **238** C3

Hollingbourne County Primary School
RMAID ME17 .... **136** B4

Holmesdale Community School
SNOD ME6 .... **85** K7

Holmewood House School
RRTW TN3 .... **205** K4

Holy Family Catholic Primary School
RMAID ME17 .... **156** A2

Holy Innocents RC Primary School
ORP BR6 .... **56** A7

Holy Trinity C of E Primary School
DART DA1 .... **23** F4

Holy Trinity C of E School
GVE DA12 .... **27** K6

Homefarm Estate
DIT/AY ME20 .... **109** K5

Homeopathic Hospital
RTW TN1 .... **10** C4

Homewood School
TENT TN30 .... **230** B5

Honeycrest Industrial Park
STPH/PW TN12 .... **198** A1

Hoo St Werburgh C P School
HOO/HM ME3 .... **50** E1

Horsmonden CP School
STPH/PW TN12 .... **194** E8

Horsted CP Junior &
Infants School
WALD ME5 .... **87** J1

Horsted Retail Park
WALD ME5 .... **67** J8

Horton Kirby
C of E Primary School
EYN DA4 .... **42** B8

Horton Kirby &
South Darenth Parish Council
EYN DA4 .... **42** B7

Horton Kirby Trading Estate
EYN DA4 .... **42** B7

Hospital
HAWK TN18 .... **234** D4

Hospital Barn Farm
MAID/SHEP ME15 .... **153** K2

Howard School
RHAM ME8 .... **70** A6

Hugh Christie School
TONN TN10 .... **148** D8

The Hundred of Hoo School
HOO/HM ME3 .... **50** D1

Hunton CP School
MAID/SHEP ME15 .... **153** H7

Hylands Clinic
MAID/BEAR ME14 .... **7** D3

Ide Hill School
RSEV TN14 .... **144** A2

Ifield School
CVE DA12 .... **45** K3

Ightham County Primary School
BGR/WK TN15 .... **104** B8

Imperial Retail Park
GVW DA11 .... **27** H5

The Industrial Estate
EDEN TN8 .... **164** B3

Invicta Grammar School
MAID/BEAR ME14 .... **7** F3

Invicta Sports Club
DART DA1 .... **23** G4

Istead Rise CP School
MEO DA13 .... **45** F6

Ivy Bower Surgery
GRH DA9 .... **25** G4

Iwade CP School
RSIT ME9 .... **73** J2

Jarvis Great Danes Hotel &
Country Club
RMAID ME17 .... **135** K5

John Goodhew Medical Centre
SIT ME10 .... **73** K5

John Mayne C of E Primary School
HDCN TN27 .... **217** J5

Joyce Green Hospital
DART DA1 .... **23** J1

Joydens Wood CP
School
BXLY DA5 .... **40** B2

The Judd School
TON TN9 .... **170** A6

Kemsing CP School
BGR/WK TN15 .... **102** E4

Kemsing Parish Council
BGR/WK TN15 .... **102** E4

Kenden Business Park
STRD ME2 .... **49** J6

Kent College for Girls
RTWE/PEM TN2 .... **191** K3

Kent County Council
DART DA1 .... **23** G5

Kent County Council
GVW DA11 .... **27** H5

Kent County Council
GVW DA11 .... **45** F1

Kent County Council
MAIDW ME16 .... **110** D5

Kent County Council
MEO DA13 .... **83** H6

Kent County Council
RDART DA2 .... **41** F2

Kent Kraft Industrial Estate
GVW DA11 .... **26** A3

Kents Potters Gallery
MAID/BEAR ME14 .... **7** D2

Kent & Sussex Hospital
STH/RUST TN4 .... **10** C3

The Kent Youth Theatre
WALD ME5 .... **88** E5

Kestner Industrial Estate
GRH DA9 .... **25** F3

Keston C of E Primary School
HAYES BR2 .... **74** C1

Kevington CP School
STMC/STPC BR5 .... **56** E2

Kincade Gallery
GRH DA9 .... **24** E6

Kingfisher CP School
WALD ME5 .... **68** C7

Kingsdown Industrial Estate
DIT/AY ME20 .... **109** F6

The Kings Family Practice
CHAT ME4 .... **4** B5

The Kings Family Practice
CHAT ME4 .... **50** C4

Kings Farm Infant School
CVE DA12 .... **45** K3

Kings Farm Junior School
CVE DA12 .... **45** K2

Kings Hill Golf Club
E/WMAL ME19 .... **129** J4

Kings Hill Primary School
E/WMAL ME19 .... **107** J8

Kings Hill Primary School
E/WMAL ME19 .... **129** J3

Kings Preparatory School
ROCH ME1 .... **2** C3

Kings Road Clinic
WALD ME5 .... **68** E5

Kings School Rochester
ROCH ME1 .... **2** B2

Kingstanding Business Park
RTON TN11 .... **191** F4

King Street Surgery
MAID/SHEP ME15 .... **7** D3

Kingswood CP School
RMAID ME17 .... **158** C4

Kingswood Surgery
RMAID ME17 .... **158** K5

Kingswood Surgery
RTWE/PEM TN2 .... **11** E4

Kit's Coty House
DIT/AY ME20 .... **87** H8

Knights Park Industrial Estate
STRD ME2 .... **2** A2

Knockholt School
RSEV TN14 .... **99** H4

Laddingford Farm Industrial
Estate
WBY/YAL ME18 .... **174** B2

Lady Boswell C of E School
BGR/WK TN15 .... **9** E4

Lamberhurst C of E School
RRTW TN3 .... **210** E8

Lamberhurst Golf Club
RRTW TN3 .... **210** E8

Lamberhurst Surgery
RRTW TN3 .... **221** J1

Langafel C of E Primary School
HART DA3 .... **44** B8

Langton Green CP School
RRTW TN3 .... **205** H2

Lansdowne County Primary
School
TIL RM18 .... **27** G1

Lansdowne CP School
SIT ME10 .... **94** D3

Lansdowne Road Clinic
RTW TN1 .... **11** D3

Larkfield Leisure Centre
DIT/AY ME20 .... **108** E3

Larkfield Trading Estate
DIT/AY ME20 .... **109** F1

Lawn CP School
GVW DA11 .... **26** D5

Leeds & Broomfield C of E School
RMAID ME17 .... **135** J7

Leeds Castle
RMAID ME17 .... **136** A7

Leesons Infant School
STMC/STPC BR5 .... **38** B8

Leigh City Technology College
DART DA1 .... **23** K7

Leigh Green Industrial Estate
TENT TN30 .... **230** E8

Leigh Primary School
RTON TN11 .... **168** D5

Leisure Centre
MAID/SHEP ME15 .... **7** F5

Leybourne Business Centre
E/WMAL ME19 .... **108** C4

Leybourne C of E Primary School
E/WMAL ME19 .... **108** C4

Limpsfield Chart Golf Club
OXTED RH8 .... **119** G8

Limpsfield C of E School
OXTED RH8 .... **119** F8

Limpsfield Grange School
OXTED RH8 .... **118** E6

Limpsfield Lawn Tennis Club
OXTED RH8 .... **118** E7

Liongate Clinic
STH/RUST TN4 .... **10** C2

Littlebrook Business Centre
DART DA1 .... **24** B2

Livingstone Hospital
DART DA1 .... **23** J6

Loaland Business Centre
STRD ME2 .... **49** J6

London Beach Golf Club
TENT TN30 .... **230** A2

London Road Trading Estate
SIT ME10 .... **93** J2

Long Mead CP Junior &
Infant School
RTON TN11 .... **170** B1

Loose Junior School
MAID/SHEP ME15 .... **133** G8

Lordswood Health Centre
WALD ME5 .... **88** D5

Lordswood Industrial Estate
WALD ME5 .... **88** D5

Lordswood Leisure Centre
WALD ME5 .... **88** D3

Lower Halston CP School
RSIT ME9 .... **72** A4

Lowfield Medical Centre
DART DA1 .... **23** H6

Lullingstone Castle
EYN DA4 .... **78** E1

Lunsford CP School
DIT/AY ME20 .... **108** E4

Luton CP Junior School
CHAT ME4 .... **4** C6

Luton Infant School
CHAT ME4 .... **4** C6

Luton Medical Centre
WALD ME5 .... **68** D5

Lynsted CP School
RSIT ME9 .... **95** H7

Madginford Park CP
Junior School
MAID/SHEP ME15 .... **134** C4

Madginford Park Infant School
MAID/SHEP ME15 .... **134** B4

Maidstone Borough Council
MAIDW ME16 .... **6** B4

Maidstone Grammar School
MAID/SHEP ME15 .... **7** E5

Maidstone Grammar
School for Girls
MAIDW ME16 .... **6** B1

Maidstone Hospital
MAIDW ME16 .... **132** A2

Maidstone Industrial Centre
MAIDW ME16 .... **6** C2

Maidstone Lawn Tennis Club
MAIDW ME16 .... **132** C1

The Malling School
E/WMAL ME19 .... **108** D7

Manor Gallery
CVE DA12 .... **27** J6

Manzoori Clinic
SWLY BR8 .... **40** C5

The Maplesden Noakes School
MAIDW ME16 .... **6** B2

Marden CP School
STPH/PW TN12 .... **196** B1

Marden Medical Centre
STPH/PW TN12 .... **176** C8

Mardyke Surgery
PUR RM19 .... **12** E4

Marlborough House School
HAWK TN18 .... **234** E4

Marlowe Park Medical Centre
STRD ME2 .... **66** C1

Marshlands Medical Practice
HOO/HM ME3 .... **48** B3

Mascalls Secondary School
STPH/PW TN12 .... **193** J2

Matrix Business Centre
DART DA1 .... **23** H4

Maundene CP School
WALD ME5 .... **88** B1

May Avenue Industrial Estate
CVW DA11 .... **27** G7

Mayplace Primary School
BXLYHN DA7 .... **22** A3

Maypole Community School
BXLY DA5 .... 22 B8

Meadows Memorial School
STH/RUST TN4 .... 189 K4

The Mead School
RTWE/PEM TN2 .... 10 C6

The Medical Centre
STRD ME2 .... 49 G6

The Medical Practice
MAID/SHEP ME15 .... 133 K7

Medway Community College
CHAT ME4 .... 68 B5

Medway Hospital
GILL ME7 .... 4 B5

Medway Little Theatre
ROCH ME1 .... 3 D3

Medway Rugby Football Club
ROCH ME1 .... 2 B6

Medway Towns Rowing Club
ROCH ME1 .... 2 A5

Medway Trading Estate
MAIDW ME16 .... 6 C4

Medway Yacht Club
HOO/THR ME3 .... 50 C3

Meopham CP School
MEO DA13 .... 63 H4

Meopham Medical Centre
MEO DA13 .... 63 H6

Meopham Parish Council
MEO DA13 .... 63 G7

Meopham School
MEO DA13 .... 63 H6

Meredale CP Infant School
RHAM ME8 .... 70 D5

Mereworth CP School
WBY/YAL ME18 .... 129 F6

Middlesex Hospital Sports
Ground
CHST BR7 .... 38 A3

Midfield Primary School
CHST BR7 .... 38 B5

Mid Kent Business Park
SNOD ME6 .... 86 A6

Mid Kent College of
Higher & Further Education
MAIDW ME16 .... 132 B3

Mid Kent College of
Higher & Further Education
ROCH ME1 .... 3 D5

Mid Kent College of
Higher & Further Education
ROCH ME1 .... 67 J8

Mid Kent School
MAID/BEAR ME14 .... 7 D2

Mid Kent Shopping Centre
MAIDW ME16 .... 110 C7

Mierscourt Primary School
RHAM ME8 .... 70 C7

Milehams Industrial Estate
PUR RM19 .... 12 E3

Milestone School
HART DA3 .... 62 A5

Millside Industrial Estate
DART DA1 .... 23 G3

Milstead & Frinsted
C of E Primary School
RSIT ME9 .... 116 E5

Milton Road Business Park
GVE DA12 .... 27 K6

Minterne CP School
SIT ME10 .... 93 J4

Mole Hill Copse CP School
MAID/SHEP ME15 .... 133 K7

Moor House School
OXTED RH8 .... 140 D3

More Park R C Primary School
E/WMAL ME19 .... 108 B6

Moreton Industrial Estate
SWLY BR8 .... 58 E1

Morley Business Centre
TON TN9 .... 170 D5

Mote Cricket Club
MAID/SHEP ME15 .... 7 E4

Mote Medical Practice
MAID/SHEP ME15 .... 133 H7

Mote Park Sailing Club
MAID/SHEP ME15 .... 134 A3

Motorway Industrial Estate
DIT/AY ME20 .... 110 C4

Murray Business Centre
STMC/STPC BR5 .... 38 C8

Murston County Primary
Infant School
SIT ME10 .... 94 C1

Murston CP Junior School
SIT ME10 .... 94 C1

Museum & Art Gallery
MAID/BEAR ME14 .... 6 C2

The Museum
CRBK TN17 .... 225 K1

Music School
MAID/SHEP ME15 .... 6 C4

Napier Road Junior School
GILL ME7 .... 5 D4

Napier Road Secondary School
GILL ME7 .... 5 D4

Neptune Industrial Estate
STRD ME2 .... 3 E1

Nevill Golf Club
RTWE/PEM TN2 .... 207 J7

New Ash Green County
Primary School
HART DA3 .... 62 A6

New Beacon School
SEV TN13 .... 8 B6

New Grove Green Surgery
MAID/BEAR ME14 .... 134 B1

New Hythe Business Park
DIT/AY ME20 .... 109 G1

Newington C of E Primary
School
RSIT ME9 .... 72 A7

Newington Industrial Estate
RSIT ME9 .... 71 J8

New Road CP School
CHAT ME4 .... 4 A5

New Road Surgery
CHAT ME4 .... 3 F4

New Surgery
BH/WHM TN16 .... 97 C8

New Swan Valley
Community School
SWCM DA10 .... 26 A6

Nizels Hotel Golf & Leisure Club
RTON TN11 .... 146 C5

The Noble Clinic
STPH/PW TN12 .... 193 K6

North Borough CP Junior School
MAID/BEAR ME14 .... 111 F7

Northcourt County
Primary School
GVE DA12 .... 28 B7

North Cray Primary School
SCUP DA14 .... 39 F4

North Downs Business Park
RSEV TN14 .... 100 E3

North Farm Industrial Estate
RTWE/PEM TN2 .... 190 E5

Northfleet Boys School
GVW DA11 .... 26 E7

Northfleet Industrial Estate
GVW DA11 .... 26 B3

Northfleet School for Girls
GVW DA11 .... 26 E8

North Kent Magistrates Court
CHAT ME4 .... 3 F3

North West Kent College
GVE DA12 .... 28 C7

North West Kent College
of Technology
DART DA1 .... 23 C6

Nugent Industrial Park
STMC/STPC BR5 .... 56 D1

Oakfield CP Junior School
DART DA1 .... 23 G8

Oakland Primary School
BH/WHM TN16 .... 97 G3

Oaklands CP Junior &
Infant School
WALD ME5 .... 88 A2

Oaklands Junior School
BH/WHM TN16 .... 97 G3

Oaks County Infant School
SIT ME10 .... 93 J4

Oak Trees CP School
MAID/SHEP ME15 .... 133 J7

Oakwood Hospital
MAIDW ME16 .... 132 A3

Oakwood Park Grammar
School
MAIDW ME16 .... 132 C3

Oasthouse Theatre
RHAM ME8 .... 70 C6

Offham CP School
E/WMAL ME19 .... 107 F6

Offham Cricket Club
E/WMAL ME19 .... 107 F7

Oldborough Manor
Community School
MAID/SHEP ME15 .... 133 H7

The Old Guild Theatre
GVW DA11 .... 26 E7

Old Judd Rugby Club
TON TN9 .... 170 B4

Orchard Business Centre
MAIDW ME16 .... 110 C6

Orchard Business Centre
RTWE/PEM TN2 .... 190 D6

Orchard Business Centre
TON TN9 .... 170 D6

Orchard Industrial Estate
MAID/SHEP ME15 .... 156 B3

Orchard Medical Centre
RMAID ME17 .... 154 C4

Orchard Place Business Centre
E/WMAL ME19 .... 106 C8

The Orchard Theatre
DART DA1 .... 23 H5

Orpington College of
Further Education
ORP BR6 .... 56 B5

Orpington Mental Health Centre
ORP BR6 .... 56 A7

Orpington Retail Park
STMC/STPC BR5 .... 56 D1

Orpington Sports Centre
ORP BR6 .... 56 B5

Orpington Superbowl
ORP BR6 .... 56 B5

Otford County Primary School
RSEV TN14 .... 101 J3

Otford Medical Practice
RSEV TN14 .... 101 K2

Our Lady of Hartley RC School
HART DA3 .... 62 A2

Our Ladys RC Primary School
DART DA1 .... 23 F5

Oxleas N H S Trust
BXLY DA5 .... 22 B8

Oxleas NHS Trust
ORP BR6 .... 56 C4

Oxted County School
OXTED RH8 .... 118 D7

Oxted Gallery
OXTED RH8 .... 118 C8

Oxted Health Centre
OXTED RH8 .... 118 D8

Oxted & Limpsfield Hospital
OXTED RH8 .... 118 B6

Paddock Wood Business Centre
STPH/PW TN12 .... 173 J7

Paddock Wood CP School
STPH/PW TN12 .... 173 J8

Paddock Wood Town Council
STPH/PW TN12 .... 173 H8

Painters Ash Primary School
GVW DA11 .... 44 E1

Palace Industrial Estate
MAID/SHEP ME15 .... 156 B2

Palace Wood County
Junior School
MAIDW ME16 .... 110 C8

Parker Industrial Centre
RDART DA2 .... 24 B6

Park Road Industrial Estate
SWLY BR8 .... 40 C8

Park Way CP School
MAID/SHEP ME15 .... 7 E6

Parkwood Hall School
SWLY BR8 .... 40 E8

Parkwood Industrial Estate
MAID/SHEP ME15 .... 156 C2

Parkwood Infant School
RHAM ME8 .... 90 B1

Parkwood Junior School
RHAM ME8 .... 90 A1

Parrock Street Surgery
GVE DA12 .... 27 J5

Pedham Place Industrial Estate
SWLY BR8 .... 58 D2

Pegasus Gallery
SEV TN13 .... 9 D4

Pembury Hospital
RTWE/PEM TN2 .... 191 G7

Pembury Primary School
RTWE/PEM TN2 .... 191 K6

Penhurst Place
RTON TN11 .... 187 K2

Penshurst C of E Primary School
RTON TN11 .... 187 J2

Perry Hall School
ORP BR6 .... 56 A3

Phoenix Industrial Estate
STRD ME2 .... 3 D1

Phoenix Surgery
ROCH ME1 .... 87 F6

Platt C of E Primary School
BGR/WK TN15 .... 105 J7

Platt Industrial Estate
BGR/WK TN15 .... 105 J6

Plaxtol CP School
BGR/WK TN15 .... 126 E7

Pluckley C of E Primary School
HDCN TN27 .... 183 J7

Police Station and
Magistrates Court
RTW TN1 .... 11 D3

Postley Industrial Centre
MAID/SHEP ME15 .... 7 D5

Poultwood Golf Club
RTON TN11 .... 149 F5

Poverest Primary School
STMC/STPC BR5 .... 56 B2

Pratts Bottom Primary School
ORP BR6 .... 76 D6

Premier Business Park
CHAT ME4 .... 68 C5

Preston Hall Hospital
DIT/AY ME20 .... 109 K5

Princes Park Medical Centre
WALD ME5 .... 68 C8

Princess Christian's Hospital
RTON TN11 .... 147 J4

Priory School
STMC/STPC BR5 .... 56 D5

Prison
MAID/BEAR ME14 .... 6 C2

Purfleet Primary School
PUR RM19 .... 12 E4

Quarry Wood Industrial Estate
DIT/AY ME20 .... 109 J7

Queenborough Yacht Club
QBOR ME11 .... 55 K1

Queen Marys Hospital
SCUP DA14 .... 38 B3

Queen Victoria Cottage Hospital
RTON TN11 .... 170 C8

Railway Street Industrial Estate
GILL ME7 .... 5 D2

Rainham Mark Grammar School
RHAM ME8 .... 70 A4

Rainham School for Girls
RHAM ME8 .... 69 K6

Ravensquay Business Centre
STMC/STPC BR5 .... 56 C2

Raynehurst CP School
GVE DA12 .... 46 C1

Rectory Business Centre
SCUP DA14 .... 38 C2

Rectory Paddock School
STMC/STPC BR5 .... 38 D7

Regional Sports Centre
TIL RM18 .... 27 J1

Regis Manor County
Primary School
SIT ME10 .... 73 K7

Reynolds Health Centre
DART DA1 .... 23 G5

Richmond County Infants School
GILL ME7 .... 4 C2

Ridge View School
TONN TN10 .... 170 D1

Riding School
E/WMAL ME19 .... 131 F2

Riverhead County Infant School
SEV TN13 .... 8 B1

Riverside Business Centre
TON TN9 .... 170 B5

Riverside Industrial Estate
DART DA1 .... 23 H4

Riverside Medical Practice
STRD ME2 .... 86 A2

Riverside Retail Park
RSEV TN14 .... 102 A6

Riverview Clinic
GVE DA12 .... 46 C3

Riverview Park Surgery
GVE DA12 .... 46 B2

Riverview Primary School
GVE DA12 .... 46 B2

The Robert Napier School
GILL ME7 .... 5 E5

Rochester Airport
Industrial Estate
ROCH ME1 .... 67 H8

Rochester Airport
Industrial Estate
WALD ME5 .... 87 H1

Rochester Grammar
School for Girls
ROCH ME1 .... 2 C6

Rochester Health Centre
ROCH ME1 .... 3 D5

The Rochester
Mathematical School
ROCH ME1 .... 67 G5

Rochester Museum
ROCH ME1 .... 2 C3

Rochester Tutors
Independent College
ROCH ME1 .... 3 D4

Rodmersham CP School
RSIT ME9 .... 94 C7

Rodmersham Squash Club
RSIT ME9 .... 94 B8

Rolvenden Primary School
CRBK TN17 .... 238 C3

Roseacre Junior School
MAID/BEAR ME14 .... 134 C2

Rose Cottage Surgery
STPH/PW TN12 .... 198 B3

Rose Hill School
STH/RUST TN4 .... 10 A2

Rosherville C of E School
GVW DA11 .... 27 F5

Rowhill School
RDART DA2 .... 41 F2

Royal Park Primary School
SCUP DA14 .... 39 F1

Royal Victoria Place
Shopping Centre
RTW TN1 .... 11 D3

Rusthall Medical Centre
STH/RUST TN4 .... 206 A2

Ruxley Corner Industrial Estate
SCUP DA14 .... 38 E4

Ryarsh CP School
E/WMAL ME19 .... 107 J2

Sackville School
RTON TN11 .... 147 G8

Sacred Heart School
RTWE/PEM TN2 .... 207 K2

St Albans CP School
DART DA1 .... 23 J5

St Andrews Medical Centre
STH/RUST TN4 .... 190 A5

St Andrews School
ROCH ME1 .... 2 C3

St Anselms RC Primary School
DART DA1 .... 23 K4

St Augustine RC Primary School
RHAM ME8 .... 90 A3

St Augustine School
STH/RUST TN4 .... 190 A7

St Barnabas C of E
Primary School
RTW TN1 .... 11 D2

St Bartholomews Hospital
ROCH ME1 .... 3 E4

St Bartholomews Hospital
SWLY BR8 .... 40 C8

St Bartholomews RC Primary School
SWLY BR8 .... 40 B8

St Benedicts School
WALD ME5 .... 88 D4

St Botolphs C of E Primary School
GVW DA11 .... 26 E6

St Francis RC Primary School
MAID/BEAR ME14 .... 7 D2

St Georges C of E
County Primary School
BGR/WK TN15 .... 105 F3

St Georges C of E School
GVW DA11 .... 27 H8

St Georges School
RTWE/PEM TN2 .... 208 B1

St Gregorys RC School
STH/RUST TN4 .... 190 A7

St Helens C of E Primary School
HOO/HM ME3 .... 31 G1

St Hilarys School
SEV TN13 .... 9 D1

St James C of E Primary School
HOO/HM ME3 .... 21 G8

St James CP School
E/WMAL ME19 .... 108 D6

St James's Junior & Infant School
RTWE/PEM TN2 .... 11 E3

St John Fisher Catholic School
CHAT ME4 .... 3 F6

St John Fisher RC
Secondary School
ROCH ME1 .... 3 E5

St Johns C of E Infant School
CHAT ME4 .... 3 E5

St Johns C of E Primary School
MAID/BEAR ME14 .... 133 K2

St Johns Hill Surgery
SEV TN13 .... 9 E1

St Johns Infant School
STH/RUST TN4 .... 10 C2

St Johns Primary School
STH/RUST TN4 .... 190 B7

St Johns RC
Comprehensive School
GVE DA12 .... 28 A7

St Johns RC Primary School
GVE DA12 .... 28 A7

St Joseph RC School
DART DA1 .... 22 B3

St Josephs Preparatory School
GVE DA12 .... 27 K8

St Josephs RC School
GVW DA11 .... 26 E6

St Katherines CP School
SNOD ME6 .... 85 J7

St Lukes School
STH/RUST TN4 .... 190 C7

St Margaret Clitherow
RC Primary School
RTON TN11 .... 148 A8

St Margarets at Troy Town
C E Primary School
ROCH ME1 .... 2 C4

St Margarets C of E Junior School
RHAM ME8 .... 70 B6

St Margarets Old School
BGR/WK TN15 .... 147 F1

St Marks C of E Primary School
STH/RUST TN4 .... 206 C5

St Marys Abbey
E/WMAL ME19 .... 108 A6

St Mary & St. Josephs RC School
SCUP DA14 .... 38 A3

St Marys C of E Primary School
SWLY BR8 .... 58 B1

St Marys CP School
STRD ME2 .... 49 G6

St Marys Infant School
GILL ME7 .... 5 D2

St Marys Island Church of
England Aided Primary School
CHAT ME4 .... 50 C5

St Marys Middle School
OXTED RH8 .... 118 C7

St Marys RC County
Primary School
TIL RM18 .... 27 G1

St Matthews C of E Infant School
ROCH ME1 .... 2 A6

St Michaels C of E Primary
Junior School
MAIDW ME16 .... 6 B4

St Michaels C of E Primary School
TENT TN30 .... 230 B3

St Michaels RC Primary School
CHAT ME4 .... 3 F5

St Nicholas School
STRD ME2 .... 2 A1

St Olaves Grammar School
ORP BR6 .... 56 C7

St Paulinus C of E Primary School
DART DA1 .... 22 B3

St Pauls C of E Infant School
RRTW TN3 .... 206 A2

St Pauls C of E Junior School
STH/RUST TN4 .... 206 A2

St Pauls C of E School
SWLY BR8 .... 40 E6

St Pauls County Infant School
MAID/BEAR ME14 .... 111 G7

St Pauls Cray C of E
Primary School
STMC/STPC BR5 .... 38 D8

St Pauls Cray Health Clinic
STMC/STPC BR5 .... 38 B7

St Peter Chanel RC School
SCUP DA14 .... 38 D3

St Peters County Infant School
ROCH ME1 .... 2 C5

St Peters Primary School
RTWE/PEM TN2 .... 11 E4

St Peters RC Primary School
SIT ME10 .... 93 J3

St Philomena RC Primary School
STMC/STPC BR5 .... 56 D4

St Saviours Surgery
MAID/SHEP ME15................... 133 K8

St Simon Stock RC
Comprehensive School
MAIDW ME16 .... 132 C2

St Stephens C of E Infant School
MAID/SHEP ME15................... 6 B5

St Stephens CP School
TON TN9 .... 170 D6

St Thomas C of E Primary School
RRTW TN3 .... 205 F8

St Thomas More RC
Primary School
WALD ME5 .... 88 B2

St Thomas of Canterbury
Primary School
RHAM ME8 .... 69 J4

St Thomas School
SIT ME10 .... 94 D4

St Werburgh CP Junior School
HOO/HM ME3 .... 50 D1

St Werburgh Medical Centre
HOO/HM ME3 .... 33 F8

St Werburgh Medical Practice
HOO/HM ME3 .... 37 G1

St William of Perth RC
Primary School
ROCH ME1 .... 2 B6

Sandhurst CP School
HAWK TN18 .... 243 K1

Sandling CP School
MAID/BEAR ME14................... 111 H6

Sandown Court School
RTWE/PEM TN2 .... 190 E8

School House Aveley School
SOCK/AV RM15 .... 13 J1

School of Health
RDART DA2 .... 24 A5

Seal St Lawrence Primary School
BGR/WK TN15 .... 125 J3

Sedleys C of E Primary School
MEO DA13 .... 44 B3

Senacre Technology School
MAID/SHEP ME15................... 133 K8

Senacre Wood CP School
MAID/SHEP ME15................... 134 B7

Sessions House
MAID/BEAR ME14................... 7 D2

Sevenoaks Business Centre
RSEV TN14......................... 101 K7

Sevenoaks CP School
SEV TN13 .... 9 D1

Sevenoaks Hospital
SEV TN13 .... 102 A8

Sevenoaks School
BGR/WK TN15 .... 9 E5

Sevenoaks Swimming Centre
BGR/WK TN15 .... 9 E4

Sevenoaks Town Council
SEV TN13 .... 9 D1

Sevenoaks Way Industrial Estate
STMC/STPC BR5 .... 38 D8

Shamel Business Centre
STRD ME2 .... 2 C1

Shawcroft School
STMC/STPC BR5 .... 57 F2

Shears Green CP School
GVW DA11 .... 45 G1

Shears Green Infant School
GVW DA11 .... 45 G1

Sheldon Business Centre
STRD ME2 .... 49 J6

Shenstone School
DART DA1 .... 22 A4

Shepway County Primary
Junior Mixed School
MAID/SHEP ME15................... 134 A6

Shepway CP Infants School
MAID/SHEP ME15................... 134 A6

Sheridale Business Centre
STRD ME2 .... 2 A2

Sherwin Knight County Junior &
Infant School
STRD ME2 .... 66 D1

Sherwood Park Infant School
RTWE/PEM TN2 .... 11 F1

Sherwood Park Primary School
RTWE/PEM TN2 .... 11 F1

Shipbourne CP School
RTON TN11 .... 148 C1

Shopping Arcades
MAID/BEAR ME14................... 6 C3

Shoreham County Primary School
RSEV TN14.......................... 78 C6

Shorne C of E Primary School
CVE DA12........................... 47 H3

Sidcup Health Centre
SCUP DA14 .... 38 B1

Sidcup Hill Primary School
SCUP DA14 .... 38 C3

Sidcup Sports Club
SCUP DA14 .... 38 A2

Sikh Temple
DART DA1 .... 23 G6

Sikh Temple
GILL ME7 .... 5 D3

Sikh Temple
CVE DA12........................... 27 J7

Singlewell CP School
CVE DA12........................... 46 A4

Siri Guru Ravidass Temple
STRD ME2 .... 49 G6

Sissinghurst Primary School
CRBK TN17 .... 215 H6

Sittingbourne Industrial Park
SIT ME10 .... 93 H1

Sittingbourne Industrial Park
SIT ME10 .... 94 A1

Sittingbourne Memorial Hospital
SIT ME10 .... 94 A3

Sittingbourne & Milton Regis
Golf Club
RSIT ME9 .... 92 A3

Sittingbourne Sports Centre
SIT ME10 .... 94 B3

The Skinners School
STH/RUST TN4 .... 10 C1

Skinner Street CP School
GILL ME7 .... 4 C2

Ski Slope
STMC/STPC BR5 .... 38 E6

Slade CP School
TON TN9 .... 170 B4

Smarden CP School
HDCN TN27 .... 202 A5

Snodland Clinic
SNOD ME6 .... 85 K6

Snodland CP School
SNOD ME6 .... 85 J6

Solefield School House
SEV TN13 .... 9 D6

Solefields School
SEV TN13 .... 9 E6

Solomons Temple
RSIT ME9 .... 139 K1

The Somerfield Hospital
MAIDW ME16 .... 6 A2

South Avenue County Infant
School
SIT ME10 .... 94 B3

South Aylesford Retail Park
DIT/AY ME20 .... 109 J6

South Borough CP School
MAID/SHEP ME15................... 7 D5

Southfields School
CVE DA12........................... 45 K3

Spa Industrial Park
RTWE/PEM TN2 .... 190 E6

Spectrum Business Centre
STRD ME2 .... 49 J6

Speldhurst Primary School
RRTW TN3 .... 188 E7

Spinnens Acre County
Junior School
WALD ME5 .... 88 E5

Spotlites Theatre Company Ltd
CHAT ME4 .... 4 A5

Springfield Industrial Estate
HAWK TN18 .... 235 F3

Stag Theatre
SEV TN13 .... 9 D4

Stansted C of E Primary School
BGR/WK TN15 .... 82 A5

Staplehurst CP School
STPH/PW TN12 .... 198 A3

Stocks Green CP School
RTON TN11 .... 169 J1

Stonecross Surgery
WALD ME5 .... 68 D5

Strood Swimming Pool
STRD ME2 .... 48 E7

Strood Yacht Club
STRD ME2 .... 2 A2

Sundridge Primary School
RSEV TN14......................... 122 A4

Surex Swimming Pools
BH/WHM TN16 .... 97 H2

Sussex Road CP School
TON TN9 .... 170 A6

Sutton at Hone C of E
Primary School
EYN DA4 .... 41 K5

Sutton at Hone & Hawley
Parish Council
EYN DA4 .... 42 A4

Sutton Valence CP School
RMAID ME17 .... 157 F7

Sutton Valence School
RMAID ME17 .... 157 G7

Swan Business Park
DART DA1 .... 23 G3

Swanley School
SWLY BR8 .... 40 A8

Swanley Town Council
SWLY BR8 .... 40 B8

Swanley White Oak County
Primary School
SWLY BR8 .... 40 B7

Swanscombe Business Centre
SWCM DA10 .... 25 K4

Sweyne CP Junior School
SWCM DA10 .... 26 A6

Swingate County Infant School
WALD ME5 .... 88 D5

Tandridge Golf Club
OXTED RH8 .... 140 A2

Target Business Centre
MAID/SHEP ME15................... 156 B2

Tatsfield Primary School
BH/WHM TN16 .... 97 H8

Teardrop Industrial Park
SWLY BR8 .... 59 F2

Temple Hill County Infant & Primary
School
DART DA1 .... 23 K4

Temple School
STRD ME2 .... 49 C5

Tennis Club
GILL ME7 .... 5 E5

Tenterden C of E Junior School
TENT TN30......................... 230 A7

Tenterden County Primary School
TENT TN30......................... 230 B7

Tenterden Golf Club
TENT TN30......................... 230 D5

Tenterden Leisure Centre
TENT TN30......................... 230 B7

Teynham Medical Centre
RSIT ME9 .... 95 K4

Teynham Parochial C of E
(Controlled) Primary School
RSIT ME9 .... 95 K4

Thames Gateway NHS Trust
RDART DA2 .... 24 B6

Thameslink Healthcare Services
N H S Trust
RDART DA2 .... 24 B5

Thames View CP School
RHAM ME8 .... 70 A4

Thamesview School
CVE DA12........................... 46 C1

The Thomas Aveling School
ROCH ME1 .... 67 H6

Thornhills Medical Centre
DIT/AY ME20 .... 108 E5

Thurrock Business Centre
WTHK RM20......................... 13 K6

Thurrock Council
PUR RM19 .... 12 D4

Ticehurst C of E Primary School
WADH TN5.......................... 232 B6

Tilbury Fort
TIL RM18 .... 27 K3

Tilbury Surgery
TIL RM18 .... 27 H1

Tonbridge Football Club
RTON TN11 .... 170 B1

Tonbridge Grammar School for
Girls
TON TN9 .... 170 C7

Tonbridge Hillview School
TON TN9 .... 170 D6

Tonbridge Market
TON TN9 .... 170 B4

Tonbridge Oast Theatre
 RTON TN11 .... 169 K2
Tonbridge School
 TONN TN10 .... 170 B3
Tonbridge Town Sailing Club
 RTON TN11 .... 169 G6
Tovil Green Business Park
 MAID/SHEP ME15 .... 6 B6
Tower Industrial Estate
 BGR/WK TN15 .... 104 D1
Town Hall
 DART DA1 .... 22 C4
Town Hall
 MAID/BEAR ME14 .... 6 C3
Town Hall
 RTW TN1 .... 10 C3
Town Hall
 TENT TN30 .... 230 A7
Town Medical Centre
 SEV TN13 .... 9 D4
Toy & Model Museum
 RRTW TN3 .... 211 F7
Trenchwood Medical Centre
 TONN TN10 .... 170 C1
Trinity Theatre & Arts Association
 RTW TN1 .... 10 C4
Trottiscliffe C of E Primary
 School
 E/WMAL ME19 .... 106 C1
Tudor Hotel Golf & Country Club
 MAID/BEAR ME14 .... 135 F3
Tunbridge Wells Borderers
 Sports Club
 RTWE/PEM TN2 .... 207 F6
Tunbridge Wells Centre
 RTW TN1 .... 10 C3
Tunbridge Wells Golf Club
 STH/RUST TN4 .... 10 A4
Tunbridge Wells Grammar
 School for Boys
 STH/RUST TN4 .... 190 A6
Tunbridge Wells Grammar
 School for Girls
 STH/RUST TN4 .... 10 B1
Tunbridge Wells Hockey Club
 RTW TN1 .... 11 D6
Tunbridge Wells
 Independent Hospital
 RRTW TN3 .... 204 E3
Tunbridge Wells Museum
 & Art Gallery
 STH/RUST TN4 .... 10 C3
Tunbridge Wells Nuffield Hospital
 RTWE/PEM TN2 .... 11 F4
Tunbridge Wells Sports Centre
 STH/RUST TN4 .... 190 A7
Tunbury Avenue Surgery
 WALD ME5 .... 88 A4
Tunbury CP School
 WALD ME5 .... 88 A5
Tunnel Industrial Estate
 WTHK RM20 .... 13 K4
Tunnel Industrial Estate
 WTHK RM20 .... 13 K6
Tunstall C of E Primary School
 RSIT ME9 .... 93 H6
Twenty Twenty Industrial Estate
 MAIDW ME16 .... 110 C6
Twydall Health & Welfare Clinic
 RHAM ME8 .... 69 J3
Twydall Infant School
 RHAM ME8 .... 69 J4
Twydall Junior School
 RHAM ME8 .... 69 J4
Tyrwitt Drake Museum of
 Carriages
 MAID/SHEP ME15 .... 7 D4
U C I Cinema
 WTHK RM20 .... 13 K4
Ulcombe C of E Primary School
 RMAID ME17 .... 158 D8
Underhill School
 RMAID ME17 .... 156 E7
Underling Industrial Estate
 STPH/PW TN12 .... 177 F4
Union Mill
 CRBK TN17 .... 225 K2

University of Greenwich
 CHAT ME4 .... 50 C6
University of Greenwich
 DART DA1 .... 23 F8
University of Greenwich
 DART DA1 .... 23 J8
University of Greenwich
 E/WMAL ME19 .... 129 J3
Upbury Manor School
 GILL ME7 .... 4 B4
Upchurch Primary School
 RSIT ME9 .... 71 H3
Upnor Castle
 STRD ME2 .... 50 A4
Valence School
 BH/WHM TN16 .... 121 F5
Valley Park Community School
 MAID/BEAR ME14 .... 7 F3
Vestry Industrial Estate
 RSEV TN14 .... 101 K6
Vigo CP School
 MEO DA13 .... 83 H6
Vigo Rugby Club
 MEO DA13 .... 83 K5
The Vine Medical Centre
 MAIDW ME16 .... 132 C3
Wainscott CP School
 STRD ME2 .... 49 J4
Wakeley CP School
 RHAM ME8 .... 70 D5
Walderslade CP School
 WALD ME5 .... 88 B3
Walderslade Medical Centre
 WALD ME5 .... 68 B8
Walnuts Leisure Centre
 ORP BR6 .... 56 B5
Warders Medical Centre
 TON TN9 .... 170 C4
Warren Road Primary School
 ORP BR6 .... 56 A8
Warren Wood CP School
 ROCH ME1 .... 67 H6
Warsop Trading Estate
 EDEN TN8 .... 164 D6
Watermill Museum
 LING RH7 .... 163 G6
Wayfield CP School
 WALD ME5 .... 68 B7
Weald CP School
 RSEV TN14 .... 145 K4
Weald Gallery
 RSEV TN14 .... 121 K5
Weald of Kent Golf Club
 HDCN TN27 .... 179 J5
Weald of Kent School for Girls
 TON TN9 .... 170 D7
Weald Sports Centre
 CRBK TN17 .... 214 D8
Wentworth County Infant School
 DART DA1 .... 22 C6
Wentworth CP Junior School
 DART DA1 .... 22 D6
West Borough County
 Primary School
 MAIDW ME16 .... 132 B3
West Borough Secondary School
 MAIDW ME16 .... 132 B3
West Borough Sports Centre
 MAIDW ME16 .... 132 C3
Westcourt County Primary School
 GVE DA12 .... 28 B8
Westgate CP School
 DART DA1 .... 23 G6
West Heath School
 SEV TN13 .... 123 K8
West Hill County Primary School
 DART DA1 .... 22 E5
West Hill Hospital
 DART DA1 .... 23 G5
West Kent College
 TON TN9 .... 170 B6
West Kent College of Further
 Education
 STH/RUST TN4 .... 190 A7
West Kent College of
 Further Education
 TON TN9 .... 170 A6

West Kingsdown Industrial
 Estate
 BGR/WK TN15 .... 80 D4
West Kingsdown Medical Centre
 BGR/WK TN15 .... 80 E4
Westlands Secondary School
 SIT ME10 .... 93 G2
West Lane Trading Estate
 SIT ME10 .... 94 B1
West Lodge School
 BFN/LL DA15 .... 38 B1
West Malling C of E Primary
 School
 E/WMAL ME19 .... 107 K6
West Malling Golf Club
 E/WMAL ME19 .... 106 E4
West Malling Group Practice
 E/WMAL ME19 .... 107 K6
West Malling Industrial Park
 E/WMAL ME19 .... 107 G4
West View Hospital
 TENT TN30 .... 229 J8
Wheelbarrow Park Estate
 STPH/PW TN12 .... 176 B7
Whitehill House Surgery
 DART DA1 .... 22 D4
Whitehill Junior School
 GVE DA12 .... 45 K1
The White House Gallery
 BH/WHM TN16 .... 120 D5
Wildernesse Golf Club
 BGR/WK TN15 .... 124 E1
Wildernesse School
 BGR/WK TN15 .... 102 C8
Wilderness Sports Centre
 BGR/WK TN15 .... 102 C8
Wilmington Grange
 Grammar School for Girls
 RDART DA2 .... 22 E8
Wilmington High School
 RDART DA2 .... 40 E1
Wilmington Parish Council
 DART DA1 .... 23 C8
Wilmington Primary School
 RDART DA2 .... 40 E1
Windmill Business Centre
 MEO DA13 .... 63 G7
Winterton Surgery
 BH/WHM TN16 .... 120 D6
Wish Valley Surgery
 HAWK TN18 .... 235 F6
Wittersham Primary School
 TENT TN30 .... 247 J4
Wolfs Wood Primary School
 OXTED RH8 .... 140 E3
Woodfalls Business Centre
 WBY/YAL ME18 .... 152 B8
Woodlands CP Junior School
 TONN TN10 .... 148 E8
Woodlands CP School
 GILL ME7 .... 5 F4
Woodlands Health Centre
 STPH/PW TN12 .... 173 H7
Wren Industrial Estate
 MAID/SHEP ME15 .... 156 B2
Wrotham Parish Council
 BGR/WK TN15 .... 81 K5
Wrotham Road CP School
 GVW DA11 .... 27 J6
Wrotham Road Health Clinic
 GVW DA11 .... 27 J7
Wrotham Secondary School
 BGR/WK TN15 .... 105 G5
Yalding C of E Primary School
 WBY/YAL ME18 .... 152 E5
Yardley Court
 Preparatory School
 RTON TN11 .... 171 F7
Yew Tree Industrial Estate
 DIT/AY ME20 .... 109 H4
York Road CP School
 DART DA1 .... 23 J6
Zobel College
 SEV TN13 .... 9 D3

Page 11

D4
1 Calverley Park Crs
2 Camden HI
3 Camden Pk
4 Catherine Pl
5 Guildford Rd
6 Meadow Hill Rd
7 Mount Pleasant Av

Page 27

G6
1 Cremorne Rd

H7
1 Weavers Cl

J5
1 Bank St
2 Bath St
3 Berkley Rd
4 Bernard St
5 Brewhouse Yd
6 Chase Sq
7 Garrick St
8 Horn Yd
9 Jury St
10 Manor Rd
11 New Swan Yd
12 Parrock St
13 Railway Pl
14 Wilfred St

Page 51

F3
1 Aster Rd
2 Bay Cl
3 Beech Rd
4 Berry Rd
5 Cherry Rd
6 Clover Rd
7 Cypress Av
8 Damson Dr
9 Elder Cl
10 Elm Rd
11 Larch Crs
12 Maple Rd
13 Marine Dr
14 Oak Cl
15 Oak Rd
16 Willow Av
17 Yew Rd

Page 56

A3
1 Cotswold Ri
2 Marlborough Cl

B3
1 Coleridge Wy
2 Wendover Wy

B4
1 Aynscombe Angle
2 Deakins Ter
3 Devonshire Rd
4 Lamorna Cl

B5
1 Mortimer Rd

C2
1 Cross Rd
2 Sidmouth Rd

D2
1 Burwash Cl
2 Copper Beech Cl
3 Roberts Cl

D8
1 Ampleforth Cl

Page 67

H8
1 Lankester Parker Rd

Page 68

A1
1 Military Rd
2 Whiffen's Avenue W

A2
1 Cambridge Ter
2 James St
3 Rhode St
4 Sir John Hawkins Wy

A4
1 Athelstan Rd
2 Freeman Gdns
3 Hillcrest Rd
4 Kingswood Av
5 Parham Rd
6 Pretoria Rd

B3
1 Chalk Pit HI
2 Hope St
3 Melbourne Rd

B7
1 Flamingo Cl
2 Goose Cl

C4
1 Chamberlain Rd
2 Waghorn St

C7
1 Kinross Cl
2 Penfold Cl
3 Snowdon Cl
4 Wheatear Wy

D1
1 Lawrence St
2 Theodore Pl

D5
1 Durrell Gdns

D7
1 Hampshire Cl

D8
1 Allen Cl
2 Judkins Cl
3 Manchester Cl
4 Ryegrass Cl

E1
1 Avondale Rd
2 Balmoral Rd
3 Buckingham Rd
4 Connaught Rd
5 Edinburgh Rd
6 Glanville Rd
7 Osborne Rd

E2
1 Marathon Paddock

Page 70

D6
1 Gloucester Cl
2 Longford Cl
3 Middlefields
4 Thompson Cl

E5
1 Banky Fields Cl
2 Bedson Wk
3 Bythorne Ct
4 Harwood Rd
5 Ten Acre Wy
6 Vineyard Crs

E6
1 Bramley Cl

Page 88

B1
1 Greenacre Cl
2 Urquhart Cl

B6
1 Bellgrove Ct
2 Spenlow Dr
3 Trotwood Cl

C2
1 Chegwell Dr
2 Greenwich Cl
3 Richmond Cl

C4
1 Hornbeam Av
2 Moonstone Dr

Page 132

E2
1 Birnam Sq
2 Goudhurst Cl
3 Kingsdown Cl

E3
1 Hever Gdns
2 Rycault Cl
3 White Rock Ct

Page 133

C1
1 Camden St
2 Cromwell Rd
3 Lucerne St
4 Princes St
5 Wheeler St
6 Woollett St

G6
1 Corrance Gn
2 Warnford Gdns

Page 134

B3
1 Laxton Cl

B8
1 Betsham Rd
2 Cheltenham Cl
3 Chiddingstone Cl
4 Chislehurst Cl
5 Doncaster Cl
6 Epsom Cl
7 Fontwell Cl
8 Goodwood Cl
9 Groombridge Sq
10 Taunton Cl

Page 206

E5
2 The Goodwins
3 School Ri

Page 207

F2
1 Belgrave Rd
2 Clarence Rw
3 Culverden St
4 Dudley Rd
5 Grosvenor Wk
6 Hanover Rd
7 Lime Hill Rd
8 Mount Ephraim Rd
9 Rock Villa Rd

F4
1 Berkeley Rd
2 Castle St
3 Cumberland Yd
4 Grove Av
5 Little Mount Sion
6 Market St
7 The Pantiles
8 South Gv
9 Sussex Ms
10 White Bear Pas

G1
1 Hill St
2 Mercer St
3 Norman Rd
4 St Barnabas' Cl
5 St Stephons Ct

G2
1 Calverley Rd
2 The Ferns
3 Garden Rd
4 Garden St
5 Lansdowne Sq
6 Monson Rd
7 Monson Wy
8 Newton Rd
9 Victoria Rd

G5
1 Beau Nash Wy

H3
1 Bucklers Cl
2 Calverley Ct
3 Cambridge St
4 Oakfield Court Rd
5 Park St
6 Prince's St
7 St Peter's St
8 Windmill St